Reconciliation, Justice, and Coexistence

Theory & Practice

Mohammed Abu-Nimer

LEXINGTON BOOKS
Lanham • Boulder • New York • Toronto • Oxford

LEXINGTON BOOKS

Published in the United States of America
by Lexington Books
An imprint of The Rowman & Littlefield Publishing Group, Inc.
4501 Forbes Boulevard, Suite 200, Lanham, Maryland 20706

PO Box 317
Oxford
OX2 9RU, UK

British Library Cataloguing in Publication Information Available

Library of Congress Cataloging-in-Publication Data

Reconciliation, justice, and coexistence : theory and practice / edited by Mohammed
Abu-Nimer.
    p. cm.
    Includes bibliographical references and index.
    ISBN 0-7391-0237-0 (alk. paper) — ISBN 0-7391-0268-0 (pbk. : alk. paper)
        1. Conflict management—Congresses. 2. Reconciliation—Congresses. 3. Ethnic
    relations—Congresses. I. Abu-Nimer, Mohammed, 1962-

    HM1126 .R43 2001
    303.6'9—dc21   00-067792

Printed in the United States of America

♾™ The paper used in this publication meets the minimum requirements of American
National Standard for Information Sciences—Permanence of Paper for Printed Library
Materials, ANSI/NISO Z39.48–1992.

*This project was made possible
by the collaborative efforts of
American University's
Center for Global Peace
and
International Peace and Conflict Resolution Division,
School of International Service.*

Contents

Acknowledgments

There are so many people to thank. This volume would not exist without the successfully organized conference Promoting Justice and Peace through Reconciliation and Coexistence Alternatives that was held at the American University in February 1999. The conference was sponsored by American University's Center for Global Peace, the International Peace and Conflict Resolution (IPCR) Division in the School of International Service, and the Abraham Fund. I am grateful to Betty Sitka, the associate director of the Center for Global Peace, whose support and encouragement made both the conference and the edited volume possible. I sincerely appreciate the efforts that the sixteen contributors invested in producing their articles, and I appreciate their patience and understanding during the sometimes frustrating process of putting together such a manuscript. I am also thankful for the assistance of Lakshitha Saji Prelis, who acted as a technical and production editor in preparing the manuscript for copyediting, and patiently communicated with the contributors and publishers to bring this manuscript to life. Mitchell Hammer, Michael Salla, and Ron Fisher are all IPCR faculty who supported and contributed to the success of the conference and this volume. Finally, I am truly appreciative and thankful to Professor Abdul Aziz Said, founder and director of the IPCR Division and the Center for Global Peace at American University, for his leadership in bringing various aspects of the conference to life.

This volume is dedicated to all practitioners and scholars of peacebuilding, particularly those who have sacrificed many aspects of their lives to promote peace and justice in areas where most people have given up.

Introduction

For many years, the field of peacebuilding has focused on the first two conflict phases: (1) the prenegotiation phase, in which researchers and practitioners focus on strategies and ways to get the parties to the table; and (2) the negotiation phase, in which the main focus is on formulating effective strategies and overcoming obstacles for productive negotiation, facilitation, or mediation processes (Fisher 1993; Kelman 1993; Montville 1990). However, since the early 1990s several political agreements have been signed in deep-rooted conflicts that a decade ago seemed impossible to settle. South Africa, Israel-Palestine, Northern Ireland, Bosnia, Guatemala, and Nicaragua are some examples of such cases. The challenges and dynamics associated with the implementation of those agreements in the postsettlement phase attracted the interest of researchers and practitioners of peacebuilding. As a result, new research on the postsettlement phase has emerged (Lederach 1997; Wallensteen and Sollenberg 1997; Chufrin and Saunders 1993; Johnston and Simpson 1994). In this phase, researchers and practitioners focus on the implementation of the agreements. Thus, obstacles and ways of overcoming new political stalemates and innovative methods of transforming the conflicting parties' relationship become core themes in this phase (to illustrate the increase in research in this area, see the various recent studies published by the U. S. Institute for Peace).

An integral part of the postsettlement phase is the parties' ability to reconcile and reconstruct a new relationship. Researchers and practitioners began describing a need for new relationship processes, such as the transformation approach (Lederach 1997; Diamond and McDonald 1996; Bush and Folger 1994). Regardless of the term used in referring to this objective in the postsettlement phase, processes of reconciliation and contradictory perceptions of justice constitute the main challenges facing parties in their attempt to resolve their conflict.

This notion of reconciliation among conflicting parties is relatively unexplored by researchers of peacebuilding (only a few studies have examined reconciliation: Vas Ness 1996; Kriesberg 1997; Rwelamira and Werle 1996; and Lederach 1997). However, there are more articles and books on justice and forgiveness, particularly from theological and ideological perspectives (Assefa 1993; Johnston and Simpson 1994; Gopin 2000; and Henderson 1996). No comprehensive research has been conducted on the dynamics of interaction between justice, reconciliation, and the pursuit of peaceful coexistence among parties.

Similar challenges exist on the application level. Peacebuilding practitioners have gained important experience in the last decade in dealing with obstacles and challenges facing them in the postconflict phase. However, few of those practitioners have managed to document their experiences (Minow 1998; Hamber, Brandon, and van der Merwe 1998). Certainly no book has documented such experiences in a comparative context in which practitioners from different conflict areas in a postconflict phase share their experiences and models of intervention with each other.

Such a need for comparative cases of peacebuilding in postconflict areas that focus on reconciliation and justice is reflected in the work of many practitioners. For example, since 1990, this author has conducted many peacebuilding training workshops in Palestine, Israel, Africa, Northern Ireland, the United States, Sri Lanka, and other areas of the world. While conducting conflict resolution workshops in Gaza (since 1994), participants typically question or test the interveners and the model by voicing one of their main concerns about the post-Oslo environment, saying, "When we take part in these peacebuilding workshops are we being trained to give up our basic rights and sense of justice?" Following such a question, participants engage in a discussion of what justice means for Palestinians in the postsettlement phase.

In another context, the Arab-Jewish dialogue and coexistence workshops in Israel (having led Arab-Jewish dialogue groups since 1980) provide a unique encounter between Jews and Arabs in a postsettlement phase (since the establishment of Israel in 1948). In two- to three-day encounters, participants attempt to negotiate their different perceptions of justice and their requirements for reconciliation. The major question in these workshops is, "What type of coexistence do Arabs and Jews want in Israel? Do they want coexistence with justice or without it?, a question they often pose to each other.

In a training workshop on religious approaches to peacebuilding conducted at Eastern Mennonite University between 1997 and 2000, African participants (often priests) from Rwanda, Kenya, and Liberia expressed their concerns on how to facilitate reconciliation between the ex-militia groups who returned to the villages after their civil wars ended. These young men were ex-soldiers who killed, tortured, and mutilated other villagers. A Liberian priest asked in one of those workshops: "How do we begin a process of reconciliation with those young men? If we do not do that, our communities will not be restored. Should those young men have a place in our postconflict peacebuilding efforts? Some people in the village may be able to forgive, but most of the people cannot forgive or forget."

These are simply a few examples and questions generated from the field that reveal the gap between research and practice. They provide the basis for this volume, which explores the relationship between reconciliation, justice, and coexistence as central concepts in any sustainable peacebuilding process.

The swelling number of practitioners, researchers, and policymakers around the world who deal with similar questions and challenges related to the postsettlement phase stimulated the idea of bringing practitioners and academicians together in an international conference to examine the relationship between the three concepts of reconciliation, justice, and coexistence on both levels of theory and practice. This volume is a publication of the papers presented at the international conference by the various panelists and of supplemental research by several other scholar-practitioners. In addition, the concluding chapter summarizes the generic lessons from the case studies and the proposed theoretical frameworks.

The initiative for an international conference titled Promoting Justice and Peace through Reconciliation and Coexistence Alternatives was launched in March 1998 by the editor of this book. The American University's Center for Global Peace, the International Peace and Conflict Resolution Division in the School of International Service, and the Abraham Fund (New York) sponsored the conference. The call for papers on these themes generated eighty-five abstracts and inquiries from different parts of the globe. Eighteen abstracts were selected, and fourteen of those were invited to participate in an international conference on the subject hosted at the American University on February 19-20, 1999. Two hundred and forty-five participants from different parts of the world, the majority from the United States, attended this two-day conference.

Like the conference, this volume aims to: (1) facilitate interaction between researchers (theory) and practitioners (application) on the nexus of reconciliation, justice, and coexistence; (2) provide an in-depth examination of some specific case studies in which practitioners have addressed issues related to reconciliation and justice (the purpose of this exploration is to allow practitioners to share their stories with others and to describe what works and what does not work in dealing with issues of justice, coexistence, and reconciliation); (3) generate generic and particular lessons based on the various cases and the theoretical analysis; and (4) make such lessons available to other practitioners, researchers, and policymakers around the world.

To accomplish these objectives, contributors to this volume were asked to address a set of specific questions, such as:

(1) What is the relationship between the concepts of reconciliation and coexistence?

(2) How do different parties to a conflict (particularly in ethnic conflicts) respond to these concepts (justice, reconciliation, and coexistence)?

(3) What are the factors that make a reconciliation process effective?

(4) What are the obstacles and challenges that face communities and practitioners who wish to engage in reconciliation?

(5) What are the major theoretical or general principles/lessons which can be drawn from different experiences in working on reconciliation and coexistence?

(6) How do certain perceptions and a sense of justice contribute to or inhibit reconciliation or peaceful coexistence?

(7) What are the various models or methods to promote reconciliation in

the field of peacebuilding?

(8)   What are the current criteria used to evaluate successful methods of reconciliation and coexistence?

(9)   What are some examples of successful reconciliation and coexistence?

(10)   How does religion contribute to reconciliation and coexistence processes?

The gathering of practitioners and researchers from diverse regions, with different sets of expertise in reconciliation, allows the exchange of experiences across specific ethnic and communal conflicts. This volume provides a unique opportunity to reflect upon and compare a wide range of experiences, and a chance to generate theoretical principles in guiding intervention programs. For example, practitioners from Northern Ireland and South Africa as well as Palestine and Israel emphasized the importance of conducting systematic intervention programs in a uni-ethnic or separate national context as a necessary first step in promoting effective reconciliation.

Finally, this volume attempts to bridge theory and practice in the field of peacebuilding. Such initiative is only one initial step to advance the field on both levels of theory and practice. Working on this volume has provided further evidence of the pressing need for practitioners from different conflict areas to document case studies and examples from their work, to explicitly generate certain principles that were effective in their intervention in the context of reconciliation and justice, and to inspire more dialogue and cooperation among researchers and practitioners. Only through such interaction can new research questions and hypotheses be drawn.

The papers presented in this volume reflect creative and pioneering work that is being done by many of the practitioners and scholars in the field of peacebuilding. These include the introduction and analysis of rituals and symbolism in the process of reconciliation, by Lisa Schirch; the dynamics of the Truth Commission in a specific region of South Africa, by Hugo van der Merwe; the challenges facing relief workers in dealing with Bosnian refugees who returned to their home, by Barry Hart; Johan Galtung's typology of twelve ways for reconciliation; Marc Gopin's in-depth examination of the concept of forgiveness and its relationship to the reconciliation process; and the use of indigenous methods of reconciliation processes in Northen Ghana, by Hizkias Assefa.

In addition to the various essays, the concluding chapter in this volume offers, in the spirit of support and assistance to the practitioners and policymakers, overarching lessons revealed by the various case studies. For politicians, there is a valuable benefit that can be extracted from the experience gathered in one volume, because they—politicians—constantly deal with issues of postsettlement and attempt to handle difficult questions related to reconciliation and justice among various conflicting parties. Reconciliation and justice are essential concepts that require the attention of policymakers and practitioners before agreements are signed or negotiated political compromises are made publicly. Such attention will serve to reduce the resistance that is often expressed by constituents, often stemming from the inability of the negotiators and their respective leaders to address those issues of justice and reconciliation. The communities' different perceptions and their criteria for justice and reconciliation are often not included, incorporated, or even considered in the political agreements. In addition, most if not all of the negotiated agreements would require parties and their constituencies to redefine their perceptions of what is a just solution. Such redefinition often does not take place automatically with the signing of the political agreement, neither on the community grassroots level nor on the political leadership level. Such reality often becomes the source of stalemates and obstacles for future reconciliation, although a negotiated agreement has been signed between official representatives of the parties. Paying attention and responding to issues relating to reconciliation and justice are crucial for lasting agreements. Thus, both policymakers and practitioners can benefit from exploring the meaning of and relationships between justice, reconciliation, and peacebuilding strategies in the postsettlement phase.

References

Assefa, H. 1993. Peace and Reconciliation as a Paradigm: A Philosophy of Peace and Its Implications on Conflict, Governance, and Economic Growth in Africa. Nairobi Peace Initiative Monograph Series, no. 1. Nairobi: Majestic Press.

Bush, B., and Folger, J. 1994. *The Promise of Mediation*. San Francisco: Jossey-Bass.

Chufrin, G. I., and Saunders, H. H. 1993. A Public Peace Process. *Negotiation Journal,* vol. 9, no. 3: 155-177.

Diamond, L., and McDonald, J. 1996. *Mutli-Track Diplomacy: A Systems Approach to Peace*. West Hartford, Conn.: Kumarian Press.

Fisher, R. J. 1993. Developing the Field of Interactive Conflict Resolution: Issues in Training, Funding and Institutionalization. *Political Psychology*, vol. 14, no. 1: 123-138.

Garcia, E., ed. 1993. *Pilgram Voices: Citizens as Peacemakers*. Manila, Philippines: Ateneo de Manila University Press.

Gopin, M. 2000. Between Eden and Armageddon: The Future of World Religions, Violence, and Peacemaking. Oxford, U.K.: Oxford University Press.

Hamber, H., Brandon, A., and van der Merwe, H. 1998. What Is This Thing Called Reconciliation? *Reconciliation Review*, vol. 1 no. 1: 12-23.

Henderson, M. 1996. *The Forgiveness Factor: Stories of Hope in a World of Conflict*. London: Grosvenor Books.

Johnston, D., and Simpson, C., eds. 1994. *Religion: The Missing Dimensions of Statecraft*. Oxford, U.K.: Oxford University Press.

Kelman, H. 1993. Coalition Across Conflict Issues: The Interplay of Conflicts within and between the Israeli and Palestinian Communities. In *Conflict between People and Groups*. S. Worchel and J. Simpson, eds. Chicago: Nelson-Hall.

Kriesberg, L. 1997. Paths to Varieties of Inter-Communal Reconciliation. Paper presented at the annual scientific meeting of the International Society of Political Psychology, Krakow, Poland, July 21-24.

Krybill, R. 1988. From Head to the Heart: The Cycle of Reconciliation. *Conciliation Quarterly*, vol. 7, no. 4: 20-32.

Lederach, J. P. 1997. *Building Peace: Sustainable Reconciliation in Divided Societies.* Washington, D.C.: United States Institute for Peace Press.

Minow, M. 1998. *Between Vengeance and Forgiveness: Facing History after Genocide and Mass Violence.* Boston, Mass: Beacon Press.

Montville, J. 1990. *Conflict and Peacemaking in Multiethnic Societies.* Lexington, Mass.: Lexington Books.

Rwelamira, M. R., and Werle, G., eds. 1996. *Confronting Past Injustices: Approaches to Amnesty, Punishment, Reparation, and Restitution in South Africa and Germany.* Durban, South Africa: Butterworths.

Vas Ness, D. 1996. Restorative Justice and International Human Rights. In *Restorative Justice: International Perspectives.* B. Galaway and J. Hudson, eds. Monsey, N.Y.: Criminal Justice Press.

Wallensteen, P., and Sollenberg, M. 1997. Armed Conflicts, Conflict Termination and Peace Agreement, 1989-1996. *Journal of Peace Research,* vol. 34, no. 3: 339-358.

Reconciliation, Justice, and Coexistence

Part I

Theoretical Frameworks
for Reconciliation in Peacebuilding

1

After Violence, Reconstruction, Reconciliation, and Resolution

Coping with Visible and Invisible Effects of War and Violence

Johan Galtung

Reconstruction, reconciliation, and resolution are extremely complex concepts; their interrelation even more so. To navigate these waters, much attention first must be paid to definitions.

Justice can be interpreted as "to each party his/her due"; the problem is determining what this means. As legal frameworks tend to carry the imprint of past injustices, it is better to lean on concepts such as parity, equality, and equity. However, justice for slaves or for women cannot mean that they share the conditions of slave owners or men, but that some social order comes about where equality and equity (not the same) are possible.

Peace can be interpreted as "negative peace," which is the absence of violence, or as "positive peace," the capacity to deal with conflict nonviolently and creatively. The more justice, the easier it is to achieve and maintain peace.

Reconciliation will be interpreted as the process of healing the traumas of both victims and perpetrators after violence, providing a closure of the bad relation. The process prepares the parties for relations with justice and peace.

Coexistence is an agreement between parties to proceed on parallel tracks, each within its own dialectic. Coexistence can be interpreted as "passive coexistence," meaning negative peace, or as "active coexistence," meaning positive peace.

We will concentrate on twelve approaches to reconciliation, as follows:

1. The exculpatory nature-structure-culture approach
2. The reparation/restitution approach
3. The apology/forgiveness approach
4. The theological/penitence approach
5. The juridical/punishment approach
6. The codependent origination/karma approach
7. The historical/Truth Commission approach
8. The theatrical/reliving approach
9. The joint sorrow/healing approach
10. The joint reconstruction approach
11. The joint conflict resolution approach
12. The ho`o ponopono approach

Only by constructing an adequate combination of these approaches can the goal of reconciliation be reached.

Reconciliation After Violence: An Overview

Reconciliation = Closure + Healing; closure in the sense of not reopening hostilities, healing in the sense of being rehabilitated.[1] Reconciliation is a theme with deep psychological, sociological, theological, philosophical, and profoundly human roots—and nobody really knows how to successfully achieve it. But first, an introduction that will become more meaningful after reading about the twelve approaches, with proposals outlining scenarios for each.

There is usually a Third Party as a source of Grace, Law, and Justice, above perpetrator and victim: God (the Church), the State (the International Community), and Society (the People). In principle, the Third Party can only administer the relation between perpetrator and victim, or change that relation into a relation to itself; punishing the perpetrator and/or comforting the victim (including trying to answer the victim's basic question: *why me*, underlying the *theodicée*).[2]

The victim can seek restitution for the harm from the perpetrator or can seek to have the perpetrator punished; or the victim can "get even" with the perpetrator through revenge. Material and nonmaterial gratification may derive from this, but hardly reconciliation or release from the trauma.

The perpetrator may seek release from his guilt: from the Third Party through submission, penitence, or punishment; from the victim through apology and forgiveness; or from himself by hard inner work. Reconciliation essentially must take place between perpetrator and victim. But that also means that either of them can withhold reconciliation, putting the trauma/guilt into the "world trauma/guilt bank" and using them as weapons.[3]

The Exculpatory Nature-Structure-Culture Approach

The relation between perpetrator and victim, whether individual or collective, involves a violent act. How that act is understood conditions the relation between the two. Hypotheses:

An actor-oriented perspective endorsing the perpetrator with free will unfettered by extenuating circumstances makes the relation particularly bitter and both closure and healing difficult to obtain. There is the possibility of a "trauma for guilt" exchange: "I live with my trauma, you with your guilt."

An actor-oriented perspective with free will reduced by extenuating circumstances may make the trauma easier to bear, but as the guilt is reduced by the circumstances, the "trauma for guilt" exchange is difficult to obtain.

A structure-oriented perspective converts the relation from interpersonal, or interstate/nation, to a relation between two positions in a deficient structure. If the parties can agree that the structure was/is deficient and that their behavior was an enactment of structural positions rather than anything more personal, then turning together against the common problem—the structural violence—should be possible: "We are both victims."

A culture-oriented perspective also converts the relation from interpersonal, or interstate/nation, to a relation spurred by a deficient culture. If the parties can agree that the culture was/is deficient and that their behavior was an enactment of that culture of violence rather than anything more personal, then turning together against that common problem—the cultural violence—should be possible: "We are both victims."

The key word in the last two hypotheses is "agree." "Outer conditions made you a perpetrator and me a victim. There is no good reason for us to hate each other; not for you to feel excessive guilt, nor for me to develop the victim psychology. Not only can we close that vicious circle and heal our psychological wounds by forgetting them, we can even reconcile with each other, put the past behind us. We can join forces and fight those conditions that pitted us against each other in horrible acts of violence."

Even if this is not the full truth, it can be more than half the truth. Moreover, it can be self-fulfilling. Outsiders, like peace workers, may suggest this perspective to the parties as a way of thinking about their own situation. This may be better done with one party at the time than with the parties together, lest the victims get upset by seeing the perpetrator grabbing the opportunity, or lest the perpetrators want to cash in more on their guilt and the victims on their trauma. Let them first arrive at an exculpatory position, then bring them together to celebrate a joint approach.

A basic problem arises when the symmetry breaks down. Parties' acts may be enactment of structural positions, but in different structures or from different positions in the same structure. And yet soldiers forced to kill by different states nevertheless enact the same lethal state war logic to kill unless both sides become conscientious objectors. And even if the landowner may prefer to keep the land of his ancestors and not yield to the landless, he may also be brought to see that position as untenable. The same applies to culture: people may be hit by violent aspects of the same culture, or violent aspects of different cultures. In either case the peace worker's task is to carefully and tactfully open the eyes of the parties to a conflict to shared victimhood and to the peaceful perspectives.

The Reparation/Restitution Approach

X has harmed Y, X is conscious of his guilt, Y is conscious of the trauma. X comes to Y and offers reparation/restitution: I'll undo the harm done by undoing the damage, repairing, restituting, and restoring the status quo. At the simplest level—buying a new vase to replace the vase broken—to the most complex level of countries and alliances at war with each other, money, goods, and services start flowing to undo the damage. Sometimes the relation is direct, sometimes via institutions such as insurance companies (e.g., for damage done to cars in accidents; countries as yet do not insure against damage in wars). But, as any house or car owner knows, there is also the time lost in the process, with opportunity costs. But reparation must always be more comprehensive than the replacement cost.

This approach only works when the violence is reversible. Irreversibility not only applies to a broken vase from the Ming dynasty that could have affective value as a family heirloom. When trauma has been wrought and is deep-rooted, any restitution borders on an insult, adding violence to violence.

Second, trying to make the victim forget what happened by filling the gap caused by the harm has an element of "buying oneself off the hook." The perpetrator is seen as trying to buy release from guilt. The harm is reduced to a commodity to be traded: "By mistake I took something from you; here, you have it back with an extra 10 percent for inconvenience and time lost."

Third, "there is no business like reparation business." With goods and services flowing, postreparation demands may be created with the possibility that it was all premeditated, or at least that somebody will think it was all premeditated. "Please bomb that factory and open for imports of my products and/or for a contract for me to rebuild."

The task of the peace worker is to explore all these arguments with the perpetrator and the victim so that they fully understand the repercussions if this is the approach chosen. They both have to accept the approach so that the perpetrator does not offer something that falls on deaf ears, or worse, increases the aggressiveness. And the victim should not start expecting a restitution that never comes, for whatever reason.

Beyond this there is something very practical a peace worker may do: suggest the concrete act of restitution. People have limited imagination, and this is not a question of finding a gift for an anniversary. The victim must want the act of restitution, but more important the act must convey the correct symbolic message. And that also goes for the perpetrator. He may, for instance, be afraid that the act of restitution is an implicit admission of guilt and can be held against him as a confession. He may also worry that the act will not lead to closure as a condition for reconciliation. He may wonder about the time perspective: Is it one act of restitution, or a series of follow-ups? Will it take place every year, like an anniversary of the evil act? Will flowers do? And so on.

Restitution is a transaction. A transaction is a two-way action, so there has to be some balance and symmetry. The instrument to ensure this is a *contract* signed by both perpetrator and victim. The peace worker should know how to draw up such a document, thus serving as a barefoot lawyer, in addition to being a theologian and a psychologist for reconciliation tasks. It may be objected that this is too formal, not sufficiently spontaneous, symbolic, or healing. True, but for those who choose this approach, this may be a minor matter.

The Apology/Forgiveness Approach

X has harmed Y; X is conscious of his guilt, Y is conscious of the harm. Both are traumatized. X comes to Y, offers "sincere apologies" for the harm, Y accepts the apologies. There is potentially a double spiritual transformation. What was initiated by violence is terminated by offering *and* accepting an apology; both-and, not either-or. Metaphors of turning a new leaf or opening a new chapter or even a new book in their relations are invoked. The slate is clean, now to be inscribed with positive acts. There is agreement that what happened is "forgotten," in the sense of not to be referred to.[4] But is it also "forgiven"? Does "I accept your apology" mean "I forgive you"? Definitely not. Some possible readings of this major drama in four acts:

"I apologize" = "I wish what I did undone and promise, no more"
"I accept your apology" = "I believe what you say, let's go on"
"Please forgive me" = "Please release me from my guilt to you"
"I forgive you" = "I hereby release you from your guilt to me"

Thus, forgiving goes one step further, relating to the trauma of guilt. Guilt is in the spirit, and it arises from the consciousness of having wronged someone. This establishes a relation to the victim, to one's own Ego, and to any God/State believed in. The victim can only release the wrongdoer from the first guilt. To some, however, this is the only important guilt.

Positive in the approach is a bond of compassion between X and Y; negative is its superficiality. Just as restitution is good for people with money, apology is for those with words. X agrees to see the harm as wrong, as something he or she wishes undone, and Y helps him or her by saying that X can now live as if no harm was wrought. But the causes of the violence are left untouched. The approach is attitude-oriented not contradiction-oriented, but hopefully with behavioral effects.

For the peace worker this is very different from the reparation/restitution approach. There is a transaction, and both parties have to be willing, meaning that either one can sabotage that process. What is needed is only for the victim not to accept the apology, or not to forgive; and for the perpetrator not to extend any apology, or not to ask for forgiveness. The drama in four acts is very vulnerable.

In addition, whereas there is something economic and contractual in the process of restitution, this transaction is spiritual/psychological. Both parties have to be "in the mood" to enter this relationship. This is probably preceded by a feeling of having looked into the abyss: it is this approach or else hatred and retribution rather than restitution, with no end.

The presumed psychological mechanism is something like this. On the surface X and Y are enacting the drama in four acts together, and relieve X of his guilt. But deeper down, in doing so, Y is also partly relieved of his or her trauma. Y, the offended party, commands the moral high ground. Extending forgiveness from that position does not leave Y's own trauma untouched.

And yet there is something missing. Like most victims in Western legal models, the victim is left asking, "What's in it for me?" This is the point where in addition to psychological mechanisms, some restitution might do much good. *The perpetrator has to deserve being forgiven.* That brings us close to the South African Truth and Reconciliation process, designed to maximize attainment of the truth about apartheid. The peace worker steers the process toward closure. Much knowledge, skills, and, above all, human tact will be needed where most of the training one would gain will be on the job.

The Theological/Penitence Approach

In the Western world this approach is associated with Christianity. It is perpe-trator-oriented in general, and guilt-oriented in particular. Above, three dimen-sions of guilt have been indicated: toward Other, the victim; toward Self; toward God/State. Matthew 25:40, for example, quotes Christ as saying, "Inasmuch as ye have done it unto one of the least of these my brethren, ye have done it unto me." Here Christ is verticalizing the guilt, lifting it out of the Self-Other context, moving it to the Self-God context (Self-Self is seen as deriving from the latter). Self-Other comes second.

The approach then proceeds in a well-described, well-prescribed chain: submission-confession-penitence-absolution; to and from God, via His repre-sentative, the Church (in the Orthodox and Catholic models), or directly (in the Protestant model). The penitence is mainly self-administered: prayer, fasting, celibacy, monastery, and flagellation. Better some pain in this life than eternal pain in the afterlife. Absolution then releases the perpetrator, the sinner, from his guilt and sin, unto God.

One problem is that this only works for the believer. There is little in this for the atheist. Nor for the Protestant not accepting the word of the Church as final; his guilt remains a burden. He needs a more direct issue of the "no guilt" certificate.

In addition, this solves neither the Self-Other problem, nor the Self-Self problem. It may even exacerbate both of them, being used as an excuse to avoid any encounter with Other, claiming that God solved the problem. If the Self-Self problem refuses to go away, doubts about God's absolution may arise. And Other is left with the *theodicée*[5] and the general *Why me?*

The title of the peace worker in this case is the priest. A double, triple vocation is nothing new for a person who very often has to be a social worker. What should the priest look out for to be a good peace worker on top of his theological role?

The basic point has already been mentioned: broaden the perspective. The priest helps by paving the way for reconciliation with God, and thereby, for the believer, with Self. To do this he may have to strengthen Self's faith, help remove doubts. But Other still remains: the victim, the forgotten party.

Consider the approaches already discussed. Broadening the perspective means taking something away from one or more of them. Obviously, the priest cannot make full use of the nature-structure-culture approach. The will to hurt or harm may be conditioned by nature, structure, or culture up to a point, but some *free will* remains, and with that, guilt and responsibility. But the priest can make use of restitution and apology.

What is recommended is that the priest who has turned peace worker includes Other, trying to pave the way for reconciliation between perpetrator and victim. The perpetrator will have to broaden the God/Self-oriented focus on absolution and include the Other-oriented focus on apology and restitution. A major problem remains, however.

The victim may say: "*Leave me alone*, I have had enough suffering; I should not have to meet him again, accept some acts of restitution, even listen to his insincere apologies. Nothing will ever undo what happened." The reaction is understandable, and the peace worker may have to be a go-between if the direct encounter is too hard on either or both. Rather than bringing them together he may have to rely on the dialogue with each one of them. The theological/penitence approach alone is simply too partial in its perpetrator-orientation; it has to be broadened.

The Juridical/Punishment Approach

This is the secular version of the above, according to the *plus ça change plus c'est la même chose* (the more things change, the more they stay the same). The successor to God is the State (in the United States often the "People"); the successor to the perpetrator is the perpetrator and to the victim is the victim; and the perpetrator-victim relation is transformed (actually deformed) into a perpetrator-State relation with the judge in the role (and almost the robes) of the priest. The prescribed process now reads *submission-confession-punishment-readmission* (to society). The logic is the same. The perpetrator is released from the guilt toward "society"; the other two forms of guilt remain. For problems, see the preceding approach.

How do International Tribunals work for collective violence? As one would expect. The accused would tend to be the perpetrators of person-to-person violence: lower-class people who kill with machetes and gas chambers, not middle-class people who kill with missiles and atom bombs. And, they would tend to be the executors of violence rather than the civilians giving the order, or setting the stage; *in bellum* rather than *ad bello*. As a result, the general moral impact will probably be relatively negligible.[6] Victor's justice.

But tribunals exist, with a major one for war crimes, crimes against humanity, and genocide coming up. As they are conceived of, within the juridical/punishment framework, they will all more or less be carriers of all the problems indicated. The key to the solution is broadening, adding other approaches.

The title of the peace worker, in this case, is the judge (and, to a much lesser extent, some of the prison personnel). Like the priest, the judge also has to add something to his juridical profession, which, like the priest, is to see to it that what happens is according to the Book. Of what should he or she be aware in order to be a good peace worker, on top of his or her juridical role?

The judge should realize that the task is not finished when the relation to the International Community (of States) is cleared because the prison sentence has been served. The perpetrator-State perspective is too narrow. Imprisonment does something to the body by limiting the movement, leaving the capacities of the spirit basically untouched, even enhanced. The judge should add the skills of the priest, and the priest may have to learn how to do the theological/penitence approach with nonbelievers.

Then there is the possibility of adding the restitution and apology approaches; in other words, of moving very close to the South African process of Truth as the road to Reconciliation. And there could be a tacit or explicit understanding that the success of that process could shorten the sentence, but not down to amnesty. The Truth has presumably already come forth through the well-tested methods of the juridical approach, with evidence, testimonies, *pro et contra dicere*, and final evaluation. What is needed is an expansion of the juridical/punishment approach to include restitution, apology, and a genuine inner change.

The Codependent Origination/Karma Approach

That Buddhism has an ethics of nonviolence (*ahimsa*) is known to most; that it also has a system analysis epistemology based on interacting causal chains/cycles is less known.[7] Concretely this means the following: although any human being at any point can choose not to act violently, the decision is influenced by his *karma*, his moral status at that moment, the accumulation of "whatever you say, whatever you do, sooner or later comes back to you,"[8] *and* by the victim's karma, *and* by their joint, collective karma; the sum total of the merits and demerits of earlier action.

Since these intertwining chains stretch into the before-lives of the past, the side-lives of the context, and the after-lives of the future, the demerit of a violent act cannot be placed at the feet of a single actor only. There is always shared responsibility for a bad karma. Hence, the way to improve the karma is through an *outer dialogue*, which in practice means a roundtable where the seating pattern is symmetric, allocating nobody to such roles as defendant, prosecutor, counsel, and judge; with rotating chairperson. But prior to this, meditation is an *inner dialogue*, with inner voices trying to come to grips with the forces inside oneself.

Thus, in Buddhist thinking there is no actor who alone carries 100 percent of the responsibility; it is all shared in space and time. Where Christianity can be accused of being too black and white, Buddhism can be accused of being too gray. But the idea of cooperating to plug the holes in the boat we share rather than searching for the one who drilled the first hole, including having a court case on board as the boat is sinking, is appealing, both for conflict resolution and for reconciliation.

In conflict theory, the concept that comes closest to this is the *conflict formation*.[9] The first task in any conflict transformation process is to map the conflict formation, identifying the parties that have a stake in the outcome, identifying their goals, and identifying the issues, meaning the clashes of goals. Since empirical conflicts (as opposed to the conflicts on a professor's blackboard) tend to be complex—high on the numbers of parties and goals—the maps are complex, but nowhere near the complexity of Buddhist causal theory.

However, the peace worker can use the mapping tool of the conflict worker and proceed basically the same way. He can have dialogues with all parties over the theme "after violence, what"? He can identify conflicts, hard and soft, and try to transcend them by stimulating joint creativity. Or, he can bring them all together and be the catalyst and facilitator around, rather than at the end of, the roundtable. Conflict work and peace work are closely related, and this approach is based on the combination of inner dialogues (meditation) and outer dialogues (mediation), with or without the peace workers as a medium.

Very few people in the world would know even the outline of all the other eleven approaches in this chapter. One of the tasks of the peace worker is to bring them to their attention. The karma approach is an excellent point of departure, given its holism, neutrality, and appeal to dialogue. In that sense it is actually a meta-approach, above or after the other approaches, accommodating all of them, like the *ho'o ponopono* approach outlined at the end of this chapter. It is an attitude, a philosophy of life, beyond the stark dichotomy of perpetrator-victim, and in that sense different from the preceding four, more similar to the rest.

The Historical/Truth Commission Approach

The basic point is to describe in great detail *wie es eigentlich gewesen* (what really happened), letting the acts, including the violent acts, appear as the logical consequences of the antecedents, with the assumption that *tout comprendre c'est tout pardonner* (to understand all is to forgive all). Although "getting the facts straight"—however ugly—is important, there are serious problems.[10]

First of all, the famous French quote may have a moral appeal to some people, but it is often disconfirmed as a descriptive hypothesis. The hideous acts are understood, including or not the names of perpetrators. But they are not pardoned: why impunity, why should they get off the hook? It may be argued that the perpetrators will also read the report that establishes their guilt to the victims, to themselves, and to the God they may believe in, and they will be tormented by that and by social ostracism. And that is punishing, not forgiving.

Second, this does not by itself produce the catharsis of the offered and received apology, the hoped for and offered forgiveness. Truth alone is merely descriptive, not spiritual.

Third, positivist historians are not good at deep culture and deep structure, at the subconscious without "sources." And *counterfactual history, what might have happened if* (history in the subjunctive, not indicative mode) and *the history of the future, how do we avoid this in the future*, are forbidden territory.

Fourth, we shouldn't limit the process to professionals whose task is to come up with the official version. Better to have ten thousand people's commissions, in each local community, in each nongovernmental organization (NGO), using round tables, involving all parties, themselves trying to arrive at a joint understanding, reconciling in the process.

The task of the peace worker is to organize those dialogues and to see to it that the findings flow into some general pool. One way of doing this is to put at the disposal of the citizens in any part of a war-torn society a big book with blank pages to be inscribed by them. The book will become a part of the collective memory, no doubt subjectively formulated, but that will also be its strengths. Rather than *the* Truth lawyers and historians think they can establish, that book will accommodate thousands of truths. Contained in the book would be descriptions of violence and traumas, not only what happened but also how it touched citizens, wounded them. Added to that would come their thoughts on what could have been done, their thoughts on reconstruction and reconciliation, on the resolution of the underlying conflict, and their hopes for the future.

In other words, the citizens would themselves establish their truths. Something like this was done by the *Opsahl* Commission for Northern Ireland some years ago,[11] and no doubt played a role in externalizing the conflict, seeing it as something objective, outside the participants, to be handled. *Soka Gakkai*[12] in Japan has also done an impressive job of collecting the war memories of many women in twenty-six volumes,[13] thereby establishing a collective memorial to be consulted by future generations. The madness of violence is amply documented.

But the major task of the peace worker is to give the search for Truth the two twists indicated while remaining truthful to empirical facts: *counterfactual history; what might have happened if*, and *the history of the future, how do we avoid this in the future*. Again, let ten thousand dialogues blossom!

The Theatrical/Reliving Approach

This approach would try exactly that: involve all parties in ten thousand exercises to relive what happened. This is not a question of documentation and "objectivity," but of reliving the subjective experiences. The ways to do so are numerous indeed.

Just telling what happened as it happened, as a witness to a historical/truth commission is already reliving, revealing, and relieving. To have the other parties do the same adds to it. To tell the stories together, in the same room, adds a dimension of dialogue, easily very emotional (*That's not how it happened!; Is that why you did it?*) Then, to stand up, reenact it up to, not including, the violence, *may* have a cathartic effect provided there is tension release through dialogue. The parties may even switch roles. But isn't that coming too close? It depends; like in a negotiation, sometimes it's better to keep them apart. The important point is to arrive at a deeper understanding, more emotional, less merely descriptive.

An alternative approach is, of course, for a professional to write the narrative histories and present it on national television for common consumption. That should not be excluded, but in plural, not with the idea of writing one play to finish all plays.

A basic advantage of the theater approach, however rudimentary and amateurish, is that it opens windows so often closed to positivist social science: *what might have happened if* and *how do we avoid this in the future*. The players can relive history up to the point where it went wrong and then, together, invent an alternative continuation. Then they go on inventing alternative futures, with theater as a workshop for visioning possible futures. A play can be rerun at any point; history, unfortunately, cannot.[14]

The peace worker would have to talk with the parties in advance, have them tell their truths about what happened and then get their general consent for the theatrical approach. If it can be done with the real parties as actors and very close to the real story, then fine. Example: a sexual harassment conflict in a school with a student complaining that the teacher made advances, the teacher denying that this was the case, and then the principal saying, "Show us what happened." In a real case, those who watched actually concluded that the teacher did not "go too far," but also that the girl had good reasons for having apprehensions about what might have happened next. In a concrete situation, there are so many dimensions to what happens that words are hardly able to catch it all. Enacting it may.

Others may be called upon as stand-ins for roles or scenes too painful for the real participants to enact. The drama can also be rewritten so that "any similarity with any real case is totally coincidental." The point is to vent emotions in a holistic setting by enacting them, taking in as much of the totality of the situation as needed. Writing the play, however, before and/or after it was enacted, is also very valuable.

Technically, videotaping may be useful not only to improve the accuracy of the enactment ("let us take that one again, I am not sure you captured what happened"), but also to be able to stop the video and say: "This is the turning point. This is where it went wrong. Let us now try to enact an alternative follow-up, what should have and could have been done."

Obviously, making and enacting conflict-related plays is an indispensable part of the training of conflict workers for reconstruction and resolution, not only for reconciliation.[15]

The Joint Sorrow/Healing Approach

We saw, as in a mirror, the immaturity of Western culture in connection with the VE and VJ (victory Europe, Japan) fiftieth anniversary celebrations May 8 and September 2, 1995. The basic content was the victory over evil forces and homage paid to those who "gave" their lives. Both contributed to the culture of war by seeing war as a legitimate instrument in struggles between good and evil and by justifying the loss of life and the bereavement. Consider this alternative:

Joint sorrow is announced for all participating countries (and others who might like to join). The myth that some people "gave" their lives is revealed for what it is: those people had their lives taken away from them by incompetent politicians, incapable of transforming conflicts, themselves incurring little or no risk but willing to send others into (almost) certain death, spreading that death to others in the process.

Without opening a new front against the political and military class as a common enemy, war as such is deeply deplored. People dress in black, sit down in groups of about ten or twenty with people from former enemy countries, and turn to the basics: How could the war have been avoided? How do we avoid wars in the future? Are there somewhere acts of peace to highlight and celebrate?

To discuss how a war could have been avoided is nothing new; any country that has been attacked may engage in that debate on every anniversary (and one conclusion is often to be better armed for next time). To discuss this together with the aggressor—jointly deploring any war as a scandal, a crime against humanity, searching for alternatives in the past and the future—is relatively new and promising. It is important to fully engage people at all levels including the elite.

The point is the togetherness. As time passes, more meetings of this kind take place, usually gatherings of veterans from both sides. They may be fascinated by the other side of the military story, evaluating victories and defeats in light of new information. If they are soldiers in the real sense there may even be no need for reconciliation. They were professionals doing a job, only destructive rather than constructive. All professionals want to know whether they did a good job; few would know this better than the other side.

The task of the peace worker is not to organize encounters of killing and demolition experts, however, but also to have veterans meet civilians, civilians meet civilians, and to have both of them meet the politicians who gave the orders. An important question is: When will acts of war, and not only cruelty on the ground, carry nametags? Who ordered that bombing, killing X civilians? Give not only the well-known names at the very top of the hierarchy (their orders are usually general) but names of the officers whose orders were more specific.

Such encounters should not become tribunals. *The focus is on healing through joint sorrow*, not on self-righteousness. The model would be a village, a town, a district recently hit by natural disaster. There are local fault lines and enmities, although nobody accuses anybody on the other side of having caused a fault line or of having even willed the disaster. There are casualties, there is massive bereavement, flags at half-mast, people in black, the shared, joint sorrow across fault lines. Of course, there is healing in this. Right after a war may be too early for joint sorrow. But after some years the time will come. That opportunity should be taken advantage of.

The Joint Reconstruction Approach

Again, with this approach the point is to do it together.[16] German soldiers in World War II for example, used a "scorched earth" tactic in Northern Norway, leaving nothing to the advancing Red Army, driving out the inhabitants. Would it be possible for those inhabitants to cooperate with the soldiers after the war was over, making the scorched earth blossom again, coming alive with plants, animals, and humans, with building and infrastructure?

The good thing, which should not be seen as an enemy of the perfect, would be to have civilians from the same nation come and participate in the reconstruction. Of course, they would not be representatives of the perpetrators of the violence, they may even be their antagonists (like sending conscientious objectors to clean up after the soldiers, the nonobjectors). But they would show that there are hard and soft aspects of that nation, as of any nation, that count toward depolarization. Moreover, there would not be the direct confrontation between perpetrators and victims; years may be needed before that event. Nevertheless that is what one should aim for, which brings us back to the point about revenge: by having violence both ways, not only harm but also guilt may be equalized (to some extent); the parties will meet as moral equals. But even better would be to build moral equality around positive acts.

Hence, the argument would be for soldiers on both sides to disarm and then meet again, but this time to construct, not to destruct. Then victims could meet with victims, commanding officers with commanding officers, and so on.[17] And this could serve as preparations for perpetrator and victim meeting each other, both of them together trying to turn their tragedy into something meaningful through acts of cooperation, rather than putting some third parties in between.

This approach was once suggested in Beirut, where there was an interesting objection: "That does not work here." In Lebanon there were not two parties fighting each other, but seventeen. Ammunition was used like popcorn, peppering houses, obviously very rarely hitting the openings, and leaving bullet scars all over. The response could be to recruit one former fighter from each group, give them a course in masonry, put seventeen ladders parallel, and have the seventeen climb up, repairing the facades as they descend. Turn the high numbers into an advantage. What a TV opportunity—provided there is also a spiritual side to the joint work.

And that last point is the crux of the matter. Rebuilding is concrete, while reconciliation is mainly spiritual. What matters is the togetherness at work, reflecting on the mad destruction, shoulder to shoulder and mind to mind. The preceding four approaches could give rich texture to the exercise:

Joint sorrow would seep in even if rebuilding can also be fun. Reflection on futility would enter. For this to happen those who did the destruction should also do the construction, facilitating *reliving* on the spot. In so doing, two or more parties will together find a deeper, more dynamic, *truth*. And they will realize how deeply they share the same *karma*, fate. Then, the peace worker should remember that there is much more to reconstruction than rebuilding physical infrastructure. Institutions have to function again; maybe the parties can exchange experiences. There are heavily war-struck segments to care for, refugees and displaced persons to resettle. There are *atomie* (fragmentation) and *anomie* (normalness) to be overcome by reconstructing structures and cultures. War hits all parties about the same way, some lightly, some heavily. It is inconceivable that nobody from the former enemies will cooperate in joint reconstruction. It is certainly worth a try.

The Joint Conflict Resolution Approach

If joint reconstruction might be possible, how about joint conflict resolution? After all, that is what diplomats, politicians, even military to some extent try to do. But there are two basic problems with their approach regardless of the quality of the outcome. It is top-heavy, antiparticipatory, and therefore in itself some kind of structural violence, often even excluding those on whose behalf they presumably are negotiating behind veils of secrecy. And they are often protected elite who may not themselves have been the physical, direct victims of violence. They may only have unleashed that violence.

So the argument here would be for general, even massive participation. Two ways of doing this should be emphasized: the *therapy of the past*, having people discuss what went wrong at what point and then what could have been done; and *the therapy of the future*, having people discuss and imagine how the future would turn out if nothing is done in favor of a more sustainable peace, and what that work would look like, starting here and now. In short, people would be active participants in conflict resolution—as subjects, not only as the objects of somebody else's decisions and deeds.

And in the process of doing so, human and cultural healing, as well as structural healing, would take place. As mentioned, a major form of horizontal structural violence before, during, and after a war is polarization; what could be more depolarizing than reconciliation through joint efforts to solve the problems? The psychological costs might be considerable, but the social gains would be enormous. All that is needed would be for the ideas to flow together in a public JIP, the joint idea pool.

Here the peace worker becomes a conflict worker again, trying Conflict Transformation by Peaceful Means.[18] Let us say efforts were made in the "before violence" phase; is it now easier or more difficult in the "after violence" phase? No doubt it is more difficult in the sense that there are two additional jobs to do: reconstruction and reconciliation. But is the resolution, or transformation, also more difficult?

We can argue both ways. On the one hand, the violence may have hardened both sides. The victor, if there is one, feels that he can dictate the outcome, having won the violent process. The loser is thinking of revenge and *revanche*, and will never accept the outcome in his heart. But there may also be acceptance, even sustainability if the terms are not too harsh. And there may be something more convincing: a fatigue effect. Whatever the outcome, never that violence again! How long that fatigue effect will last is another matter.[19]

One problem, as mentioned earlier, is that the tasks of reconstruction are so pressing that reconciliation, as well as resolution, recedes into the background. The peace worker has to keep the resolution *problématique* alive. Above are many examples of how reconstruction and reconciliation can transform the whole setting so that a conflict that once was very hard can become softer. Thus, Germany, for example, will probably ultimately have no border problems, because borders wither away within the same supranational organization, the European Union. An overarching structure reduced the polarization in Europe's midst and made transformations possible, at least in the longer run. So the task is to steer "2R" (Reconstruction and Resolution) so that they have a positive effect on resolution, never forgetting that the task is "3R" (Reconstruction, Resolution, and Reconciliation).

The Ho`o ponopono Approach

A man is asleep in his home. He is awakened by some noises, and he gets up in time to catch a young boy fleeing the home with some stolen money. The police are called. The young boy is known to the police, obviously a "delinquent," and as they say: "Three strikes and you're out."

The place is Hawaii. In Polynesian culture there is a tradition combining reconstruction, reconciliation, and resolution. The ho`o ponopono (setting straight)[20] is known to others through cultural diffusion, for example, to the owner of the burglarized house. He looks at the boy and thinks of him spending twenty years in prison. He suggests to the police, "Let me handle this one." It transpires that the boy's sister is ill, and the family is too poor to pay for medical care. Every dollar counts.

Ho`o ponopono is organized. The man's family, neighbors, and the young boy and his family sit around a table; there is a moderator, not from the families and neighbors, but the "wise man/woman." There are four phases: facts, sharing responsibility, joint reconciliation, and closure. Each one is encouraged to *sincerely* present his or her version: why it happened, how, and what would be the appropriate reaction. The young boy's reason is questioned, but even if the reason is accepted, his method is not. Apologies are then offered and accepted; forgiveness is demanded and offered.

The young boy has to make up for the violation by doing free garden work for some time. The rich man and neighbors agree to contribute to the family's medical expenses. And in the end the story of the burglary is written up in a way acceptable to all. *That sheet of paper is then burnt*—symbolizing the end to the burglary but not to the aftermath.

Is this rewarding the burglar? If this restores all parties, reconciles them, and resolves the conflict, then what is the harm?

It may all sound simple, but it is not. This approach requires deep knowledge and skills from a conflict/peace worker bringing the parties together and acting as the wise person who is chairing the session. No approach has so many of the "3R" elements as this one. There is rehabilitation of the victim, respecting his feelings and giving him a voice; there is apology and restitution. There can be manifestations of sorrow, even joint sorrow. Better than restructuration/-culturation, a new structure is being built to bring people together who never met before, sharing the karma of this conflict, imbued with the culture of this way of approaching a conflict. There are efforts to see the acts in light of extenuating circumstances: nature, structure, cultures. But then restitution and apology followed by forgiveness are built in. So are elements of penitence and punishment, but in a way building ties between victim and perpetrator. We have mentioned the karma element. The Truth element is obvious, only that all parties have to tell their truths (making it easier for the perpetrator to do so). No doubt the result will be like a replay of Kurosawa's *Rashomon*.[21] This is also theater: *ho`o ponopono* is a reconstruction of what happened, with the parties as actors. And it is all very *joint*.

In short, Polynesian culture puts together what Western culture keeps apart. There is coherence to these processes, and that coherence got lost in the Western tendency to subdivide and select, and more particularly to select the punishment approach. So, perhaps a culture that managed to keep it all together is at a higher level than a culture that out of this holistic approach to "after violence" (including "after economic violence") selects only a narrow spectrum.

Conclusion

Some conclusions flow from these explorations.

There is no panacea. Taken *singly* none of the approaches is capable of handling the complexity of the "after violence" situation, healing so many kinds of wounds, closing the violence cycles, and reconciling the parties to themselves, to each other, and to whatever higher forces there may be.

One reason is that they are all embedded in dense nets of assumptions, some of them cultural. Westerners would have no difficulty recognizing *ho`o ponopono* as culturally specific, or "ethnic," but tend to claim that the theological and juridical approaches are universal, using Western = universal; however, human stupidity has to be tempered with human wisdom, which, in turn, has to be taken from wherever we find it. Cultural eclecticism is a must in the field of reconciliation; we cannot draw on any one culture alone.

Taken *combined,* these approaches may make more sense. The problem is to design good combinations for a given situation, and that obviously requires knowledge, skill, and experience.

Some of the twelve approaches work best in groups of two or three:

- 1 and 5: the `exculpatory approach (nobody is guilty) and the karma approach (we are all guilty/responsible); together, these perspectives may have great conciliatory effect.
- 2 and 3: reparation/restitution and apology/forgiveness complete each other and may work if the case is not too difficult.
- 4 and 5: the penitence and the punishment approaches also complete each other and may release the perpetrator from guilt.

- 7 and 8: the historical and theatrical approaches complete each other, providing an image of factual and potential truths.
- 9, 10, and 11: the joint sorrow, joint reconstruction, and joint resolution approaches are based on the same methodology.
- 12: the *ho`o ponopono* approach is very holistic, in a sense incorporating all the eleven other approaches.

As there is some validity to each approach, why not try them all? The nature-structure-culture approach may blunt the trauma and the guilt and pave the way for more symmetric approaches, with shared responsibility. *Ho`o ponopono* practiced high and low in society might deepen that sharing. The three "joint approaches" could be initiated at an early stage, at a modest level, to gain experience. At the same time history commissions and theater groups could start operating. If somebody has broken the law by committing crimes of war and genocide, they will of course have to be brought to justice, facing the State, the Community of States, and his or her God. (There is no argument against that here; the argument is that the approach taken alone does not necessarily lead to reconciliation.)

The time has then come for the two approaches that together give the meaning of reconciliation that most people probably have in mind: forgiveness, to the aggressor/perpetrator who has deserved being forgiven. In a two-way transaction, reciprocity is needed. What flows in the other direction is a combination of a deeply felt apology based on a deep truth, and restitution—in some cases to be televised nationally.

But that transaction will only lead to healing-closure-reconciliation in a context of all the other approaches, as a crowning achievement. Done too early it may fall flat, particularly if outsiders enter and say, "Well, you surely have been through tough times, but it is all over now, so why not shake hands and let bygones be bygones?" Trauma, including the trauma flowing from guilt, may fill a person to the brim and beyond. Feelings that overwhelming will have to be treated with respect. And respect takes time.

In all of this, two classical traditions have crystallized with clear contours: the priest and the judge. They carry prestige in society because they know the book that can open the gates to heaven or hell, to freedom or prison. The other ten approaches are less professionalized if we assume that historians do not have a monopoly on truth, nor playwrights on drama. For all approaches, a versatile, experienced peace worker would be meaningful. He is not certifying people as damned/saved or guilty/nonguilty. He is trying to help them come closer to each other, not to love each other but to establish reasonable working relations that will not reproduce the horrors. The bitter past should become a closed book; what happened should be forgiven but not forgotten. In doing so the peace worker will have to work with the priest and the judge without letting the asymmetry of their ways of classifying human beings become his own.

One simplified, superficial, but not meaningless way of doing reconciliation work is to invite the parties to discuss the various issues. They all more or less know what happened, but they may be divided over why and what next. The twelve approaches are presented, possibly with the peace worker acting out some of the roles. The parties around the table are then invited to discuss, maybe to arrive at a good combination for their own situation. This is possible, even in war zones. And something important may happen: *as they discuss reconciliation, some reconciliation takes place.* The approaches start touching their hearts even if the outer setting is only a seminar. Of course, this is nothing but an introduction to the real thing. But from such modest beginnings, waves of togetherness may spread even from the most turbulent centers.

Notes

1. ABC triangle to understand conflict: Attitude, Behavior, and Contradiction. Thus, closure is B-oriented; whereas healing is A-oriented. Neither really deals with the contradiction; C-orientation is left to resolution. In a very A/B-oriented conflict culture, as in the United States, reconciliation will loom large and be easily embraced, like reconstruction, because there is nothing controversial. Thus, after the Vietnam war much work was done to close verbal, antagonistic behavior between "hawks" and "doves," to heal the wounds derived from that controversy without really touching the underlying contradiction within and between two countries. Twenty years had to pass for that to be initiated with Robert MacNamara's book—immediately rejected by establishment, veterans, and so on. Time will come even for that.

2. If God is both omniscient and omnipotent, how could He have permitted this to happen? But that is only a theological formulation; we all have that question when disaster strikes.

3. Ms. Trauma: "You think you can buy me off with those cheap things, words and exercises? My wound needs much more than that to heal; in the meantime vengeance remains my right!"

Mr. Guilt: "What I have done is so terrible that there is no way you can release me back to a normal life in general and to normal relations with you in particular. I'll live with that forever."

They both obtain the same thing with such maneuvers: Neither has to heal the wound in the other and (re)build a normal relation (which, as often said, does not mean loving Other).

4. Famous cases of apologies from statesmen would include the very moving act by Chancellor Willy Brandt, kneeling down in front of the 1947 monument to the Heroes of the Ghetto in Warszawa, and President Bill Clinton's Public Law 103-150 on November 23, 1994, apologizing for the overthrow of the Hawai'i monarchy in 1893. For an analysis of the difference between how Germany and Japan try the "Vergangenheits-bewältigung" (coming to terms with the past), see Ian Buruma, *The Wages of Guilt: Memories of War in Germany and Japan* (London: Meridian, 1994).

5. Here interpreted as, "If God is omniscient, omnipotent, and omnipresent, why does He permit so much evil to happen?"

6. Among the arguments for an International Tribunal is the right of the victim to voice and ear. This right, can, of course, also be taken care of by a Truth and Reconciliation process, South African model.

7. For one excellent text, see Richard Causton, *The Buddha in Daily Life* (London: Random House, 1995, pp. 168ff, "The Buddhist View of Causality").

8. An inscription found by the author on the former wall around the former West Berlin.

9. See J. Galtung, *Peace by Peaceful Means*, Part II, chapter 1 "Conflict Formations" (London: SAGE Publishers 1996).

10. For an example both of an excellent report and of the problems, see Comisión de la verdad de la ONU, De la locura a la esperanza, La guerra de 12 años en El Salvador, San Sebastian/Donostia: Tercera Prensa, 1993. No turning point is identified with identifiable action that could have made a difference in the past; action is recommended for the future with the implication that they might have been meaningful at an earlier stage. The recommendations are neither cultural nor structural in the broad sense, but institutional: division of power, institutionalization of human rights guarantees and democracy in general, reforms of the army and the national police. Some pages (233-238) are devoted to reconciliation. The report identifies "collective introspection" as a necessary condition (p. 233), pardon (p. 234), punishment of the guilty, restitution for victims and their families. The commission is convinced that knowing the truth is already a step forward, as a "pedagogy for reconciliation" (p. 240). It also recommends a national monument in the capital naming all identified victims, and a national day to honor the victims and foster national reconciliation. Thus, the report is a good example of the limitations of the thinking and action in the field.

11. Andy Pollak, ed., *A Citizen's Inquiry: The Opsahl Report on Northern Ireland* (Dublin: Lilliput Press, 1993). Permit me at this point to pay homage to my late friend, Torkel, a great international lawyer, deeply inspired by humanitarian ideals.

12. Soka Gakkai, Shinjoku-ku, Tokyo, 160, Japan.

13. I am particularly indebted to the late Robert Jungk for his inspiring work with future workshops.

14. The author has used this for many years. One approach that has been tested in many countries is to give different roles (even difficult ones, such as "two Gods, two chosen peoples, one Satan, one conflict worker"). Eighteen or twenty-four students are then divided into groups, each one taking the roles as a point of departure for the play to be written and enacted. The exercise could be done in the first week for students to become acquainted with each other (extremely strong for bonding) and then toward the end; one difference between the plays being what was learned about conflict in the meantime. A problem with the approach is that it does not always travel well across cultures. U.S. students usually perform very well, as do Mediterranean Europeans, with Northern Europeans (and Japanese) being more reserved. Once the ice is broken, however, there is general enthusiasm.

15. See Centro de Estudios Sociales, *Demobilized Soldiers Speak: Reintegration and Reconciliation in Nicaragua, El Salvador and Moçambique* (Managua: Centro de Estudios Internacionales, 1996).

16. This is some kind of opposite number diplomacy. The twinning of cities is another example of weaving societies together. The same would apply to a meeting of NGOs with the same kind of membership; physicians meet physicians, and so on. An interesting negative experience from Caucasus would apply to having historians meet

historians, not strange given that many of them are state-paid carriers of the national myths.

17. Obviously, what is recommended here is the mini- and maxi-version of the TRANSCEND/UN manual with that title, published in 1998 and 2000, respectively.

18. So often heard in Germany and some other large countries: "Another war comes when there is a new generation who does not know the horrors of war." War comes every twenty to thirty years, in other words. Fortunately, there are more factors in the picture.

19. See E. Victoria Shook, *Ho'o ponopono* (Honolulu: East-West Center, 1985). For a more general perspective, see Bruce E. Barnes, "Conflict Resolution Across Cultures: A Hawaii Perspective and a Pacific Mediation Model," *Mediation Quarterly*, vol. 12, no. 2, winter 1994, pp. 117-133.

20. This is the famous movie where parties to an event tell their truths, all of them true from their perspectives, yet told as if they lived in different places, at different times. And the truths do not add up to the truth.

21. It is incredible to note how our civilization chooses materialistic criteria such as the size of settlements, the height of buildings and other structures, and the mastery of metals (including for warfare) to evaluate whether a civilization is "primitive" or "advanced." How about the ability to handle conflicts? To love? To just be happy?

2

Social-Psychological Processes in Interactive Conflict Analysis and Reconciliation

Ronald J. Fisher

One of the most serious global problems facing the world as it lurches into the new millennium is how to manage destructive and protracted conflict between groups with differing identities who are interacting within the same political system or geographic region. In their recent annual review, Wallensteen and Sollenberg (1997) register a total of 101 armed conflicts in the 1989-1996 period, of which only six were interstate conflicts, and in which only 71 of 254 parties were internationally recognized states. Most of these destructive conflicts are between different identity groups defined in racial, religious, ethnic, cultural, or ideological terms, and most have a long history. The costs of these violent and apparently intractable, ethnopolitical conflicts are enormous in both human and economic terms, especially when compared to the potential benefits of cooperative and peaceful relationships. The seriousness of this problem is multiplied because of the resistance that many such conflicts exhibit toward methods of management and resolution over the long term.

According to Azar (1990) and other analysts, these conflicts are based in deep-seated intergroup cleavages that persist over long periods of time with sporadic outbreaks of violence. As such, they are not amenable to the traditional diplomatic or military methods of conflict management, which seek termination, settlement, or accommodation, without adequately addressing the basic human needs for security, identity, recognition, participation, and equity, the frustration of which lies at the heart of the conflict. Since typical settlements or continuing stalemates do not address these underlying concerns or provide for a sense of justice, these unresolved, simmering conflicts are vulnerable to reescalation. They are therefore characterized by a continuing cycle of violence, often over generations, which is extremely difficult to break (Lumsden 1997). Unilateral or reciprocal atrocities committed by one generation become the basis for retributive, vengeful atrocities perpetrated by the next generation. Over decades or centuries, it often becomes unclear, if not irrelevant, as to who the original persecutor was, or who is most responsible for a condition of mutual victimization.

It is the intransigent nature of escalated ethnopolitical conflicts that has in part resulted in the development of innovative, largely unofficial methods of intervention. Professionals from a variety of disciplines working in the field of conflict resolution have brought forward fresh analyses, new models, and creative methods for supplementing and supplanting traditional adversarial and authoritative procedures. One stream of activity, labeled Interactive Conflict Resolution (ICR), involves small-group, problem-solving discussions between unofficial and influential representatives of identity groups engaged in destructive conflict; the discussions are facilitated by an impartial third party of social-scientist practitioners (Fisher 1993). In a broader manner, ICR is defined as "facilitated face-to-face activities in communication, training, education, or consultation that promote collaborative conflict analysis and problem solving among parties engaged in protracted conflict in a manner that addresses basic human needs and promotes the building of peace, justice, and equality" (Fisher 1997, 8).

The leading prototype of ICR is the conflict analysis or problem-solving workshop, which seeks to increase mutual understanding and to create alternative directions for conflict resolution and peacebuilding that the participants can transfer to the leaderships and thereby to the relationship between the parties. Another important variant of ICR is intercommunal dialogue, which seeks to increase understanding and trust between members of conflicting groups that may eventually have some positive effects on public opinion or policymaking. In the broader context of approaches to peace, both conflict analysis and dialogue are often used as peacebuilding interventions at the stage of prenegotiation, to help move the parties toward settling their differences and rebuilding their relationships (Fisher 1997). Once settlement has occurred, however, there is often a glaring need for ICR interventions directed toward reconciliation, so that the outcomes of negotiation can be rendered durable. In this critical domain of reconciliation, the field of ICR is relatively underdeveloped in both conceptual and practical terms.

Reconciliation involves reestablishing harmony and cooperation between antagonists who have inflicted harm in either a one-sided or reciprocal manner. According to Kriesberg (1997), reconciliation refers to developing a mutual conciliatory accommodation between antagonists and establishing an amicable relationship after a rupture involving extreme injury. At the intercommunal level, Kriesberg describes the phenomenon as follows:

> Reconciliation here refers to accommodative ways members of adver-
> sary entities have come to regard each other after having engaged in
> intense, and often destructive struggle. They have become able to put
> aside feelings of hate, fear, and loathing, to put aside views of the other
> as dangerous and subhuman, and to put aside the desire for revenge and

retribution. To put aside does not mean not to have such feelings, perceptions, and goals, but not to make them paramount nor to act on them
against the former adversary. (1997, 2)

In a systematic, sociological manner that is additive to existing literature,
Kriesberg (1997) identifies several basic elements of reconciliation, including the
units involved (individuals, officials, groups, peoples), the dimensions of
reconciliation (acknowledgment, acceptance, apology, redress, forgiveness), and
the possible degrees of reconciliation (full or partial, accommodation, coexistence).
He also discusses the obstacles to reconciliation, the motives for reconciliation, and
the policies and strategies that can result in it. On a sobering note, Kriesberg
observes that postconflict relationships typically involve only a few elements of
reconciliation, and yet he concludes that some form of equitable coexistence
leading toward reconciliation is essential to prevent one-sided domination or
recurrent destructive conflict in intercommunal relations. He thus identifies a
central challenge facing the field of conflict resolution.

Kriesberg and other authors (e.g., Henderson 1996; Lederach 1997; Montville
1993; Tavuchis 1991) have described a variety of reconciliatory activities at
various levels involving different actors. One common distinction is official versus
unofficial activities, which often coincides with public versus private interactions.
Contrast, for example, a public, one-sided apology by a political leader to an
aggrieved group, with a small, private meeting of religious figures from the two
adversaries in an exchange of acknowledgments and apologies or with a public
statement of contrition by a military leader found guilty of war crimes. At a policy
level, Kriesberg (1997) encompasses this variety by listing structural approaches
(e.g., reducing inequities, developing crosscutting ties, creating human rights
safeguards), experiential methods (e.g., trials, truth commissions, public education),
and interpersonal approaches (e.g., small group dialogues, training workshops). He
also notes that reconciliation strategies can take a top-down, lateral (mid-level), or
bottom-up approach, and can be enacted from inside one of the adversary groups
or from the outside. In this taxonomy, reconciliation work from an ICR base would
be a combination of interpersonal and experiential methods, typically involving
middle-range leaders or influentials coming together with the assistance of an
outside intermediary who works inside both collectivities. It is clear that the ICR
approach is only one limited form of reconciliation in a wide range of possibilities.

One unique and powerful element of the ICR approach to reconciliation is that
the method is based in social-psychological principles, concepts, and practices that
focus on the centrality of relationship in conflict resolution. Herbert Kelman, one
of the pioneers of ICR, has on a number of occasions articulated the social-
psychological basis of his workshop method of interactive problem solving, which
involves both analysis and reconciliation. Kelman (1979) notes that social
interaction, which is at the heart of the development a resolution of conflict, is the
central focus of social psychology, a discipline that seeks to understand the
interface of individuals and society. Thus, it simultaneously looks for explanation
to both individual and institutional factors, the interaction of which fuels

intercommunal and international conflict. With regard to the individual level, it is assumed that conflict is always partly a subjective, social process (Fisher 1989) in that the perceptions, attitudes, and behaviors of parties in conflict are central to the interaction between them. At the institutional level, it is essential to understand the social norms, the policies, the political systems, and the cultures of the conflicting entities, and to weave these into the analysis of conflict evolution and expression.

It follows that social-psychological insights are complementary to political analysis, in that while conflict often arises out of objective and ideological differences, its escalation and intractability are typically the result of psychological and social factors (Fisher 1997). Thus, an assumption of social-psychological methods is that the conflict has arisen through the social interaction of the parties and can only be resolved through their direct, bilateral interaction (Kelman 1992). The conclusion is that relationship issues (e.g., misperceptions, mistrust, and frustrated basic needs) must be addressed through innovative, mutually agreeable solutions, developed through joint interaction, in order to reach a lasting resolution (Fisher 1997).

The social-psychological underpinnings of ICR lead to the working assumption of this chapter: full, successful reconciliation between alienated groups cannot take place without an adequate degree of genuine dialogue and conflict analysis of a mutual, interactive nature. That is to say, the conditions and outcomes of successful dialogue and conflict analysis lay the groundwork for the reciprocal enactment of the necessary elements of reconciliation: acknowledgments of transgressions, apologies for these, forgiveness of these, and assurances that such acts will not occur in the future. In order for individuals from the mutually aggrieved parties to move toward reconciliation, they must come to understand the other side—its perceptions, cognitions, motives, strategies, and failings—and the history of interaction that escalated and maintained the conflict within the context of a destructive relationship characterized by misperception, miscommunication, mistrust, deceit, manipulation, threat, defensiveness, coercion, and violence. A related point is made by Joseph Montville, a scholar-practitioner with considerable experience in facilitating reconciliation:

> Healing and reconciliation in violent ethnic and religious conflicts depend on a process of transactional contrition and forgiveness between aggressors and victims which is indispensable to the establishment of a new relationship based on mutual acceptance and reasonable trust. This process depends on joint analysis of the history of the conflict, recognition of injustices and resulting historic wounds, and acceptance of moral responsibility where due. (1993, 112)

Montville emphasizes the importance of reconciliation in conflict resolution and affirms the necessity of understanding the history of the conflict in order to move forward. This step is operationalized, according to Montville (1993), by initiating a "walk through history" as the first stage of a problem-solving workshop in order to elicit the grievances of one group that have not been acknowledged by the other side. While this aspect of diagnosis is essential, it is only one element of the conflict analysis that is proposed here to prepare the way for complete reconciliation. In addition to unraveling the process of mutual victimization in their history, it is necessary for parties to understand many other aspects of their conflict in order to move into reconciliatory interaction.

The purpose of this chapter is to spell out some of the requirements, processes, and outcomes of conflict analysis and dialogue that underpin subsequent reconciliation. Similarly, the conditions and interactions that promote and constitute genuine reconciliation are identified. The conclusion addresses, among other questions, how the personal experience and change of influential individuals might be transferred to their respective collectivities. This is essential if small-group reconciliation work is to be part of a wider process of conflict resolution and peacebuilding between former adversaries.

Processes of Conflict Analysis and Dialogue

Designing and Implementing Constructive Confrontation

The conflict analysis or problem-solving workshop involves bringing together a small number of participants (typically four or five from each side) with a third-party panel of skilled scholar-practitioners (typically for three to five days). The participants are invited because they are influential in their respective communities in terms of affecting public opinion, official decision making, or both, and they often come with the knowledge and blessing of their leaderships. Usually, participants are chosen to represent the spectrum of political thinking in their communities in regard to the conflict. Thus, it is important to have "hawks" as well as "doves" present, but extremists and fanatics are usually ruled out, either by their own choice or because they would be unwilling or incapable of interacting respectfully and constructively with people from the other side. The focus in the initial discussions is on the history and development of the conflict, and it is hoped that this analysis will result in increased understanding, mutual realizations, and a broadening of thinking which will allow for joint problem solving directed toward peacebuilding activities or alternative ways of dealing with the conflict.

The agenda of the workshop is not fixed, but usually contains some standard elements which follow a rough progression from the main issues and current state of the conflict and the relationship, to underlying hopes, fears and needs, factors and interactions underlying and fueling escalation, constraints and resistances to deescalating, innovative directions or solutions, and finally to collaborative ways of transferring or applying insights to the back-home situation. The discussions are moderated and controlled if necessary by the third-party team, members of which are chosen for their knowledge of conflict processes and their ability to facilitate small-group interaction. The workshop thus provides a neutral, unofficial, low-risk, and noncommittal venue for parties to explore their relationship in a private (quiet but not secret) manner free from the glare of publicity or official scrutiny. Varying descriptions of the basic characteristics of workshops are available from a number of sources, including Azar (1990), Burton (1987), Chufrin and Saunders (1993), Fisher (1983, 1997), Kelman (1979, 1992), Mitchell (1981), and Volkan (1991).

The implementation of the agenda is largely the responsibility of the third-party team, who sets ground rules for the interaction and operationalizes a number of strategic functions to facilitate productive confrontation, that is, the direct engagement of the issues and other contentious topics by the parties. Ground rules generally emphasize the open, flexible, and analytic nature of the discussions as opposed to an adversarial debate, negotiation, or argument. Participants are encouraged to engage in respectful and honest interchanges that are compatible with an academic seminar or problem-solving session. In order to support freedom of expression, strict confidentiality is requested, specifically that no statements made in the workshop will be attributed afterward to particular individuals, even though it is understood that general reports will go back to the respective leaderships and/or constituencies. Participants are asked to see the third-party not as a judge or an audience, but as an impartial moderator and consultant whose role is to help increase the shared understanding of the conflict.

The core functions of ICR as expressed in conflict analysis workshops have been largely captured in Fisher's (1972, 1997) model of third-party consultation. First, the third-party works to induce mutual motivation for problem solving by tactics such as maintaining optimum tension and balancing situational power. Second, the consultant spends a lot of time, especially in the early stages, working to improve communication between the parties through human relations skills such as paraphrasing, empathizing, clarifying, and summarizing. Third, the third-party serves a unique purpose beyond simple facilitation by entering into the diagnosis of the conflict, injecting concepts and models from social science that may help explain the etiology and escalation of the conflict in ways that participants may not have previously considered. Finally, the third-party also regulates the interaction, controlling disruptive interchanges that contradict ground rules, and pacing the problem-solving phases of the workshop from differentiation to integration. Given these strategic functions and the tactics necessary to carry them out, it becomes clear why panel members need to be skilled practitioners in group processes as well as scholars who understand conflict dynamics.

When the focus of the workshop is on dialogue to increase understanding between members of conflicting groups, as compared to inducing problem solving between unofficial representatives, additional guidelines are useful. The emphasis in dialogue is on increasing shared knowledge and building trust among the participants, as opposed to developing options to influence public opinion or affect policymaking. Nonetheless, the same ground rules and strategic functions more or less apply, underscoring the importance of dialogue as an essential element of conflict analysis and reconciliation. In addition, several authors have articulated principles and guidelines that help further define the nature of dialogue (e.g.,

Chasin and Herzig 1993; Fisher 1997; Schindler and Lapid 1989; Schwartz 1989). Common to these statements are norms of open and genuine expression, attentive and respectful interaction, and a willingness to look for commonalities as well as differences. Dialogue participants are encouraged to speak from personal experience rather than to make rhetorical or abstract statements. The essence of dialogue is often articulated by asking participants to speak in order to inform and educate rather than to persuade or deter, and to listen in order to understand and learn rather than to refute and argue. In addition, the sequence of developing dialogue over time is given careful attention.

The goals of both conflict analysis and dialogue include changes in the thinking, feelings, and behavior of participants. It is generally hoped that misperceptions will be corrected, attitudes will be improved, positive emotions toward the other side will be rekindled or developed, and that a cooperative orientation will begin to re-emerge or be established. The model of third-party consultation specifies the objectives of improved intergroup attitudes, an improved relationship, and conflict resolution, in the sense of mutually acceptable and self-sustaining solutions. From a social-psychological perspective, the emergence of improved attitudes is critical in a number of ways. The model indicates that this involves more complex, veridical, and favorable attitudes toward the other party; that is, it is not simply emotional elements that are important. Cognitive aspects are paramount in that the adversaries must increase the complexity and differentiation of their thinking about the other side and must gain a more accurate picture of the other, if there is to be realistic movement toward reconciliation and resolution. These cognitive changes will then support more positive feelings and more cooperative behavior toward the other party.

Inducing Cognitive Changes in Participants' Thinking

The overall design of workshops as well as the ground rules, strategic functions, and guidelines for conflict analysis and dialogue are intended to create conditions that are conducive to cognitive changes in the direction of mutual realization and learning among the participants. Individuals are now face-to-face with the hated and feared enemy other, and they are encouraged and influenced to enter into open and authentic exchanges designed to help reestablish a trusting and cooperative relationship. This is a significant challenge in a number of ways, not the least of which from a social-psychological perspective is the induction of a considerable amount of cognitive dissonance. In the first place, it is incongruent to interact with the enemy other, and in the second place, it is difficult to receive increasing amounts of direct information that is dissonant with many of the perceptions, beliefs, and judgments that each side holds regarding the other.

It is common in intergroup conflict that each group holds simplified beliefs or stereotypes of the other, or at a minimum has a less differentiated image of the other than of itself. Thus, as more and more information comes forth as to the intentions, motivations, strategies, constraints, frustrations, concerns, complexity, and variety of the other group, each participant experiences some degree of cognitive dissonance (unpleasant tension due to incongruence among cognitive elements) between this and his or her existing images and attitudes. Such information can of course be filtered out, discounted, seen as exceptional, or assimilated to existing beliefs in all the cognitive ways that human beings have of deceiving and defending themselves. However, it is likely that some degree of dissonance will be induced, and the resulting pressure to regain consonance will lead to some amount of attitude change in positive directions. It is also dissonant to be interacting within the workshop in constructive and even pleasant ways with the negative, rejected other. Thus, the authentic interaction of conflict analysis and dialogue simply produces information and experiences that are difficult to ignore or explain away, at least in the first instance, and the ensuing attitude change is predicted to affect future perceptions and behaviors toward the other party (Fisher 1989). Whether these attitudinal changes will generalize to include additional members of the other group and whether they will hold up when participants return home are issues of some controversy in social psychology and interactive conflict resolution (see Fisher 1990, 1997).

Among the most pervasive cognitive errors that individuals, and thereby groups, involved in destructive conflict make are misattributions about the characteristics and motives of the other side. Attribution is the process by which we infer causation about the behavior of another actor, and these judgments are critical, because they tend to guide both our immediate reaction and our future behavior toward that actor. The processes of making and changing attributions are therefore central to conflict escalation, analysis, and deescalation (Baron 1997; Berkowitz 1994; Fisher 1990). The making of attributions in conflict causation and escalation is particularly insidious because negative events, such as the contentious tactics and their effects, which are common in conflict, tend to induce negative attributions about the actor, because this is cognitively consistent (Berkowitz 1994).

In the social-psychological study of attribution, a central question is the degree to which individuals make personal attributions to internal causes within the other actor, or situational attributions to environmental factors impinging upon the other actor (Fisher 1982). A common finding is that humans have a tendency to make personal attributions about others when they are an observer and yet situational attributions about their own behavior, that is, when they are the actor (Jones and Nisbett 1972). This so-called fundamental attribution error is partly explained because individuals as actors are more aware of the environmental forces that are reasons for their behavior, whereas to the observer, it is the actor's dispositions that are apparently front and center. In intergroup relations involving prejudice or hatred, this bias is extended into the "ultimate attribution error" (Pettigrew 1979) through which members of one group will consistently make personal and negative attributions about any undesirable behavior by members of the other group. Usually, they will see the behavior as due to common or innate characteristics of that group of people. However, if desirable behaviors are perceived, these will be explained away by making situational or other attributions that ignore the possibility of positive personal or group dispositions, for example, by attributing the behavior to luck or an exceptional situation. In essence, the target of prejudice can't win—if they do something bad, they are held responsible, but if they do something good, they are not.

In the conflict analysis workshop, the attributions that individuals and parties make about their own behavior and the other side's behavior are enumerated, exchanged, and held up for scrutiny, partly through the third-party function of diagnosing the conflict. Thus, each side is able to present its analysis of the causes of its behavior, as it knows it, in a respectful and yet challenging environment. The other side is able to listen in a more open fashion, typically to an attributional analysis that is highly divergent from the one it holds. Much of the discussion of past and present actions and policies focuses on the intentions and perceived situational factors behind behaviors that had negative effects on the other side. Typically, each party sees its contentious actions as defensive in a preventive or retaliatory manner (i.e., justified), while the other party sees these as aggressive and malevolent (i.e., unjustified). Typically, each party has difficulty seeing or accepting the environmental factors, including its own behavior, that have been part of the causation and justification for the other's contentious tactics. This is partly because parties in conflict, as any observer of another's behavior, tend to see their attributional analysis of the other's actions as accurate with a high degree of certainty (Berkowitz 1994).

Through the process of mutual analysis, the complexity of thinking on both sides is expanded from a stereotype of the evil, aggressive, and immutable other to an appreciation of behaviors that have multiple causes in a system of escalating interactions. Participants come to see more of the total field of forces acting on their adversary in both the past and the present, and the certainty of their initial attributional analysis begins to weaken as they encounter new explanations that are credible (see Berkowitz 1994). This is in part because the old and new attributions are incongruent, producing cognitive dissonance that induces change. In content terms, participants come to see the inherent dynamics of conflict escalation that have been fueled by their mutually adversarial approach, including how the use of threat and coercion has fueled defensive reactions and reciprocal behaviors. They come to see that each party has been making difficult choices in this complex environment, which each believes will protect and extend its interests. They often come to see that both parties are driven by some of the same underlying needs, for security, recognition of identity, participation, and so on. In attributional terms, the observer's analysis comes to incorporate more of the field of forces that the actor has in its own analysis, and thus becomes more accurate as judged by the actor—arguably the most appropriate measure of accuracy (Berkowitz 1994). As this process is reciprocated, widening sets of mutual realizations about the other and about the conflict significantly increase the complexity of thinking on both sides. Cognitive changes (reperceptions, reattributions, and improved attitudes) begin to occur that are prerequisites to later affective and behavioral changes. Thus, while each side remains unable to condone the other's transgressions or accept their negative effects at this stage of the analysis, each comes to see that the contentious tactics of the other are in some ways as understandable and reasonable as its own.

of the other are in some ways as understandable and reasonable as its own.

Related more to the affective changes necessary for reconciliation is the process of self-disclosure in conflict analysis and dialogue workshops (Fisher 1989). Individuals in these sessions are encouraged to speak for themselves and from their personal experience in the conflict. In addition to analytical comments, this involves a degree of authentic self-disclosure about opinions, feelings, and experiences that seldom occur in wider interactions and that are difficult to discount or explain away. As noted above, this genuine exposure and explanation of the field of forces acting on individuals and parties begins to lessen the certainty of the attributional analyses held on the other side. The social norm of reciprocity encourages self-disclosure to become a mutual process, thus revealing basic similarities among the participants that builds a basis for positive regard (Fisher 1982). Consistent with theory and research on interpersonal self-disclosure, this exchange typically increases shared understanding and begins to rebuild trust in the relationship, at least among workshop participants. What is also occurring is a rehumanization of the other, which casts a whole new light on their behavior and appropriate reactions to them. If the other party can no longer be rejected as subhuman, then the universal norms of fair and proper treatment again apply and must be taken into account in policy and strategy development. The cognitive reappraisal and rehumanization of the other party also opens the door for affective reconciliation with them.

Processes of Reconciliation

Reconciliation as an interpersonal or intergroup encounter is a difficult and delicate process that is not simply a matter of the head, but more so of the heart (Kraybill 1988). That is to say, values and conscience tell people they ought to reconcile and help set direction for it, but emotions are more powerful and move at their own pace. Thus, Kraybill concludes:

> True healing involves a unity of head and heart. The head sets the goal
> and keeps things on track. The heart provides the content of the emo-
> tions. Given a chance, the two will converge in common purpose. What
> makes the difference is a process which values and gives space to both
> (1988, 8).

Reconciliation is related to a domain of potential change identified by Kelman (1963, 1972) as "corrective emotional experiences," a concept drawn from the group therapy literature, which refers to the simultaneous occurrence and examination of intense feelings. Such experiences occur regularly in ICR workshops in relation to the conflict and are an essential element of the analysis and learning which occurs. However, this is not to confuse such workshops with psychotherapy, since these two fields of practice have different foci, purposes, and understandings (contracts) with participants and parties (Kelman 1991). ICR is not concerned with personal development or rehabilitation in mental health terms, but with fostering individual changes in perceptions and attitudes that have relevance to changes in policymaking and the conflict system. In addition, the focus in ICR is intergroup interaction, rather than personal and interpersonal. Nonetheless, the encouragement and elicitation of reconciliation is a very personal matter because of the intense feelings of alienation, anger, fear, loathing, and hatred that individuals often feel toward members of the other party.

The cognitive changes outlined so far bring the agenda of reconciliation to the fore, because it becomes increasingly discrepant in the workshop interaction to continue to hold such intense negative feelings toward the other party when you are starting to see much of the party's negative behavior in a new light. The opportunity to examine these feelings, and to entertain and develop more consonant positive feelings toward the other side, is a unique and powerful element of ICR workshops.

Conditions for Authentic Exchanges

Reconciliation is a very challenging process, partly because it means realigning so much in one's cognitive and emotional world. This may even include one's own sense of group or national identity, since in ethnopolitical conflict one group's identity often incorporates the rejection of the other's identity and legitimacy as a people. The challenge of reconciliation can be approached more effectively by adopting some working assumptions and by realizing the paradoxes that are built into the process (Lederach 1997). First, we must see relationship as the basis of both conflict and its resolution, because reconciliation requires engaging the parties as human beings in relationship. Second, the process of reconciliation assumes an encounter of several streams of experience—the past with its trauma, anger, and grief, and the future with the possibility of mutuality and interdependence. Third, Lederach assumes that the field of conflict resolution and peacebuilding must look outside the discipline of mainstream international discourse and practice to find innovative methods of reconciliation.

The working assumptions relate to three paradoxes that link seemingly contradictory yet interdependent forces (Lederach 1997). First, the open expression of a painful past is linked with the search for a shared future. Second, the truth about what has happened needs to be exposed, and yet parties must express mercy and let go of transgressions against them in favor of a renewed relationship. Third, there is a need to achieve a sense of justice in redressing wrongs, and at the same time, parties must enter into a vision of peace with a common future. It is a requirement that ICR workshops with a reconciliation focus provide space for each of these paradoxes to be expressed and to be worked through to a successful resolution.

The functions of the third-party are essential to establishing a climate for reconciliation, because they establish related conditions that enable the process. The groundwork in establishing mutual motivation for problem solving is essential to enable the parties to stand back from their conflict and to come to see it as a shared problem to be solved, as opposed to a war to be won. A successful problem-solving atmosphere encourages participants to see that their relationship may be salvageable, and impresses upon them their interdependence with the other party. Thus, the question becomes how to shape the future to their shared interests, rather than to their joint disadvantage.

In working to improve communication and establish dialogue, the third-party creates a relatively unique experience for the antagonists. They are able to communicate with each other in a more open and accurate fashion, and while they may not like all that they hear, they are usually able to increase their understanding of the other side significantly. Cognitively, participants develop a more realistic and differentiated view of the other side, and emotionally they come to appreciate and even empathize with the complexity and difficulty that the other side faces as human beings caught in the many painful dilemmas of destructive conflict. Full and reflective listening to the experience of the other, often facilitated by third-party involvement, allows for a cognitive and emotional appreciation that is very rich in comparison to adversarial modes of communication.

The diagnosis of the conflict extends to developing cognitive and emotional reassessment, as participants come to see how the field of forces driving their side's strategies and tactics is amazingly similar to that of the other party. The mutual realization is that to some degree, both parties have been caught in the insidious dynamics of escalating and protracted conflict. This is not to say that the parties are absolved of the responsibility for their choices that had negative effects on the other, or that the parties share equal responsibility for their mutual disasters, but this does create an appreciation of similarity and humanity that is difficult to discount. As is true in interpersonal attraction, these similarities can begin to rebuild some of the liking—that is, positive attitudes—between the participants as members of two different groups.

The function of regulating the interaction helps to create and maintain a climate in which participants follow the norms of respectful, genuine, and analytical interaction. This results in a sense of safety and creativity, in which participants can self-disclose and explore avenues of experiencing and learning that are typically closed to them. In relation to the paradoxes of reconciliation, participants are able to engage in the open expression of a painful past, and to mutually explore the truth of what has happened between them. Furthermore, the problem-solving flow of the discussions from differentiation to integration allows for the sequential addressing of the paradoxes. As mutual understanding and appreciation develop around the past and about how justice may be achieved, participants are better able to consider how to construct a shared future and rebuild their relationship. In doing so, it becomes apparent that some degree of reconciliation is essential if they are to move out of the paradoxes and into a new and more consonant social reality.

Another aspect of ICR workshops that helps establish the conditions for reconciliation is found in Kelman's (1986) concept of "working trust." Recognizing that it is unrealistic to generate interpersonal trust between participants from the two sides, Kelman sees the third-party as an initial repository of trust for both sets of participants. Then, after some time in the workshop process, they can come to establish a working trust in each other, which recognizes their common interests despite their profound differences. This working trust allows them to engage in analysis and problem solving, while their common trust in the third-party assures them that their interests, sensitivities, and confidences will be protected. As Kraybill (1988) points out, in order to enter into the process of reconciliation, the parties do not need to rebuild trust, but they do need a willingness to risk again. The establishment of a working trust, along with other conditions, is essential for problem-solving workshops to be able to serve a healing purpose by contributing to a reconciliation between the parties, that is, a transformation of their relationship (Kelman 1991).

The Sequenced Elements of Reconciliation

The conditions favoring reconciliation set the stage for the actual behaviors of reconciliation that can lead to a renewed relationship between the parties. In the context of ICR workshops, certain statements and responses are necessary to operationalize the process and produce the outcomes of reconciliation. In the public domain, with political leaders or other influentials, similar behaviors are necessary to stimulate reconciliation on a mass scale. However, regardless of the level of social interaction, the essential elements and their necessary sequence appear to be similar: acknowledgment, apology, forgiveness, and assurance.

With particular reference to destructive ethnopolitical conflict, Montville (1993) affirms the importance of dealing with victimization, that is, "a history of violent, traumatic aggression and loss; a conviction that the aggression was unjustified by any standard; and an often unuttered fear on the part of the victim group that the aggressor will strike again at some feasible time in the future" (113). He also points out, in agreement with the experience of this author and other scholar-practitioners who work in this field, that typically both sides have a sense of victimhood and spend considerable time in neutral fora competing over who is the most aggrieved and legitimate victim. This is understandable, because each party is looking for redress of the losses they have suffered. It is important here to recognize that while the physical reality of victimization is seldom equal or balanced, it is very often shared to some degree. This creates a social-psychological reality of mutual victimization which third-party consultants must accept and attempt to work with.

The analytical work that creates the conditions for reconciliation directly contradicts the phenomenon of mutual victimization. In analyzing the conflict, it becomes apparent that both sides are employing a simplistic "aggressor-defender model" to understand the conflict and portray their victimization (Rubin, Pruitt, and Kim 1994). Each sees the other as the aggressor who has created the conflict and engaged in an escalating series of contentious tactics. Each side sees that it has simply responded with defensive reactions (some of which may be "preventive"), but to no avail as the aggressor has persisted and wreaked further destruction. However, as the analysis proceeds, the participants come to see that a more complex conceptualization, such as the "conflict spiral model," is necessary to adequately understand the conflict to their joint satisfaction. This model portrays a vicious circle of action and reaction, in which one party's contentious tactic elicits a contentious reaction from the other, which in turn prompts a further and more serious contentious tactic, and so on, each time to a higher level of escalation (Rubin, Pruitt, and Kim 1994). Through this analysis, the parties come to see that while it is true they are both victims, it is also true that they are both persecutors. Theoretical inputs such as White's (1984) concept of "defensively-motivated aggression" enable the parties to see the double-edged sword in many of their behaviors. It therefore becomes apparent that each side has some destructive behaviors to acknowledge and to apologize for if they are to move toward rebuilding a cooperative relationship.

In discussing intercommunal reconciliation, Kriesberg (1997) outlines several "dimensions" noted earlier which include the essential elements identified here. In a similar vein, Montville (1993) speaks of the necessity of the aggressor acknowledging grievances, accepting responsibility, expressing contrition, and seeking and receiving forgiveness from the aggrieved party. A sociological analysis of reconciliation is provided by Tavuchis (1991), who is concerned with situations where one party violates a norm or moral imperative, harms the other party, thus endangering their own social standing, and therefore takes steps to restore social harmony. For Tavuchis, the critical act is that of apology, that is, "to plead *mea culpa* (my fault) and apologize to the wronged party. In doing so, we acknowledge the fact of wrongdoing, accept ultimate responsibility, express sincere sorrow and regret, and promise not to repeat the offense" (1991, vii). However, he points out that the making of a satisfactory apology is a delicate process and is only successful when it eradicates the consequences of the wrongdoing by successfully evoking forgiveness as a prelude to reconciliation. Tavuchis indicates that the basic interaction in apology is between two parties, whether they are individuals or collectivities, and that the elements of apology are the same in all relationships.

The first step in moving toward apology in ethnopolitical conflict is an ac-knowledgment by one side, or typically and ideally both sides, that it has engaged in acts that brought suffering to the other—transgressions often to the level of atrocities that are well outside the realm of human moral acceptance. In the context of an increased complexity of thinking and the establishment of a working trust, participants in ICR workshops often become able to openly recognize and accept responsibility for the actions of their side that caused hurt—physical, psychologi-cal, moral—in the other (see, for example, Fisher 1992). This typically follows the analysis of the sources and escalation of the conflict, and of the underlying concerns, because the parties are now in a position to acknowledge the transgres-sions of the past and to give and seek assurances that will address their fears and needs for the future. Tavuchis (1991) notes that the acknowledgment is the naming of the offensive behaviors in a way that mutually identifies these as apologizable actions. This is important because "apologetic discourse presupposes cognitive and evaluative congruence in the form of the shared definitions of the violation, its severity, history, and implications" (57). The acknowledgment may or may not be in response to a call from the aggrieved party for an apology. In either case, the challenge in ICR workshops is to attain some adequate degree of congruence between the parties on the nature and severity of apologizable transgressions. This is more readily done when there have been reciprocal violations against their common humanity, because their shared sense of morality and the norm of reciprocity influence them toward exchanging acknowledgments. Following a shared analysis, the third-party is well positioned to move participants into a consideration of the acknowledgments that they wish to provide to the other or want from the other.

The act of apology expresses regret (remorse, sorrow) for a transgression that has injured or wronged another party (Tavuchis 1991). By so doing, the offender hopes to repair damaged feelings and restore the relationship and social harmony. However, to apologize is extremely difficult and unsettling, and rather contradictory, because the offender is seeking forgiveness for behaviors that are unreasonable, unjustified, and so on, and is being exposed to justifiable retribution while asking for unconditional remission (Tavuchis 1991). Apology thus renders the offender vulnerable in the moment, in the relationship, and in the eyes of the wider community. It clearly is an "act of risk" which a skilled facilitator can help bring forward through a good sense of timing and an atmosphere of respect (see Kraybill 1988). In addition to the personal fears and inadequacies that render apology difficult, consideration should also be given to gender and cultural factors, such as captured in White's (1984) concept of "macho pride." In any case, the heart of apology, according to Tavuchis (1991), is the authentic expression of regret, rather than an appeal to reason, thus underscoring the emotional essence of reconciliation over the rational aspect. It is therefore critical that the apology be perceived as genuine, as involving true remorse and contrition, because this is primarily what the offender is offering in exchange for forgiveness. Only the offended party has the power to forgive and has the options of accepting the apology, refusing it and thus rejecting the offender, or acknowledging the apology but deferring a decision (Tavuchis 1991). When successful, according to Tavuchis, "apology . . . is a decisive moment in a complex restorative project arising from an unaccountable infraction and culminating in remorse and reconciliation" (45).

In discussing how to break the cycle of victimization and vengeance in intractable ethnic conflict, Irani notes that "to embark upon the challenging process of reconciliation, victims and victimizers must find a way to acknowledge and apologize for past hurts and suffering inflicted by the other in order to achieve forgiveness, the key component of true conflict resolution" (1997, 2). However, as Irani, Arendt (1958), Montville (1993), and others have indicated, forgiveness as a concept or a process has not received much attention in the scholarly disciplines and professions from which the multidisciplinary field of conflict resolution has grown. The significance and salience of forgiveness have been more noticeable in the domains of religion and psychotherapy (Kriesberg 1997; Montville 1991). And yet we now see the essential role of mutual forgiveness in achieving reconciliation between longtime enemies who have perpetrated violence and taken vengeance on each other. Henderson (1996) provides a variety of case descriptions of internal and international conflict in which forgiveness and reconciliation were significant factors in resolution. An edited collection by Garcia (1993) includes examples of reconciliation work as well as commentaries by leading practitioners from the scholarly, religious, and other domains. In many cases, religious actors and a spiritual element have played an important role in fostering reconciliation and resolution (see Johnston and Sampson 1994).

The moral aspect of forgiveness is worthy of consideration, because as Tavuchis notes, the power to forgive "entails a profound moral obligation since the helpless offender, in *consideration for nothing more than a speech,* asks for nothing less than the conversion of righteous indignation and betrayal into unconditional forgiveness and reunion" (1991, 35, italics in original). However, this is not entirely true at the intercommunal and international levels, because restitution or compensation can also be part of the wider conflict resolution process. As Kriesberg (1997) indicates:

> [M]any persons who have suffered from oppression and atrocities in the course of an intense struggle seek redress for the injustices they endured. Reconciliation often entails some degree of such redress. This may be in the form of tangible restitution or compensation for what was lost; it may take the form of punishment for those who committed injustices; or it may be exhibited in policies which offer protection against future discrimination or harm. (3)

Usually these forms of restitution are carried out at the public level, such as in compensatory payments to aggrieved groups, trials of those charged with committing atrocities, or truth commissions to gauge responsibility and require reparations where possible.

While public strategies for restitution may be discussed in ICR workshops, the focus in reconciliation is on forgiveness as a social-psychological process and a moral act. Some scholar-practitioners in ICR specialize in workshops that have forgiveness and healing as a major focus (e.g., Borris forthcoming; Montville 1991, 1993). Montville (1991) contends:

> There is a strong case to be made that the sense of victimhood can only be relieved through the experience of profound psychological processes by the victim group as a whole. Here there would seem to be powerful linkages between the acts of oppressors acknowledging their wrongs and asking forgiveness for them, the victims forgiving the aggressors— and we must note that victims may also have committed dehumanizing crimes of violence—and finally both sides completing a mourning of their losses so that a new equilibrium and a true sense of mutual respect and security can describe the relationship. (181)

In order to bring about mutual and complete forgiveness, Montville (1987), Kriesberg (1997), and others see the necessity of a combination of interpersonal methods such as workshops and public strategies in educational, economic, and other spheres.

In the context of a conflict analysis workshop, statements of forgiveness can follow naturally on the acknowledgments and apologies from the other side. Again, the increased attitudinal and attributional complexity regarding the other, and the perceived genuineness of their statements, are precursors to accepting the apology and offering forgiveness. Scholar-practitioners who focus on forgiveness emphasize the importance of the victim increasing his or her understanding of the offender and developing a new perspective from which to see the hurtful past. Dealing with forgiveness mainly as a personal, unilateral process in the context of interpersonal relationships, Smedes (1984) tells a fable called "The Magic Eyes" to illustrate how the offended person must find a new way of looking at the offender. This allows the offended one to see the deeper truth about the offender, which separates the offender from the hurtful act and creates new insight that leads to new feeling, including a sense of release and renewed empathy and goodwill toward the offender. In a similar vein, Borris (forthcoming) maintains that forgiveness entails a shift in understanding of the other party, the development of a sense of compassion toward the other, and a personal release of anger, pain, and suffering which leads to inner peace. Her analysis and prescriptions for achieving forgiveness are relevant to situations of mutual victimization between identity groups as well as to individuals in interpersonal relationships.

The act of mercy that is part of forgiveness and the release it engenders effectively dissolve the paradox with the truth of what has happened. The significance of emotional and moral processes of the heart in this very meaningful experience far outweighs that of rational calculations. Justice may still be sought, often through the terms of a negotiated settlement, but when forgiveness is reciprocal, the parties are now free to move toward a vision of a shared future.

Often in situations of protracted, violent conflict, the deep fears and perceived risks of moving into the future with the other party outweigh the benefits that are expected. Therefore, the parties remain trapped in the status quo, and the conflict is intractable. Thus, one essential element of reconciliation is the assurances that the parties can give each other in order to overcome the fears and reduce the risks (see Fisher 1992). One type of assurance indicates that contentious and hurtful actions of the past will not be repeated, while another type articulates the benefits that can be anticipated in a shared future. The former is sometimes better expressed at the point of apology (Tavuchis 1991), while the latter may more appropriately follow on mutual forgiveness. In the workshop setting, as with acknowledgments, the third-party can appropriately call for assurances that the parties want to give or would like to receive, following the analysis of needs and fears and some mutual articulation of the benefits of a renewed relationship. This is not a political discussion or negotiation, but involves participants expressing the sentiments or actions of their group that are useful in allaying the fears or meeting the needs of the other side. Often, such positive aspects in the behavior of the other party are not perceived or are distorted in terms of intentions, and the potentially beneficial elements are lost. This stream of necessary assurances, however, must flow through to the political level and can be addressed through mechanisms such as security guarantees, economic payments, dispute resolution structures, and so on. As Kriesberg (1997) notes, it is essential that the parties anticipate mutual security and well being as a final element of reconciliation.

Conclusion

The intractability of violent ethnopolitical conflict has stimulated the search for innovative and more effective methods for its management and resolution. This search has also highlighted the necessity of reconciliation in order to prevent recurring cycles of vengeance. It is assumed that social-psychological processes are an essential element of the understanding and practice required to deal with this massive human problem. The focus in this chapter has been on processes of social cognition and social interaction in the context of ICR workshops, which bring together influential representatives of the antagonists for intense and open discussions. It is proposed that the analysis and interaction in these sessions bring about attitudinal changes in terms of perceptual accuracy, cognitive complexity, the rekindling of positive emotions, and the stimulation of behavioral orientations for cooperation. These changes prepare the way for enacting the elements of reconciliation—acknowledgment, apology, forgiveness, and assurance—which also constitute a social-psychological process of considerable fragility and difficulty. Cognitive analysis and constructive confrontation set the stage, but the sequence of reconciliation needs to be facilitated and managed skillfully for a genuine outcome, as opposed to false, superficial statements that may be partly motivated by social desirability.

The major challenge facing ICR methods is that of transfer; that is, how the changes and ideas from the small-group setting are taken back to the host societies in ways that positively affect public opinion and policymaking toward accommodation and mass reconciliation. Fisher (1997) provides an initial model of the transfer process that allows for differential effects on the various constituencies (leadership, public-political, governmental-bureaucratic) in the home communities. Assessment to date indicates that ICR methods can play an important role in affecting public opinion and policymaking: for example, in the Middle East conflict, the work of Kelman and other ICR practitioners is generally credited with having a positive effect on the political discourse and potential options over the last twenty-five years (Kelman 1995; Rothman 1993).

Unfortunately, with reference to reconciliation, there is little evidence of direct transfer from ICR programs to the public level, partly because few projects focus mainly or exclusively on reconciliation. Of course, many of the existing cases of reconciliation (e.g., Henderson 1996) involved various forms of small-group interaction, but it is not clear how much these followed the various ICR models.

Further analyses along this line would be valuable. What is also required are systematic attempts to develop reconciliation programs based on our existing theories of practice and to follow the effects of such interventions to the political and public levels. At the same time, it must be kept in mind that ICR approaches are only one small part of the wide array of reconciliation strategies required at multiple levels of society to break the cycle of violence.

References

Arendt, H. 1958. The Human Condition. Chicago: University of Chicago Press.

Azar, E. E. 1990. The Management of Protracted Social Conflict. Hampshire, U.K.: Dartmouth.

Baron, R. A. 1997. Positive Effects of Conflict: Insights from Social Cognition. In Using Conflict in Organizations. C. K. W. de Dreu and E. Van de Vliert, eds. London: Sage Publications.

Berkowitz, N. H. 1994. An Attributional Model of Conflict Escalation: Implications for Training Lay People in Escalation Management. Paper presented at the annual scientific meeting of the International Society of Political Psychology, Santiago De Compostela, Spain.

Borris, E. R. Forthcoming. The Healing Power of Forgiveness and the Resolution of Protracted Conflicts. Journal of Social Issues.

Burton, J. W. 1987. Resolving Deep-Rooted Conflict: A Handbook. Lanham, Md.: University Press of America.

Chasin, R., and Herzig, M. 1993. Creating Systemic Interventions for the Sociopolitical Arena. In The Global Family Therapist: Integrating the Personal, Professional, and Political. B. Berger Gould and D. Hilleboe DeMuth, eds. Boston: Allyn and Bacon.

Chufrin, G. I., and Saunders, H. H. 1993. A Public Peace Process. Negotiation Journal, vol. 9, no. 3, 155-177.

Fisher, R. J. 1972. Third-party Consultation: A Method for the Study and Resolution of Conflict. Journal of Conflict Resolution, vol. 16, no. 1, 67-94.

———. 1982. Social Psychology: An Applied Approach. New York: St. Martin's.

———. 1983. Third Party Consultation as a Method of Intergroup Conflict Resolution: A Review of Studies. Journal of Conflict Resolution, vol. 27, no. 2, 301-334.

———. 1989. Prenegotiation Problem-Solving Discussions: Enhancing the Potential for Successful Negotiation. In Getting to the Table: The Process of International Prenegotiation. J. G. Stein, ed. Baltimore: Johns Hopkins University Press.

———. 1990. The Social Psychology of Intergroup and International Conflict Resolution. New York: Springer-Verlag.

———. 1992. Peacebuilding for Cyprus: Report on a Conflict Analysis Workshop, June 1991. Canadian Institute for International Peace and Security, Ottawa, Ontario, Can.

———. 1993. Developing the Field of Interactive Conflict Resolution: Issues in Training, Funding and Institutionalization. Political Psychology, vol. 14, no. 1, 123-138.

———. 1997. Interactive Conflict Resolution. Syracuse, N.Y.: Syracuse University Press.

Garcia, E., ed. 1993. Pilgrim Voices: Citizens as Peacemakers. Manila, Philippines: Ateneo de Manila University Press.

Henderson, M. 1996. The Forgiveness Factor: Stories of Hope in a World of Conflict. London: Grosvenor Books.

Irani, G. E. 1997. Breaking the Cycle: Acknowledgement, Forgiveness, and Reconciliation in Conflict Resolution. Paper presented at the United States Institute of Peace, Washington, D.C.

Johnston, D., and Sampson, C., eds. 1994. *Religion: The Missing Dimension of Statecraft.* Oxford, U.K.: Oxford University Press.

Jones, E. E., and Nisbett, R. E. 1972. The Actor and the Observer: Divergent Perceptions of the Causes of Behavior. In *Attribution: Perceiving the Causes of Behavior.* E. E. Jones, D. E. Kanouse, H. H. Kelley, R. E. Nisbett, S. Valins, and B. Weiner, eds. Morristown, N.J.: General Learning Press.

Kelman, H. C. 1963. The Role of the Group in the Induction of Therapeutic Change. In *International Journal of Group Psychotherapy*, vol. 13, 399-432.

———. 1972. The Problem-Solving Workshop in Conflict Resolution. In *Communication in International Politics.* R. L. Merritt, ed. Urbana: University of Illinois Press.

———. 1979. An Interactional Approach to Conflict Resolution and Its Application to Israeli-Palestinian Relations. In *International Interactions*, vol. 6, no. 2, 99-122.

———. 1986. Interactive Problem Solving: A Social-Psychological Approach to Conflict Resolution. In *Dialogue Toward Interfaith Understanding*, W. Klassen, ed. Jerusalem: Ecumenical Institute for Theological Research.

———. 1991. Interactive Problem Solving: The Uses and Limits of a Therapeutic Model for the Resolution of International Conflicts. In *The Psychodynamics of International Relationships. Volume II: Unofficial Diplomats at Work.* V. D. Volkan, J. V. Montville, and D. A. Julius, eds. Lexington, Mass.: Lexington Books.

———. 1992. Informal Mediation by the Scholar-Practitioner. *In Mediation in International Relations: Multiple Approaches to Conflict Management.* J. Bercovitch and J. Rubin, eds. New York: St. Martin's.

———. 1995. Contributions of an Unofficial Conflict Resolution Effort to the Israeli-Palestinian Breakthrough. *Negotiation Journal*, vol. 2, no. 1, 19-27.

Kraybill, R. 1988. From Head to Heart: The Cycle of Reconciliation. *Conciliation Quarterly*, vol. 7, no. 4 (fall), pp. 2-3, 8.

Kriesberg, L. 1997. Paths to Varieties of Inter-Communal Reconciliation. Paper presented at the annual scientific meeting of the International Society of Political Psychology, Krakow, Poland, July 21-24.

Lederach, J. P. 1997. Building Peace: Sustainable Reconciliation in Divided Societies. Washington, D.C.: United States Institute for Peace Press.

Lumsden, M. 1997. Breaking the Cycle of Violence. *Journal of Peace Research*, vol. 34, no. 4, pp. 377-383.

Mitchell, C. R. 1981. *Peacemaking and the Consultant's Role.* Westmead, U.K.: Gower Publishing.

Montville, J. V. 1987. The Arrow and the Olive Branch: The Case for Track Two Diplomacy. In *Conflict Resolution: Track Two Diplomacy.* J. W. McDonald and D. B. Bendahmane, eds. Washington, D.C.: Foreign Service Institute, Department of State.

———. 1991. Psychoanalytic Enlightenment and the Greening of Diplomacy. In *The Psychodynamics of International Relationships. Volume II: Unofficial Diplomats at Work.* V. D. Volkan, J. V. Montville, and D. A. Julius, eds. Lexington, Mass.: Lexington Books.

———. 1993. The Healing Function in Political Conflict Resolution. In *Conflict Resolution Theory and Practice: Integration and Application.* D. J. D. Sandole, and H. van der Merwe, eds. Manchester, U.K.: Manchester University Press.

Pettigrew, T. F. 1979. The Ultimate Attribution Error: Extending Allport's Cognitive Analysis of Prejudice. *Personality and Social Psychology Bulletin*, vol. 5, no. 4, 461-476.

Rothman, J. 1993. Unofficial Talks Yielded Mideast Peace. *The Philadelphia Inquirer*, September 14.

Rubin, J. Z., Pruitt, D. G., and Kirn, S. H. 1994. *Social Conflict: Escalation, Stalemate, and Settlement*. 2d ed.. New York: McGraw-Hill.

Schindler, C., and Lapid, G. 1989. *The Great Turning*. Santa Fe, N. Mex.: Bear and Co. Publishing.

Schwartz, R. D. 1989. Arab-Jewish Dialogue in the United States: Toward Track II Tractability. In *Intractable Conflicts and Their Transformation*. L. Kriesberg, T. A. Northrup, and S. J. Thorson, eds. Syracuse, N.Y.: Syracuse University Press.

Smedes, L.B. 1984. *Forgive and Forget: Healing the Hurts We Don't Deserve*. New York: Harper and Row.

Tavuchis, N. 1991. *Mea Culpa: A Sociology of Apology and Reconciliation*. Stanford, Calif.: Stanford University Press.

Volkan, V. D. 1991. Official and Unofficial Diplomacy: An Overview. In *The Psychodynamics of International Relationships, Volume II: Unofficial Diplomacy at Work*, V. D. Volkan, J. V. Montville, and D. A. Julius, eds. Lexington, Mass.: Lexington Books.

Wallensteen, P., and Sollenberg, M. 1997. Armed Conflicts, Conflict Termination, and Peace Agreements, 1989-96. *Journal of Peace Research*, vol. 34, no. 3, 339-358.

White, R. K. 1984. *Fearful Warriors: A Psychological Profile of U.S-Soviet Relations*. New York: Free Press.

Note

This chapter has previously appeared in *Conflict Resolution: Dynamics, Process, and Structure*. Ho Won Jeong, ed. Permission to reprint this chapter has been granted by: Ashgate Publishing Limited, Gower House, Croft Road. Aldershot, Hants GU11 3HR. Tel: (01252) 331551. Fax: (01252) 317446. Web: http://www.ashgate.com

Note: The author is indebted to Herbert Kelman for his integrative insights and contributions as a coconsultant in fusing conflict analysis and reconciliation considerations in workshop design and implementation. The author would also like to thank Martin Rempel for contributing to the literature search for this chapter and for sharing his experience as a coconsultant in some of the conflict analysis and reconciliation work that stimulated part of the thinking for this chapter.

3

Changing Forms of Coexistence

Louis Kriesberg

Throughout history, relations between different peoples often have been characterized by great brutality. They have included enslavement, forced conversion, and genocide. However, relations between peoples have also been characterized by respectful coexistence, equitable opportunities, and shared governance. Moreover, these relations are not static, becoming increasingly oppressive at times and increasingly equitable at other times. The purpose here is to explore how accommodations between communal groups can and do become more integrated, peaceful, and just. Those who would support movement in such directions have a never-ending task but one that is always possible to undertake, often with good effect.

To begin, the grand concepts of peace, justice, reconciliation, and coexistence will be distinguished. After mapping out different kinds of coexistence, varying in mutuality and integration, the factors affecting various forms of coexistence and their changes are discussed. Then the focus shifts to movements toward greater integration, peace, and justice. In concluding, the role of reconciliation in affecting such movements is examined.

Conceptual Issues

The words *peace, justice, reconciliation*, and *coexistence* are used in various senses and often overlap in meaning. For purposes of this chapter, each term is used in a relatively narrow sense so that the terms do not subsume each other and become analytically useless.

Peace has a great variety of meanings, ranging from imposed order to loving harmony. It may refer to the absence of direct physical violence or to relations in which no group experiences structural violence; the former condition is often called *negative peace* and the latter *positive peace* (Galtung 1996; Stephenson 1994). *Negative peace,* then, refers to the absence of war; it may connote order and security, but it may also connote suppression of struggles to redress injustice. *Positive peace* refers to at least a minimal level of equity in the life conditions of the people in the same social system. To distinguish the word *peace* from the term *justice,* the word *peace* is generally used here to refer to personal and group security and legitimate order.

Justice here refers to a multifaceted, ongoing set of processes moving toward social relations that are regarded as equitable by the people engaged in them. Justice is never fully realized, involving as it does contradictory qualities and changing standards. We are most concerned here with varying degrees of justice among parties in social relations, as assessed by the members of those parties themselves. The often heard chant, "No justice, no peace; no peace, no justice," suggests the desirability of advancing peace and justice together, but also the frequent failure to do so.

Reconciliation refers to the processes by which parties that have experienced an oppressive relationship or a destructive conflict with each other move to attain or to restore a relationship that they believe to be minimally acceptable. It is a way, then, of advancing peace and, optimally, justice as well. Reconciliation also is understood to be an aspect of an existing relationship, marked by varying degrees of mutual acceptance. In this sense, it may be a feature of a peaceful and just relationship. But, as we shall see, reconciliation involves so many aspects that some aspects, at a given time, may contribute to peace and justice, while others do not.

Coexistence generally refers to an accommodation between members of different communities or separate countries who live together without one collectivity trying to destroy or severely harm the other (Weiner 1998). This minimal level of coexistence is compatible with competition and even conflicts, if conducted through legitimate channels. It is also compatible with significant differences not only in values and cultural patterns, but also in economic standing and political power. It can be viewed as a minimal level of peace.

Coexistence, however, is often understood to go beyond this minimal level, to include a sense of mutual tolerance and even respect. Also, it sometimes is understood to entail relative equality in economic position and political power. Great differences in economic conditions and power are likely to mean that one party dominates another and that the accommodation is not symmetrical. Accommodations marked by great asymmetry and unilateral imposition are usually regarded as unjust and are not treated here as relations of coexistence.

The character of the coexistence between peoples matters. One or more parties may judge a form of coexistence as unjust, as a violation of their sense of equity or fairness. What is just and what is unjust depends upon the standards of judgment parties use, and all sides in a social relationship often do not share those standards. Discrepancies between the actual form of coexistence and the standards of justice held by one or more parties in the relationship are a fundamental source of discontent and frequently of intense struggle.

Forms of Coexistence

Coexistence is one set of possible relations between different collectivities. To help examine the many possible forms of coexistence, two dimensions of any kind of intercommunal relationship are stressed: the degree of integration and the degree of unilateral imposition (Kriesberg 1999b).

A crucial dimension of the relations between ethnic, religious, linguistic, or other communal groups is the degree to which the members of the groups are integrated with each other. High integration refers to high rates of social interaction between members of the coexisting peoples and high levels of interdependence in their economic and political relations. It also entails shared institutional arrangements and cultural patterns. Consequently, members of the different communal groups also share some common identities.

These various aspects of integration tend to vary together, but integration may be much greater in one way than another. For example, in societies with considerable ethnic discrimination, people of different ethnicities may live segregated lives and have low rates of social interaction, but nevertheless share important societal identities and function within the same major institutions.

The second important dimension discussed here is the extent to which the relationship either is mutually constructed or is unilaterally imposed and sustained. Unilateral imposition is high insofar as the nature of the accommodation is determined and harshly imposed by one party and not accepted by the other party. Unilateral imposition is widely regarded as unjust, and this is particularly so among the people subjected to the imposition.

In this chapter, the focus is on relations between members of collectivities who share ethnic, religious, linguistic, or other communal identities and so regard themselves as a people or nation (Smith 1991). Such identities are based on a socially constructed common history and on having a sense of common fate. This means that the identity is shaped by persons who are not members of the group as well as by the members themselves. After all, being treated as a distinct people tends to make the persons so designated believe that they have a common destiny (Nagel 1994).

Peoples, communities, and societies, however, are not unitary entities. Because of the diversity among the members of such collectivities, no single characterization of the accommodation fully captures the degree of integration and of imposition that the diverse members experience. For example, even where one people is forced to live in segregation by another, the conditions and expectations of the segregated vary somewhat as do those of the people imposing the segregation. Such variations, as well as the shared qualities providing the bases for solidarity, provide sources for changing the form of accommodation.

Relations between collectivities that entail at least a modest degree of integration and not extreme unilateral imposition are of primary interest here. In such accommodations, the peoples are regarded as coexisting. Relationships that are largely imposed by one side, or whose integration results in assimilation, are not viewed as relationships of coexistence. Relationships that are unilaterally imposed may entail considerable integration between distinct peoples, but be regarded as unjust and resisted by the dominated side; such relationships are generally not treated here as reaching the level of coexistence. Thus, the relations between Jews and Arabs in Palestine between 1948 and 1993 were so widely regarded as unacceptable by the Arab Palestinians that the relationship is viewed as not attaining the coexistence level for most people for most of the time (Kriesberg 2000).

**Table 3.1: Dimensions and Forms
of Intercommunal Accommodation**

Imposition Level	Integration Level		
	Low	**Moderate**	**High**
Unilateral & Severe	Expulsion Secession Direct Colonial Rule	Apartheid	Slavery
Mixed & Moderate	Indirect Colonial Rule	Domination Segregation Preeminence	Forced Assimilation
Mutual & Little	Negotiated Separation	Autonomy Multiculturalism Pluralism	Free Assimilation

Several relatively common forms of intercommunal coexistence warrant discussion. They are presented in table 3.1. First, consider the forms in terms of the degree to which distinct peoples are integrated with each other. At one extreme are independent countries whose governments are at peace with each other; for example, during the Cold War, relations between the Soviet and American governments were often characterized as ones of peaceful coexistence. Members of different communities within the same country sometimes have come to regard *political separation* between them as a mutually satisfactory form of relationship. This has been the case for Norwegian separation from Sweden in 1905, the Slovenian withdrawal from Yugoslavia in 1991, the division of Czechoslovakia into two republics in 1993, and the establishment of several countries from what had been the Soviet Union in 1991. Social, cultural, and economic integration can accompany political separation into two or more sovereign states.

Even the creation of independent states, of course, does not guarantee peaceful coexistence. Borders cannot be drawn that neatly separate distinct peoples. Persons with different ethnic, religious, linguistic, and other bases for communal identities are intermingled throughout every region and in the world at large. Such intermingling can be the source of destructive conflicts when secessions are attempted, as has been made brutally evident in much of the territory of the former Yugoslavia. Such terrible cases demonstrate that peaceful and mutually acceptable separations generally need to be reached by a process the peoples deem legitimate.

Many forms of coexistence within a country have been tried; some of them have been peaceful for extended periods of time. One set of forms involves substantial separation between people with different collective identities. This may involve regional *autonomy* where, for example, a country's constitution provides that different languages have primacy in various regions (Lapidoth 1996). This is the case in contemporary Switzerland, Spain, and Canada. In the United States, autonomy includes reservations for indigenous peoples; it also includes a commonwealth relationship with Puerto Rico.

Separation may also take the form of *segregation*, often imposed by one group upon another. The segregation is sometimes enforced by law, as was true with apartheid in South Africa and with the Jim Crow system in the American south. Such segregation, rejected by the subjugated group, does not constitute coexistence. Segregation, however, also may result from blends of informal imposition and self-selection, as is the case currently with residential and occupational discrimination against African Americans and the choice of some African Americans to live and work with each other. That relationship is a marginal kind of coexistence.

Another type of coexistence involves relatively high integration, but distinguishes among peoples in terms of their ethnic, religious, linguistic, or other cultural markers. One form this takes is *power sharing*. That is, particular religious and linguistic groups are allocated fixed roles in the political system, as in Lebanon. A second form of this coexistence type is cultural *pluralism*, ranging from informal self-designations to institutionalized multicultural arrangements, as exemplified in contemporary Canada and the United States. In the third form of this type, *preeminence*, one ethnicity, religious community, or linguistic group accords primacy to itself. Thus, in some countries, members of a dominant group, adhering to an ethnonationalist ideology, may enact rules that place obstacles to obtaining citizenship by those who they regard as having different historical origins (Smith 1991). In many countries or empires, a single religion is recognized as the state religion or a single language is designated as the country's official language. In conjunction with this system, varying degrees of personal and group autonomy for persons practicing other religions and using other languages may be found.

In another set of forms with a high degree of integration, *assimilation* is possible but not imposed. In countries where people generally adhere to an ideology of civic nationalism (Smith 1991), acquiring certain cultural markers or expressing political allegiance suffices to become a citizen of the country with equal rights.

These various forms of coexistence are ideal types; no country purely exemplifies any one of them. Rather, for different groups within a country and for different aspects of integration, there may be varying amounts of domination and of pluralism. Thus, while people in the United States generally claim to follow an ideology of civic nationalism, some Americans think that others do not "look American," implicitly adopting an ethnonationalist ideology.

Although these forms of coexistence have been discussed thus far largely in terms of their degree of integration, referring to the degree of unilateral imposition associated with them could not be avoided. That matter will now be discussed directly. The forms of coexistence vary greatly in the degree of imposition involved. For example, one people, against the desires of another people who do not wish to assimilate, may harshly impose assimilation. In such cases, members or representatives of the dominating ethnic, religious, or linguistic community may insist that members of subordinated groups not practice their religion or not use their language and adopt the cultural markers of the dominating ethnic group. Such impositions may be quite coercive and insofar as that is the case, the relationships are not regarded here as cases of coexistence. This has often been true for peoples in Europe who do not move but become a minority as the political boundaries shift or find that the demands of the majority group change and require assimilation. The situation of many Kurds in Turkey is illustrative.

Assimilation may not be imposed, but be allowed. If assimilation is what many members of the minority or subordinated groups seek, then the relationship would not be regarded as to be unilaterally imposed and would be treated as a form of coexistence. This has been the case for many European immigrant groups in the United States. Of course, this can result in the disappearance of a distinct people in that territory, which also marks the end of coexistence.

Particular forms of autonomy, power sharing, and multiculturalism also vary in their degree of imposition by one side and the methods used to sustain them. Typically, no one side wholly determines the way these forms are structured. Rather, particular forms are frequently the result of conflict, often waged constructively (Kriesberg 1998). The terms of the form of coexistence generally are formally negotiated and enacted into laws, as occurred in Spain after Francisco Franco died in 1975. Terms often also result in some degree from tacit bargaining by different people in various parts of a country.

Having sketched out many kinds of coexistence, it should be evident that they are subject to change. Some forms are more stable than others, and certain sequences of changes are more likely than others. To consider these matters, the conditions and the processes fostering stability and constructive change in these forms of coexistence will be discussed.

Sequences

Although changes in the form of coexistence may be inevitable, some relationships are more enduring than others. Stable relationships are often regarded as peaceful. Furthermore, if the changes that do occur are the result of orderly and legitimate methods, and not destructive fighting, they too are generally viewed as peaceful. In this section, the focus is on movements toward more stable and peaceful accommodation, toward less unilaterally imposed and more just accommodations, and toward those marked by increasing integration.

Four sets of factors affect the forms of coexistence and their sequential changes: (1) Features of the coexistence arrangements, (2) The social context for the coexisting parties, (3) Internal features of each party, and (4) The structure and interactions between the coexisting parties. The effects of each on the stability, mutuality, and integration of the relations between communal groups will be examined.

Coexistence Arrangements

The terms of any particular form of accommodation are likely to have implications for future changes of that form. They tend to affect movements toward (1) increased stability of the form of coexistence, (2) greater mutuality in determining the form of coexistence, and (3) increased integration between communal groups.

Many features of the form of coexistence affect its stability. Its adaptiveness is particularly important. Changes in the social context and in the relations between the coexisting entities, as well as their internal features, also have impacts on the form of coexistence. Consequently, rigidity in the terms of coexistence makes the form susceptible to rupture, often accompanied by intense and destructive struggle. Lebanon is illustrative of this possibility. According to a National Covenant agreed to in 1943, the president would be a Maronite Christian and the prime minister a Sunni Muslim. As the years went by, the relative size of the Muslim communities grew, and the relative role of the Shiite Muslims especially increased. The power-sharing formula was not changed, and this contributed to the civil war that broke out in 1975, ending in a new formula.

Another major factor contributing to stability is consistency among the characteristics of the form of coexistence. Some features may have contradictory implications for each other. For example, high economic integration and social-political segregation are difficult to sustain, unless considerable coercion is exercised. This certainly produces severe strains. For example, in South Africa considerable economic interdependence existed from the beginning of European settlement in the region (Greenstein 1995). This generated many problems in social relations and economic motivation. Apartheid was an attempted solution to these problems. Established in 1948 by the government led by the National Party, apartheid produced additional strains, nevertheless surviving in somewhat changing forms for fifty years. In the United States, the American Creed of individual rights and equal opportunity was inconsistent with the enforced segregation and subordination of African Americans (Myrdal, Sterner, and Rose 1944). That contradiction contributed greatly to the transformation of Black-White relations in the 1950s and 1960s.

One other notable feature of a relationship is the nature of the creed or ideology that characterizes its form of accommodation. The values, norms, and practices that are part of a creed or ideology may pertain to the legitimacy of the class, status, and power differences, and to the legitimacy of procedures for changing them. Ideologies vary in the way religious, linguistic, ethnic, and other communal groupings are viewed. Thus, the Stalinist Soviet Union and Hitlerite Germany both had been totalitarian societies. The Nazi ideology, however, glorified authoritarian control from the top and the racial superiority of Aryans, while Communist ideology glorified people's democracy and national rights of the Soviet Union's constituent peoples. The Nazi system was overthrown from the outside. The Communist ideology was used by opponents of centralized totalitarian rule and contributed to the nonviolent transformation and then dissolution of the Soviet Union.

Changes toward more or less symmetry in intercommunal relations also are greatly affected by various features of the actualized coexistence arrangements. Thus, some features provide opportunities for members of different groups to sustain their culture and interests as they see them. These characteristics include shared norms supporting diversity. Another important feature is the provision of opportunities and structures enabling vulnerable groups to legitimately participate and raise challenges to aspects of the arrangements that they believe to be asymmetrical.

Other features of coexistence arrangements, on the other hand, tend to increase the asymmetry of the relations between communal groups. Insofar as different entities have unequal resources, the more powerful have the capability and the temptation to use that power to increase their domination. Consequently, rules and institutions are established to buttress their authority and hamper challengers.

Finally, many features of accommodation arrangements affect further integration. This is examined by functionalists, according to whom international organizations may increase and expand in order to serve the initial functions for which they were created (Mitrany 1966). The way the European Coal and Steel Community, established in 1953, contributed to forging a European common market and a series of European institutions is illustrative (Haas 1958).

Some coexistence accommodations help create vested interests in expanding the compact and the integration it entails. One mechanism that helps generate such vested interests is the establishment of an agency to implement particular provisions of the form of coexistence. Leaders of such agencies tend to seek an expansion of their activities and of the staff to perform the activities (Kriesberg 1984). This may be seen in the effects of official and nonofficial organizations in the fields of affirmative action and human rights, as well as of organizations working to subjugate challenging communal groups in the society.

The creed associated with a particular form of coexistence also has implications for the direction in which that form changes. Members of an ethnic, religious, or other communal group, for example, may adhere to an ideology that proclaims their superiority to other communal groups. Such ideologies tend to propel communal groups toward greater separation. On the other hand, some creeds may be relatively inclusive; they varyingly emphasize ideas of tolerance, liberty, equal opportunity, civic nationalism, and the separation of church and state. Such creeds can contribute to increasing equality and assimilation.

Certain characteristics of the form of coexistence foster increasing separation between different collectivities. Thus, coexistence arrangements may give privileged positions to intellectuals and politicians within each collectivity. Some of them, particularly those from the subordinated collectivity, would have a vested interest in advancing separatism, which in turn would further enhance their status and power

Contextual Factors

Whatever the features of the accommodation may be, alone, they do not determine its future. In addition, many changing external conditions affect the direction that any accommodation takes. Coexisting entities interact within larger social systems, which themselves undergo changes. Societal and global social systems are important sources of changing circumstances for coexisting communal groups. Societal and global changes help determine the stability of any accommodation that has been achieved and the movement toward or away from increased integration and greater mutuality.

The stability of any given form of coexistence is greatly impacted by developments in the society and in the world as a whole. First of all, continuity in relevant institutions and patterns of conduct in the society and the world helps perpetuate already established forms of coexistence. Thus, economic stability, persistence in ideologies, and continuities in demographic balances generally reinforce current forms of coexistence.

Large and abrupt changes in a society or the global system, on the other hand, undermine established coexistence arrangements. Thus, breaking up an empire creates new countries with sets of peoples living with each other in new relationships. This was evident after the dissolution of the Ottoman, Austria-Hungarian and Soviet empires, when new borders created new dominant and subordinate communities.

Particular contextual changes tend to support certain kinds of coexistence. Thus, implementing policies to increase mutuality and integration in economic activities tends to be aided by an expanding economy. For example, this played an important role in the relatively effective affirmative action policies in Malaysia, with a rapidly expanding economy (Mauzy 1993). In general, economic well-being and prospects of continuing improvement ease problems of mutual accommodation.

Governmental and nongovernmental organizations that are not directly engaged in a particular intercommunal relationship often mediate or otherwise help the engaged parties to reach an accommodation. This kind of intervention is increasingly happening in intercommunal conflicts. The survival of the accommodation reached often depends upon ongoing efforts by such intermediaries, as a study comparing the survival of peace settlements in Cyprus, Namibia, Angola, El Salvador, and Cambodia indicates (Hampson 1996).

Asymmetries in the relations between communal groups are also greatly impacted by various changes in the regional and global context. The changes may help groups with relatively fewer resources to improve their position. This occurs when the external allies of the dominated group improve their relative position and therefore can provide increased support. This may also follow from changes in the salience of particular ideological, religious, or other normative ideas. Thus, subjugated peoples are now better able to make claims for greater civic equality, buttressed by the new global salience regarding human rights and self-determination.

A wide variety of contextual developments affects the degree of integration between communal groups. These include facing a new common external enemy. If an external threat arises, and is not too severe, it often contributes to solidarity against the common enemy. As most frequently studied, the common enemy is another country making war on the country in which the communal groups coexist (Coser 1956; Kriesberg 1998).

As the prevailing regional or global ways of thinking about social identities and forms of organization change, so does the salience of various shared identities by coexisting communal groups. Increasing global attention to religious, racial, or linguistic identities is echoed within each society and region. Consequently, old divisions in a society may decline in salience while new-shared identities rise in salience. The result is declining integration among some groups and increased integration among others. For example, the decline in Soviet and Communist identity and increased importance of religious identity in central Asia alters many integrative bonds throughout central Asia and the Middle East.

Internal Factors

Changes within each party coexisting with other parties also affect the collectivities' form of coexistence. These internal factors to a significant degree have their own dynamic in affecting stability, integration, and mutuality.

Among other factors, stability of the form of coexistence is strongly affected by the continuity in leadership of each collectivity. Changes in leaders or in the relative authority of different elites, on the other hand, undercut past arrangements. For example, in Quebec, the growing urbanization of French speakers increased the role of intellectual and political elites compared to the

Catholic Church hierarchy. This fostered a shift in identity and strengthened separatist sentiments.

Changes within each party also affect the degree of imposition by one party relative to another. Members of a dominant collectivity may come to doubt the justifications for their dominance. Religious doctrine may have provided an acceptable justification for members of the dominant community, but changes in the doctrine weakened their sense of righteousness about their superiority. A significant step in this change among Afrikaners in South Africa occurred in 1986, when the general synod of the Dutch Reformed Church resolved that there was no biblical imperative for the forced separation of peoples.

As a consequence of such doubts or acknowledged past unfairness by members of the relatively dominant group, members of the subordinated group have better opportunities to effectively achieve coexistence on more equitable terms. In the United States after World War Two, anti-Semitism expressed in conventional discriminatory practice and other widespread overt behavior markedly decreased. This was partly a consequence of recognizing how anti-Semitism could lead to the Holocaust experienced by Jews in Europe and how it contributed to the failure of the United States to act more energetically to prevent or to ameliorate the tragedy.

The degree of integration between the coexisting parties is affected by internal changes within each collectivity. Thus, as members of one collectivity become more specialized and less self-sufficient as a collectivity, their dependence on relations with members of other communal groups tends to increase. Consequently, they experience a greater need for closer connections with those others with whom interdependence has grown. Thus, the apartheid system was undermined by the growth of economic dependence of Whites on Black workers and managers (Kane-Berman 1990).

Relational Factors

The internal factors of each party influence the form of accommodation particularly as they impact on the interactions between the parties. Changes within each party alter the relative positions between interacting parties. Consequently, thus, demographic, economic, cultural, political, and many other aspects of the relations between coexisting parties inevitably change over time. Those changes necessarily affect coexistence arrangements.

The persistence of forms of accommodation is affected by many relational factors. Thus, continuity in the demographic balance among the coexisting parties helps sustain their established arrangements, if the arrangements had not been unilaterally imposed. The persistence of the demographic balance in Switzerland has contributed to the stability of the form of existence in that country, while the changes in the demographic balance among communal groups in Lebanon contributed to the 1975 rupture of the arrangements established in 1943.

The changing composition of the Canadian population has contributed to the search for a new formula for relations between the French speakers of Quebec and the English speakers throughout Canada. Canada, in many ways, began as a state consisting of two nations. The high levels of immigration of diverse European and non-European peoples, however, relegated the French to one people among many others in a largely English-speaking multicultural country.

Relational factors also affect the degree of symmetry in intercommunal forms of accommodation. If members of the minority or relatively disadvantaged people acquire more resources and capabilities, they may become able to renegotiate the terms of their coexistence with the relatively advantaged people. This contributed to the changes in the relations between the Walloons and the Flemish in Belgium, as economic development in the Flemish region of Belgium improved more rapidly than in the Walloon region, whose residents had previously been preeminent. The anticipation of a changing relative balance also can have such an effect. For example, the declining proportion of Whites in South Africa contributed to their willingness to renegotiate the terms of their relationship with the non-Whites of South Africa before they decline further.

An important relational component is the history of the relationship. One or more sides in an intercommunal relationship often harbor grievances from past suffering inflicted by the other. The nature of such grievances affects the standards used by each side to make claims against the other in the present and for the future.

The acquisition of certain resources and capabilities helps groups make greater claims. Long dormant claims may be renewed when the capability to do so emerges. For example, the land claims of indigenous American peoples have only recently been strongly raised after many decades of dormancy. The revival of claims owes something to the new generation in the native groups who have legal skills to pursue the claims.

The level of integration is affected by changes in the nature of intercommunal relations. Thus, insofar as members of different communities increasingly believe they share important values, identities, or interests, their level of integration is likely to be enhanced. Thus, too, as members of different communities become more equal in class, status, and power, they are likely to increase in mutual respect and social interaction.

Combining Factors and the Direction of Change

The effects of each factor depend upon the features of the other factors. For example, if the demographic balance between communal groups is changing, then rigid terms of coexistence with fixed arrangements are unlikely to be enduring. This would also be the case if the prevailing norms and standards of fairness were changing for one or more of the major coexisting parties or their social environment.

Some changes in the social context, whether they be new technological developments or shifts in terms of discourse, may enable one party to gain relatively more advantage and thus alter its relationship with its coexisting partners. Thus, subordinated groups may more effectively make claims for greater equality based on new views about the right of self-determination or of democratic participation. This argument is supported by the evidence that numerous effective struggles for democracy or for national liberation occurred during particular historical periods (Gurr 1994).

Intercommunal accommodations that move toward greater mutuality sometimes also move in the direction of greater integration. As the relationship between peoples is more symmetrical and viewed as more just, social interaction is more equal and integration enhanced. The changing terms of accommodation between Blacks and Whites in South Africa is illustrative, as apartheid ended and new accommodations were forged. Similarly, in the southern United States, the integration between Whites and Blacks increased in many regards as the discriminatory Jim Crow accommodation was dismantled in the American south in the 1950s and 1960s.

Movement toward greater mutuality, however, can result in accommodations with reduced integration between communal groups. Increased freedom by one people from the domination of another can foster the expression and elaboration of cultural differences and the preference for autonomy or independence. Thus, the reduced Israeli control over Palestinians in the West Bank and Gaza was accompanied by increased separation between Israel and the emerging Palestine. Similarly, in Canada, increased mutuality between French-speaking Quebec and the rest of Canada has been accompanied by increased separation between them.

Which course of development is followed depends on the interaction among many of the factors that have been previously discussed. For example, each party's creed or ideology tends to sustain the existing mutuality and integration of the intercommunal accommodation; but a change in the creed then would lead to a change in the level of integration or mutuality. The degree of integration characterizing an accommodation also would tend to be self-sustaining. In the case of South Africa, many Whites came to view apartheid as unworkable and morally wrong, and that undercut the effort to impose apartheid (Giliomee 1997). The integration of Blacks and Whites in the South African case was so high, however, that separation was not possible. Consequently, both increased mutuality and integration mark the post-apartheid accommodation. In the case of Israeli-Palestinian relations, the Israeli Jews did not lose faith in Zionism, and the integration between Arab Palestinians and Israeli Jews had been relatively limited. Consequently, the increased mutuality of control is accompanied by reduced integration, in many regards, as separate states are being established (Savir 1998).

Reconciliation in Sequencing Forms of Coexistence

In recent years, we have seen a remarkable surge in efforts to further reconciliation between former enemies. Representatives of one side or more have expressed regret and apologized, have prosecuted perpetrators of gross violations of human rights, and have provided compensations to the aggrieved party. Reconciliation, it must be stressed, has many aspects, and each aspect varies in the degree to which it is attained. Reconciliation is never total, never including all members of former antagonistic parties, not including every dimension of reconciliation completely, nor being fully reciprocal between the parties (Kriesberg 1999b).

The varying levels of reconciliation impact greatly upon changes in the form of coexistence. Reconciliation is a very complex set of processes. It occurs between individuals, peoples, governments, and other groups and combinations of them. It may occur among a few or among most members of one or more reconciling sides. It occurs in many different settings, including families, communities, and countries. It occurs over varying time periods after the rupture, oppression, or atrocity about which the reconciliation is occurring.

Reconciliation occurs along at least four dimensions: (1) truth, in the sense of shared understandings of it and at least recognition of varying views of it, (2) justice, whether in the form of punishment of wrongdoers or of a new, more equitable system of relations, (3) remorse and forgiveness, either of which may be expressed independently of the other or that are carefully exchanged, and (4) person and/or group safety and security (Lederach 1997). Reconciliation may vary in degree along each dimension, by the proportions within each side who participate in it, and in other ways. What is of importance here is the kind and degree of reconciliation among different members of each side that contribute to transforming enemy relations and building integrated and mutually acceptable forms of coexistence.

In the transformation from enmity to cooperation in Franco-German relations after World War II, some degree of reconciliation along each dimension was achieved (Ackermann 1994). Justice was advanced by West German provision of some compensation to victims of Nazism, Nazi perpetrators of gross human rights violations were put on trial, and the West German government passed legislation to prevent recurrences of Nazism. Security was advanced by close economic integration through institutions such as the European Coal and Steel Community and then by other economic institutions and by military alliances. Truth was advanced by official and nonofficial reports about the Nazi regime and the atrocities committed throughout the territories controlled by Germany. Reports about French collaboration emerged much later. Official German apologies and German expressions of remorse were evident, and official acceptance of the new Germany by France was also evident. Expressions of forgiveness and of remorse were made by French and German individuals in various settings (Henderson 1996).

In other relationships, the lack of significant reconciliation efforts has been followed by destructive violence, long-lasting antagonism, or at best a mutually mistrusting and hostile accommodation. This is illustrated by the denial of past human rights violations by one or more sides in Serb-Croat relations in the former Yugoslavia, in Turkish relations with Armenians and with Kurds, and in relations between Israeli Jews and Arab Palestinians.

Based on the preceding discussion of coexistence and related work on reconciliation, a few observations can be ventured. First, to achieve more than minimal coexistence, that is, peaceful accommodations marked by moderate to high integration and by moderate to little unilateral imposition, significant and broad reconciliation is important. Reconciliation can be quite limited between groups in accommodations that involve little integration and/or high unilateral imposition.

Second, in relations between large-scale groups, a significant degree of reconciliation between the authorities on each side is usually crucial. Subjective reconciliation and even manifest reconciliation between grassroots or unofficial middle-rank leaders by itself is generally inadequate to transform animosity and antagonism. Reconciliation at those levels, however, can encourage and speed reconciliation at higher levels and make them credible. Undoubtedly, also, reconciliatory actions taken at the highest levels can bring about fundamental changes within and between coexisting communal groups.

Third, among the major dimensions of reconciliation, exposing the truth of past and current oppression and atrocities is crucial and in many instances easier to pursue than admissions of guilt and remorse and expressions of mercy and forgiveness. Developing a shared understanding about the reality of past and present relations provides a base upon which justice, remorse/forgiveness, and peace can be gradually constructed. This is one of the great achievements of the Truth and Reconciliation Commission in South Africa. It was designed to maximize the attainment of the truth about apartheid and the struggle between those who tried to sustain it and those who tried to end it. It was conducted and used to make that truth known as widely as possible in South Africa.

Finally, progress toward an enduring and equitable coexistence is in itself a significant aspect of reconciliation. Progress toward peace encompasses personal and group security and the protection of basic human rights. Increasing security and protection of human rights is a way of manifesting reconciliation, since institutionalizing such assurances reduces the chances that past atrocities and oppression will recur. On the basis of that kind of peace, other aspects of reconciliation, even involving remorse and expressed apologies, become possible. Such sentiments and actions may occur generations after the perpetration of large-scale violations of human rights, as occurred in many colonized parts of the world.

Conclusion

There are worse conditions than coexistence. Furthermore, coexistence can be the prelude to increasing peace, advancing reconciliation, and achieving greater justice. The forms of coexistence constantly undergo change, sometimes slowly but other times abruptly; sometimes the changes are slight but other times transforming, and sometimes the changes are in the direction of increased peace and justice but other times moving in the other direction. The changes result from developments within one or more parties in the conflict, from developments in the relations between the contending sides, and also developments in the social context.

History and the reality of the relations between antagonistic parties profoundly affect the course of changes in the form of coexistence and the possible roles of various aspects of reconciliation for those changes. Developing a shared history, or at least a mutually acknowledged varied set of histories, is an important aspect of reconciliation.

Justice is never wholly achieved nor wholly absent, but it varies in degree and for different members of the groups in a social relationship. Furthermore, the degree and character of justice is not static. Social conditions change, and standards of judgment vary over time. Within this broad context, only a few observations are made about justice in relationship to coexistence.

Coexistence and justice have different relationships, depending on the concept of justice that is accepted. When people believe justice to be based on particular absolute standards, their attempts to realize it would interfere with the achievement of coexistence. In such circumstances, a group may regard those who do not share their standards of justice to be acting unjustly and try to correct their conduct or to destroy them. On the other hand, if justice is understood to be totally relative, then no universal basis for valuing coexistence exists. Justice, however, is regarded here neither as absolute nor as wholly relative. Some standards are almost universally regarded as important in determining what is justice, while other standards are widely disputed. Accepting a conventional conception of justice, the focus here is on those standards of justice about which there is high consensus (Kriesberg 1999a; Welch 1994). These include condemnations of genocidal policies, coerced unidirectional exploitation, and gross violations of human rights.

Furthermore, the priority people place on any single goal, be it peace, justice, or even coexistence, should not be absolute. Each is desirable, as is freedom, security, and economic well-being. At some level, there are trade-offs among all these values that each of us would seek and defend. People are likely to differ, within given historical circumstances, about the relative priority of various goals, but such differences between adversaries can contribute to constructing mutually acceptable settlements.

The analysis presented here has implications for theory and policymaking about problem-solving conflict resolution and about the transformation of intercommunal conflicts so that relations between adversaries become more just and peaceful. Every accommodation is embedded in a wider context that profoundly affects subsequent intercommunal accommodations.

The interconnections between justice, peace, reconciliation, and coexistence are profound and should be more fully recognized and examined. A first step in such an examination is to distinguish among them. The inevitability of changes in each of these aspects of social relations has been emphasized here. Several points about such changes deserve mentioning. The analysis indicates that the stability of any particular coexistence arrangements and the direction of their sequence of changes are not determined solely by the character of those terms. The continuity of any particular kind of accommodation is greatly shaped by contextual, relational, and internal factors. The persistence of the terms of coexistence, and the way they change when they do, depends upon the interaction between the changes in contextual, relational, and internal conditions and the already existing form of coexistence. An effective accommodation is one that meshes well with future changes.

The quality of the accommodation, its fairness, is affected by contextual, relational, and internal factors. The parties have ultimate responsibility for their relations, but many groups outside the relationship also affect the course of changes in the forms of coexistence. Whatever those groups do or do not do, they have some effect and therefore some responsibility.

Analysts and peacemakers should anticipate that the terms of coexistence change over time. They should expect to modify or restructure the terms of any accommodation. Taking that perspective recognizes actual experience, and it may well serve to reduce the tasks and burdens of each negotiation, recognizing that it is not final. Finally, accommodation formulas should allow for change and build in considerable flexibility.

References

Ackermann, A. 1994. Reconciliation as a Peace-Building Process in Postwar Europe. *Peace & Change*, vol. 19, no. 3, 229-250.

Coser, L. A. 1956. *The Functions of Social Conflict*. New York: Free Press.

Galtung, J. 1996. *Peace by Peaceful Means: Peace and Conflict, Development and Civilization*. London: Sage Publishers.

Giliomee, H. 1997. Surrender without Defeat: Afrikaners and the South African Miracle. Braamfontein, South Africa: South African Institute of Race Relations.

Greenstein, R. 1995. *Genealogies of Conflict: Class, Identity, and State in Palestine/Israel and South Africa*. London: Wesleyan University Press.

Gurr, T. R. 1994. *Minorities at Risk*. Washington, D.C.: United States Institute of Peace Press.

Haas, E. B. 1958. *The Uniting of Europe*. Stanford, Calif.: Stanford University Press.

Hampson, F. E. 1996. *Nurturing Peace: Why Peace Settlements Succeed or Fail*. Washington, D.C.: United States Institute of Peace Press.

Henderson, M. 1996. *The Forgiveness Factor*. London: Grosvenor Books.

Kane-Berman, J. 1990. *South Africa's Silent Revolution*. Johannesburg: South African Institute of Race Relations.

Kriesberg, L. 1984. Policy Continuity and Change. *Social Problems,* vol. 32 (December), 89-102.

———. 1998. *Constructive Conflicts: From Escalation to Resolution*. Lanham, Md.: Rowman & Littlefield.

———. 1999a. On Advancing Truth and Morality in Conflict Resolution. *Peace and Conflict Studies*, vol. 6, no. 1, 7-19.

———. 1999b. Paths to Varieties of Intercommunal Reconciliation. Pp. 105-129 in *From Conflict Resolution to Peacebuilding*. H. Jeong, ed. Fitchburg, Md.: Dartmouth.

———. 2000. Negotiating the Partition of Palestine and Evolving Israeli-Palestinian Relations. *The Brown Journal of World Affairs*. vol. 7 (winter/spring), 63-80.

Lapidoth, R. 1996. *Autonomy: Flexible Solutions to Ethnic Conflicts*. Washington, D.C.: United States Institute of Peace Press.

Lederach, J. P. 1997. *Building Peace: Sustainable Reconciliation in Divided Societies*. Washington, D.C.: United States Institute of Peace Press.

Mauzy, D. 1993. Malaysia: Malay Political Hegemony and "Coercive Consociationalism." In *The Politics of Ethnic Conflict*. J. McGarry and B. O'Leary, eds. London: Routledge.

Mitrany, D. 1948. The Functional Approach to World Organization. *International Affairs*.

Myrdal, G., Sterner, R., and Rose. A. 1944. *An American Dilemma: The Negro Problem and American Democracy*. New York: Harper and Brothers.

Nagel, J. 1994. Constructing Ethnicity: Creating and Recreating Ethnic Identity and Culture. *Social Problems,* vol. 41, 152-176.

Savir, U. 1998. *The Process: 1,100 Days That Changed the Middle East*. New York: Random House.

Smith, A. 1991. *National Identity*. Reno: University of Nevada Press.

Stephenson, C. M. 1994. New Approaches to International Peacemaking in the Post-Cold War World. 14-28. in *Peace & World Security Studies: A Curriculum Guide*. M. T. Klare, ed. Boulder, Colo.: Lynne Rienner.

Weiner, E., ed. 1998. *The Handbook of Interethnic Coexistence*. New York: Continuum.

Welch, D. A. 1994. Can We Think Systematically about Ethics and Statecraft? *Ethics and International Affairs*, vol. 8, 33.

4

The Attainment of Justice through Restoration, Not Litigation

The Subjective Road to Reconciliation

Mica Estrada-Hollenbeck

Disputing parties' attainment of reconciliation relates to the process by which the parties attain their justified outcomes. At the time of this writing, there are twenty-two recent peace agreements and cease-fires (INCORE 1999). These agreements and cease-fires were the result of many different conflict resolution processes that resulted in very different types of justified outcomes. In Nagaland, parties agreed to a cease-fire in order to engage in talks that an American Baptist group sponsored. The cease-fire has been extended but no peace agreement has yet been adopted. In Guatemala, Norwegians acted as mediators in 1996 to facilitate the drafting of a peace treaty that entailed decreasing the size of the army and granting amnesty for the military, providing for land reform, and providing education and retraining for ex-guerillas. Russian and Chechen presidents negotiated and signed a series of peace agreements, which state that they will not use force and that they will abide by international law. However, border skirmishes continue to flare occasionally. In Mozambique, after twenty-eight years of civil war, the United Nations (UN) supported the establishment of a democratic process and sponsored elections two years ago. There has now been peace for four years. These are just a few examples of the many conflict resolution processes used to stop violence between peoples. Some agreements result in long-lasting peace agreements where parties attain reconciliation—a relationship in which parties no longer harbor animosity toward the other and agree to behave in a manner that does not threaten the other's basic human rights—and peacefully co-exist. Other agreements are temporary, with a return to violence and war. Still other agreements result in something in between these two examples. How do we know what processes, which seek to *justly* resolve a conflict, create the conditions for reconciliation? There are certainly many variables that establish the foundation upon which reconciliation develops. This chapter describes (a) conceptions of justice, (b) the conflict resolution processes used to attain "justice," and (c) how these conflict resolution approaches promote restorative justice and potentially establish a foundation upon which reconciliation between groups can occur.

Social Science Conceptions of Justice

In the social sciences, "justice" is understood as (1) procedural justice, and (2) distributive justice. Procedural justice occurs when parties perceive the procedure by which a people attains justice as fair and legitimate. Distributive justice occurs when participants in a situation of injustice perceive that the distribution of what is owed and paid is equitable, fair, and legitimate. Justice, then, occurs when the conflict resolution process includes both fair processes and distributions. Interestingly, this definition of justice does not require the use of a specific type of conflict resolution process or distribution to exist in order for justice to occur. On the contrary, this approach to justice simply requires that there is a *perception* of fairness in the process and distribution. There has been a great deal of research in the social sciences demonstrating that these two parts are distinct from each other (Welbourne 1998; S. Williams 1999), and yet both are related to people's assessment of whether justice occurred and their overall satisfaction with an outcome. Social scientists have used procedural and distributive justice to discuss the merits and limitations of the U. S. criminal justice system (i.e., the legalistic justice approach). Social scientists have not begun to study how restorative justice (described later) relates to either procedural or distributive justice. Both justice systems share in common intent to provide procedural and distributive justice to the disputing parties. However, legalistic and restorative justices differ in their definition of what constitutes *justice*.

Legalistic Justice

Historically, in the United States, the common process of formally resolving conflicts has been through a *legalistic justice* system (Van Ness 1996). Zehr (1997a) characterizes this same conflict resolution process as a retributive justice system. In this system, perpetrators commit crimes against the state, not against other people (Hudson and Galaway 1996). Crimes, in these cases, are any act or omission to act that the authoritative governing body has declared punishable and hence lawbreaking.

History

As common as the legalistic justice system appears to be, the idea that crimes are the result of breaking government laws is actually a relatively recent development that occurred "during the rise of centralized governments in Europe during the Middle Ages" (Van Ness 1996, 22). Legal systems prior to that time viewed crime primarily as wrong done to victims and their families. To maintain community peace, community members encouraged perpetrators to provide restitution and gestures of atonement in order to repair their injury to the victims and restore peace to their communities. This changed between the tenth and eleventh centuries, when kings recognized the power of viewing breeches in social relations as a direct offense against their governing rules (i.e., laws) that maintain peace. Wilkinson (1997) dates the paradigm shift to the Norman Invasion of Britain. He writes that by the end of the eleventh century, crime was not perceived as an injury to a person but as an offense against the state. Specifically, scholars attribute the shift to William the Conqueror, who was known to have developed a legal system that centralized power. To sharpen the judicial orientation, his son, King Henry I, "issued laws detailing offenses against the 'king's peace'" (Wilkinson 1997, 6). By identifying crimes as offenses that jeopardize the "king's peace," they were able to take control of the courts from local rulers and from the Roman Catholic Church (Van Ness 1996). In spite of this new approach to attaining justice, victims continued to initiate the majority of criminal proceedings in England and the United States until the late nineteenth century (Hay and Snyder 1989). Still, the judicial system that Kings William and Henry I developed, which oriented crime and the focus of the conflict resolution process away from victims and toward the state, has survived for centuries.

In Modern Times

Today in the United States, the government initiates the majority of prosecutions. Victims are encouraged *not* to directly seek revenge, retaliation, or punishment except via the criminal justice system, through representatives such as legal prosecutors. Steinberg (1984) attributes this to a rise in professional police forces, public prosecutions, and professional correctional officials. Whatever the reason, court authorities (i.e., judges and juries) typically resolve conflicts between defendants (i.e., the accused perpetrators) and the state—*not* victims. The administration of criminal justice has become the exclusive responsibility of the government. The government grants authority to court authorities to act as binding arbiters, which means that court authorities are "witnesses" to the court proceedings and given the right to judge disputes between defendants and prosecutors. The judgments are binding in that defendants and prosecutors must abide by the court authorities' decisions (or appeal to higher courts) or face punishment. Thus, court authorities resolve disputes when they decide the guilt or innocence of defendants, the just punishment for defendants, and the suitable compensation for victims. Theoretically, the state law and previous interpretations of that law (legal precedence) guide all court decisions.

Ideal justice occurs when nonguilty perpetrators are freed and the guilty perpetrators are equitably and justly punished. Just punishment, what some refer to as *retribution*, follows the principle: "For your hurt [that you caused], we [the state] hurt [you] in return, but not necessarily in kind" (Shriver 1995, 31). According to Zehr (1997b), the courts ensure just punishment when they:

1. Find out what laws were broken
2. Identify lawbreakers
3. Determine deserved actions to take against lawbreakers
4. Carry out the "deserved action"

The ideal outcome of this process is to reestablish equity such that the harm offenders' cause will be balanced by harm done to those offenders. The victims, at best, are often secondary concerns of justice (Zehr 1997a). Official acknowledgment that crimes cause breeches in relationships between victims and perpetrators, that breeches should be mended, and that parties should attempt to reconcile, is irrelevant in the attainment of legalistic justice. Clearly, the primary concern of legalistic justice is to maintain rules, laws, and civil order.

Reconciliation

Regarding the role of reconciliation in legalistic justice processes, Minow (1998) wrote the following:

> Reconciliation is not the goal of criminal trials except in the most abstract sense. We reconcile with the murderer by imagining he or she is responsible to the same rules and commands that govern all of us; we agree to sit in the same room and accord the defendant a chance to speak, and a chance to fight for his or her life. But reconstruction of a relationship, seeking to heal the accused, or indeed, healing the rest of the community, are not goals in any direct sense (26).

In this passage, Minow is describing trials that international officials conducted in the aftermath of mass atrocities, specifically international war tribunals. She argues strongly that the goals of war tribunals (which seek legalistic justice) do not include reconciling perpetrators and victims. Similarly, the U.S. criminal justice system systematically promotes a legally fair outcome for perpetrators but *not* reconciliation between victims and perpetrators (Van Ness 1996). Structurally, victim-perpetrator reconciliation (or any restoration of a civil relationship) is discouraged since in most criminal cases, norms and regulations prohibit perpetrators and victims from directly communicating with each other during trials.

Legitimate System

Although there are criticisms, imperfections, and empirical evidence of bias in the system (Brown 1986), in many ways this legalistic system is a legitimate system that functions without threat of dissolution. U.S. courts do effectively resolve thousands of criminal cases daily. In fact, the majority of perpetrators and victims involved in criminal cases submit to the judgments of the court authorities. One reason this system works is that court authorities have the power to make perpetrators and victims abide by their verdicts. If perpetrators and/or victims do not submit to verdicts, governmental agents such as police, federal agents, and other protective agents of the state will enforce (coercively, if necessary) verdicts so that justice prevails. Although there are examples of imperfections in this system, in the majority of criminal cases, perpetrators and victims do perceive the court's power as legitimate and real.

Another reason the U.S. criminal justice system maintains an image of fairness and legitimacy is because ideally, objectivity guides legal proceedings and verdicts. There is an underlying assumption that objectivity is obtainable and that it lights the road to truth and justice. To put this in social science terms, there is a mass perception that third-party[1] objectivity creates a context in which procedural and distributive justice can occur. To assure objectivity, court authorities are not supposed to have any personal interests in the cases in which they participate. If their objectivity is in question, they can be and are removed from cases. To facilitate objective and impartial analysis, prosecutors and defendants both attempt to provide information that is "factual" and free from subjectivity. Court authorities' objective analysis and decision making are the cornerstone upon which the legitimacy of the legalistic justice system lies.

Limitations to a Legalistic Approach to Justice

Uniqueness of Ethnic and Intercommunal Disputes

There are limitations to the legalistic justice system. Specifically, several problems arise when third parties transfer principles of the legalistic system to the international political scene and attempt to use them to "resolve" ethnic and intercommunal conflicts. To "resolve," of course, is to do more than stop the violence. To resolve is to leave the conflicted parties with institutions and attitudes that favor peaceful interactions. This sort of resolution also requires the establishment of *working trust*. *Working trust* refers to a level of trust that enables parties to participate (sometimes cautiously) in problem-solving activities such as negotiations or mediation. Kelman (1993a) describes it as "a trust sufficient to allow them [the parties] to proceed with the coalition work of joint analysis, interactive problem solving, and planning implementation" (244). Working trust is akin to "instrumental" trust in that it does not require a shift in sentimentality toward the other party (see Rubin, Pruitt, and Kim 1994, 30). Sometimes parties establish working trust entirely for pragmatic and strategic reasons. Ethnic conflicts, however, distinguish themselves from other types of conflicts by the parties' intensity of mistrust, duration of hostility, and resistance to long-term peace. To begin to understand the intensity of the mistrust and a reason why these conflicts are so resistant to resolution, examine table 4.1, which depicts schematically some of the trade-offs that parties feel they are confronting.

Table 4.1: An Oversimplified Schematic of an Ethnic Conflict

	And Party B Cooperates	And Party B Competes
If Party A Cooperates	• Abandon hope of *ideal peace and justice* • Potential for peace and some justice	**For Party A** • Abandon hope of *ideal peace and justice* • "Worst nightmare" occurs
If Party A Competes	**For Party A** • Potential of getting ideal peace and justice is high exploiting Party B's "softening"	• Maintain hope of ideal peace and justice • Continue violence and loss of life

In table 4.1, each party has a choice to either cooperate (e.g., negotiate, mediate, be willing to talk informally, and so on) or compete (e.g., continue hostility and violence). If both parties cooperate, then they each concede that there is no chance of their ideal justified outcome occurring, but there is a potential for peace, some justice, and possible reconciliation. If one group cooperates and the other group does not, the cooperating group abandons any hope of achieving its ideal outcome and risks everything: the group's "worst nightmare" in which there is permanent loss of the group's security, identity, and any justified outcome. The price each group pays for competing is, at the very least, continued loss of lives, but in exchange, the group can continue to believe that ideal justice (as the party defines it) may someday occur when the group "wins." Kelly (1966, 60) summarized the dilemma when he wrote the following:

> To believe everything the other person says is to place one's fate in his hands and to jeopardize full satisfaction on one's own interests. . . . On

the other hand, to believe nothing the other says is to eliminate the possibility of accepting any arrangement with him.

Two forces can move groups toward cooperation: (1) increased trust that other groups will cooperate, too, and thus will not attempt to annihilate them, rob them of their identity, or fully rob them of their sense of justice; and/or (2) the cost of competing becomes unbearable relative to the potential of a justified outcome occurring (i.e., winning). Third parties can affect either or both of these forces. If these parties are to coexist and have a potential for reconciliation, following a settlement, number two alone (i.e., increasing the cost of competing) is insufficient, because it does not improve trust between the parties. Without "trust," parties will not have the capacity to depend upon or place confidence in the truth and accuracy of others' statements or behaviors (Moore 1996). Clearly, a lack of trust undermines the parties' abilities to improve their long-term relationship. Numerous researchers and practitioners confirm that trust is important in the convening and conducting of productive conflict resolution processes (see Moore 1996). However, building trust between hostile ethnic groups is often a slow and difficult process because of the structural, strategic, and psychological barriers that exist during intense conflicts (Ross and Ward 1995; and see Fisher in this volume). Several characteristics of legalistic justice undermine the building of trust, making conflict resolution processes less stable and reconciliation less likely. As stated before, reconciliation occurs when parties no longer harbor animosity toward the other and/or agree to behave in a manner that does not threaten the other party's existence. The following is a discussion of the three most obvious limitations to resolving ethnic disputes in a legalistic manner if building trust and a foundation upon which reconciliation can occur are the end goals.

(1) In most ethnic conflicts, it is not clear who are victims and who are perpetrators since all parties have their set of crimes committed and perpetrated. During times of hostility, violence, and war, members of all parties have experiences of being victims and also of being perpetrators. It is often the rhetoric of victimhood that motivates peoples to rise and perpetrate against others. For victims, perpetrations are justified revenge and not criminal offenses. Attempting to label parties as either "victims" or "perpetrators," which is necessary in a legalistic system, then becomes very problematic because most parties do not view themselves as "perpetrators." In fact, such a label is inconsistent with parties' national narrative and identity. For example, Israelis typically consider themselves victims of years of Arab hatred, prejudice, and persecution. Israelis view their own military actions as a necessary response to Arab nations, who threaten their security and question Israelis' right to live in the Middle East. In contrast, Palestinians view themselves as victims, and not perpetrators, in the conflict, because Israelis displaced them by physically robbing them of their land, homes, and national unity. Palestinians use violent actions against Israelis in order to make Israelis recognize that Palestinians are a national group with rights that the Israelis violated. In this case, and many other

ethnic conflicts, a story of victimhood is central to all parties' national narratives, their histories, and their own identities. Further, these national narratives are powerful enough to mobilize members into actions that sometimes lead to death. Thus, in intense ethnic conflicts, *a conflict resolution process* (whether it be a problem-solving workshop, mediation, negotiations, international tribunals, and so on) *that requires the labeling of one party as the perpetrator and the other as the victim is inherently problematic*. When third parties impose such labels, following a legalistic approach to resolving the conflict, at least one conflicted party will perceive the third-party as "taking sides," being biased and inappropriate brokers of peace. Third-party labeling obviously undermines the legitimacy of the entire conflict resolution process, the perception that the third party will facilitate a just and fair outcome, and the willingness of the parties to abide by the outcome (if they feel it is unjust). Without both parties perceiving the process and outcome as just, the context for building working trust and establishing a foundation for reconciliation is diminished, making these outcomes unlikely.

(2) A second limitation, arising when third parties transfer the principles of the legalistic judicial system to the international political scene, is that *third parties* (typically the world community and/or UN) *overestimate their power and try to arbitrate the dispute and impose peace agreements*. One often-used method to impose third-party solutions is to make the cost of continuing to compete very high by issuing sanctions, threatening military force, publicly condemning the group, or actually using military force. When trying to achieve a long-term peace, primarily using coercive tactics is problematic for at least two reasons. First, forcing parties to cooperate by making competing very costly does not produce or improve trust between parties. In fact, it does the opposite, since both parties know that cooperation, if it occurs, is not a willing choice of "the enemy." If the third party reduces the cost of competing (e.g., the world community loses interest in the conflict), the "enemy" may return to competing in the form of severe violence. Second, even if third-party coercion does bring about a peace settlement, the ability of the third party, typically the UN or other large militarized third parties such as the North Atlantic Treaty Organization (NATO), to enforce long-term peace initiatives is highly questionable. As stated earlier, in the U.S. legalistic justice system police and other enforcement officers all are willing to act if anyone does not abide by the decision of court authorities. The U.S. courts system acts in concert with a centralized power to enforce obedience to the courts' ruling—acting coercively, if necessary. In contrast, the world community has a decentralized international enforcement structure. Thus, the world community does not have the equivalent of a police force or other enforcement officers to command obedience.

In place of police and enforcement officers, most recently there has been the proliferation of "peacekeeping forces" (PKF). The UN PKF are multinational military forces that are currently (as of February 1999) present in sixteen areas of the world (UN Department of Public Information 1999). There is ongoing debate as to what role PKF should play in the world and to whom they should ultimately answer—to the UN or to each country's own national authority. Perhaps because of the many ambiguities surrounding the building and maintaining of PKF, the actual forces now present in the world vary in their jurisdiction, authority, and role from conflict to conflict. For example, the UN considers PFK to have an "Observer Mission" in Angola and Sierra Leone, to be a "Military Observer Group" in India/Pakistan, and to have a "Civilian Police Mission" in Haiti (UN Department of Public Information 1999). Yet, in spite of the active role of PKF in the world today, PKF are not the equivalent of a universal police force, and it remains questionable whether they are sufficient to enforce imposed settlements—especially long-term settlements.

(3) What binds parties to an agreement if the third party cannot impose a solution? When external forces alone are insufficient to bind parties to an agreement, then there have to be internal forces that will bind disputing parties to an agreement. One such internal force is the parties' subjective perception that the agreement is just. This occurs when parties perceive that the agreement responds to their and the other parties' basic interests and needs in an adequate and acceptable manner. In such situations, parties trust the process and the other, because there is mutual recognition that it is pragmatic to do so, not just because it is externally imposed. In the legalistic system, third parties' impartial decision making and objectivity are the most important contributors to the shape of an agreement and not the conflicting parties' subjective understanding of the conflict. Thus the third limitation, arising when third parties transfer the principles of the U.S. legalistic system to the international political scene, is that *third parties* (primarily trained in the U.S. legalistic system) *underestimate the importance of the parties' subjective perceptions of the conflict contributing to the shape of the agreement.*

By allowing subjective perceptions to contribute to the shape of the agreement, conflicting parties can overcome some psychological barriers to resolution. One such barrier occurs when what appears to be objective and rational to third parties is viewed as suspicious and unreasonable to those engaged in the conflict (Ross and Ward 1995). There are many examples of parties in ethnic disputes not adopting or, when forced to adopt, eventually rejecting, objectively fair, rational third-party solutions to conflicts. For example, in Cambodia, the UN supported a plan to develop a permanent coalition arrangement with two prime ministers—an objectively fair arrangement. The UN's largest-ever peacekeeping operation facilitated the elections in 1993. In July 1997, Cambodia's second prime minister, Hun Sen of the Cambodian People's Party, launched a coup against his coalition partners. Many of the leaders of the other party, FUNCINPEC, were killed and others, including Prince Norodom Ranariddh, were forced into exile (INCORE 1999; see J. L. Rasmussen in this volume for a more complete discussion). There are many complex explanations for why the UN arrangement did not work. At the very least, analysts must agree that the "objectively fair" political arrangement was not perceived as truly "objective" or "fair" to anyone but the third party. In the end, parties who mutually develop "subjectively fair" agreements are more likely to bind themselves psychologically to the conflict resolution process and the agreements they forge. In theory, these sorts of agreements make it more likely that parties will abide with agreements—even in the absence of violent external forces. Further, this process increases the likelihood that agreements address the basic needs of the parties (or else why would they agree to it?), which then provides a firm foundation upon which long-term resolution and potentially reconciliation can develop.

Restorative justice is an alternative criminal justice approach that responds to the limitations just described and provides a viable alternative to the prevalent legalistic justice system.

Restorative Justice

To understand restorative justice, the praxis of legalistic justice must be set aside, and a reorientation of how we think about crime and justice must be embraced (Zehr 1997a). Unlike the legalistic approach, the restorative justice approach identifies crime primarily as conflict between individuals that results in injuries "to victims, communities, and the offenders themselves, and only secondarily as a violation against the state" (Hudson and Galaway 1996, 2). The aim of the judicial system, then, is to reconcile conflicting parties while repairing the injuries from the crimes. Peachy (1989) describes the ultimate goal of restorative justice as "making right the wrong" (302). This is also true of legalistic justice, but the process by which "right" is attained and how theorists define "right" vary greatly. In the restorative justice approach, equitable compensation, punishment, and restitution are not an end in themselves, but simply an element of a wider solution to the conflict (Netzig and Trenczek 1996). Van Ness (1996) describes the principles that are the foundations of restorative justice theory in the following manner:

Crime is primarily conflict between individuals resulting in injuries to victims, communities, and the offenders themselves; only secondarily is it lawbreaking. The overarching aim of the criminal justice process should be to reconcile parties while repairing the injuries caused by crime. The criminal justice process should facilitate active participation by victims, offenders, and their communities. The government to the exclusion of others should not dominate it.

In short, within this system, if there is no restoration of the social relationships that the conflict affected, true justice does not occur. Not surprisingly, those who support a restorative justice system are critical of the legalistic justice system, because it ignores the fact that criminal acts are often entangled in complex interpersonal structures (Netzig and Trenczek 1996; Fattah 1992). In contrast, restorative justice requires parties not only to have trust in the process, but also encourages parties to increase trust in each other.

History

Restorative justice systems date back thousands of years. In 1700 B.C., the Babylonian Code of Hammurabi prescribed restitution as a sanction for property offenses, and the Sumeria Code of Ur-Nammi (2030 B.C.) required restitution for violent offenses (Wilkinson 1997). Roman Law of the Twelve Tables (449 B.C.) and Germanic tribal laws (496 B.C.) also described restitution schedules. What these laws and codes had in common was the assumption that lawbreaking was the result of an offense between two or more people of their community. The codes and tables provided instructions for disputants to follow in order to restore order to their relationships and to the community in which they resided. The conception that lawbreaking is a breach in social relation and that justice occurs when this breach is mended between the disputing parties comes from an ancient system of justice. According to Wilkinson (1997), the modern reemergence of restorative justice began in Kitchener, Ontario, 1974, when a Mennonite probation officer and a volunteer service director convened a group to develop a humane and efficient criminal justice system. These practitioners observed that victims and offenders appeared to be more satisfied with mediation as opposed to adjudicated justice (i.e., legalistic justice processes) (Van Ness 1996). Many studies show a reliable finding: satisfaction with the process, *not* the outcome, is a better predictor of overall satisfaction with the resolution (Bush 1999). Restorative justice writers initially sought to describe such satisfactory processes.

Historically and in modern times, restorative justice systems exist outside the Western world. Arguably, a form of a restorative justice system has co-existed with legalistic justice in Japan for over forty years (Haley 1996). In this system, officials and culture "reinforce values of confession, repentance, forgiveness, and leniency" (349). In some instances, Japanese courts even favor repentance over "just" retribution. There is evidence that many forms of restorative justice systems have remained in practice for centuries in smaller communities. For example, in the Kpelle Moot, a public apology and the acceptance of an apology are central features to the process of resolving disputes among members. If victims of offenses still feel angry, "the community holds a dance in a circle and they sing and ask the gods to remove the bitterness in your heart" (Ury 1990, 235). Ultimately, restorative justice systems share in common the end goal that the disputing parties will be able to live in the same community without animosity, discord, or distrust. Thus, reconciliation between the victim and perpetrator is a desirable and attainable goal.

In recent times in the United States, if restorative justice occurs in a legalistic system of justice, it occurs through victim-offender mediation and reconciliation programs. Typically, disputing parties meet together with a trained mediator to resolve the conflict by constructing a settlement that achieves justice (as the conflicting parties define it). "Victim" and "perpetrator" labels are not necessary to initiate the restorative justice process, since it is not always clear which parities are perpetrators and which are victims (Netzig and Trenczek

1996). Ideally, parties assume responsibility for the wrongs they have done, apologize (if appropriate), and are willing to provide compensation or make reparation. It is important to note that compensation is *not* the end in itself. It is "simply an element within a framework of a wider solution to the conflict that mediation was designed to achieve" (Netzig and Trenczek 1996, 244). Also, parties must be willing to accept expressions of remorse and to even forgive. Forgiveness may seem like an unreasonable expectation, but there is much evidence that humans are capable of forgiveness—even in response to the most atrocious actions (Henderson 1996; Shriver 1995; Minow 1998). Third parties "facilitate" the resolution process; they do not mandate or coerce parties into agreement. Community members support the conflicting parties' resolution process when they provide opportunity for the settlement to occur and publicly endorse the parties' settlement (Hudson and Galaway 1996*). Reconciliation*—a relationship state in which parties no longer harbor animosity toward the other and agree to behave in a manner that does not threaten the other's basic human rights—*is a common and desirable outcome of today's restorative justice system*. Ultimately, the restorative justice system assumes that settlements that rest on conflicting parties' *subjective* perceptions of fairness are longer lasting and more likely to promote reconciliation than imposed (i.e., adjudicated or arbitrated) settlements (Van Ness 1996). The assumption is that "humans beings do not live in an objective world; rather, through observation, awareness, thinking, acting, and communication, they produce their own empirical reality" (Netzig and Trenczek 1996, 242). Thus, in this approach the third parties' objective understanding of the conflict is secondary to the conflicting parties' subjective perceptions. The parties use their subjective understanding of the conflict to identify the problem, to shape the course of the interaction, to collectively and integratively create a settlement, and to bind them psychologically to the settlement. A criminal justice system that facilitates conflicting parties' active participation in the resolution process and gives weight to participants' subjective understanding of the conflict is best suited to achieve restorative justice. The following section identifies several conflict resolution approaches that contribute in varying degrees toward the attainment of restorative justice in the context of an ethnic or intercommunal dispute.

Identifying Conflict Resolution Approaches that Promote Restorative Justice

As described before, when parties have endured years of intense hate, violence, and conflict, they will have little trust in each other. Institutional, strategic, and psychological barriers to resolution exist that contribute toward the escalation and sustaining of the non-trusting relationship between the parties (Ross and Ward 1995). In the face of such an intractable situation, third parties may resort to what they know works—transporting the principles of the legalistic system to the international scene. At the extreme, this is international relations guided by the "big stick" approach to peace in which third parties (based upon their ideas of fairness) design a peace agreement and make the parties abide. Third parties achieve peace, meaning the ceasing of violence and adoption of a just outcome,[2] by making competing *very* costly. For example, the use of violence was NATO's strategy for "restoring peace" to Kosovo in the spring of 1999.[3] This "realpolitik" approach to resolving the conflict provided a seemingly "fast" solution, but only time will reveal if the "resolution" adequately creates the conditions for a lasting peace or the potential for reconciliation. Based upon the amount of post-peace hostility in Kosovo, one can extrapolate that the conflicting parties are not psychologically committed to peace, that as in many cases of "resolved" ethnic conflicts, working trust has not developed, and that reconciliation remains an absurd idealist's dream.

In resolving ethnic conflicts, the restorative justice approach provides an alternative and more effective approach by which to navigate the road to reconciliation than the dominant legalistic approach. The restorative justice approach suggests that if reconciling conflicting parties while repairing the injuries from crimes is a goal, then imposing a settlement (conducted in a legalistic manner) is the least effective means to achieve it. Either in addition to or in place of a legalistic justice approach, several conflict resolution approaches can be used to resolve international ethnic conflict and provide methods by which restorative justice can potentially occur. Ideally, these approaches seek to not simply resolve the conflict but to transform the relationship between the conflicting parties. Lederach (1995) describes the transformation process as entailing a change in social structures such that there is opportunity for cooperation, just relationships, and nonviolent mechanisms for handling future conflict. This "transformed" relationship establishes a firm foundation upon which reconciliation may grow. In short, this type of comprehensive peace is not simply getting parties to the "table," nor achieving a cease-fire. However, all this discussion of transformation and reconciliation remains irrelevant if the parties feel there is no reason to stop competing and begin engaging in a conflict resolution process.

Problem-Solving Workshops (PSWs)

When trust is entirely eroded, which is characteristic of ethnic conflicts, agreeing to come to the mediation or negotiation table is, in itself, a gesture of cooperation and trust that parties are unwilling to take. Thus, in order for parties to agree to cooperative behaviors, either intense external pressure has to make the cost of competing unbearable or trust building must begin prior to official talks. Several forms of nonofficial negotiations or "track II diplomacy" have been used to enable people from conflicting parties to talk "off the record" and confidentially about the potential for a peaceful settlement. None of these approaches intentionally or explicitly seeks to begin the restorative justice process. However, several contribute to a restorative justice process inadvertently. For example, the PSW (1) restores communication between the conflict-ing parties (which does not rely on "victim" or "perpetrator" labeling), (2) relies heavily on noncoerced participation, and (3) creates a context in which the parties can use their subjective understandings of the conflict to problem solve (Chataway 2000). All these characteristics contribute toward the long-term establishment of working trust.

Kelman and his colleagues have facilitated many workshops between Israelis and Palestinians over the past twenty years (Kelman 1993a, 1993b; Cohen, Kelman, Miller, and Smith 1977). The majority of those years have been spent trying to create the conditions for negotiations to occur between Israelis and Palestinians, which included establishing working trust. The Israeli-Palestinian workshops increased trust between segments of each of these groups in several ways. It should be noted, however, that the building of trust has often been incremental and tenuous—developing over the course of nearly twenty years of confidential meetings.

Initially, the PSW provided politically influential Israeli and Palestinian persons with opportunities to meet "the enemy" in a confidential setting (Kelman 1991). At the very least, the workshops provided evidence to each side that there were people from the other side willing to talk with them about the potential for peace. Participants were motivated to participate in the workshops for various reasons, but often they shared in common the belief that neither side was going to "win" soon and that they did not want another generation to live with the violence. Regardless of participants' reasons for attending workshops, however, their very presence and willingness to discuss the conflict was often a significant statement of hope that working trust could develop even during times of intense conflict between Israelis and Palestinians (Chataway 2000). This is true even when communication is tense, emotional, and difficult.

Within a PSW, participants are able to listen to several people from the "enemy" group talk about their perspectives of the conflict and how to solve it. This structure provides opportunities for participants to differentiate their enemy image. The differentiation process included breaking down monolithic views of the enemy camp, distinguishing between the enemy's ideological dreams and operational programs, and differentiating between negative and positive components of the other's ideology and symbols of legitimacy (Kelman 1987). Participants' knowledge of the other group became more sophisticated, and over the course of years, an uneasy coalition forms across the conflicting lines (Kelman 1993a) as an expression that working trust is building.

The PSW also provides opportunities for parties to identify mutually reassuring steps (Kelman 1993b) that they can take to incrementally build working trust, such as issuing statements of recognition, introducing mutually favorable ideas into political discussion, and writing about the other's perspec-tive of the conflict as legitimate. Parties with a history of violent and intense conflict have many reasons to mistrust each other, and so developing working trust is a slow process built upon many mutually reassuring steps.

One limitation to the use of the PSW, as opposed to the "realpolitik" approach to resolving conflict, is that it does *not* provide a quick solution to a conflict and often only begins the long road toward restorative justice and reconciliation. It does not quickly cease violence, death, or destruction as "realpolitik" approaches seemingly can. The Israeli-Palestinian case is a perfect example of a slow process which, even during negotiations, has been an incremental walk toward peace. However, the Israeli-Palestinian long-term peace process, which includes the PSW, has attributes that make this peace potentially long lasting and restorative in nature. The history of unofficial problem solving, unofficial diplomatic efforts, and many grassroots trust-building activities has contributed to the recognition, by segments of each community and their leadership, that coexistence is inevitable and tolerable (Joint Working Group on Israeli-Palestinian Relations 1998). It cannot be said that Israelis and Palestinians feel reconciled. Yet, there are large segments of the Israeli and Palestinian communities that now identify their conflict as a mutual problem that must be solved together. Thus, building trust and seeking a mutually agreed-upon just outcome is the pragmatic alternative to continued violence. By identifying and enacting mutual confidence-building measures, and incrementally building working trust, a foundation is set on which to continue improving their relationship such that reconciliation may someday occur.

Mediation

Mediation, executed in the traditional manner, is the most common form of resolving domestic conflicts used by restorative justice advocates. Like the PSW, mediation typically (1) requires communication between the conflicting parties to occur (which does not rely on "victim" or "perpetrator" labeling), (2) relies heavily on noncoerced participation, and (3) provides opportunities for every parties' subjective perspectives to contribute to the shape of the agreement. Unlike the PSW, however, mediators typically plan a very active process in which they encourage conflicting parties to identify the problem, brainstorm possible alternative outcomes, and design a concrete agreement to which all parties can agree (Beer and Stief 1997; Moore 1996).

According to C. Williams (1999), in diplomatic circles the traditional mediator has been an outsider, impartial and full of objectivity. These mediators are typically from North America and Europe, nearly always middle-aged or elderly men and trained as lawyers, diplomats, or politicians (C. Williams 1999). Mediators work almost exclusively with leaders and act as facilitators to improve communication. The end goal is typically to cease violence. More recently, mediator teams have become mixed (including people inside and outside of the conflict) and are from different levels of the community (including people from the political leadership to the grassroots level). Broader ranges of individuals are conducting mediation, and its application is more diverse. Mediators with personal knowledge of the conflict (i.e., having a subjective perspective) are viewed as a resource to guide interventions rather than as a biased observer to ignore.

In the end, those mediation efforts that seek a restorative justice outcome are transformative for the disputing parties. As in Northern Ireland or South Africa, the end goal of mediation is not simply to end the violence but to construct a stable and restoratively just peace (see Bush and Folger 1994). Mediation that promotes restorative justice is a part of a larger process that Williams summarizes as follows:

> Mediation only makes sense in the context of all the work that has to be done before and afterward, so that a settlement is not the way to silence the loser, but is the first step in building a society which is genuinely acceptable to all groups (C. Williams 1999, 4).

Mediation, however, is not always conducted with an end goal of building working trust and restoring justice. In fact, quite often it still resembles the older version of mediation in which the mediator is an outsider more eager to impose an agreement than to facilitate parties in designing their own agreement. Richard Holbrooke (1999) describes this sort of mediation process in his book, *To End a War.*

According to Holbrooke's account of the development of the Dayton Peace Accord (DPA), signed in November 1995, a "ninety-two-page draft peace agreement and volumes of backup materials" were presented to Warren Christopher days before the official Dayton talks between the Serbian, Croatian, and Bosnian representatives began (1999, 223). This draft agreement was based upon Holbrooke's and his colleague's previous interactions with each party, and, it is commonly understood, it also contained provisions that the United States and other "Contact Group" members felt were necessary to secure a lasting peace. This draft agreement was open to modification, but the third party ultimately was the primary party who felt psychologically bound to the agreement (meaning that the third party was fully committed to and believed in the agreement). Holbrooke, as mediator, used both military threat, personal skill, and political pressure to gain the parties' agreement. The third party could "own" the agreement, because it made sense to them and was consistent with their objective understanding of the conflict. It is not clear that the conflicting parties felt ownership of the agreement as much as they felt resignation.

According to the DPA, Bosnia was to be a multinational democratic state where previously disputing parties would coexist. In spite of this seemingly logical solution, today the three principle ethnic parties—Croats, Bosnians, and Serbs—continue to "hold very different perspectives about how the country should look," and when there is cooperation in the implementation of the DPA "it is only grudgingly and under intense international pressure" (International Crisis Group 1998, 1). Whether Bosnia is an example of "making the best of a bad situation" or an example of the problems of pressuring parties into an agreement, most agree there is currently an uneasy peace there, and it is not a stable foundation upon which reconciliation can occur. Although mediation is a common approach used to achieve restorative justice (which has the ideal goal of reconciling the disputing parties), the way in which it is conducted affects its effectiveness in achieving this goal. Mediators have a great deal of flexibility in how they control the agenda, the degree to which they impose (or offer) solutions, and the way in which they personally exert power over the disputants (Beer and Stief 1997). Needless to say, mediators have a lot of control over whether the foundation for reconciliation is set, since they can affect how much mutual trust is built between the disputing parties during the conflict resolution process. Mediators can facilitate reaching the goals of restoring justice, reconciling parties, and attaining a peaceful solution. In rare cases, the parties themselves seek these goals through a process of interest-based negotiations.

Interest-Based Negotiations

Mediation and negotiation are the most commonly used methods of dealing with ethnic conflict when the parties are willing to sit in a room together. In several cases, mediations become negotiations when third parties no longer participate in the settlement process. Negotiations can take many forms but typically occur when (1) two or more parties make a decision about interdependent goals or objectives, (2) parties commit to a nonviolent means of resolving their dispute, and (3) the method or procedure for making the decision is not predetermined (Lewicki, Saunders, and Minton 1999). When parties recognize that peaceful and just coexistence is the best outcome for all, interest-based negotiations can be the most direct process for achieving restorative justice. In theory, the negotiation process requires the disputing parties to be responsible for (and, therefore, psychologically own) every aspect of their conflict resolution process. Unaided or hindered by a third-party facilitator, mediator, or judge, conflicting parties are free to define their own roles, remain a part of the process by choice, and use their subjective perceptions of the conflict exclusively in creating the shape of the agreement.

The current South African government emerged as the result of negotiations in which the country transformed from violent ethnic relations to peaceful coexistence. How did this come about? Tremendous world pressure in the form of economic sanctions and condemnation made the cost of continuing to compete with (in this case, suppress) the weaker party too high. Although seemingly forced into negotiation, the negotiators from the two major parties decided at the beginning of the negotiation to attempt to build an agreement in which all parties could coexist peacefully as South Africans (Eloff 1999). After many years of a policy of apartheid, the white ruling power negotiated with the African National Congress, led by Nelson Mandela, to have a peaceful end to South Africa's apartheid and instill a truly democratic government. In doing this, the white minority willingly gave up their ruling power in exchange for some form of amnesty. Based on their subjective understandings of the conflict, these parties constructed their agreement and were psychologically committed to its success. The international community supported the agreement and facilitated the peace process by overseeing fair elections, lifting economic sanctions, and making public acclamation in favor of the agreement. Ultimately, the negotiating parties were psychologically committed to a settlement in which their groups would coexist in a peaceful and just state. This set the foundation for a negotiation in which the parties embraced the principles of restorative justice by endorsing a rhetoric of reconciliation and establishing mechanisms such as the Peace and Reconciliation Commission through which restoration could (theoretically) be achieved.

Of course, when parties are willing to negotiate and feel that it is in their best interest to create a long-lasting settlement in which all parties can continue to peacefully coexist, negotiations can be a productive and effective restorative justice process. This sort of negotiation assumes that some working trust exists and that the parties are willing to transform their relationship away from hostility toward reconciliation. However, conflicting parties are not always willing to partake in this type of negotiation. More often, ethnic groups with a history of conflict do not desire to coexist in a mutual society, live as peaceful neighbors, or transform their relationship in a reconciliatory direction. In these cases, negotiations can degenerate into a series of strategical and tactical maneuvers that undermine the building of trust and the restoration of justice and can, in the end, only serve to escalate the conflict (Rubin, Pruitt, and Kim 1994). This sort of negotiation typically occurs during distributive bargaining, but the same dynamics can occur during interest-based negotiation as well. All nego-tiators are susceptible to institutional, strategic, and psychological barriers to resolution that exist in intense conflicts, because there is no third party to stop the "enemy dynamics" that fuel these barriers. However, negotiators trained in interest-based negotiation (see Fisher, Ury, and Patton 1991 or Lewicki Saunders, and Minton 1999) are probably less likely to succumb to these barriers and recognize the interdependence of their futures. Any negotiated agreement that all parties endorse as relatively just serves a restorative function. It becomes public evidence that the disputing parties have established working trust and that they acknowledge that their futures are intimately tied to the other. This is a strong foundation upon which reconciliation can eventually develop.

Conclusion

This chapter argues that conflict resolution processes that promote restorative justice rather than legalistic justice are more likely to lead to reconciliation. Based upon this analysis, the following three characteristics of conflict resolu-tion processes that are consistent with the restorative justice system have been identified:

1. Identification of parties as either victims or perpetrators is not necessary to the conflict resolution process.

2. Third parties do not impose settlements.
3. The disputing parties use their subjective understanding of the conflict to identify the problem, shape the course of the interaction, collectively and integratively create a settlement, and bind them psychologically to the settlement.

Conflict resolution processes that have these characteristics make reconciliation more likely because they improve the chances that conflicting parties will trust the process and potentially each other. Although trust is not a necessary component for a cease-fire to occur, it is necessary for the restoration of a relationship between conflicting parties, and as a precursor to and component of reconciliation. Further, these three characteristics create a context in which conflicting parties are more likely to be psychologically committed to the resolution process and the agreement.

It is important to note that this chapter has taken a domestic[4] conception of achieving justice—that is, the legalistic and restorative justice systems—and theorized how these systems express themselves in the international political scene. This sort of extrapolation has its limitations. For instance, it must be noted that unlike the restorative justice approaches used in domestic disputes that list reconciliation as an immediate goal, "reconciliation" between the conflicting parties of an ethnic conflict should be considered a long-term goal that rests upon a lasting settlement. In the end, whether third parties employ legalistic or restorative justice systems to resolve interethnic conflicts, reconciliation requires a comprehensive conflict resolution process that incrementally transforms the relationship between the conflicting parties from enemies to neighbors.

Notes

1. *Third party* refers to the party that is not directly engaged in a dispute and is acting in some way as a settler of the dispute. *Third parties* may actually be the third, fourth, fifth, and so forth. party depending upon the number of parties actively engaged in a dispute or conflict. In this paper, *third party* is a generic term.
2. This refers to a third-party defined "just" outcome.
3. At this writing, the outcome of this strategy is yet unknown.
4. This refers to the United States of America's domestic scene.

References

Beer, J., and Stief, E. 1997. *The Mediator's Handbook.* Gabriola Island, B.C.: New Society Publishers.

Brown, R. 1986. *Social Psychology.* New York: Free Press.

Bush, R. A., and Folger, J. P. 1994. *The Promise of Mediation: Responding to Conflict through Empowerment and Recognition.* San Francisco: Jossey-Bass.

Bush, R. A. B. 1999. What Do We Need a Mediator For?: Mediation's Value-Added for Negotiations. In *Negotiation: Readings, Exercises, and Cases*. R. Lewicki, D. Saunders, and J. Minton, eds. 3d ed. Boston: Irwin McGraw-Hill.

Chataway, C. 2000. Paradigms of Conflict and Conflict Resolution: Requirements for Realizing the Value of Track II Diplomacy. In *(Dis)Placing Security: Critical Reevaluations of the Boundaries of Security Studies*. S. Arnold and J. Beier, eds. Toronto, Canada: Center for International and Security Studies, York University.

Cohen, S. P., Kelman, H. C., Miller, F. D., and Smith, B. L. 1977. Evolving Intergroup Techniques for Conflict Resolution: An Israeli-Palestinian Pilot workshop. *Journal of Social Issues*, vol. 33, 165-188.

Eloff, T. 1999. Developing Peace: The South African Experience of the Role of Civil Society in Facilitation and Mediation. <http://INCORE.ulst.ac.uk/publications/research/mediation/sue.html>

Fattah, E. 1992. Beyond Metaphysics: The Need for a New Paradigm. In *Criminal Law Theory in Transition* R. Lahti and K. Nuotio, eds. Helsinki: Finnish Layer's Publishers.

Fisher, R., Ury, W. L., and Patton, B. 1991. *Getting to Yes: Negotiating Agreement without Giving In*. New York: Penguin.

Haley, J. O. 1996. Crime Prevention through Restorative Justice: Lessons from Japan. In *Restorative Justice: International Perspectives*. B. Galaway and J. Hudson, eds. Monsey, N.Y.: Criminal Justice Press.

Hay, D., and Snyder, F. 1989. Using the Criminal Law, 1750-1850: Policing, Private Prosecution, and the State. In *Policing and prosecution in Britain, 1750-1850*. D. Hay and F. Snyder, eds. Oxford, U.K.: Clarendon Press.

Henderson, M. 1996. *The Forgiveness Factor: Stories of Hope in a World of Conflict*. London, U.K.: Grosvenor.

Holbrooke, R. 1999. *To End a War*. (Revised ed.) New York: Modern Library.

Hudson, J., and Galaway, B. 1996. Restorative Justice and International Human Rights. In *Restorative Justice: International Perspectives*. B. Galaway and J. Hudson, eds. Monsey, N.Y.: Criminal Justice Press.

INCORE. 1999. Recent Peace Agreements and Cease-fires.<http://INCORE.ulst.ac.uk/>

International Crisis Group. 1998. Whither Bosnia? <http://intl-crisis-group.org/>

Joint Working Group on Israeli-Palestinian Relations. 1998. *General Principles for the Final Israeli-Palestinian Agreement*. Cambridge, Mass.: Program on International Conflict Analysis and Resolution, Weatherhead Center for International Affairs, Harvard University.

Kelly, H. H. 1966. A Classroom Study of the Dilemmas in Interpersonal Negotiations. In *Strategic Interaction and Conflict: Original Papers and Discussion* (49-73). K. Archibald, ed. Berkeley, Calif.: Institute of International Studies.

Kelman, H. C. 1987. The Political Psychology of the Israeli-Palestinian Conflict: How Can We Overcome the Barriers to a Negotiated Solution? *Journal of Political Psychology*, vol. 8, 347-363.

———. 1991. Informal Mediation by the Scholar/Practitioner. In *Mediation in International Relations*. J. Bercovitch and J. Z. Rubin, eds. London, U.K.: St. Martin's Press.

———. 1993a. Coalitions Across Conflict Lines: The Interplay of Conflicts Within and Between the Israeli and Palestinian Communities. In *Conflict Between People and Groups*. S. Worchel and J. Simpson, eds. Chicago: Nelson-Hall.

———. 1993b. *Social Psychological Approaches to Peacemaking in the Middle East.* Paper presented at the Third Symposium on the Contributions of Psychology to Peace, August. Randolph-Macon College, Ashland, Virginia.

Lederach, J. P. 1995. Conflict Transformation in Protracted Internal Conflicts: The Case for a Comprehensive Framework. In *Conflict Transformation* K. Rupesinghe, ed. London, U.K.: St. Martin's Press.

Lewicki, R. J., Saunders, D. W., and Minton, J. W. 1999. *Negotiation: Readings, Exercises, and Cases.* 3d ed. Boston: Irwin McGraw-Hill.

Minow, M. 1998. *Between Vengeance and Forgiveness: Facing History after Genocide and Mass Violence.* Boston: Beacon Press.

Moore, C. 1996. *The Mediation Process: Practical Strategies for Resolving Conflict.* San Francisco: Jossey-Bass.

Netzig, L., and Trenczek, T. 1996. Restorative Justice as Participation: Theory, Law, Experience and Research. In *Restorative Justice: International Perspectives.* B. Galaway and J. Hudson, eds. Monsey, N.Y.: Criminal Justice Press.

Peachy, D. 1989. What People want from Mediation. In *Mediation Research.* K. Kressel, D. Pruitt, and Assoc., eds. San Francisco: Jossey-Bass.

Rubin, J., Pruitt, D., and Kim, S. H. 1994. *Social Conflict: Escalation, Stalemate, and Settlement.* 2d ed. New York: McGraw-Hill.

Ross, L., and Ward, A. 1995. Psychological Barriers to Dispute Resolution. *Advances in Experimental Social Psychology,* vol. 27, 225-304.

Shriver, D. 1995. *An Ethic for Enemies: Forgiveness in Politics.* New York: Oxford University Press.

Steinberg, A. 1984. From Private Prosecution to Plea Bargaining Criminal Prosecution, the District Attorney, and American Legal History. *Crime and Delinquency,* vol. 30, no. 4, 592-598.

United Nations Department of Public Information. 1999. Current Peacekeeping Operations. <http://UN.org/dept/dpko>

Ury, W. L. 1990. Dispute Resolution Notes from the Kalahari. *Negotiation Journal,* vol. 6, no. 3, 169-229.

Van Ness, D. 1996. Restorative Justice and International Human Rights. In *Restorative Justice: International Perspectives.* B. Galaway and J. Hudson, eds. Monsey, N.Y.: Criminal Justice Press.

Welborne, T. M. 1998. Untangling Procedural and Distributive Justice. *Group & Organization Management,* vol. 23, no. 4, 325-326.

Wilkinson, R. 1997. Back to Basics: Modern Restorative Justice Principles Have Their Roots in Ancient Cultures. *Corrections Today,* vol. 59, no. 7, 6.

Williams, C. 1999. A Need to Talk—Internationally. <http://INCORE.ulst.ac.uk/publications/research/mediation/sue.html>

Williams, S. 1999. The Effects of Distributive and Procedural Justice on Performance. *Journal of Psychology.* 133(2), 183.

Zehr, H. 1997a. Restorative Justice: The Concept. *Corrections Today,* vol. 59, no. 7, 68-70.

———. 1997b. Restoring Justice: Envisioning a Justice Process Focused on Healing—Not Punishment. *Other Side,* vol. 33, no.5, 22-27.

5

Forgiveness as an Element of Conflict Resolution in Religious Cultures

Walking the Tightrope of Reconciliation and Justice

Marc Gopin

Forgiveness as a way of healing human relationships and solving human conflicts is an age-old practice that appears in numerous religious traditions. There are problems, however, with defining what exactly this activity is or has been in these traditions, what its significance is within these meaning systems, and, finally, what usefulness, if any, these traditions play in contemporary analysis of conflict and peacemaking. In particular, forgiveness as a means of peacemaking, depending on how it is realized, brings into sharp relief the perennial challenge of balancing peace and justice in the pursuit of conflict resolution. Often, at least on the surface, it appears that forgiveness is at odds with the demands of justice, at least, as either side of a conflict perceives justice. One would imagine that the first task of this exploration is to attempt definitions of the term *forgiveness* in a representative sampling of religious cultures. But this is no easy task. The definition seems to change with the religious agent.

As an example, in the lived religion of many—certainly not all—Christians, the reality of forgiveness is so important as a faith principle that its exact moral parameters and interpersonal characteristics can change, as long as the living reality of forgiveness is acknowledged. They may agree that a true presence of forgiveness may have to result in much more just social arrangements. But, in any case, believing in forgiveness is a sine qua non of believing in the living reality of God. Thus it takes on an entirely different meaning than for those people—religious or otherwise—who see forgiveness as a stage in a human relationship that probably involves many other stages and moral requirements. This clearly seems to have much to do with the metaphysical meaning of forgiveness; that is, its centrality to the life, death, and message of Jesus. This makes its role as a conflict resolution device hard to distinguish, in certain cases, from its role as a means of teaching or spreading the faith. It is vital, therefore, in evaluating the benefits of forgiveness to conflict resolution, to study the highly varied cultural uses of the concept in the conflict situation. This is not to suggest any criticism of the use of forgiveness in one particular cultural way. It simply requires that we put all of these different styles of forgiveness into their proper context.

The Lived Characterizations of Forgiveness

There are many contradictory characterizations of "forgiveness" that include, for various people: verbal acts and formal gestures; confession, apology, repentance, and acknowledgment of the past; a willingness to suffer punishment as part of forgiveness; ritualized bilateral exchanges that give efficacy to forgiveness only in a prescribed set of interactions; unilateral expressions; bilateral expressions of the gesture; forgiveness that is offered and received that cancels all other obligations; forgiveness only in the context of legal compensation, justice, restoration, or the righting of past wrongs; and finally, interpersonal versus collective executions of remorse, apology, and forgiveness.

This latter practice raises the problematic issue of collective responsibility and the dangers of forgiveness playing into one of the most conflict-generating human tendencies, namely, the tendency to hold whole groups or even one individual responsible for the actions of large groups. Often in public gatherings involving forgiveness in some Christian contexts, there is a tendency for people to take on themselves the sins of their own group, whether or not they personally committed those sins. This is the precise foundation of the first stages of most ethnic violence, where victims are guilty because of their ethnicity and are held responsible as if they have committed all the offenses of a group. Indeed, there can be no mob psychology without this cognitive and emotive construct of the world. But being responsible for an entire group is a foundational religious notion. This is, in essence, the Christian notion of Jesus taking on the sins of the world, suffering for it, and providing forgiveness for those who believe in him by dying for their sins.[1] Thus, we must at least raise the question of the wisdom of collective patterns of apology and forgiveness, when they have a tendency to hold responsible the innocent, or at least the less guilty, for the high crimes of others. There is also a tendency for members of victim groups to offer forgiveness in the name of those who have not consented to such a process and who demand a closer attention to justice, restitution, and even large-scale punishment. Thus it may satisfy the emotional and spiritual needs of those present, but only enrage those who are not present.

The discussion in this chapter, for reasons of space only, needs to be limited to the Abrahamic faiths, and cultures deeply affected by them. Much more needs to be investigated in other religions of the world. In order to understand the use of forgiveness in explicitly religious conflict resolution, it is necessary to see it embedded in its other theological uses, specifically in terms of the God-human, and God-human or God-tribal community, relationship. Furthermore, in its pristine religious form, we need to divide it into the uses of receiving versus offering forgiveness. Receiving forgiveness from God is a key to being in the good graces of God and to avoiding punishment and receiving rewards—in addition to the inherent reward of restoring a close relationship to God. The forgiveness may be necessary for specific sins committed, or, in the case of Christianity, it may be because the human being by nature, due to original sin, requires forgiveness from God, which can then lead to a rebirth in grace without the burden of original sin. The latter is accomplished only through acceptance of God's only begotten Son, Jesus. Thus, forgiveness is a key to the restoration of relationship to God, and, in the conservative Christian case, it is the key to becoming legitimate as a Christian and as a human being. Furthermore, that legitimacy is wrapped around an exclusive character to forgiveness, namely, that it can only be accomplished through faith in Jesus, not just God. Many more liberal Christians today may dispute this exclusivity, though not necessarily the central myth of the sinful human being in need of a forgiving God.

Offering forgiveness, in the Christian case, is also an opportunity to be close to God, in that one emulates this central divine characteristic. It should be noted that this has old Hebrew biblical roots in terms of a God who, according to the myths, repeatedly forgave first humanity and then the Israelites for their various trespasses, until God could no longer avoid punishment. But patience with human failing, infinite compassion, and forgiveness are seen as basic characteristics of God in the Hebrew Bible, the New Testament, and the Qur'an. God is not seen as exclusively forgiving, and He is even seen to punish for several generations, as mentioned earlier. However, the forgiveness element of the divine character lasts infinitely, or in biblical terms, for a thousand generations.[2]

In the Jewish and Islamic case, God is presented as infinitely compassionate, as well as forgiving.[3] Divine wrath and punishment are also liberally expressed in both the Bible and the Koran. To what degree God's compassion or forgiveness requires human emulation of God is an interesting question. Let us first address this issue in Judaism.

The standard emphasis of rabbinic Judaism rests squarely on forgiveness as embedded in a process of change that is initiated by the person who did something wrong. In this sense, crime, change, and forgiveness are embedded in the much larger practice and metaphysical reality of *teshuva*, repentance. Teshuva, the capacity to transform oneself or a community, is considered to be one of the most sublime elements of faith in a good, forgiving God. The fact that repentance can change a guilty verdict is a great blessing. Resh Lakish exclaimed, "Great is repentance, for it transforms intentional sins [zedonot] into sins of negligence or forgetting [shegagot]." And in another version, "Great is repentance for it turns intentional crimes into testimonies for a person's goodness."[4]

There is also an important rabbinic idea, which is critical for Jewish consciousness, that true repentance comes when the person stands again in the same place, with the same opportunity to do the crime, and then resists it.[5] This suggests some concern with whether processes of repentance and confessions of wrongdoing are really authentic unless they have some external reality.

There are several interacting themes of forgiveness. There is, as stated, the idea of teshuva, repentance. There is *mehila*, which is the standard word for forgiveness, but there is also *seliha*, which is sometimes translated as pardon and sometimes as forgiveness. Seliha is translated in Psalms 130:4 as "the power to forgive."[6] All of these divine qualities entail forgiveness, forbearance, patience, and a resistance to anger, in addition to the obvious quality of mercy in overlooking someone's guilt. God's continuing to sustain human beings, to nurture their bodies from moment to moment, knowing full well the extent of their failings, is seen as a perpetual commitment to mercy, forgiveness, and patience.

This theological foundation is critical to understanding what is hoped for in the personality of the human being who is called upon to forgive those who have hurt him or her. The rabbis characterize forgiveness as something that should come immediately if it is clear that someone is embarrassed by what he or she has done or if he or she feels guilty about it.[7] In fact, there is a notion of a person having a right to forgiveness when he or she has clearly repented and is now living a decent life. The person may even insist upon it.[8] The right to forgiveness is an interesting concept that should be explored further.

In all of the above cases forgiveness is seen as a kind of quid pro quo for the moral transformation of the person. In interpersonal terms, it involves a bilateral, formal process that also has internal elements. But it seems that the rabbis saw something in forgiveness that goes beyond a bilateral process. They stated, for example, that anyone who cries at the death of a good person is forgiven for all his or her sins,[9] that if someone is a good, kind man but he buries a child, then all his sins are forgiven,[10] that if even one person does authentic teshuva, repentance, it is enough to forgive the entire world.[11] This last point is particularly astonishing, and it suggests that there is an independent power of forgiveness that extends well beyond a simple tit for tat of one sin, one repentance and one forgiveness for that sin. But it is also clear that much of the emphasis of this literature is the power and responsibility of individuals who have hurt someone else, or sinned against God, to initiate the process of change, and only then receive a response from the injured other.

There is an important interplay of several related concepts here. Arrogance or "hardness of the face" (*azut panim*), which is considered the opposite of humility, characterizes someone who never surrenders or wipes away his own principles. He always stands in a hard way before people. He is vengeful. The vengeful person never forgives his friends who have injured him. This, in turn, causes conflict and hatred. The person who is perpetually angry is also the one who cannot surrender his own positions, and this too leads to revenge.

The formula for forgiveness and its role in conflict resolution is that this gesture must be preceded by the cultivation of the kind of person who has humility, who avoids a "hard face" in his presentation of self to others, who learns to control his anger, and who is willing to surrender his positions sometimes, even if he is in the right.[12]

These sources also reveal, however, one of the fundamental weaknesses of religious traditions. The very same sources suggest that when it comes to dealing with those who are "wicked," who are against the Torah, it is permissible to be arrogant with them and to display all the negative qualities just mentioned, in order to "fight them" and their influence successfully.[13] Thus, we have two dilemmas with this and many other sources: First, who decides when the prosocial side of these texts is operationalized, and when the antisocial side is operationalized? Who decides who is wicked? Second, in the contemporary pluralistic age, most people could be classified as "wicked" or "against God," and, thus, does this not neutralize these sources as building blocks of forgiveness and conflict resolution?

This is at the crux of the problem of the hermeneutic variability of historical religions, the fundamental ambivalence that we sense in approaching them as resources for conflict resolution. Generally speaking, it has been religious authorities, often connected with reigning structures of economic and police power, who decide who is wicked and who is righteous, to whom pro-social values must be directed, and to whom they must not. And this marriage of religious authority, embedded in larger power structures, as well as the selective application of religious values, has generally been a prescription for disaster in human history. This is not only due to the removal of large groups of people from the purview of ethical responsibility, but it is also due to the selective application of the ethics of submission, passivity, and humility as a tool to pacify the faithful. Thus forgiveness can potentially be selectively withdrawn from the most in need of being engaged, while forgiveness can also be applied more narrowly to keep religious groups from expressing anger at unjust situations.

This is a problem that must be confronted, and it lies at the heart of whether forgiveness will become an authentic, carefully crafted component of a mature system of conflict resolution that honestly confronts injustice and the issue of the distribution of power, or whether it becomes a pious tool of pacification, selectively applied by authorities or public opinion to conflicts that disturb the harmony of the acceptable order of religious society. For example, it might be applied, as this author has witnessed, to fellow Christians, all involved in furthering the mission of the Christian faithful, but not to, say, communists, who are the "sworn enemies of the Church." The examples proliferate. Forgiveness may be encouraged and insisted on for a wife when it comes to an unfaithful husband, but not even considered when it comes to a distant "infidel" one may be slaughtering with perfectly righteous indignation. Thus forgiveness in this context, from the perspective of today's concepts of conflict resolution, might be considered an unfortunate adjunct to barbarism.

Furthermore, it should be noted that religious patterns of forgiveness are only as good as the moral system they serve. For example, if a religious system condones slavery or the death penalty for adultery, as all the biblical religions did at one time or another, would the issues of apology, confession of guilt, and forgiveness even arise? Did they historically when religious traditions embraced slavery? Was it possible, in a society and a religion that accepted slavery, to strongly encourage a master to apologize for his act of slavery in a moral structure that did not condone it to begin with? Conversely, if a man was caught not standing before his elders would it not be certain that contrition and apology would be the first order of business, even as everyone involved is on a battle-field fighting some religious enemy? Is this an impossible scenario? Not in this author's experience. In other words, religious forgiveness, in terms of conflict resolution and justice, is only as helpful as the moral system that it accompanies and buttresses.

Islam and Forgiveness

Let us turn our attention now to Islam, with a focus on texts of forgiveness and compassion as they may relate to peacemaking. Here we find some remarkably similar hermeneutic dynamics. Forgiveness is mentioned in at least twenty-three verses of the Qur'an. As in Judaism, much of its usage refers to God's kindness. God is referred to as "oft-Forgiving." In this sense, it is parallel to divine mercy (Surah 39:53). One commentator suggests that there are three usages in the Qur'an: (1) forgiveness as forgetting, (2) forgiveness as ignoring or turning away from, as a defensive maneuver if someone insults you, and (3) divine forgiveness (*ghafara*) which refers to Allah's covering up of sins.[14]   Allah's forgiveness extends especially to minor sins that should not be dwelled upon (53:32), but Allah does not forgive for joining other gods to Allah (4:48), the primary betrayal of Allah. Furthermore, repentance after a life of sin only when facing death is considered inauthentic, and forgiveness is not offered (4:17-18). Throughout, both implicitly and explicitly, it seems clear that divine forgiveness is contingent on human repentance. As in Judaism, it is a bilateral process, and forgiveness is inextricable from that bilateral relationship.

There is evidence of forgiveness even for idol worship, presumably with the requisite human repentance. Allah is seen as forgiving the "Jews" for the Golden Calf episode (4:153), and at least being patient with Abraham's slow search for God that involved initial belief in other deities (4:76-78). Furthermore, the general character of God is portrayed as forgiving. In fact, the angels are seen as praying for the forgiveness of all beings on earth (42:5), and this text, at least, presents this, apparently knowing full well that a large portion of humanity does not only commit sins but also engages in the sin of joining other gods to Allah.

Needless to say, all of this language of forgiveness comes in the context of a literature that very explicitly approves and ordains this-worldly, violent encounters with nonbelievers, when this is legitimate and appropriate, according to Islamic law, just as we see in the historical sources of Judaism and Christianity. We will not go into here the justifications of jihad in Islam. It is certainly the case that there are extensive limits to the brutality of jihad, and that there is no compulsion allowed in terms of conversion. But suffice it to say that every collection of hadith, reports on the Prophet, has a special section dedicated to jihad, which recounts the exploits against "heathens," those who would not become Muslim, who would not accept Allah. Thus, as in Judaism, which has an extensive and subtle moral interpersonal system that exists side by side with legitimated violence, especially against idolaters, here too, this literature must be seen in context.

Continuing with a study of Islam, let us turn now from forgiveness and Allah to human models of forgiveness. The Qur'an records that one of the instructions to Muhammad is "Hold to forgiveness" even as he resists evil (7:199). It is expected that people have the right to repay evil for evil. However, it is also stated that those who, even when they are justifiably angry, can forgive have the highest reward (42:37). Ideally, the Qur'an suggests that people deal with their differences by a process of "consultation," which is not specified in the Qur'an at least, but no doubt has been developed over the centuries. This consultation reference could and should become the basis for religiously sanctioned processes of conflict management. There is no blame for those who cannot forgive; however, forgiveness combined with reconciliation yields a reward from Allah (42:40). Forgiveness combined with compensation for injury appears to be a preferable path to retaliation even if retaliation is permitted (Hadith Sahih Bukhari 3.49.866). This is an interesting position in that it recognizes that the recompense of injury is injury, following along the lines of Exodus 21:24, the *lex talionis*, or eye for an eye, legal principle. Judaism never accepted the literal reading of this Middle Eastern principle. Islam, too, sees forgiveness as the preferable act. Most important, forgiveness is seen as the act of a "courageous will" (42:43). "A strong person is not the person who throws his adversaries to the ground. A strong person is one who contains himself when he is angry" (Malik's Muwatta 47.3.12).

This has important implications for allowing the forgiving man to think of what he does as not cowardly but as an act that confirms his strength as a person. This is important in response to some troubling questions that a conflict resolver would have with forgiveness in conflict resolution, namely, what it accomplishes and does not accomplish in terms of the empowerment of both sides.[15] In addition, in order for the need for justice to be achieved in authentic conflict resolution, there also needs to be a resolution of the sense of powerlessness felt often by victims of violence. If forgiveness is merely a religious requirement, but is not seen or felt as some form of empowerment, then its effectiveness in truly resolving and transforming the conflict may be limited. The religious act may repress hidden anger and turn into a formalistic act that does not address the person's deeper needs. It is vital that forgiveness, if it is to be done, is seen and felt as an empowering act. This text would affirm this inner process, as does the rabbinic dictum, "Who is the greatest hero among the heroes? He who turns an enemy into a friend."[16] Once again, classical Judaism and Islam share a strategy of how particularly to get the male to become a peacemaker. This is particularly vital in terms of both traditions, the biblical and the Qur'anic, having religious prophets and heroes who were warriors, such as Abraham, Moses, Joshua, David, and Muhammad.

The hadith literature yields some interesting ideas on forgiveness and conflict resolution as well. Malik's Muwatta states, "Every Muslim forgives except a man who has enmity between him and his brother. Leave these two until they have made reconciliation" (47.4.17), and the following text adds, "Leave these two until they turn in tawba." It seems that this text refers to a fellow Muslim. But whether, under what circumstances, and according to whose interpretation, it could be extended to Muslim-non-Muslim relations is an important hermeneutic challenge for Islamic peacemakers. Clearly, however, the forgiveness is not simply an internal act, but rather an external act of reconciliation that parallels an inner process.

It is this proactive element that is important to highlight here, as we did in Judaism. Just as there must be an active interaction of human repentance and divine forgiveness, here, too, human forgiveness is inextricably related to a process that has both internal and external formal aspects. On the internal level, the hadith stress anger as a key impediment to forgiveness and reconciliation.[17] It is not considered hallal[18] to shun one's brother for more than three days. The shunning is attributed variously to envy, anger, suspicion, spying, and competition (Malik's Muwatta 47.4.13-16). The better of the two people greets his fellow first. Shaking of hands is considered an important act that cures the rancor. Thus, there are specific symbolic/ethical acts, such as being the first to greet and shaking hands, that provided important clues to this deep, cultural process of reconciliation and forgiveness which stem from the oldest strata of Islamic culture.

The Interaction of Arab Culture and Islam

The proactive element in forgiveness and reconciliation that we have seen in Islam has old monotheistic roots, as we have demonstrated in Judaism. But it is also rooted in the old Arab method of reconciliation referred to as *sulha*. George Irani refers to several Arab methods of dealing with conflicts, including *wasta* (patronage-mediation), and *tahkeem* (arbitration).[19] *Sulh*, which Irani translates as "settlement," and *muslaha*, which Irani translates as "reconciliation," are rituals that are formally institutionalized in Arab cultural institutions of the past, as well as the present, to some degree. Sulh is conducted between believers and is a form of contract, legally binding on both sides. According to some authorities, salaam carries the connotation of permanent peace, whereas sulh may be temporary but could lead to permanent peace. In any case, it is action- and ritual-oriented.[20] Public sulh, according to one Jordanian expert, is conducted between large groups, such as tribes, whether or not the original parties to the conflict are known or are still present, historically speaking. Permanent peace among them requires compensation for those who have suffered the most and a pledge from all the parties to forget everything and create a new relationship. Private sulh takes place between known parties, and the purpose is to avoid the cycle of revenge. For example, if a murder is committed, the families go to *muslihs* or *jaha* (those who have esteem in the community). A *hodna* (truce) is declared.

The task of the sulh is not to judge, according to Irani, but to preserve the good name of both families and reaffirm the ongoing relationships of the community. This has what Mennonite peacemakers refer to as a restorative quality to it, which suggests that the process is much more than a judgment of who is right and wrong. Nevertheless, this judgement does occur, and the process is an arbitrated one. If one party is guilty of something as serious as murder, for example, there may be *diya* (blood money) that must be paid in order to avoid bloodshed. Finally there is a formal process of *muslaha*, a public event in the village center. The families line up, the parties shake hands (*musafaha*), the family of the perpetrator may visit the family of the injured or murdered, and they drink bitter coffee (in some traditions it is *mumalaha* [partaking of salt and bread]). Finally, the family of the offender hosts a meal.

There are many important elements in this process. The use of symbolism is critical. The ritual use of food and the body for the handshake is key, involving all the senses, especially touch, between the parties. The bilateral way in which the parties relate, each with its own assigned symbolic role, is critical and plays the role that all ritual plays in critical turning points of life and death. It gives the parties an ordered universe of peace, predictability, and security, when this is precisely what the violence or offense stole from them.

The contractual element of this process is critical here to the culture. Treaties of an oral or custom-based nature are important to Middle Eastern cultures; they can and should play a role in any intercultural process of Middle Eastern peacemaking.

Generally speaking, the literature focuses on the conduct of sulh when there is one guilty party. Of course, it is the nature of complex conflicts that there is usually a large amount of injury to innocents and crimes on both sides, and usually it is lopsided in ways that the combatants can never agree upon. However, it is possible that combatants can agree on specific crimes on both sides that are regrettable and/or subject to restitution and processes of reconciliation and apology. Thus, how sulh could be applied to complex conflicts is an interesting question. Furthermore, applying sulh to intercultural and interreligious conflicts is certainly a challenging question. There is the obvious problem of religious authorities on both sides calling into question the orthodoxy of extending the process in this way. But there is also a deeper question of how and whether the symbolic process can be meaningful when it has primordial roots for only one side. A syncretistic process typical of modern interfaith experimentation would only be appealing to some and probably appalling to the most religiously conservative on both sides, who probably need the process of reconciliation more than most. Thus, the problems of application are clear.

For example, how would sulh apply to situations of massive wrongdoing and injury to large groups of people, even over generations? Most descriptions of sulh presume, in classic court style, that there is one guilty party, although the written literature on this may not reflect the subtle variations of its lived reality at the hands of elders and arbitrators. But this is not the nature of long-standing interethnic culture, where there is usually extensive injury on both sides, and recognizing this is half the battle of conflict resolution. Certainly, these village-based methods could not automatically translate into applicability to complex conflicts facing the Middle East. However, they may prove to be, in altered form, a crucial adjunct or parallel process to formal negotiations over matters of justice, war, and peace that speak to peoples' hearts and deeper needs in a way that virtually nothing currently proposed by diplomacy is accomplishing.

Conclusion

This author has been involved in an ongoing, high-level effort to elicit the beginnings of a reconciliation process between Jewish and Islamic clerical leadership. It is certainly leading to statements of reconciliation or peacefulness that may or may not see the light of day, depending on the security of the parties involved. Forgiveness ceremonies, apologies, sulha, and teshuva-type ceremonies remain only a theoretical possibility at this point, but we are closer than ever to preparing the political and religious ground for such a possibility. The symbolic and transformative power of leading sheikhs and rabbis embracing in such a ceremony is an image that drives all of us forward in this difficult work, because we believe that this is the missing ingredient of the so-called peace process. It is the human element that is needed to transform this bitter, merciless, haggling struggle into a deeper process of trust-building, honest bilateral conversations about justice, and even reconciliation. It behooves us to work strenuously now to provide possible models of how this could occur. We want especially to guide this process in such a way that it truly responds to the human needs expressed on all sides, so that peacemaking and its cultural ceremonialization do not undermine deep conflict resolution and the pursuit of just solutions to complex wars.

In sum, we have explored the various parameters and uses of forgiveness in Judaism and Islam and, to some degree, in the lived experience of Christianity. It is clear that there is potential in all three religions for this phenomenon of forgiveness to prove important in processes of conflict resolution. However, there are several major conditions, particularly if we are to think of this in terms of the deadly conflicts facing the Middle East.

1. Religious forgiveness must be seen in the context of a range of other religious moral values, such as justice, in order for it to work well with our basic understanding today of what truly resolves conflicts and stops deadly violence in the long term.

2. Assuming number one, it can still be said that there are times when an act that involves apology, remorse, or forgiveness should stand on its own as a powerful symbol of a stage in relationship building. Forgiveness need not at every moment be tied to justice, because its powerful psychological—spiritual if you like—impact drives the process forward toward rational negotiations about justice, power sharing, and fair solutions.

3. Timing in forgiveness-type activities (apology, remorse, symbolic reconciliation, gestures of repentance and restitution, unilateral forgiving, expressions of care) is critical, and it varies from culture to culture. Generally speaking, most people are prepared for acts of forgiveness in the context of some progress in justice issues, as a kind of glue that binds rational processes to the hearts of the parties. Conversely, forgiveness too early is offensive to many injured parties. But in some cultures and in some intractable situations, it seems that forgiveness-type activities are actually the first, not the last, activity, in that they break the psychological impasse to rational negotiation.

4. Religious forgiveness should never be exclusively verbal. Actions, symbolic actions, surprising gestures, ceremonies, and rituals are vital for most people who feel deep injury. For many, it is the only kind of reconciliation that they seem able to handle. This is especially true in many families. Thus, while in some ideal universe of psychological healing it would be better if everyone could place into words what their adversaries need most to hear, we should not eliminate from conflict resolution the majority of humanity who cannot bring themselves to say the words, "I am sorry," to an enemy. There are many other modes of forgiveness to be utilized that will lessen violence, restore everyone to a dignified life based on just solutions, and even create reconciliation.

5. Forgiveness must be a critical adjunct to rational negotiations and justice seeking, because in virtually every long-standing conflict, from families all the way to genocide, there is never complete justice; there is no way to recover the lost lives, the lost time, or the emotional scars of torture and murder. And there is rarely the possibility of achieving everything each group envisioned at the height of struggle and battle. Thus, in the context of mourning what cannot be restored, forgiveness and the creation of new bonds with those who one fought is a vital form of comfort for irrecoverable losses. It offers the possibility of a new matrix, a new cognitive and emotive structure of reality that cannot replace the losses but does create a surprisingly new reason to live nonviolently and

believe that such a life can be worth living. People recovering from geno-cide and feeling guilty over their survival, people who have been forfeit-ing their sons' lives for generations, often need a jolt, an unexpected rea-son that they may be able to live normally, a reason to believe that a new way of life is not only possible but will actually be better than continuing to mourn their losses and punish those who inflicted those losses. For-giveness processes can be the soul that animates this new vision of reality in the heart of those who have suffered for so long.

Notes

1. Of course, this is not just a Christian notion. It has old Jewish roots, though it is certainly not as dogmatically central to Jewish belief and practice as is the death of Jesus for the sake of forgiveness. There is an ancient idea that the death of the righteous atones for the sins of a generation. See Midrash Tanhuma (Buber ed.), Ahre mot 10.

2. Exodus 34:7. This verse is said countless times on the holiest day of the Jewish year, the Day of Atonement, and is emphasized as the most important characteristic of God.

3. There are numerous sources in the Torah (the term is used interchangeably with the Hebrew Bible). See, for example., Micah 7:18-20. For Allah as merciful, see in the Qur'an, Surahs 6:26; 5:74; 15:49; 16:119. For Allah as forgiving, see 4:25; 5:74; 85:14.

4. The last phrase is a translation of *zekhuyot* in this context only.

5. T. B. Yoma 86b.

6. Tanakh: The Holy Sriptures (Philadelphia: Jewish Publication Society, 1985).

7. T.B. Hagigah 5a; T.B. Berachot 12b.

8. Avot of Rabbi Nathan 40:5, statement of Rabbi Elazar ben Rabbi Yossi.

9. T.B. Shabbat 105b.

10. T.B. Berachot 5b.

11. T.B. Yoma 86b; Otzar Midrashim, Gadol u'Gedualah 6.

12. Orhot Tzadikim (n.d.; rpt. Jerusalem: Eshkol, 1946), chapters 4, 8, and 12.

13. Orhot Tzadikim, chapter 4. The problem here is the implied limitation of many of these methods of interaction to fellow Jews. See Rabbi Moshe Cordovero, Tomer Devorah (rpt. New York: Feldheim, 1993): 13-17. This is an old crux in Jewish tradition, and it is extended to the other monotheistic faiths. In all of them, traditional ethical language usually circumscribes many of the most important ethical principles to fellow believers, "those who accept Allah," or who call themselves Muslims, or those who are "brothers and sisters in the body of Christ," and so forth. It certainly affects the ethical values that today would be vital in establishing universal human rights. This is the essential problem of a group that has a "special" relationship to God. And yet, I have argued elsewhere that we cannot escape the need of ethnic groups, and the need of religious groups, to feel special, unique. See Marc Gopin, *Between Eden and Armaged-don: The Future of Religion, Violence and Peacemaking* (New York: Oxford University Press, 2000).

14. See The Holy Qur'an, ed. and trans. "Abdullah Yusuf' Ali (Brentwood, Md: Amana Corp., 1989), Surah 2:109, no. 110. Scholars should investigate the connection between this last notion of divine forgiveness as a covering and the Biblical and rabbinic notion of over *al pesha*, or *moheh pesha*, mentioned above.

15. On the importance of empowerment in conflict resolution, or specifically the conflict transformation, see B. Bush and J. Folger, *The Promise of Mediation* (San Francisco: Jossey-Bass, 1994).

16. Avot of Rabbi Nathan 23:1.

17. Yahya related to me from Malik that Yahya ibn Said said that he heard Said ibn al-Musayyab say, "Shall I tell you what is better than much prayer and sadaqa?" They said, "Yes." He said, "Mending discord. And beware of hatred—it strips you of your deen." Malik's Muwatta 47.1.17.

18. Hallal also refers to Islamic food that is considered acceptable for eating.

19. George Irani, "Rituals of Reconciliaiton: Arab-Islamic Persectives," p. 3. Delivered at the United States Institute of Peace (unpublished paper of a Peace Fellow). See also Elias Jabbour, *Sulha: Palestinian Traditional Peacemaking Process*, Jefforson, N.C.: House of Hope, 1996).

20. Irani, p. 27

6

Negotiating a Revolution

Toward Integrating Relationship Building and Reconciliation into Official Peace Negotiations

J. Lewis Rasmussen

> *In a world where war is everybody's tragedy and everybody's nightmare, diplomacy is everybody's business.*
>
> —Lord Strang[1]

The changing temper of the times has indeed brought with it new concerns that demand new approaches toward the study and conduct of global political relations in general and, in particular, how we will prevent, manage, and resolve destructive sociopolitical conflict. In other words, because we are just beginning to understand that successful peacemaking is the product of a series of coordinated interventions on the part of official and unofficial actors at the grassroots, national, regional, and global levels that stretch from the immediate to over the long term, the challenge before us is how best to meet that challenge.

Indeed, how can the global community continue to assist with rebuilding countries that face such severe problems as Angola, Cambodia, Haiti, or Somalia—especially with yet another *crisis du jour* just around the corner? Will the Dayton Agreements governing the former Yugoslavia collapse during the implementation phase? Despite the 1995 political agreement between Palestinians and Israelis, why is peace in desperate need of consolidation, the promising recent resumption of talks notwithstanding? Similarly, why is Cambodia at a crossroads? Why indeed, since following the 1991 Agreements for a Comprehensive Settlement of the Cambodia Conflict (signed in Paris by the four major Cambodian factions and eighteen countries), the international community spent over $2.5 billion in less than two years on a two-part United Nations (UN) mission, UN Advance Mission in Cambodia (UNAMIC) and UN Transitional Authority in Cambodia (UNTAC) designed to begin the implementation process and to help put the country on the path toward a sustainable peace and a functioning democracy.

Peacebuilding, especially reconciliation and reconstruction during the postsettlement phase, has only recently begun to receive the attention of scholars and practitioners. The majority of early research focused on assisting donors in better understanding the transition from crisis to relief to development but did not address key issues surrounding postsettlement reconciliation and reconstruction.[2] In fact, as Lederach (1998, 135) argues, we are still in the early stages of developing frameworks for resolving wars.

Academic analysts—operating largely within prescribed realist parameters—have disproportionately focused on how parties get to the table (prenegotiation), the substantive nature of negotiations, and the processes or stages through which negotiation unfolds (Hampson 1996). Unfortunately, a longer term orientation toward conflict resolution has not been well advanced (Stedman and Rothchild 1996), despite the fact that peacebuilding has begun to receive serious attention over the past several years within the UN system, the U.S. government and other governments, regional organizations, and relief and development nongovernmental organizations (NGOs) (see Boutros-Ghali 1992, 1995; Ball 1996; Colletta, Kostner, and Wiederhofer 1996; Crocker and Hampson, with Aall 1996; Kumar 1996; Maynard 1999; USAID 1999; World Bank 1998).

At issue is an interrelated series of problems. First, although the term *peacebuilding* entered the mainstream lexicon several years ago, a consistently shared set of connotations has not permeated the mass consciousness. In other words, if meaning arises from use, the perspectives, objectives, and means brought to bear by political, military, and humanitarian actors differ so widely both within and across national and international institutions—as well as across the official/unofficial divide—that designing and making operational strategies proved extremely challenging (de Soto and del Castillo 1994; Crocker, Hampson, and Aall 1996; Seiple 1996; Chopra 1999).

Second, little systematic, reflective work has been done on operationalizing reconciliation and relationship building during the postsettlement phase of peacebuilding. Such analysis will be forthcoming, of course, as conflicts mature and as strategic consciousness continues to broaden to include such foci. Finally, there has been virtually no study of how to prepare for the postsettlement reconciliation needs by incorporating relationship building and reconciliation activities into (1) the arduous *process* of brokering an official agreement and (2) the *terms* of an official agreement.

Consequently, much like the clarion call Saunders (1984, 1985) made to broaden the negotiation process to include "prenegotiation," we again find ourselves in a period of history when the process of official peace negotiation must be expanded. Only this time it is necessary to selectively involve non-governmental actors in the process and to integrate a strategic focus on relationship building and reconciliation. Both additions are elements of a peace process that previously have been ignored, undervalued, or largely left off the official table by virtue of being more germane to the postsettlement environment. The imperative for change, though, is indeed clear. The problems that initially gave rise to and supported the conflict must be dealt with prior to and during the implementation of a peace agreement if a lasting resolution is to be obtained. Countries such as Angola, Bosnia, Cambodia, Rwanda, Sierra Leone—to name but a few—have at one point reached negotiated agreements to end their civil wars, and yet all continue to struggle toward a sustainable peace.

Unfortunately, a negotiated settlement does not necessarily bode well for a lasting peace. In fact, only one-third of settlements to civil wars negotiated between 1945 and 1993 have resulted in a stable, lasting peace (Licklider 1995). This suggests, among other things, that (1) the struggle for political power during the implementation of an agreement is where the battle for sustainable peace is truly waged, and (2) there may be shortcomings associated with the manner in which official negotiations (to end civil wars) are designed and conducted.

Power Sharing, Democratization, and Negotiating Sustainable Peace

Implementation of agreements should be considered "no less formidable a task than negotiating them" (Crocker, and Hampson 1996, 55). In their effort to understand better how to make peace settlements work, Crocker and Hampson concluded that peace agreements are much more likely to collapse "in cases of civil or intrastate conflict where effective political authority is either non-existent, fragmented and faction-ridden, or too weak to overcome the self-sustaining patterns of hostility and violence that characterize struggles to assert political identities" (1996, 55).

In this regard, one function of a peace agreement is to provide terms for a just realignment of political authority. One method for changing the social and political order is through the adoption of preferential policies. According to Horowitz, such action can also reduce ethnic (or intergroup) conflict—although he notes that preferential policies "once adopted are difficult to reverse, even when . . . policymakers are convinced reversal is warranted," and can thus perpetuate conflict (1985, 679). The paradox is that effectively changing such political systems in the aftermath of intense conflict requires recognition and tolerance of diversity, as well as access to participation in the processes that determine the conditions of security and identity (broadly defined to include economic, physical, physiological, and psychological aspects).

Generating more equitable participation in such processes often requires such electoral innovations as engineering power-sharing formulas among previous combatants, either as part of the terms of a formal agreement or as an outcome of postsettlement negotiation during the initial implementation period leading up to democratic elections.[3] The fundamental tenet supporting power-sharing theory is the belief that such appropriate engineering will "help construct a democratic political system capable of withstanding the centrifugal tendencies that tear deeply divided societies apart" (Sisk 1996, 77). Unfortunately, though, a "negotiated settlement to a civil war is likely to result in veto groups that will not surrender power for social change" (Licklider 1995, 685).[4]

Several interrelated obstacles are likely to hinder the successful application of a power-sharing approach toward sustainable peace. One problem is that leaders (of a legitimate government or political party, or of an insurgent group) generally have little leeway—either within the hierarchy of their party or among their constituents—on issues of tolerance and cooperation in a climate where existential politics is often seen as a continuation of the former war by different means. Second, a negotiated settlement to a civil war is likely to produce gridlock (or worse), as the former ruling party (or parties) is unlikely to surrender power easily by agreeing to elections, or abiding by "unfavorable" results. Getting leaders to change the political and social structures that have kept them in positions of privilege is extremely difficult, as this is not necessarily in their best interests as rational electoral actors.

Third (and closely related to the second), a negotiated settlement that was brokered with heavy external pressure may lead parties to believe that the best way to consolidate power—once the external pressure (and general presence) is removed—is through zero-sum electoral arrangements. Fourth, participation in cooperative mechanisms is predicated on trust and on physical and psychological security—rather uncommon commodities following years (if not decades) of civil war. People who feel insecure are likely to be less tolerant of political or ethnic diversity and less trusting of their counterparts and the newly defined political processes. Consequently, a fifth obstacle (closely related to the second) is that opposition parties are likely to "contest" the elections if the results do not bear out the legitimacy of their claims supporting years of armed struggle.

The historical frailty of negotiated settlements and the risks associated with adopting power-sharing as a strategy for peaceful sociopolitical change suggest strongly that the manner in which power sharing formulas are engineered and applied should require greater attention to the processes of relationship building and reconciliation.

The transition toward a sustainable, peaceful democracy should be premised on a sense of national reconciliation from the bottom up and from the top down. In divided societies, a peace process must not only broaden "the moderate political center [by] persuading rejectionist parties to participate in negotiations," elections, and the renewed social institutions that follow, but must also deepen the practice of moderation within the *overall society* (Sisk 1996, 85). The philosophy, values, and beliefs necessary to support a democratic society must be given time to sprout and take root; above all, they must be nurtured prior to, during, and after elections. While the first new election in an emerging democracy is important, the second and third elections are even more so.

In this regard, the 1993 elections in Cambodia were ostensibly not just about choosing new leaders but, rather, an entirely new process of governance and leadership; democratic elections were to have signified a watershed change in the relationship between state and society in Cambodia.[5] It was remarkable that nearly 90 percent of eligible voters turned out that May to vote in what could best be described as a climate of armed, cold peace.

However, although the civil war no longer raged with the same intensity in 1993, a report prepared by UNTAC's human rights component concluded that in just the two and a half months immediately preceding the elections there were 200 deaths, 338 injuries, and 114 abductions that were determined to be "politically motivated." The report went on to state unequivocally that "numerous, almost systematic, attacks on political party offices or serious acts of harassment and intimidation" occurred during this preelection period (Moser-Puangsuwan 1995, 119-120). Moreover, the Khmer Rouge was not singularly culpable. The State of Cambodia (SOC; now known as the Cambodian People's Party, or CPP) was found to have perpetrated numerous acts of violence against its opposition; although to a considerably lesser extent, the Royalist party, known by its acronym FUNCINPEC, and other minor parties were not without sin either.

Unfortunately, in the recent aftermath of institutionalized political violence, national reconciliation remains a much-discussed concept, especially in the guise of political rhetoric. Very little reconciliation, however, was achieved among the major political parties (including the Khmer Rouge, the recent integration of defectors into the national army notwithstanding)[6]—and to a significant degree within political parties themselves—prior to the initial 1993 elections, and between then and the July 1997 coup. This lack of reconciliation has long been the case among those at the top-level national leadership all the way down to the level of communal chiefs in the villages; to a substantial degree, the political divisions are mirrored throughout society at large.[7]

"[T]he division between Khmers grows more deep, and this is owing to the increasingly open hostility between the Hun Senists and Ranadariddhists," wrote King Sihanouk in a letter to his exiled half-brother, Prince Norodom Sirivudh.[8] Expressing regret that granting amnesty would not sufficiently guarantee his safety, since Hun Sen did not approve of such a pardon (although Ranariddh did), Sihanouk lamented the fact that "acts of violence are multiplying. . . . The life of a human being in our country is no longer valued."[9] In addition, respect for national and international law seemed to matter little to then Co-Prime Minister Hun Sen, who was reported to have openly told Prince Sirivudh that his plane would be shot down should he attempt to return to Cambodia.[10]

National reconciliation must be based on accepted legal principles, democratic will, sincere respect for human rights, and an overall commitment to nonviolent approaches for dealing with political differences and conflict. Regrettably, Kem Sokha (a member of the Cambodian parliament and chair of the Commission on Human Rights and Reception of Complaints) warned in March 1997 that the current approach to national reconciliation "is not a genuine national reconciliation which can be beneficial to the Cambodian people and nation. Rather it is simply the gathering of one force in order to attack another force."[11]

Sustainable peace clearly remains an illusive objective in Cambodia, a country where the bases of national reconciliation remain conspicuously absent at a critical time when sociopolitical change—in the form of democratic electoral competition—was again driven by increasingly equal parts of rhetoric, intimidation, and violence. Following the 1997 coup and the 1998 elections, Hun Sen was installed as a single head of government, despite wide controversy surrounding allegations of fraudulent abuse of the electoral system and significant abuse of political and military power.

Such conditions were not at all what the 1991 Paris Agreements were supposed to portend. Unfortunately, a critical examination of the process leading to the negotiations, and of the negotiations themselves, exposes a disheartening inattention toward relationship building and reconciliation (Rasmussen 1998). When so illuminated, the volatility of Cambodian political (and hence social) life is more easily understood and therefore all the more regrettable.

Oversight in Overseeing Peace Negotiations: Additional Examples from Cambodia

The key to sustainable peace is perhaps found in the notion that action must be taken prior to, during, and following elections. This suggests that greater attention should be given to the nexus between peacemaking (the larger processes leading up to and including brokering a formal peace agreement) and the needs of postsettlement peacebuilding. For example, the first Paris Conference on Cambodia (held July 30 to August 30, 1989) adopted the following mandate:

> To reach, through a consistent, balanced and co-ordinated approach, a comprehensive agreement providing for the internationally supervised withdrawal of foreign troops, restoring the independence of Cambodia, guaranteeing its sovereignty, territorial integrity and neutrality, *promoting peace and national reconciliation in the country*, ensuring self-determination for the Cambodian people through internationally supervised elections, arranging for the voluntary return of refugees and displaced persons to their country and paving the way towards the economic reconstruction of Cambodia. (Text Adopted by

the Paris Conference on Cambodia Document, 1 August 1989
CPC/89/4, emphasis added)

To fulfill the mandate five committees were set up. One committee was to establish an international control mechanism to oversee various aspects of the settlement, including the military, political, and electoral components. The second was to address what was called "the guarantee questions," in particular the legal dimensions of commitments made by states to ensure the durability of the settlement. Refugee matters and reconstruction were the responsibility of the third committee, and the fourth, or the Ad Hoc Committee, was charged with organizing internationally supervised free and fair elections under an interim authority led by Prince Norodom Sihanouk. Finally, the Coordinating Committee was responsible for preparing and presenting the draft final document. While the first three committees produced substantial areas of agreement, including a statement covering issues where no consensus had been reached, the first session of the conference collapsed, as the Ad Hoc Committee could not reach an agreement governing power-sharing arrangements among the four main factions (Ratner 1993, 5-6).

Despite the innovation of including refugee issues as an integral component of a peace agreement, the absence of a committee designed to actively promote the transition toward a democratic civil society is a major shortcoming. More important, though, is the conspicuous absence of a committee to address issues related to the general promotion of *peace and national reconciliation in the country*—a cornerstone of the conference mandate and the 1991 Agreement for a Comprehensive Settlement of the Cambodian Conflict. Quite simply, though economic reconstruction (the domain of the third committee) and a vibrant civil society are critical for postsettlement success, neither will be obtained without building more functional relationships. The negotiators lost a potentially critical opportunity to have taken into account, strategically and operationally, the significance of rebuilding a social infrastructure.

Granted, it is one thing to gain a peace agreement and quite another to get the modalities of the new relationships and mechanisms for further reconciliation within society expressed in the terms of an agreement. It is important that this occur, however, as a negotiated agreement serves as a guide for a variety of postsettlement endeavors leading toward a sustainable peace. Moreover, it is a challenge of altogether greater significance to enable people to either begin or resume living together following years of violent conflict. Indeed, this is what the secretary-general reported to the forty-fourth session of the General Assembly. Following the failure of the first Paris Conference at the end of August 1989, Pérez de Cuéllar stated in his October report that "the most important outstanding issue was national reconciliation" (UN Department of Public Information 1992, iv). Unfortunately, this statement proved to be of much greater rhetorical significance than practical value, as evidenced by the total lack of attention to this issue in numerous missions deployed in advance of UNTAC.

During the first Paris Conference, a fact-finding mission was sent by the secretary-general to ascertain "necessary technical information" to support "the deployment of an international control mechanism" from August 6-19, 1989 (UN Department of Public Information 1992, iv). Similarly, in 1990 four UN fact-finding missions were sent without any mandate to study how to improve the *social infrastructure*. Instead, two missions explored communication and transportation infrastructure, water supply and sanitation, and the housing infrastructure. The third mission examined the political administrative infrastructure of the current Cambodian government, while the fourth analyzed the conditions associated with the repatriation of refugees (UNIDR 1996, 10).

Later the UN secretary-general sent a survey mission to Cambodia from August 19 through September 4, 1991, to help "prevent further deterioration of the political and military situation." The mission was to begin preparations for the military aspects of what was to become UNTAC by evaluating the modalities necessary to maintain the cease-fire and halt foreign military support (UNIDR 1996, 13-14). Again, no charge was given to assess the sociopolitical factors necessary to support an agreement, build confidence in the peace process, and begin to enhance trust among the warring factions—all factors extremely critical to disarmament and demobilization.

Finally, based on findings from the above survey mission, the UN Advance Mission in Cambodia (UNAMIC) was approved by the UN Security Council on October 16, 1991, for deployment immediately following the signing of the Paris Agreements. Unfortunately, UNAMIC was also not designed to promote confidence-building measures, enhance interfactional cooperation, or in any other way lay the groundwork for the relationship building and reconciliation activities that were so desperately needed. Instead, the signatories to the Paris Agreements requested that the UN secretary-general provide good offices associated with monitoring the cease-fire agreement prior to the deployment of UNTAC, begin mine awareness and clearing initiatives, and repair roads and bridges (see Article 9 of the Paris Agreements; see also the Report of the Secretary General on Proposal for a United Nations Advance Mission in Cambodia [UNAMIC], UN document S/23097, September 30, 1991).[12]

It seems rather shortsighted to have excluded such pragmatism from the policymaking decisions associated with the process and outcome of brokering the October 23, 1991, *Agreements on a Comprehensive Political Settlement of the Cambodia Conflict*. Though the global political community has since learned a great deal about the causes and dynamics of violent sociopolitical conflict and the needs of a postsettlement environment, it was then either not well informed by some of its nongovernmental counterparts or it chose to ignore such advice. Regardless, new tools need to be developed and new approaches need to be tried.[13]

Upon reflection, and in light of more recent events, it appears that the international community's dedication to a comprehensive settlement that would promote peace and national reconciliation was premised on a limited vision of reconciling *political* differences within and around the country. Instead, the international community used the process of the Paris Agreements, particularly the failed first round, as an opportunity to contest and further maximize their own objectives within the pretext of helping to find common ground among the Cambodian factions (see Haas 1991a, 190-226). It appears that while the eventual agreements were not totally *forced* upon the factions, the document unquestionably bore the imprimatur of the French and Indonesian cochairs and the Perm 5. It was in this regard that Uch Kiman (Cambodian secretary of state for foreign affairs) proclaimed that "the four Cambodian factions, despite serious reservations, signed the Paris Peace Accords in October 1991 as the price of creating that level playing field designated for Cambodian players only" (1995, 62).

The eventual agreement was reached primarily because it represented the product of the political reconciliation among several major external powers, operating in a spirit of cooperation among states that was hitherto unmatched in the tenure of the UN. In essence, UNTAC—as the implementation mechanism—was "the first exercise of *global authority* in all of history" (Chopra 1994, 13; original emphasis). As such, it also represented a watershed breakthrough in terms of international peacemaking. However, as Ambassador Tommy Koh, the representative of Singapore, noted of the failed first round, gaining agreement among "the five Great Powers is a necessary, but not a sufficient, condition for the resolution of regional conflicts" (Koh 1990, 86). Indeed, both the vision of the eventual 1991 agreements and the state of concord among external players were not to be found inside Cambodia. In retrospect, the ability of the international actors to cooperate in a process of postsettlement peacebuilding and, in particular, the May 1993 elections in Cambodia became "the politically tolerable substitute for the inability of the factions to reconcile themselves" (Doyle 1994, 96).

The geopolitical orientation that drove the process did enable an agreement to be reached in a little over two years of formal negotiation and mediation after nearly two decades of intermittent talks, political maneuvering, and ongoing civil violence. The agreement was possible only because of the withdrawal of Russians and the Chinese support at the conclusion of the Cold War, which then also led to the Vietnamese withdrawal and what was at the time a secret bilateral agreement between China and Vietnam. In fact, many participants of the Paris negotiations suggested that this was the major reason the Cambodian factions signed the agreement—they had no other viable choice without their respective patrons (Doyle 1994).

Again, unfortunately for Cambodia, the negotiation and mediation processes that led to the Paris Agreements did not adequately comprehend nor address relationship factors. Chopra concluded that both the accords and the UN implementation mission (UNTAC) severely "underestimated the depth of distrust between the factions"—to the extent that one senior official described the relationships as "mutual hate" (1994, 72). Instead, the negotiation process, the terms of agreement, and the implementation mechanism (UNTAC) "assumed excessive good faith and substantial reconciliation [that was, after all, what the parties had 'signed' in the Paris Agreements]. In particular, they assumed that what was lacking was coordination" (Doyle, 1995, 69).

This is not to imply that foreign affairs professionals believe relationships are unimportant, rather that patterns of communication and relationships are, by comparison, too often taken for granted in peacemaking. Ronald Fisher presents well the parameters of two different general orientations. One approach stresses that gaining agreement on the substantive issues first (i.e., the conflicting objectives and positions) will lead to improvement in the relationships among the parties. Conversely, the other extreme emphasizes the subjective dimensions of conflict, focusing more on the relationship between antagonists. The presumption is that improving perceptions, attitudes, emotions, trust, and communication among parties "will facilitate a more collaborative and integrative approach to dealing with the objective side of the conflict" (Fisher 1995, 47).

In most instances, both strategies should be employed. A review of the Paris Agreements and the annexes, however, illustrates the lack of explicit structural consideration given to relationship building and reconciliation. If improvements in relationships and national reconciliation are desired, parties to the process of negotiated sociopolitical change must plan accordingly and provide sufficient opportunities and resources to effect change in the social infrastructure, not just the political and physical infrastructures. In the end, the notion of a "comprehensive political settlement" had much less to do with a comprehensive, holistic approach toward national reconciliation and sustainable peace within Cambodia, than it did with marrying the international and the intranational *political* aspects of the conflict. This marriage was a necessary step in order for the international partners to gain a clean (legal) divorce from a dysfunctional relationship.

The thinking behind official peacemaking (i.e., the efforts to determine what the problems are and how they should be solved) has long been guided by a Cold War, realist mentality. The foundations of such a mindset were designed to support policies for dealing with conflicts between nation-states in an era governed by highly different political rules and normative considerations. Dr. Richard Solomon (the former U.S. assistant secretary of state who led the U.S. participation in the Cambodian peace process) confirmed that the mindset governing the Cambodian peace process indeed corresponded more to traditional *geopolitics* than to what this chapter begins to describe as *geosocial politics*.

In an interview, Solomon indicated that little specific attention was given to enhancing trust and improving the relationships among the antagonistic negotiators. Nor was any consideration given to building into the Paris Agreements any type of mechanisms designed explicitly to foster reconciliation during the postsettlement period. Similarly, Solomon acknowledged that no consideration was given by the major powers to instituting postsettlement mechanisms—such as the South African system of local, regional, and national peace commissions (see Gastrow 1995)—for preventing or managing disputes and conflict and for further promoting a sustainable peace. The efforts leading up to the Paris negotiations and the negotiations themselves, Solomon concluded, were not principally about bringing peace to the eight million Cambodian citizens. Rather, this process was first and foremost about the unfolding of *geopolitics* among the three superpowers of the day—China, Russia, and the United States.[14]

The competition for (and efforts to control) regional hegemony, development of strategies to enhance regional stability, and designing a way for international actors to withdraw from Cambodia were of greatest *geopolitical* concern. The absence of a *geosocial* political approach toward the Cambodian conflict has left the country in a state of violent turmoil and but one step removed from becoming a "failed state." With relationship building and reconciliation having been left largely outside the political equation leading up to and governing the Paris peace process, the Paris Agreements, and the UN implementation mission, one wonders the extent to which the roughly eight million Cambodian people were conceived of as the ultimate stakeholders and beneficiaries. In essence, past and recent events surrounding the Cambodian conflict demonstrate the "fallacy of basing world politics on realpolitik alone" (Haas 1991b, 121). In fact, Michael Haas's analysis of the Cambodian conflict concluded that "[p]ractioners of the theory of realpolitik denied peace and stability to small states, while large states exulted in narcissism, believing that war is inevitable unless a country is armed to the teeth" (Haas 1991b, 121).

Although Haas offers a highly illustrative and critical assessment, which might appear consistent with Solomon's remarks, Solomon (1999) makes a quite clear and compelling case for the absolute necessity of major power involvement. Without broader strategic objectives and without the political and financial support, leadership, and long-term commitment of certain countries, the 1991 Paris Peace Agreements would not have been signed. He also notes that the agreements would not have been possible without "serendipity," in particular, the unexpected collapse of the Soviet Union and the sea change in Vietnamese policy toward China and the region.

The complexity of peacemaking within an international system should be readily apparent. As the world painfully feels its way through what should still be considered a transitional era, the current environment of dealing with violent sociopolitical conflict can be best summarized as "new rules, new actors, new roles" (Rasmussen 1997). In order to enhance the prospects for sustainable peace we should endeavor to understand and utilize the strengths of both official and unofficial approaches. For example, care should be exercised to incorporate relationship building and reconciliation activities into such deciding functional areas as security policy, resettlement, rehabilitation, and reconstruction. Postsettlement policymaking should deliberately take relationship building and reconciliation into consideration; however, it is critical that such planning be done prior to implementation. "By waiting until the latter stages of a peace operation . . . the clout of the international community will likely have faded, and a window of opportunity will probably have been lost" (Oakley and Dziedzic 1998, 486-487). Accordingly, the ability to formulate appropriate policy must be based on an understanding of the impact that relationship building and reconciliation have on functional areas of peacemaking. This requires, however, a priori, a pragmatic conceptual orientation toward reconciliation and relationship building and reassessing our understanding of the structure, process, and purpose of peace negotiations.[15]

Rethinking the Content and Process of Peace Negotiations

In respect to negotiating peace in civil wars, varying degrees of external assistance (including the use of a wide range of incentives and disincentives) are usually necessary to broker an agreement. Consequently, both the negotiation process and the resulting agreement become extremely powerful mechanisms for shaping what a society should look like and how it should function; in other words, it is a question of who will rule and according to what rules. As such, brokering and implementing a peace accord is a highly invasive procedure (not unlike major surgery). Good intentions and necessity notwithstanding, this act becomes a highly normative undertaking, regardless of the extent to which the majority of terms are reached and decisions are made freely by the representatives of the protagonists.

In essence, official peace negotiations and peace agreements—regardless of whether they contain detailed power-sharing provisions—have not been designed to facilitate reconciliation or otherwise even build good relationships among former warring parties and their constituencies. One reason is that official negotiation, as a conflict management and resolution technique, is designed (through codification) to gain the agreement of individuals representing their respective constituencies (broadly speaking) to produce macrolevel *changes in behavior. Attitudinal* or *value-based change* in the individual negotiators, or (and even more important) among the members of society, is not an inherent objective of such negotiations.[16] A second related factor is that negotiated agreements ending civil wars have not generally addressed the deeper problems that gave rise to and perpetuated a given war (Ball 1996). For example, although refugee returns and human rights abuses are typically dealt with in peace negotiations, they are not treated as symptoms of deeper underlying causes. Similarly, postsettlement decisions of noncompliance are both a symptom and cause of mistrust and often lead to the resumption of hostility and violence, if not the reemergence of all-out civil war.

Finally, most negotiations have not sought to explicitly address how to best enable former enemies and divided societies not to just live in the shadow of a peace agreement but to actually cooperate side by side in (re)constructing a functional and just civil society—including the institutionalization of nonviolent mechanisms for preventing and managing future sociopolitical disputes as they arise. Unfortunately, given that virtually all contemporary violent conflict is being waged on an *intra*state basis (Wallensteen and Sollenberg 1995, 1997,

1999), this omission is critical, as communities in divided societies must first learn to cooperate and coexist before any true chance for reconciliation can occur on a large scale.

Ideally, a peace negotiation process should be about designing the architecture for "cooperative, mutually enhancing relationship[s] that contribute to the welfare and development" of all groups or societies by addressing their respective fears and needs (Kelman 1996, 104). Needs have a greater chance of being met when relevant groups are (or perceive themselves to be) represented in the society's government; a society sharply divided into high-identity groups may require political power-sharing practices to meet this condition. Parties to a conflict need to learn to view the situation in which they find themselves not as autonomous entities locked into a win-lose contest where the terms of their relationships are defined by maintaining a static symbolism of noncooperation, aggressive posturing, and violent exchanges. Rather, by discovering the terms of mutual interdependence the situation can begin to be transformed into a common set of problems to which joint solutions must be found.

Accordingly, Sisk points out that power sharing is predicated on an acceptance by the groups in conflict "of a *shared or common destiny*" and an expectation that they "will in fact go on living together." They must also adopt "a pragmatism that leads to collaborative problem solving through negotiation (that is, when negotiation is chosen not as a course through which to subdue the opponent, but for the purposes of jointly determining solutions)" (Sisk 1996, 78; original emphasis). Thus, if power sharing is necessary, and for it to be effective, both the process of reaching an agreement and the agreement itself should become a blueprint for transforming relationships. In no uncertain terms, relationship building and reconciliation are necessary to turn over in an expeditious manner the responsibility for implementation, reconstruction, and governance to the indigenous parties (see Kiman 1995).

Such considerations are consistent with lessons Cameron Hume gleaned while assisting the Mozambican peace process as a principal representative of the United States. In a well written and insightful book, *Ending Mozambique's War*, Hume reached four main generalizable conclusions: a peace process should (1) "center attention on the core causes of the conflict," (2) "take place in a framework designed to build order," (3) "accelerate changes in the relations between the parties," and (4) ensure that the "process of dialogue and reconciliation continue beyond the signing of the agreement" (Hume 1994, 144-147). Undertaking such comprehensive economic, social, political, and military transformation is an enormous challenge, truly nothing short of attempting to "negotiate a revolution" (de Gruchy 1997).

In order to produce such agreements, however, Saunders argues that governments must begin to organize differently, both "substantively and politically." Citizens outside governments have an important and complementary role to play (Saunders 1996, 431).

Functional relationships are the sine qua non of sustainable peace. After all, a series of interim agreements may well culminate in a political settlement and the cessation of a conflict; however, good, functional relationships among adversaries are essential for implementing and sustaining a peace agreement (Laue 1991). Although such functional relationships are no guarantee of a successful implementation of a peace agreement, the lack thereof will unequivocally hinder all progress to that end. Therefore, we must attempt to improve the official negotiation process to deal more effectively with such needs, including enhancing coordination with Track II actors.

This suggests that, as it is necessary for the momentum supporting a peace process to be maintained, the (re-) establishment of functional relationships within divided societies cannot wait until after a formal peace agreement has been brokered. Rather, relationship building activity as a precursor to reconciliation should occur prior to and during the process of negotiating a peace agreement. After all, if peace is to be sustained, the modalities of the formal agreement must have former adversaries work closely together on sociocultural, economic, political, and military reconstruction efforts; if reconstruction is to succeed, more positive, functional relationships among former adversaries must develop. Additionally, relationship building and reconciliation activities should be recognized as formal objectives of an agreement, and the process of peacemaking should therefore be designed accordingly. Similarly, implementation mechanisms should take into account the need to further repair human relationships and to further the sociopolitical capacity for coexistence.

The negotiation *process* of reaching such an agreement should be strategically designed and implemented with an eye toward enhancing the foundations of a social infrastructure. Regrettably, official peacemaking seems to give greater attention (disproportionate to need) to the reconstruction of the *physical* infrastructure than to the *social* infrastructure. Moreover, the tasks of relationship building and reconciliation within divided societies should not be postponed until the postsettlement period and should not be left entirely to the unofficial sector.

Relationship Building and Reconciliation as Process and Outcome Objectives of Peace Negotiations

Metanoia, as a Christian construct, suggests "a change of heart" (Fox 1988, 6) or "a change of mind" (Arendt 1958, 240).[17] Referred to by the New Testament as "conversion," *metanoia* calls for "internal change that shows itself in practical conduct. . . . This interior transformation blossoms out into a change of awareness, vision, attitude, and conduct" (Gula 1984, 28-29). Although the biblical concept of conversion to God has relevance, conversion represents an apt metaphor for process of reconciliation when concurrently seen from a secular perspective as well.

In contrast with a strict theological approach, reconciliation in the context of protracted, violent, and sociopolitical situations is more than restoring an individual's sense of self, their relationship with God, and their relationship(s) with others as victim or aggressor. It is also about restoring a sense of community and purpose to society at large—spiritually, psychologically, and physically. Such reformation is centered on healing a society that has, in effect, through the ravages of war, become sick, dysfunctional, and in great need of physical reconstruction.

In this sense, the process of reconciliation is both restorative and constructive. Therefore, reconciliation is a three-pronged process of conversion and change that must occur within people, as individuals and groups, as well as in regard to the postsettlement reconstruction of society. Reconciliation, in one sense, is the reconstruction of relationships, which, in turn, constitute the thread necessary to reweave the social fabric of community *and* to (re)construct the physical infrastructure of the nation.[18] Both a strong social fabric and physical infrastructure are essential to support and yet serve as a complement to a functional state.

Analogous to the importance of timing and ripeness inherent to intervening in an active conflict, there are times when reconciliation efforts may be premature. People who have suffered great physical loss and psychological trauma need time to deal cognitively and emotionally with the idea of reconstructing relationships with those whom they hold responsible for their misfortune, sorrow, and suffering. As Dwyer (1999, 87) notes, "[I]ndividual psychological capacities may render reconciliation impossible for some." However, as John Menzies (a former U.S. Ambassador to Sarajevo during the war) noted about the former Yugoslavia, at a very practical level people may be willing and able to work through their anger and animosity. In effect, they may be able to "build down their differences" by accomplishing tasks representing the most basic functional aspects of normal social life, for example., agreeing to turn on water or electricity, or open telephone lines in a given neighborhood in which another ethnic group resides.[19] While reconciliation may be premature, basic functional cooperation may be possible and may serve as a precursor to reconciliation. Thus, although reconciliation and reconstruction represent distinct sets of activity, they are in many ways coterminous; each is necessary but not sufficient for a sustainable peace.[20] (See Galtung in this volume).

Reconciliation is also necessary for the design and implementation of mechanisms and systems to manage and resolve future disputes and conflict in a state marked by ethnic, if not also political, pluralism. Without the sustainability of a peace agreement that provides mechanisms to address both symptoms and causes of a chronically ill society, the reparation of societal breaches will be severely tested.

Considering factors such as lack of accountability, legitimacy, the breakdown of shared values and civil order that often results in the inability of the state to meet its obligations as a fair and just sovereign, and vice versa, brokering a formal peace agreement among the leaderships of former combatants is an imperative first step. It is equally imperative that this include confidence building and trust building and other efforts toward reconciliation among the leadership of former combatants, as either military factions or political parties.

Cambodia and several other countries currently suffer the consequences of the failure to pay attention to relationship building and reconciliation among the official negotiators. As a second step, striking a social contract that brings together again the disparate groups within civil society is just as critical. Eventually, a sustainable peace also requires striking a similar social contract between civil society and the state.[21]

Thus, it is postulated that reconciliation as a change of heart and mind must take place in three sociopolitical domains across three levels of relationships. Such transformation must (1) occur among the combatant signatories of an official peace agreement, (2) be inherent to a social contract that society must make with itself, and (3) be reflected in an eventual social contract between the state and civil society. Accordingly, relationship building and reconciliation must take place on an intrapersonal level, at an interpersonal level, and on an intergroup level. Relationship building and reconciliation are therefore multifaceted concerns of both the public and private realms over an extended period of time—the separation of state and civil society notwithstanding.

This premise represents a significant shift from the manner in which official peacemaking has traditionally occurred, one reason being that international attention toward intense violent conflict has, until recently, been heavily focused on conflict between states. In such situations, there was less need for reconciliation and relationship building in an immediate sense; détente was the default mechanism. Internally, various sectors of society pulled together to rebuild following the cessation of hostilities. Gradually, sufficient time would pass for the rebuilding of trust necessary for the avenues of relationships to again emanate from various sectors of society toward and eventually across borders, that is, post-World War II Franco-German relations (see Ackermann 1994). However, with virtually all violent conflict currently occurring within states (the vast majority of which are severely underdeveloped [see the recent editions of the Ploughshares Armed Conflict Report]), adversaries—including their "constituents"—must begin immediately to work much more closely and cooperatively if the nation is to have any chance of meaningful physical reconstruction. And if a divided society is to "pull together," the relationships among its members must again become more positive, more functional—hence, the concurrent need to reconstruct the social infrastructure.

Thus, there must be a change in the way the antagonists view the nature of the conflict, options for dealing peacefully with such hostility, the perceptions of their role in the conflict, their perceptions of other relevant actors, and their relationship with those other actors. In other words, if a peace is to be sustained, individuals—as official negotiators or as an everyday-human-as-neighbor—must undergo a change of heart and mind. Like conflict transformation, the journey toward reconciliation and a sustainable peace must begin with individual change and must be predicated on a sense of trust and imbued with a sense of hope.

Trust Building

Living and working in trust frees people to accept the responsibilities of relationships, to embrace a sense of personal and social responsibility, and, in so doing, acknowledge and accept a moral responsibility for one another and for their respective constituents. To live and work in trust is to have the capacity to hope for and believe in a better future than the continuation of war and existential politics. To not do so is to give way to the fear and anger inherent to mistrust. Fear leads a person to shirk such responsibilities, as it "is suspicious of all that makes up life. Fear builds walls of protection, seeks the control of domination, and the power of manipulation" (Gula 1984, 20). Separation, suspicion, and estrangement not only characterize life ruled by fear, but also capture well unfortunate and pervasive aspects of the Paris peace process.

Trust, as Schreiter (1992, 36) writes, is concurrently both an intrapersonal act and a transactional phenomenon. As such, both the act of trusting (because it involves considerable risk) and violence leave people quite vulnerable. Moreover, both the foundations and the mortar of community and society are built entirely on trust. Violence, by betraying both acts of trust and the very ability to trust, chisels and cracks those foundations. Peace agreements are in fact a blueprint for the reconstruction of a war-torn society, it is imperative that the foundations of that society be anchored by the (re)generation of trust among the political and military leadership represented at the bargaining table.

Enhancing trust should serve to help illuminate and clarify the significance of decision making surrounding the allocation of resources, as overcoming fear and mistrust are deeply interrelated and critical to moving toward a lasting peace; inadequate attention to these factors will indeed hinder or prevent all such progress. For example, the UN's inability to disarm the Cambodian factions was intimately linked with the mistrust of one another and the peace process exhibited among the factions' leaders. Although one would not normally think of disarmament in this light, disarming is truly an act of reconciliation; through such action, each side gives permission to begin trusting the other.

Rediscovering Self and the Other

Like the transactional dimension of trust being dependent on another, the notion of self is also other-dependent. Consequently, for the transactions of trust building and reconciliation to take place, understanding who the "other" is and how that sense of otherness was constructed is critical.[22] In other words, it is important to identify those events, behaviors, perceptions, values, and judgments that enabled "us" *to make them* "other" if this form of alienation is to be overcome (Lederach 1999). This is a fundamental ingredient for (re)constructing relationships, community, and society in the name of reconciliation and the pursuit of a lasting peace.

A number of aspects integral to the process of religious conversion are relevant to the type of intense (and sometimes secular) transformation that must occur for peace to be sustained. However, there must first be a conscious decision to alter old images of our selves and our world. A sense of moving on, of letting go, of being mindful that we have changed, and a desire to not be as we were before must come about. Correspondingly, individuals must rediscover or reappropriate meaning in their lives in order for past, present, and future experiences and relationships to be integrated into a new perspective. This letting go of what is no longer significant or "life-giving" allows us to make room for that which is new.

Such change, Montville (1993) argues, can only occur if individuals are willing to acknowledge past behavior, claim responsibility, and demonstrate contrition or remorse. This ability to envision new self-images as individuals and in relation to others is critical. Conversion of this nature, Gula argues (1984), is predicated on the reformation of imagination; seeing anew allows people to understand critically what has happened to them and to think creatively about what is possible in the future. In this manner, negotiating counterparts would be able to generate an interpenetration of perspective into one another's respective experiences. This exchange is more than simply generating empathy, though. It is a process which "involves a hermeneutical relocation whereby we see, hear, and understand in a different way" (Villa-Vicencio 1997, 34). As Gula concludes, "Reconciliation cannot happen without these new images and the power they release to recreate not only personal relationships, but also the whole of our society" (1984, 35).

This type of change is not typical to official peace negotiations. Concerted attention must be paid to the human dynamics of relationship building in the processes leading to the table as well as while at the table. This is not to suggest that such endeavors are beyond the scope of negotiators or the negotiation process. Peace negotiations should, to the extent possible, pay attention to the need to engender a sense of personal conversions predicated on trust, hope, and forgiveness among the adversaries-as-negotiators. However, formal negotiations should also not get bogged down by an over emphasis on relationship building. Accordingly, the structure through which official peacemaking is pursued must be transformed to include mechanisms designed to address deeper, underlying *causes* of conflict, including the need to improve human relationships. For enemies to engage in a cooperative relationship to reconstruct a functional and just society, a fundamental rethinking of both the purpose of peace negotiations and how they are structured is required. Some of the questions that need to be posed are: Who is involved in such negotiations? What should the process of negotiating look like? To what degree can and should a negotiation process endeavor to specifically shore up the social infrastructure as well as the political and physical infrastructures? To what degree should official negotiations address concerns and issues relevant to the interpersonal relationship among the negotiating adversaries?

As previously suggested, a major consideration for dealing with contemporary internal conflict is how to best enable former enemies and divided societies to learn how not just to live in the shadow of a peace agreement but to cooperate side by side in (re)constructing a functional and just society—including the institutionalization of participatory politics. This requires a fundamental rethinking of both the purpose of peace negotiations and how they are structured. Who is involved in such negotiations? What should the process of negotiating look like? Is the purpose of official negotiation to exact promises of behavioral change sans any accompanying attitudinal or value-based change? Is the purpose to simply stop the fighting and provide a basic outline for the reconstruction of a ravaged society, leaving for the implementation process the real challenge of navigating the significant gaps between the idealized terms of the agreement and the actual reality of daily life? To what degree can and should a negotiation process endeavor to specifically shore up the social infrastructure as well as the political and physical infrastructures? To what degree should official negotiations address concerns and issues relevant to the interpersonal relationship among the negotiating adversaries? Likewise, to what degree should the terms of any agreement include mechanisms to address similar dynamics within society?

Regrettably, practitioners of traditional diplomacy have tended to look upon the calls of the conflict resolution community for relationship building and reconciliation as being an emotional appeal for dealing with emotional problems. Psychosocial concerns have been too easily dismissed as not terribly relevant to the immediate needs of dealing with disputes between sovereigns over power and resources. Attending to the quality of human relationships has often been viewed as "soft politics" (well meaning but "touchy-feely"), especially when compared to the "hard politics" traditionally associated with cease-fires; disarmament and demobilization; questions of territorial control; technical and political aspects of refugee and internally displaced people (IDP) returns; resource allocations; power-sharing formulas and technical aspects of staging elections; and macroeconomic reconstruction and reform.

The appeal to include a focus on human relationships should not, however, be understood as a naive supplication of those peddling soft politics. Rather, such counsel should be understood on an *in-context* basis.[23] It is in this sense, notes Robert Seiple—a veteran bombardier of the Vietnam War and president of World Vision International—that reconciliation "needs to be incarnated in real world situations. Lighter-than-air idealism without tangible demonstration will betray both hope and opportunity" (1994, 11).

Thus, relationship building and reconciliation should be considered from both a strategic and tactical vantage point, as improving relationships based on trust, hope, and forgiveness is important and highly complicated. It is critical, however, to keep in mind that reconciliation transcends forgiveness.[24] As Wink (1998, 14) notes, "[F]orgiveness can be unilateral; reconciliation is always mutual." Additionally, forgiveness can take place within the heart and mind; reconciliation, though, because of the relational context, must be embodied in deed as well (see Wink 1998). Therefore, relationship building and reconciliation must be also viewed as specific outcome objectives of a peace process, not just as strategic and tactical elements of negotiation. Hence, the negotiation process must be designed to include mechanisms for enhancing relationship building and reconciliation, and the outcome (an official agreement) must include terms and modalities to expressly further relationship building and reconciliation during postsettlement implementation.

Guiding such social and political change peacefully will require both a concerted and creative approach toward developing and/or maintaining crucial relationships and coordinating better activities among bodies politic across the official/unofficial divide as it exists within and between countries. The real challenge, however, is not just how to bridge the official/unofficial worlds in general, but how to incorporate a changing and expanded relationship-based philosophy toward sustainable peace and *geosocial* politics into the practical, hard-nosed reality of official, binding negotiations, whose overarching milieu remains based on *realpolitik*.

Conclusion

It is hopefully quite apparent that peace negotiations, such as the 1991 Paris Accords governing the Cambodian conflict, should no longer be designed and carried out exclusively within a *geopolitcal* paradigm, if the objective is to do more than simply stop the fighting. Rather, an additional orientation, best described as *geosocial politics,* must supplement such endeavors. Quite simply, internal conflicts are usually fought over issues of structural and resource control; consequently, peace negotiations and peace agreements tend to focus on such issues because they are perceived to be the source of the conflict. However, such issues can also be seen as secondary expressions of the relationships which lie at the center of conflict—structural and resource problems can also be considered "symptoms of underlying causes" (Kraybill 1996, 111).

An approach to peacemaking based on an operating framework grounded on the as-of-yet-loose notions of *geosocial politics* reverses these *realpolitik*-based assumptions. "The purpose of politics is relationships," Kraybill explains. Politics is naturally concerned with resource allocation and structural power arrangements. However, these factors "are not ends in themselves, their purpose is to support just and satisfying relationships" (Kraybill 1996, 111). In this sense, politics should be defined as "how humans 'get along' with each other in spite of their conflicts. . . . Politics can be, ought to be about the business of learning how to live with neighbors, some too different to be likable, [yet] who have too many interests in common with us to be dismissed from our civic company" (Shriver 1995, 3-6). Thus, a fundamental tenet of this alternative paradigm (*geosocial politics*) calls for the "conscious conduct [of] politics in the service of relationships" (Kraybill 111).

In essence, if a lasting peace is to be consolidated, reconciliation—as a change of heart and mind—must eventually take place in three relationship domains. First, a change of heart and mind must take place among the combatant signatories of an official peace agreement and their respective leadership cadres. Second, a social contract must be struck among the various groups within society; a state of reconciliation among these groups is necessary for maintaining such a social contract, itself necessary for a sustainable peace. Finally, relationship building and reconciliation are necessary precursors for brokering the more traditional social contract between the state and civil society. Reconciliation within this third domain, though, is probably not possible without reconciliation occurring in the first two domains. Although reconciliation in the second domain does not entirely depend on parallel success within the first domain, the rehabilitation and reconstruction of society will be severely impeded by an unstable environment marked by violent competition for political power and control.

Consequently, appropriate consideration must be given to the design and implementation of a peace process that takes into account the need for change to occur on an intrapersonal, interpersonal, and intergroup basis in the context of enhancing relationships among a wide range of key individuals. This is especially salient when power sharing is an explicit outcome objective of any given peace negotiation.

Somehow bridges must be built, breaches mended, and gaps narrowed. A process of reparation, of *drawing back together*, of restoring a sense of trust—restoring even the most basic faith in the possible existence of goodwill (moral will)—must be brought about. In this sense, the leaderships of parties to a conflict (along with their respective constituents) must learn to trust both each other and the peace process itself. In many instances, it may be initially easier to trust the latter than the former. Consequently, the process of negotiating peace in civil wars must be broadened to better help achieve such confluence. Given the track record of such negotiations, there is no reason not to try a different approach.

Notes

1. Quoted in Norman A. Graebner, "Public Opinion and Foreign Policy: A Pragmatic View." In *Interaction: Foreign Policy and Public Policy*, Don C. Piper and Ronald J. Terchek, eds., Washington, D.C.: American Enterprise Institute, 1983.

2. In fact, there is not even agreement on what to call this stage of a conflict. For example, the UN and the World Bank prefer the term *postconflict* to *postsettlement*. The former term is literally inappropriate, however, as few violent sociopolitical conflicts are truly resolved by a political accord having been reached. Such wishful thinking is not unique to the Bretton-Woods system, though. For example, Rothchild (1997, 2) concludes that many "[s]eemingly intractable ethnic-related conflicts have been concluded in recent years by means of negotiations." His list of sixteen examples contain

numerous countries where civil war still wages, as well as ones where all-out civil war has been terminated but where lower-level violence remains as many of the deeper causes of conflict have not been resolved.

3. See Sisk (1996) for an excellent review of the theory and application of power sharing approaches.

4. The lack of a power sharing option was a major determinant in Savimbi's decision for the National Union for the Total Liberation of Angola (UNITA) to breach the 1991 settlement that temporarily ended Angola's civil war. The inclusion of a power sharing option was a major component of the 1994 Lusaka agreement that terminated the renewed fighting. On the other hand, despite the fact that power-sharing in Cambodia (suggested and brokered by King Sihanouk following a threat of a seven-province secession on the part of the Cambodian Peoples' Party (CPP) after it lost the May 1993 elections) between the CPP (led by the second prime minister, Hun Sen) and the FUNCINPEC party (led by the first prime minister, Prince Ranariddh) lasted until July 1997, both co-prime ministers have stated that the power-sharing approach has not worked and that no such arrangements would be considered for the upcoming elections in 1998. The purging of Ranariddh by Hun Sen during the July 1997 coup bears out the arguments on the limitations of power sharing, the fragility of negotiated settlements, and the immense challenge of the democratization process.

5. I have avoided the term *civil society* because Cambodia has not historically had a civil society, as the term is generally used in the West—although the philosophic and physical seeds of such are beginning to take root.

6. Provisions were being made to integrate Khmer Rouge (KR) defectors only into the army; there were no current plans, though, to provide any positions within the civilian government. Moreover, the two ruling parties were competing to attract defectors into their respective armed forces; this competition was a major factor in Hun Sen's decision to stage a "military crackdown against such illegal activity" (his terminology).

7. Personal interviews with Om Radsady, chair, Foreign Affairs Commission of the Cambodian National Assembly (March 25, 1997); Kao Kim Hourn, executive director of the Cambodian Institute for Cooperation and Peace—a recently established, semiautonomous think tank (March 27, 1997); Ok Serei Sopheak, chief of cabinet to the second prime minister of the Interior (March 27, 1997); and Nanda Pok, executive director, Women for Prosperity, an indigenous NGO working to promote women's participation in positions of leadership (March 28, 1997). It should be noted that Sopheak thought that while much more trust and relationship building needs to be accomplished, identifiable progress was being made at that time.

8. Sirivudh had been in exile for having allegedly masterminded a failed coup attempt and plotting to assassinate Hun Sen.

9. Reuters News Service, January 4, 1997 (taken from Internet service, Camnews v.001.n187, January 7, 1997).

10. Personal conversation with Prince Sirivudh at the U.S. Institute of Peace, Washington, D.C., February 21, 1997. This was confirmed during a personal conversation with Ok Serei Sopheak, March 25, 1997.

11. Written speech delivered at a working conference on Cambodia, sponsored by The Asia Society and The Asia Foundation and held at Johns Hopkins University's School of Advanced International Studies in Washington, D.C., March 23-25, 1997.

12. Prince Sihanouk first requested such assistance in the middle of July 1991.

13. The creation and deployment of a Conflict Analysis and Resolution Team (CART) would provide an additional mechanism designed to help achieve a variety of

objectives related to a sustainable peace. The CART should be comprised of individuals representing different functional areas of expertise, that is, a political component, a military component, humanitarian relief, democratization, human rights, conflict resolution, rule of law, religion, and so on. The exact composition and size could vary according to the particular situational needs; however, the team should be of manageable size and have a core foundation of conflict resolution expertise. The composition could be homogenous, that is, representing one government (or an organizational body) and serving as an interagency tool. A heterogeneous composition could further enhance coordination efforts within the larger international community. Finally, whenever appropriate, the CART should include local representatives. Specifically, the mandate of a CART should be related to a more comprehensive assessment of the psychosocial elements and how they in turn affect and are affected by the more traditional political-military elements. Similarly, a CART should be utilized *during* a peace operation in order to feed recommendations into the ongoing strategic planning and operational policy processes. This is particularly important during the postsettlement implementation phase, which is where the most difficult battle for sustainable peace is waged. For example, a CART could have been deployed during Paris peace negotiations and/or during the predeployment planning of the peace operation to feed information back into the negotiation and/or implementation planning process as well as to test ideas and/or evaluate elements of the actual implementation.

14. Personal interview with Richard Solomon, Washington, D.C., April 1998.

15. The concept and application of relationship building and reconciliation is further explored below. For now, it is sufficient to state that reconciliation is essentially about the reconstruction of relationships, which, in turn, constitute the most basic material necessary to both reweave the social fabric of community and to (re)construct the physical infrastructure of the nation. In this sense, the process of reconciliation is both restorative and constructive. However, for any transformation to occur, a change of awareness, attitude, and conduct must begin on an individual basis and eventually spread to the collective. Consequently, reconciliation should be explored as a process of conversion and change that must occur within people, as individuals and groups, as well as in regard to the postsettlement reconstruction of society.

16. This supposition was confirmed by eight current or former highly senior U.S. government officials, each of whom has been deeply involved in peacemaking efforts.

17. Arendt refers to the connotations attached to the New Testament Greek term *metanoein* in Luke 17:3-4. She suggests that it also renders the Hebrew *shuv*—to return, or to trace back one's steps, as opposed to repentance.

18. Under normal circumstances the organized collective of families (households) is what we call *society* and the political form of such organization is what we call the *nation* (see Arendt 1958, 28-29), whereas the term *state* refers to the formal structures of governance constructed to guide and serve the nation.

19. Personal interview, June 20, 1997.

20. Although functional cooperation may under certain conditions and to varying degrees precede full reconciliation, such cooperation should be construed as part of the larger processes of relationship building and reconciliation, especially at a communal level. Though the role of reconstruction in the reconciliation process is not explored here, it must suffice at this point to suggest that the type of sustained, major (re)construction necessary to rebuild war-torn societies is unlikely to occur without significant progress in reconciliation.

21. Civil society is comprised of the corporeal networks of associations and organizations and their analogous sociocultural, economic, and political interests and values that permit individual and collective participation in the processes that determine the mechanisms of governance and the manner in which they function. It is recognized that the Western concept of civil society does not apply to all societies; in some cases it may be more appropriate to speak of a "public realm."

22. The notion of "otherness" is a constitutive dimension for both individualistic and collectivistic cultures. However, it is very important to understand whether people develop their identity largely on the basis of an individualistic view of self or on a collectivistic basis where their concept of who they are is only definable in relation to others.

23. This parallels Goffman's (1972) analysis of behavior in a *behavior-in-context* approach and Knorr-Cetina's (1988) adaptation to understanding situational dynamics on the basis of a *situation-in-context* approach.

24. Dwyer (1999) suggests that reconciliation is actually quite distinct from forgiveness.

References

Ackermann, A. 1994. Reconciliation as a Peace-Building Process in Postwar Europe: The Franco-German Case. *Peace and Change*, vol. 19, no. 3, pp. 229-250.

Arendt, H. 1958. *The Human Condition*. Chicago: University of Chicago Press.

Ball, N. 1996. *Making Peace Work: The Role of the International Development Community*. Washington, D.C.: Overseas Development Council.

Boutros-Ghali, B. 1995. *An Agenda for Development*. New York: United Nations.

———. 1994. *Building Peace and Development: Annual Report on the Work of the Organization*. New York: United Nations.

———. 1993. *An Agenda for Peace*. New York: United Nations.

Chopra, J. 1999. *Peace Maintenance: The Evolution of International Political Authority*. New York: Routledge.

———. 1994. *United Nations Authority in Cambodia*. Occasional Paper No. 15, Watson Institute for International Studies, Brown University.

Colletta, N. J., Kostner, M., and Wiederhofer, I. 1996. *The Transition from War to Peace in Sub-Saharan Africa*. Washington, D.C.: World Bank.

Crocker, C. A., and Hampson, F. O. 1996. Making Peace Settlements Work. *Foreign Policy*, vol. 104 (fall), pp. 54–71.

Crocker C. A., Hampson, F. O., and Aall, P., eds. 1996. *Managing Global Chaos: Sources of and Responses to International Conflict*. Washington, D.C.: United States Institute of Peace Press.

de Gruchy, J. W. 1997. The Dialectic of Reconciliation: Church and the Transition to Democracy in South Africa. In *The Reconciliation of Peoples: Challenge to the Churches*. G. Baum and H. Wells, eds. Maryknoll, N.Y.: Orbis Books.

de Soto, A., and del Castillo, G. 1994. Obstacles to Peacebuilding. *Foreign Policy* vol. 94 (spring), pp. 69-83.

Doyle, M. W. 1995. *UN Peacekeeping in Cambodia: UNTAC's Civil Mandate*. International Peace Academy Occasional Paper Series. Boulder, Colo.: Lynne Rienner.

———. 1994. "UNTAC: Sources of Success and Failure." In *International Peacekeeping: Building on the Cambodian Experience*. H. Smith, ed. Canberra, Australia: Australian Defense Studies Centre.

Dwyer, S. 1999. Reconciliation for Realists. *Ethics and International Affairs*, vol. 19, pp. 81–98.

Fisher, R. J. 1995. Pacific, Impartial Third-Party Intervention in International Conflict: A Review and an Analysis. In *Beyond Confrontation: Learning Conflict Resolution in the Post Cold War Era*. J. A. Vasquez, et al., eds. Chicago: University of Chicago Press.

Fox, M. 1988. *The Coming of the Cosmic Christ*. San Fransisco: Harper.

Gastrow, P. 1995. *Bargaining for Peace: South Africa and the National Peace Accord*. Washington, D.C.: United States Institute of Peace Press.

Goffman, E. 1972. The Neglected Situation. In *Language and Social Context*. P. P. Giglioli, ed. Harmundsworth, Middx: Penguin.

Gula, R. M. 1984. *To Walk Together Again: The Sacrament of Reconciliation*. New York: Paulist Press.

Haas, M. 1991a. *Genocide by Proxy: Cambodian Pawn on a Superpower Chessboard*. New York: Praeger Publications.

———. 1991b. *Cambodia, Pol Pot and the United States: The Faustian Pact*. New York: Praeger Publications.

Hampson, F. O. 1996. *Nurturing Peace: Why Peace Settlements Succeed or Fail*. Washington, D.C.: United States Institute of Peace Press.

Horowitz, D. L. 1985. *Ethnic Groups in Conflict*. Berkeley, Calif.: University of California Press.

Hume, C. 1994. *Ending Mozambique's War: The Role of Mediation and Good Offices*. Washington, D.C.: United States Institute of Peace Press.

Kelman, H. C. 1996. Negotiation as Interactive Problem Solving. *International Negotiation: A Journal of Theory and Practice*, vol. 1, no. 1, pp. 99-123.

Kiman, U. 1995. Cambodia: Our Experience with the United Nations. *Pacifica Review*, vol. 7, no. 2, pp. 61–68.

Knorr-Cetina, K. 1988. The Micro-Social Order: Toward a Reconception. In *Actions and Structure: Research Methods and Social Theory*. N. Fielding, ed. London: Sage Publications.

Koh, T. T. B. 1990. The Paris Conference on Cambodia: A Multilateral Negotiation that Failed. *Negotiation Journal*, vol. 6, no. 1.

Kraybill, S. 1996. An Anabaptist Paradigm for Conflict Transformation: Critical Reflections on Peacemaking in Zimbabwe. Unpublished Ph.D. dissertation, Department of Religious Studies, University of Cape Town, South Africa.

Kumar, K., ed. 1997. *Rebuilding Societies after Civil War: Critical Roles for International Assistance*. Boulder, Colo.: Lynne Rienner.

Laue, J. H. 1991. Contributions of the Emerging Field of Conflict Resolution. In *Approaches to Peace: An Intellectual Map*. W. S. Thompson and K. M. Jensen, eds. Washington, D.C.: United States Institute of Peace Press.

Lederach, J. P. 1999. *The Journey toward Reconciliation*. Scottsdale, Pa.: Herald Press.

———. 1998. *Building Peace: Sustainable Reconciliation in Divided Societies*. Washington, D.C.: United States Institute of Peace Press.

———. 1995. Beyond Violence: Building Sustainable Peace. In *Beyond Violence*, A. Williamson, ed. Belfast, Ireland: Community Relations Council.

Licklider, R. 1995. The Consequences of Negotiated Settlements in Civil Wars, 1945-1993. *American Political Science Review*, vol. 89, no. 3, pp. 681–690.

Maynard, K. A. 1999. *Healing Communities in Conflict: International Assistance in Complex Emergencies*. New York: Colombia University Press.

———. 1997. Rebuilding Community: Psychosocial Healing, Reintegration, and Reconciliation at the Grassroots Level. In *Rebuilding Societies after Civil War: Critical Roles for International Assistance*. K. Kumar, ed. Boulder, Colo.: Lynne Rienner.

Montville, J. 1993. The Healing Function in Political Conflict Resolution. In *Conflict Resolution Theory and Practice: Integration and Application*. D. Sandole and H. van der Merwe, eds. Manchester, U.K.: Manchester University Press.

Moser-Puangsuwan, Y. 1995. UN Peacekeeping in Cambodia: Whose Needs Were Met. *Pacifica Review*, vol. 7, no. 2, 103-127.

Oakely, R. B., and Dziedzic, M. J. 1998. Conclusions. In *Policing the New World Disorder: Peace Operations and Public Security*. R. B. Oakley, M. J. Dziedzic, and E. M. Goldberg, eds. Washington, D.C.: National Defense University Press.

Project Ploughshares. 1995. *Armed Conflicts Report 1995*. Waterloo, Ontario: Institute of Peace and Conflict Studies, Conrad Grebel College.

———. 1996. *Armed Conflicts Report 1996*. Waterloo, Ontario: Institute of Peace and Conflict Studies, Conrad Grebel College.

Rasmussen, J. L. 1998. *Negotiating a Revolution: Transforming the Orthodoxy of International Relations toward the Resolution of Violent Socio-Political Conflict*. Ann Arbor, Mich.: UMI Dissertation Services.

———. 1997. Peacemaking in the Twenty-First Century: New Rules, New Roles, New Actors. In *Peacemaking in International Conflict: Methods and Techniques*. I. W. Zartman and J. L. Rasmussen, eds. Washington, D.C.: United States Institute of Peace Press.

———, and Oakley, R. B. 1992. *Conflict Resolution in the Middle East: Simulating a Diplomatic Negotiation between Israel and Syria*. Washington, D.C.: United States Institute of Peace Press.

Ratner, S. R. 1993. The Cambodia Settlement Agreements. *The American Journal of International Law*, vol. 87, no. 1, pp. 1–41.

———. 1990. *Turbulence in World Politics: A Theory of Change and Continuity*. Princeton, N.J.: Princeton University Press.

Rothchild, D. 1997. Ethnic Bargaining and the Management of Intense Conflict. *International Negotiation: A Journal of Theory and Practice*, vol. 2, no. 1, pp. 1-20.

Saunders, H. H. 1996. Prenegotiation and Circum-Negotiation: Arenas of the Peace Process. In *Managing Global Chaos: Sources of and Responses to International Conflict*. C. A. Crocker, F. O. Hampson, with P. Aall, eds. Washington, D.C.: United States Institute of Peace Press.

———. 1985. We Need a Larger Theory of Negotiation: The Importance of Prenegotiating Phases. *Negotiation Journal*, vol. 1, no. 3.

———. 1984. The Prenegotiation Phase. In *International Negotiation: Art and Science*. D. B. Bendahmane and J. W. McDonald, eds. Washington, D.C.: Foreign Service Institute, U.S. Deparment of State.

Schreiter, R. J. 1992. *Reconciliation: Mission and Ministry in a Changing Social Order*. Maryknoll, N.Y.: Orbis Books.

Seiple, C. 1996. *The U.S. Military/NGO Relationship in Humanitarian Interventions*. Carlisle, Pa.: U.S. Army Peacekeeping Institute.

Seiple, R. A. 1994. Reconciliation: A Return to Vietnam. In *Reconciliation in Difficult Places: Dealing with Our Deepest Differences*. Monrovia, Calif.: Office of Advocacy and Education, World Vision.

Shaw, T. M. 1996. Beyond Post-Conflict Peacebuilding: What Links to sustainable Development and Human Security. *International Peacekeeping*, vol. 3, no. 2, pp. 3-16.

Shriver, D. W., Jr. 1995. *An Ethic for Enemies: Forgiveness in Politics*. New York: Oxford University Press.

Sisk, T. D. 1996. *Powersharing and International Mediation in Ethnic Conflicts*. Washington, D.C.: United States Institute of Peace Press.

Solomon, R. H. 1999. Bringing Peace to Cambodia. In *Herding Cats: Multiparty Mediation in a Complex World*. C. A. Crocker et al., eds. Washington, D.C.: United States Institute of Peace Press.

Stedman, S. J., and Rothchild, D. 1996. Peace Operations: From Short-term to Long-term Commitment. *International Peacekeeping*, vol. 3, no. 2, pp. 17-35.

UN Department of Public Information. 1992. *Agreements on a Comprehensive Political Settlement of the Cambodia Conflict*. New York: UN Department of Public Education.

UNIDR (United Nations Institute for Disarmament Research). 1996. *Managing Arms in Peace Processes: Cambodia*. Geneva, Switzerland: UNIDR.

USAID (United States Agency for International Development). 1999. *Promoting Social Reconciliation in Postconflict Societies: Selected Lessons from USAID's Experience*. USAID Program and Operations Assessment Report No. 24. Washington, D.C.: Center for Development Information and Evaluation, USAID.

Villa-Vicencio, C. 1997. Telling One Another Stories: Toward a Theology of Reconciliation. In *The Reconciliation of Peoples: Challenge to the Churches*. G. Baum and H. Wells, eds. Maryknoll, N.Y.: Orbis Books.

Wallensteen, P., and Sollenberg, M. 1999. Armed Conflict, 1989–98. *Journal of Peace Research*, vol. 36, no. 5, pp. 593-606.

———. 1997. Armed Conflicts, Conflict Termination and Peace Agreements, 1989–96. *Journal of Peace Research*, vol. 34, no. 3, pp. 339-358.

———. 1995. After the Cold War: Emerging Patterns of Armed Conflict, 1989–1994. *Journal of Peace Research*, vol. 32, no. 3, pp. 345-60.

Wink, W. 1998. *When the Powers Fall: Reconciliation and the Healing of Nations*. Minneapolis, Minn.: Augsburg Fortress Press.

World Bank. 1998. *Post-Conflict Reconstruction: The Role of the World Bank*. Washington, D.C.: World Bank.

Zartman, I. W., and Rasmussen, J. L., eds. 1997. *Peacemaking in International Conflict: Methods and Techniques*. Washington, D.C.: United States Institute of Peace Press.

7

Justice and the Burdens of History

Joseph V. Montville

Justice may be one of the most useful concepts in coming to grips with the challenge of peacebuilding. A good deal of the discussion of justice focuses on retribution, how a social system protects its members from various forms of harm, or transgressions by other members. Here, the threat and imposition of punishment against perpetrators is seen as basic to the functioning of a society. Recently, there has been increasing interest in the concept of restorative justice that goes beyond simple punishment to seeking healing of conflicted relationships as the most reliable way of defending against recurrence of crime. This chapter deals with an aspect of restorative justice as it relates psychologically to the dignity and self-esteem of individuals and the design of reconciliation strategies for peacemaking.

In its most general sense, justice implies order and morality. That is, justice means predictability in the daily life of a community and its individual members and the observance of basic rules governing right and wrong behavior. Justice serves the interests of life and the advancement of the human species, because it is perhaps the most fundamental element of peace. Indeed, it is a truism that there is no peace without justice. But from both a moral and dynamic perspective, it is very important to define peace and justice not only as the absence of war and the enforcement of laws, but also as progress toward the optimum environment for the fulfillment of human developmental potential.

Observers of human behavior in society, from Hobbes and Marx to Freud and Durkheim, have worked to construct analytical theories to predict human behavior and the course of politics and history. More recently, the eclectic community of scholars who have created the discipline of political psychology has illuminated the conceptual landscape by combining the knowledge of human development and motivation with the knowledge of social systems and institutions. One of political psychology's most important contributions has been the development of human needs theory to explain the biological and psychosocial imperatives of human existence and how frustration of natural instincts and needs leads to conflict and reactive violence. Human needs theory is essential to understanding the genesis of political conflict in general and of ethnic and sectarian conflict and violence in particular. It is also critical to the design of effective conflict resolution intervention strategies in the cause of genuine peace and justice.

Human Needs and the Defense of the Self

Adapting Abraham Maslow's (1954) graduated listing of needs genetic to every human being, there are (1) the basic physical survival needs for food, shelter, clothing, reasonable health, and safety from attack. Then come (2) the relational or social needs for affection and connectedness to nuclear family and wider identity group. The more psychologically complex needs for self-esteem and the esteem of others—for dignity—which are critical for a basic sense of security follow as (3), and the self-actualization stage, or the opportunity to fulfill one's developmental potential, is at (4) humankind's luxury aspiration.

In preindustrial societies, the possibilities for individuals discovering their gifts for science, the arts, scholarship, athletics, or other life skills are harshly limited by the need to devote most of their waking hours to securing enough food and maintaining shelter to stay alive and physically functional. In industrial societies there are far more opportunities to discover individual talents because of the division of labor and variety of specialties the marketplace and community require. Yet even in these cases, sudden loss of a job or serious illness quickly knocks one back down to the level of survival anxiety unless there are family or social safety nets that guarantee basic needs regardless of the individual's ability to earn. Thus, as James Chowning Davies (1986) puts it,

> Physical needs are well secured only where people are living in the most developed, integrated, prosperous, interdependent, and nonviolent industrialized societies—and only among perhaps ten to twenty percent of the people living in these advanced, emancipated societies. It has taken more than four hundred years—from the wars of the Reformation to the second generation after World War II—to secure the good life for what remains a minority in the most orderly and open conditions. (51)

Davies also notes the sense of powerlessness that accompanies the inability of the vast majority of people to secure their basic physical and esteem needs. It is clear that this level of analysis raises the broadest issues of social and distributive justice that are beyond the scope of this chapter. The focus here is on identity and esteem needs, which are extremely vulnerable to political violence and aggression. Sadly, for many nations and peoples, traumatic loss dominates their memory of history. It is these losses, these wounds, that constitute the burdens of history and the enduring sense of injustice that make peacebuilding so difficult for traditional diplomats and political leaders.

The psychology of victimhood is an automatic product of aggression and resultant traumatic loss in individuals and peoples. The refusal of aggressors to acknowledge the pain of the hurts inflicted on victims, and therefore the absence of remorse by the aggressors, creates an overwhelming sense of injustice in the victims. A society, a leadership, a world, and, indeed, a universe the victims had heretofore assumed would shield them from harm have all let them down. Their new psychology would henceforth keep the victimized people highly suspicious and on permanent alert for future acts of aggression and violence. It would also make them strongly resistant to pressures to make peace before the aggressors acknowledge the victims' losses and ask forgiveness for their violence. The victims' collective sense of security in their identity, their self-concept, their basic dignity, and a future for their children have been dealt a devastating blow.

This concept of victimhood psychology is derived from dynamic or depth psychology, especially the subfield called ego psychology or psychology of the self. But it is interesting, and gratifying, to note that some specialists in philosophy and law have come to similar conclusions about the impact of the harm caused by criminal acts to the victim's self. Thus, Jeffrie Murphy (1988), dealing with the issues of forgiveness, mercy, and justice, sees the resentment in victims of crime, and their consequent demand for retributive justice, as defense, above all, of the self. Murphy writes,

> In my view, resentment (in its range from righteous anger to righteous hatred) functions primarily in defense, not of all moral values and norms, but rather of certain values of the self. . . . I am suggesting that the primary value defended by the passion of resentment is self-respect, that proper self-respect is essentially tied to the passion of resentment. (16)

Gregory (1978), emeritus professor of psychiatry at the Harvard Medical School, has written from the perspective of a clinician at a community-based psychiatry department at Cambridge Hospital. In *Man's Aggression: The Defense of the Self*, Rochlin reported on his experience in treating patients in addition to his scholarly research. He found that insults to or aggression against the self-concept produced an automatic reactive aggression in defense of the self. His thesis is that narcissism, which he defined as love of the self, is a fundamental part of the human being's psychological security system. Narcissism is critical to the defense of the self. Thus, when the love of the self is jolted either through threat or insult, especially physical assault, there is an automatic, fear-based psychophysiological reaction. Everett Worthington (1999) has described the fear-based stress response system of the victim as elevations in epinephrine, corticosteroids, and other stress hormones. This stress-response system can be mobilized by the sight of the aggressor, by hearing sounds associated with him or them, or simply through recalling from memory the original threat or attack.

The initial reaction of the victim is to avoid or withdraw from the offender. If this is not possible, then anger (narcissistic rage), retaliation, or fighting (in defense of the wounded self) occurs. And, as Worthington writes, "if such fighting is unwise, self-destructive, or futile, the person might exhibit the human equivalent of a submissive gesture—depression, which declares that the person is weak or helpless and needs succor; depression usually elicits help and inhibits aggression" (113-114). It should be noted that animals show similar patterns of flight, fight, or surrender as part of an instinctive physical defense system when under attack.

Thus, in victimhood psychology, the individual or group, which by definition has sustained traumatic loss, is overwhelmed with a sense of existential injustice, and yet, in the absence of acknowledgment and remorse from the aggressor, still fears further attacks. Memory sustains fear, which activates stress-related hormones, which overall mobilize individuals or groups into militance in defense of the self. In this high state of narcissistic rage, sense of injustice, basic distrust, and continual fear, it is little wonder that ethnic and sectarian conflict has always been and continues to be so resistant to traditional diplomacy and negotiating processes. As with individual victims of trauma, peoples and nations require complex healing processes to get beyond their psychological and physiological symptoms to become full partners in reconciliation and peacebuilding.

Individual and Group Reaction to Traumatic Loss

Conflict resolution and reconciliation strategies often must deal with contemporary victims of traumatic violence and loss as well as members of identity groups or nations that have a memory of violent aggression in the past decades or centuries. This produces a victimhood psychology based on group memory of the violent loss accompanied by an enduring injustice. Sometimes we must deal with both historic and personal loss in the same people. Thus, Jews in Israel might be recent victims of Palestinian terrorist bombings in buses or outdoor markets. But they also have an internalized memory of Christian oppression in Europe throughout the ages and the nightmare of the Holocaust. Catholics in Ireland have burned into their memory Cromwell's genocidal aggression, repression, and degradation in the seventeenth century, the passive British genocide of the potato famines in the nineteenth century, and the experience of combat with the British police and army in the twentieth century. Palestinians share the collective Arab memory of humiliation by European imperialism starting with Napoleon's landing in Egypt in 1798, and more specifically their own defeat, displacement, and expulsion when the Jewish state was formed in 1948. As China defines its future relationship with the rest of the world, it is haunted by the memory of humiliation by Britain in the Opium Wars of 1839 and 1856, and the futile Boxer Rebellion of 1899 against victorious Western powers. Japan's "rape" of Nanking in 1937 only nourished China's sense of victimhood and its determination under Mao Tse Tung to regain its self-respect and the respect of other nations by whatever means necessary.

Psychiatry and clinical psychology continue to be the most important sources of scientific knowledge of the effect of political violence and traumatic loss on individuals and nations. Another Harvard psychiatrist from the Cambridge Hospital has written what may be the most definitive study to date on the effects of traumatic loss. It is of equal value to individual rape or torture victims as it is to entire groups and nations that have suffered violent defeat. In *Trauma and Recovery* (1992), Judith Lewis-Herman has distilled a description of the effects of traumatic loss and a prescriptive approach that, as the cases below attempt to show, is as relevant to ethnic and sectarian conflict resolution processes as it is to individual victims.

In a chapter entitled "Remembrance and Mourning," Lewis-Herman emphasizes a theme derived from her clinical experience that has been dominant in the work of the leading psychiatric political psychologist, Vamik Volkan (1988, 1997), and this writer (Montville 1993, 1995). She writes,

> Trauma inevitably brings loss. Even those who are lucky enough to escape physically unscathed still lose the internal psychological structures of a self securely attached to others. Those who are physically harmed lose in addition their sense of bodily integrity. . . . Traumatic losses rupture the ordinary sequence of generations and defy the ordinary social conventions of bereavement. The telling of the trauma story thus inevitably plunges the survivor into profound grief . . . [which] is the most necessary and the most dreaded task . . . of this stage of recovery. (188)

From the perspective of psychologically sensitive conflict resolution interventions, the challenge in dealing with victimhood psychology is that of reviving the mourning process, which has been suspended as a result of the traumatic experience and helping to move it toward completion. Storytelling is a central part of the process, not only for the victim reconstructing the story, but also for the persons representing the aggressor group. This form of telling and listening is best accomplished in the problem-solving workshop, the dominant tool of the conflict resolution practitioner. But as detailed below in the matter of the South African Truth and Reconciliation Commission, storytelling can also achieve its purpose in large, public settings.

For contemporary victims of political trauma, the process of eliciting details of the violence and loss can be difficult. Not knowing is one way of describing the victim's strong reluctance to recall the terror and pain associated with the event or events. For representatives of groups or nations that have suffered traumatic loss in the past, the memory of which is passed from generation to generation, the problem is somewhat easier to overcome. But even here, it is critically important for the third party in a dialogue to show great sensitivity in assuring the workshop participants of the safety of the dialogue setting and constantly validating their personal dignity and the experience they are relating.

Storytelling is also a form of ritual testimony that has healing powers. As Lewis-Herman (1992) writes, "Testimony has both a private dimension, which is confessional and spiritual, and a public aspect, which is political and judicial. The use of the word testimony links both meanings, giving a new and larger dimension to the [victim's] individual experience" (181). Lewis-Herman cites a therapist working with Southeast Asian refugees who says that in the telling of the story it is no longer an account of shame and humiliation. Rather it becomes a story about dignity and virtue. Victims in the process restore and regain their lives so that they can move on. There are several examples below of individual stories told in small workshops or as public testimony before a truth and reconciliation commission.

At this point, the author recalls the story of a Croatian Protestant minister who described to a group of Serbs, Croats, and Muslims in 1996 how Serb militiamen cut a two-foot gash in his back with a bayonet and raped his daughter in his presence. His listeners were stunned by the brutality of the acts but also deeply moved by his courage and commitment to rebuilding community with the Serbs of eastern Croatia. The minister had regained his dignity and established himself as an exemplar of moral power. Skeptics may still challenge the contention that the therapeutic treatment of individual victims of trauma can be used to guide the design and implementation of conflict resolution strategies in ethnic and sectarian conflicts. Thus, it is again gratifying to turn to another practitioner of the law for support of this thesis.

Public Acts of Healing

Justice Richard Goldstone of the South African Constitutional Court is a veteran of commissions of inquiry and international criminal tribunals. In 1991, he organized and led an important commission in South Africa investigating public violence, and he headed the tribunal in The Hague for Bosnia and Rwanda from 1994 to 1996. In January 1997, Goldstone gave a speech at the U.S. Holocaust Museum, entitled "Healing Wounded People." In light of the foregoing discussion on the psychology of healing, the following excerpts are quite remarkable. Goldstone said,

> The most important aspect of justice is healing wounded people. I make this point because justice is infrequently looked at as a form of healing—a form of therapy for victims who cannot begin their healing process until there is some public acknowledgement of what has befallen them. In South Africa, how do we deal with the past? Should we brush it under the carpet? Why reopen the sores? In Rwanda, how can we deal with a country that suffered one million dead in geno-

cide? In attempting to answer these questions, the people who should be consulted more than anyone else are the victims. What do they want and need for themselves and their families? One thing I have learned in my travels in former Yugoslavia, Rwanda, and South Africa is that where there have been egregious human rights violations which have gone unaccounted for, where there has been no justice, where the victims have not received any acknowledgement, where they have been forgotten, where there has been national amnesia, the effect is a cancer in the society and is the reason that explains the spiral of violence that the world has seen in former Yugoslavia for centuries and in Rwanda for decades, as obvious examples. (Author's transcription of audio tape.)

The healing effect of truth and reconciliation commissions varies considerably from one set of victims to another. The family of the late Steve Biko in South Africa has strongly criticized the provisions of the Truth and Reconciliation law that provides for impunity for military or police political torture or murder if confessed to the Truth and Reconciliation Commission (TRC). And a recent unpublished memorandum from Wilhelm Verwoerd in South Africa quotes a Black South African saying, "What really makes me angry about the TRC and [its chairman, Archbishop Desmond] Tutu is that they are putting pressure on us to forgive. . . . I don't know if I will ever be ready to forgive. I carry this ball of anger inside me and I don't even know where to begin dealing with it. The oppression was bad, but what is much worse, what makes me even more angry, is that they are trying to dictate my forgiveness."

This is a valuable piece of evidence in support of the point Judith Lewis-Herman makes in *Trauma and Recovery*. In trying to work through the psychological impact of traumatic violence, victims may generate a fantasy of forgiveness—or be urged to forgive by outsiders. In this situation victims imagine that they can rise above their rage and "erase the impact of the trauma through a willed, defiant act of love." "But," Herman continues, "it is not possible to exorcise the trauma, either through hatred or love . . . the fantasy of forgiveness often becomes a cruel torture. True forgiveness cannot be granted until the perpetrator has sought and earned it through confession, repentance, and restitution" (189-190).

Yet, for all its obvious imperfections, the Truth and Reconciliation Commission has made a major contribution to South Africa's transition to majority rule. Storytelling has had its impact. A program on National Public Radio in Washington, D.C., in September 1997 carried a statement by one of the members of the TRC named Mary Burton, a well-known human rights activist. She says,

> One of the amazing things is the effect that telling their story has on people. . . . I think of three mothers, for example, of young men who were killed, [the mothers] who were really bowed down by not only grief but long grief; long, exhausted grief. . . . They were witnesses

when some of the police who were involved in the incident were
questioned at a public hearing. . . . I still couldn't understand exactly
why it seemed to have such a transforming effect on them, because
on the final day of the hearings they went home singing and smiling
and dancing. . . . And one of them said to me: 'Now everybody
knows, my neighbors know, that my son was not a criminal. He was a
freedom fighter.' For years she had been looked at as the mother of a
criminal, and now she could hold up her head in her own circles. And
so for her it was the public acknowledgment that was important.
(September 15 1997, 4)

Even without expressions of remorse or repentance by perpetrators, a TRC
performs the crucial task of acknowledgment of the victim's loss. The violation
of basic human rights becomes a permanent part of the state's public record, and
the state assumes a protective stewardship for the victim. This provides an
essential assurance to the victims that their future safety is protected. There is a
noteworthy example of a public acknowledgment of the losses of one side in an
ethnic conflict that was unilateral and not part of an interactive process. Yet
there is no question that this act, by a chief of state, was an important contribution to an evolving peace process between two wartime enemies. On January 1,
1978, *October*, a widely read Egyptian magazine, published a New Year's
interview with President Anwar Sadat. Far and away the favorite leader of
political psychologists, it was Sadat who, in his stunning visit to Jerusalem in
November 1977, had told the Israeli Knesset that 70 percent of the problem
between Israel and the Arabs was psychological. In the January interview, Sadat
again displayed his amazing insight into the victimhood psychology of Israelis,
notwithstanding the fact that Israel had defeated Egypt militarily in 1948, 1956,
1967, and 1973. (Many believe that Egypt nevertheless won a significant
psychological victory in 1973, in the surprise Yom Kippur attack across the.
One of the consequences was the fall of the Golda Meir government in Israel.)

In the interview Sadat tossed several bouquets to his eventual Israeli partners in peacemaking. Of Menachem Begin, "I have read his writings and
concluded that he is a man with whom understanding can be reached." On
Moshe Dayan and Ezer Weizman, "Dayan is a hawk which is natural after his
great victory in 1967 and after what happened to him in the October [1973] war.
However, Dayan was flexible during our talks. . . . Weizman is a real gentleman
and is witty. [Noting that Weizman's son had been seriously wounded in
fighting along the Suez Canal] How can a man like this not want peace. There
is a bereaved father and mother in every Israeli home."

To the Israeli people as a whole Sadat said the following

All Israelis are under arms until age fifty-five. They know war and
know it is loathsome. Death is loathsome and destruction harder to
bear than death. Jews are victims of war, politics and hatred. They
have special problems, which we must know so as to understand their

positions. Jews have lived in fear for thousands of years, exposed to many massacres and persecutions. When they established Israel, imagination became reality and fear a certainty. They are strangers in a strange land. They are surrounded by millions of hostile Arabs. (*October* Magazine, January 1, 1978)

It would be difficult to overestimate the impact of Sadat's words on Israeli public opinion and especially that of the political leadership at the time. He undertook an act of clear and unambiguous acknowledgment of the pain involved in being Jewish (without so saying explicitly) in a Christian, European environment throughout the centuries. He not only communicated to the Jewish people that he understood, but he also used his leadership position in Egypt and the Arab world—Cairo being the communications capital of the Arab world—to educate his own people in the psychology of Jewishness. This act helped Arabs to understand a little better the vigor of Israeli aggressiveness in defense of the collective self and set the stage for the ultimate Camp David accords by providing a rationale for ending the state of war and making some sort of peace. The robustness of Israeli-Palestinian attacks and counterattacks continued down through the signature of the Oslo agreements in 1993, but the state of (cold) peace between Israel and Egypt endured, even after Sadat's assassination, despite provocation on other Arab fronts.

Private Acts of Healing

The problem-solving workshop or seminar for representatives of groups in conflict is practically always successful in beginning a healing process if the third-party facilitators are psychologically sensitive. The safe environment within which individuals can present grievances permits each side to gradually educate the other in the dimensions of loss felt by the other. Quite naturally, one or the other side may become very defensive in the face of broadside accusations, especially if it feels that its losses in the conflict have not been recognized or appreciated, which in the beginning is almost always the case. This situation can be characterized as a competition of victimhoods. Indeed, the sense that the other side never truly understands one's fear and pain usually endures long into a reconciliation process.

However, there is one tool in the problem-solving workshop that consistently overcomes the defenses of sides that believe they are victims of unfair collective attack. This is the telling of personal stories of loss. As Justice Goldstone and other witnesses stated about the South African Truth and Reconciliation Commission, storytelling usually had a cathartic effect on the victim telling the story, which, as has been noted, became part of the official, public record of the state. But in the private confines of the small, facilitated workshop, storytelling also penetrates the defenses of the other side that has stoutly resisted the broadside accusations. This writer participated in several workshops in which this phenomenon was apparent.

In a workshop in Austria in 1983, facilitated by an interdisciplinary group from the American Psychiatric Association, Israelis, Egyptians, and Palestinians met and unburdened themselves of broad political and personal complaints, and they got along reasonably well as intellectuals, professionals, and former government officials. But they did not engage at a profound emotional level until a physician from Gaza told the story of his nephew whose eardrum had been broken by an Israeli soldier who had struck him on suspicion of having thrown a stone. The physician insisted that the boy of twelve years had not participated in the stone throwing. He had just had the bad luck to be in the wrong place at the wrong time.

The story was painful—and entirely credible—for the Israelis. The story-teller was their companion in the Austrian workshop. They shared meals with him, went on outings, and sang songs in the evenings after meetings with him. There was no saving distance between the victim and the victimizers—representatives of the society that sent the military occupiers to Gaza. The same would have been true if the victim had been an Israeli child harmed by a Palestinian aggressor.

In this case, a Likud-associated Israeli in the workshop, who admitted to having made letter-bombs in London to be used against British targets during the mandate period, was clearly affected by the story of the deafened nephew. He said he had good contacts in the Israeli defense ministry, and he provided a telephone number for the Gazan to call him directly if and when he ever endured another act of violence at the hands of the Israeli occupation force. Thus a personal Israeli-Palestinian alliance was forged which, if nourished after the meeting, promised to endure. Even if this alliance were to wither over time from lack of use, the exchange between the occupier and the occupied established a moral symmetry in the workshop that permitted subsequent collaborative engagement by all the parties in serious exploration of next plausible steps in the peace process.

In 1992, this writer was part of a third-party team assembled by Vamik Volkan, M.D., founder and director of the Center for the Study of Mind and Human Interaction at the University of Virginia, to run a Baltic-Russian workshop in Kaunas, Lithuania. The dynamic in the early stages of the work-shop was similar to that in the Austrian meeting of Arabs and Israelis. The humiliation of Soviet occupation of the Baltic countries—Lithuania, Latvia, and Estonia—was very fresh in Baltic minds. Indeed, despite the global recognition of the three states' independence, there were still residual Russian military forces in each. This situation generated enormous resentment.

For their part, the Russian participants, some who were residents in the Baltic States, some from Moscow, including government officials and the Russian ambassador to Estonia, were very defensive. Some complained about the way the Balts used the terms *Soviet* and *Russian* interchangeably. They said the Soviets, the oppressors, were by definition multiethnic—Ukrainians,

Georgians, Armenians, Uzbeks. The Russians, on the other hand, were not only identifiable by their Russianness, but were also the greatest victims of the Soviet system. They were forced to sacrifice their standard of living so that other Soviet nationalities, including the Baltic peoples, could have a better life.

The broadsides continued to be exchanged, as in the Israeli/Arab workshop in Austria. Then a Lithuanian-American woman told her story. She had been a student in the medical faculty. The day in 1939 that the Red Army entered Kaunas, she had been walking to the apartment building where her best friend, also a medical student, lived with her family. As she approached the building, she saw a Soviet military truck pull up to its entrance. Soldiers stepped out and entered the building. Shortly thereafter, the soldiers reappeared, leading her best friend and her parents, who were put into the truck and taken away. In the hushed conference room, the Lithuanian-American physician ended her story. She never saw her best friend again.

This first-person account of painful loss, which could never be forgotten, did much to bring home to the Russians in the workshop the sense of helplessness and humiliation the Baltic people experienced because of the Soviet occupation. Again there was no escape from this truth. The Russians and the Latvians, Estonians, and Lithuanians were taking meals together, and even singing together during evening recreation. There was no chance to use the traditional psychological devices of avoidance or denial of unpleasant facts. Thus the level of discourse changed meaningfully in the workshop. A retired Russian People's Commissariat of Internal Affairs (NKVD) (predecessor of the Committee of the State Security [KGB]) officer spoke as much to herself as to the others:

> Looking back over history it is hard to understand what happened, how and why. My father was a military man. His duty was to save the Baltics from fascism. This seemed normal to us. We did not know of the Molotov-Ribbentrop pact. We were all unfree and victims. Six people in my family were put in concentration camps. This was, sadly, routine at the time.

> After World War II, we set out to rehabilitate the countries that had suffered under fascism. We saw the Baltic countries joining in this effort. I first saw that the Balts were fighting Soviet domination at C.S.C.E. [Conference on Security and Cooperation in Europe] meetings. It was a slow realization for me and painful to understand. I am ashamed of Russian behavior in Eastern Europe and the Baltic countries. We behaved badly in these countries. [Author's unpublished memorandum]

There is much more about the Russian-Baltic Track II diplomacy interactions than can be described here. Suffice it to say that these unofficial interventions were buttressed by the active role of the high commissioner on National Minorities of the Organization on Security and Cooperation in Europe. The commissioner, former Dutch Foreign Minister Max van der Stoel, succeeded in emotionally defusing and legally moderating the language issues requiring Russian speakers to learn Estonian or Latvian. The third-party assistance in the aggregate contributed to a relatively smooth transition in the three Baltic States. Russians found ways to acknowledge and express levels of remorse for the moral debts the Soviet Union had accumulated in the Baltic States. In the process these small states were able to sense that a measure of justice and equity was returning to their relationship with their giant neighbor. However, they worked to fortify this new feeling of relative security by pushing eagerly for membership in the Council of Europe, the European Union, and even the North Atlantic Treaty Organization (NATO).

This chapter concludes with an account of only partial success of reconciliation efforts in an enduring sectarian conflict, that of Northern Ireland. There has been an impressive, one could say heroic, struggle to negotiate a settlement of the conflict as seen in the Good Friday Agreement of 1998. There have been enormously gratifying referenda in support of the agreement by all the major parties and the Protestant and Catholic voters. These majorities in both communities have made the rational choice to end the sectarian terrorism, organize their self-government, and get on with their lives in the broader context of the European Union. And yet, the burdens of history on this conflict have only received perfunctory attention. There is an enduring sense of unatoned loss on the part of Irish Catholics in their struggle for justice and dignity under the long rule of Britain. And there is deep-seated fear in the Protestant, Unionist community because of the Irish Republican Army (IRA) reluctance to decommission its weapons. Even if and when the disarming process begins, it is likely that the Protestants will continue to suspect the motives of the IRA culture. And it is also likely that armed Republican units will continue to exist for the foreseeable future.

The complexity of the reconciliation process for Northern Ireland—indeed for Britain and Ireland—was revealed in a long dinner conversation between a Unionist and a Catholic nationalist, constitutional politician who were participants in a Track II workshop organized by the author in Strasbourg, France, in 1993. The Unionist entered the discussion deeply suspicious of what his people called a "Pan-Nationalist conspiracy" that brought together the Catholics of Northern Ireland, the Irish Republic, and the Irish Catholics of the United States to work relentlessly for the reunification of the island of Ireland. For Protestants, this meant not only losing their identity in a sea of Irish Catholics, it meant also the prospect of Catholic revenge against them for centuries of British depredations.

The task for the Catholic politician in this three-hour conversation was to ease the Protestant's fears by explaining how he had personally suffered at the hands of the IRA. He described attacks on his home, threats to his family, even the bones that IRA thugs had broken in his body. The man had paid a big price for his commitment to constitutional government and nonviolence. In the telling of his story, he convinced the Unionist that there was not a Pan-Nationalist conspiracy. This was significant, because the politician went on to become a strong advocate of the peace process. Yet he ultimately became identified with the opposition to the Good Friday Agreement, reflecting the Protestant community that continues to be suspicious of the motives of Catholics.

There are few experts on the thinking of the IRA and its splinter groups. The most seasoned observers were profoundly impressed by the long effort of John Hume, leader of the constitutional Catholic Social Democratic Labor Party, to persuade the IRA, through Sinn Fein leader Gerry Adams, to declare a cease-fire and join the peace process. John Hume and David Trimble, leader of the Ulster Unionist Party, had earned their Nobel Peace Prize. Yet there has been little evidence of any of the healing necessary to begin a genuine reconciliation between Protestants and Catholics. There is instead a deal supported by majorities and sincerely friendly governments in London, Dublin, and Washington, D.C.

Yet the requisite acknowledgment of British/Protestant moral responsibility for past wrongs has not been part of the Catholic-Protestant dialogue among politicians in Northern Ireland. There was the significant exception of initiatives taken by British Prime Minister Tony Blair in acknowledging England's responsibility in the starvation of Irish men, women, and children in the potato famines in 1846 and 1848. Blair also supported the building of a monument at Liverpool Cemetery in memory of the Irish famine victims buried there. And he also reopened the official inquiry into British police responsibility for the killing of unarmed Catholic demonstrators on "Bloody Sunday" in Londonderry in 1972. It is safe to say that Tony Blair played a big part in the success of the pro-peace referenda among Catholic voters in 1998. But from the psychological point of view, there is so much more to acknowledge.

There may be a clue in the assessment of Paul Arthur (1997), a highly respected Ulster University professor, and Catholic, who has won the confidence of Unionists and worked mightily in Track II diplomacy. In describing the impact of the Catholic hunger strikers in Belfast in 1980-1981, Arthur notes that those who died were in a long tradition of Irish Catholics who offered up their lives in the struggle for dignity and justice against British rule. The strike was redolent of martyrdom and religious symbolism, even though IRA members were for the most part anti-Church and atheistic followers of Marxist revolutionary ideology.

There was great drama in the strikes and deathwatches. An iconography emerged with barbed wire from prison represented as crowns of thorns and the dying men seen in postures of Crucifixion. The sacrifice of the masses was being enacted. Images and evocations of the Blessed Virgin as consoler were seen and heard. The sense of persecution and loss and the almost spiritual and existential feeling of injustice are the substance of the memory of the hunger strike, but also of the potato famine and Cromwell's armies in the seventeenth century.

It is well that the 1998 peace agreement was made on Good Friday. But the Resurrection for the Protestants and Catholics of Northern Ireland has yet to take place.

Conclusion

The inescapable lesson of this analysis of the burdens of history on ethnic and sectarian conflicts is that even the most brilliant negotiator can at best help make a temporary deal between adversaries, unless he or she also advances a genuine process of healing the wounds of history. It is distressing, even tragic, that diplomats, most politicians, and almost all professors of political science and international relations are ignorant of this relentless reality. The scientific evidence for the critical importance of healing is available, as are methods and processes for carrying it out. Political leaders can acknowledge publicly the moral debts of their nations; senior clergy can do the same for their followers. Historians can undertake their own truth commissions in reviewing and revising tendentious studies and textbooks the way French and German scholars did after World War II. Television documentaries and public affairs programs can address the burdens of history. Educational tourism for both sides in a historic conflict can help people to come to terms with the past, or even rediscover some shared past glories with their contemporary enemies. Poets, playwrights, painters, sculptors, and composers can use their media to communicate messages of atonement.

There have been brave, if fitful, attempts to integrate healing processes into formal peacemaking. The important gestures of British Prime Minister Tony Blair toward the Irish cited above are an example. Another example occurred when the U.S. State Department's Middle East peace team of Dennis Ross and Aaron Miller tried, unsuccessfully, to arrange for Yasser Arafat to visit the Holocaust Museum in Washington, D.C., in 1998. The diplomats thought that Arafat's symbolic acknowledgment of the burdens of history on the Jewish people might increase Jewish trust in the peace process. Ironically, while Arafat was ready to make the visit, an official of the Holocaust Museum, unmoved by the gesture toward healing, blocked it.

But the struggle to raise public consciousness of the critical importance of actual healing in political relationships must and will continue. Perhaps the skeptics will be impressed finally by the efforts of the halt and lame Pope John Paul II. In the Jubilee Year 2000, he is exerting every fiber of his body to travel to the appropriate sites to acknowledge the moral debts of Christendom to its victims throughout the centuries: the Orthodox, the Muslim and Christian victims of the Crusaders, those savaged by the Inquisition, but above all to the Jewish people. Perhaps a new definition of *realpolitik* will emerge from these efforts that emphasizes the essential role of reconciliation in diplomacy and peacemaking. Perhaps the idea of justice, in its broadest sense, will find its way into the thinking and agendas of diplomats and statesmen.

References

Arthur, P. 1997. 'Reading' Violence: Ireland. In *The Legitimization of Violence*. D. Apter, ed. London: McMillan.

Davies, J. C. 1986. Roots of Political Behavior. In *Political Psychology*. M. Hermann, ed. San Francisco: Jossey-Bass.

Lewis-Herman, J. 1992. *Trauma and Recovery*. New York: Basic Books.

Maslow, A. 1954. *Motivation and Personality*. New York: Harper.

Montville, J. V. 1993. The Healing Function in Political Conflict Resolution. In *Conflict Resolution Theory and Practice: Integration and Application*. D. Sandole and H. van der Merwe, eds. Manchester, U.K.: Manchester University Press.

———. 1995. Complicated Mourning and Mobilization for Nationalism. In *Social Pathology in Comparative Perspective: The Nature and Psychology of Civil Society*. J. Braun, ed. Westport, Conn.: Praeger.

Murphy, J., and Hampton, J., eds. 1988. *Forgiveness and Mercy*. Cambridge, U.K.: Cambridge University Press.

October Magazine. 1978. January. (Arabic).

Rochlin, G. 1978. *Man's Aggression: The Defense of the Self*. Boston: Gambit.

Volkan, V. D. 1988. *The Need to Have Enemies and Allies*. Northvale, N.J.: Jason Aronson.

———. 1997. *Bloodlines: From Ethnic Pride to Ethnic Terrorism*. New York: Farrar, Straus and Giroux.

Worthington, E. L. 1998. *Dimensions of Forgiveness: Psychological Research and Theological Perspectives*. Philadelphia: Templeton Fund Press.

8

Ritual Reconciliation

Transforming Identity/Reframing Conflict

Lisa Schirch

Promoting Justice and Peace through Reconciliation and Coexistence Alternatives

Most of the early Western writings in the field of conflict studies sought to understand conflict through an objective, analytical lens that downplayed the subjective realm of culture and worldview and tried to control the perceptual and emotional factors that make conflict so messy and complex. This "rational" approach sees conflict arising over land, water, money, or other material resources. This approach to conflict uses logical problem-solving methods to bring about settlement or resolution.

A second approach describes conflict as a relational problem between individuals and groups characterized by power imbalances, poor communication and dysfunctional social structures that are unable to meet human needs. Conflict interventions based on these relational theories of conflict draw on a host of new communication technologies that assist humans in relating to each other and a variety of ideas on how to design social structures to meet human needs.

While the "rational" and "relational" approaches bring important insights into how to understand and intervene in conflict, the field of conflict studies is still lacking in how to address the leftovers in the "theoretical trashbin," the psychological and cultural dimensions of conflict. The concepts of worldview, culture, and identity form the core of the study of the "symbolic" approach to conflict. These messy aspects of conflict are central to reconciliation processes, which emphasize forgiveness, healing, and growth.

An increasing number of conflict scholars and practitioners are writing about symbolic approaches to conflict, lending legitimacy to its inclusion in conflict theory and giving the field new language to use in its analysis of conflict (Docherty 1998; Nudler 1990; Volkan 1990; Lederach 1997; Montville 1991). Docherty notes that the rational, relational, and symbolic approaches to conflict shape how theorists and practitioners analyze and intervene in conflict (1998). Some theorists and practitioners choose to use only one approach, while others use a combination. Table 8.1 below gives further exploration of how each approach describes conflict and prescribes intervention.

Table 8.1. Approaches to Conflict

Approaches to Conflict	Description of Conflict	Prescriptive Conflict Intervention
Rational	Competing interests over an issue or scarce resource cause conflict	• Remove and control emotions • Think analytically/rationally about the problem • Improve problem-solving skills • Separate the people from the problem
Relational	Poor communication patterns, competitive social attitudes, an imbalance of power, and/or poor social structures cause conflict	• Improve communication skills of the parties • Switch from a competitive to a cooperative model of relationships • Address power imbalances • Construct social structures that meet human needs
Symbolic	Differing perceptions, cultures, and worldviews create conflict	• Conceive the process of reconciliation as transforming perceptions of identity and reframing conflict • Create opportunities to bridge worldviews by engaging people through their bodies, senses, and emotions • Develop common symbolic "frames" for talking about conflict through myth, metaphor, and ritual

(Schirch 1998)

Symbolic approaches to conflict grow out of an understanding that humans have a need to symbolically understand who they are and how they relate to their environment. Worldviews are shaped by personal experiences, the cultural groups to which an individual belongs, and cosmological understandings of the world. Each individual's worldview is a dynamic lens used to sense, experience, and perceive the world. Worldviews are expressed, confirmed, and re-created through all types of symbolic forms including metaphors, myths, and rituals that explain why the world is as it appears to be and builds designs for what the world could or should be (Geertz 1973; Maturana and Varela 1987).

Efforts to move parties in conflict toward reconciliation and coexistence are partly dependent on addressing divergent cognitive worldviews and cultural identities. Perceptions of what is just and what constitutes peace rely on the symbolic lenses of people in conflict. If we are to help change or align the way people in conflict define justice and coordinate their efforts to create peace, the field of conflict studies must be ready to work with the symbolic worldviews of those people.

For example, what appears to be just and designed for what would constitute a vision of peace differs greatly according to the differing worldviews of Greek and Turkish Cypriots on the ethnically divided island of Cyprus. Both sides believe that they are the victims of aggression. A symbolic approach to the Cyprus conflict could begin with a worldview analysis of how the Greek and Turkish Cypriots view the conflict, each other, and their own identities. What metaphors and potent stories are used in their conflict language to talk about the island?

While symbolic concepts such as worldview and perception help describe conflict, finding symbolic tools for addressing conflict is still largely uncharted territory. Ritual is posed in this chapter as a tool for bringing competing views of justice and peace into converging visions of coexistence and reconciliation. Ritual can complement and enrich, rather than replace, rational and relational approaches.

Ritual: Rummaging in the Theoretical Trashbin

Since the beginning of time, ritual has held an important place in human societies. Ritual and ritual-like contexts are the age-old ways the symbolic aspects of conflict are addressed in cultures around the world. Rituals regulate relationships in communities, serving as ways of defining identity and providing the social lubricant to relate to others and to the surrounding world. Reaching back into history toward one of the oldest habits of humanity, perhaps we can find a new key to the future of working with conflict. *Rituals are special contexts conducive to the symbolic transformation of identity and the reframing of conflict toward sustainable, coexisting relationships.*

Despite its ancient origins, ritual is still a dragon on the edge of our medieval map of conflict. Ritual holds a more prominent role in the fields of anthropology, theology, and psychology, and there is a growing body of interdisciplinary literature in the new field of ritual studies itself that has its own journals and textbooks (see Grimes 1995, 1996). We don't often hear of ritual's role in solving complex, deep-rooted conflicts. Instead, we have become accustomed to hearing of serious negotiations, rational discussion, and problem-solving efforts.

My awareness of ritual's role in reconciliation was born on the island of Cyprus during a series of workshops in the skills and practice of conflict analysis and resolution. A consortium of conflict resolution trainers and facilitators brought together Turkish and Greek Cypriots for these intensive workshops. During the day, trainers led participants through exercises in improving communication, problem solving, and negotiation skills to increase the capacity of the Cypriot participants to work together to manage their conflict. Almost every evening after the training, the group of Turkish and Greek Cypriots ate dinner together and danced and sang together in local restaurants. These social rituals seemed to be important to the process of transforming the participants' understanding of themselves, perceptions of their "enemies," and their view of the conflict as a whole.

How and why do rituals work to bring about reconciliation? An understanding of the dynamics of identity is crucial to relating the possible functions of ritual in reconciliation processes.

Culture and Identity

Each person belongs and interacts with many different cultures during his or her life. An individual gains a sense of identity when he or she explicitly "belongs" and relates to a group. One's "identity," then, is simply a metaphor for the relationship of an individual to his or her cultural context. The self is defined in the context of relationship to others (Fitzgerald 1993).

Cultural groups share socially significant traits such as gender, age, religion, or class. Families, organizations, churches, sports teams, and other groups within society each hold a unique culture that may share aspects with other cultures, but have distinct rules for behavior and interaction among the culture's members. Individual worldviews make up and shape a group's culture and, reflexively, cultures are reflected in and shape individual worldviews. An individual's worldview will reflect a varying mix of cultural influences unique to that individual.

For example, this author belongs to a number of different cultural groups. I am Mennonite, politically active, educated, White, female, married, a teacher, and live in the Shenandoah Valley of the East Coast of the United States. Belonging to each of these "cultural identity categories" gives me a particular set of cultural values (some more loosely defined than others) and has exposed me to particular experiences that have shaped my unique worldview.

The diagram below maps how an individual's identity and worldview are constructed out of their cultural groups such as age, sex, race, religion, and other socially significant categories (marked with a "?").

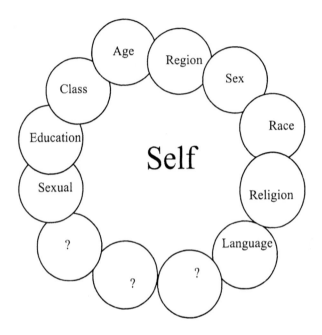

Identity and Conflict: Symbolically Constructing the "Other"

The illusive nature of identity is a subject of many theorists in various disciplines, including conflict studies (Burton 1990; Gurr 1993; Montville 1990; Fisher 1990; and Northrup 1989). Scholars have explored the need for identity and how that need influences the dynamics of conflicts. There are three major findings of many of these studies. One, people have a human need to define themselves in relation to others. Two, people are willing to both kill and die defending certain sociocultural identities. And three, people's understanding of who they are is often based on perceptions and constructions of an adversarial "other."

Conflict appears to be basic to the construction and maintenance of identity. In his classic work, *The Functions of Social Conflict*, Lewis Coser described the benefits individuals and groups derive from engaging in conflict. He claims that conflict is an "essential element in group life and formation" and is premised on the identification of an "other" (Coser 1956, 31). Vamik Volkan's work on the apparent psychological need for enemies and allies supports this claim (Volkan 1988). It appears as if conflict shapes and strengthens the identity of one's own group by stripping the humanity from the enemy, creating unidimensional objects to hate.

For example, the U.S. identity is constantly re-created behind the trigger of ever-larger guns pointed at any country or group of people appearing to threaten the capitalist identity and all that it entails. In the long term, it appears that it does not matter who plays the adversarial identity targeted. It is more important, it seems, to find or even create some target to justify a capitalist economy grounded in the production of weapons. As the Soviet Union collapsed and the Cold War ended, the United States quickly helped to create "Iraq's monster." Public discourse in the United States is now fraught with dehumanizing messages about Iraq's leadership. It appears as if the United States can only maintain its cowboy, frontier identity by maintaining an adversarial relationship. Without a transformation of U.S. identity or the discovery of a new enemy, it is unlikely that weapons inspections or negotiations with Saddam Hussein will result in peaceful coexistence.

Dehumanizing: Stripping Off Identities

Many psychologists have explored how individuals and groups search for cognitive consistency by ignoring or rejecting information that contradicts their worldview (see Fisher in this volume). In conflicts, these psychological processes become active in shaping perceptions of the enemy, the "other." It is difficult for people to find anything good or redeemable in their enemies. Information about an enemy's identity that might reveal positive characteristics is avoided by either conscious or unconscious removal of the incongruent information.

The psychological process of dehumanization assists in achieving cognitive consistency. Enemies are dehumanized to minimize any ambiguous or guilty feelings about killing and hating the enemy (see Montville in this volume). Dehumanization functions to dissociate the enemy with any of the symbols of humanity that might emphasize the similarities between conflict parties. Coser and Volkan posit that keeping one's own sense of identity requires an ongoing denigration of an "other" (Coser 1956; Volkan 1988). As humans strip the humanity of the "other" in conflict, they negate the identities they may share with their enemy, leaving a one-dimensional understanding of both their own and their enemy's identity.

In fractured societies, individuals and groups seem to focus on one aspect of their own and their adversary's identity. Divisions between cultural groups are more complete and may even be reinforced by multiple identity divisions, as in societies where class and religion fall along the same societal fault line.

Some types of identity become overemphasized so much that people begin seeing each other as only having one identity. People's understanding of their own and their adversary's identity may become frozen into a system where the conflict itself is dependent on the "conflict habituated" identities of the people in conflict (Diamond and McDonald 1996). Northrup claims that conflicts that focus on one aspect of the identities of the parties, such as the way the Arab-Israeli conflict focuses on the Jewish and Arab identities of the parties, tend to be intractable, because efforts to humanize the enemy threaten the core identity of each group. Northrup claims that conflict cannot be fully addressed until the identity issues are fully included (Northrup 1989, 55).

The diagram below shows how one identity, such as race, may become overemphasized in defining people. In the United States, for example, the persistence of racism can be attributed to the societal fault line dating back to slavery, when White people began dehumanizing African people for economic profit. In the early days of the slave trade, White authorities intentionally stripped the rich and varied sources of identity away from Africans, leaving until today a perception that the social construction of "race," more than any other cultural category, defines peoples of African origin. Because of the unique set of historical and current experiences of African Americans, race continues to be an identity that overshadows other potential sources of identity.

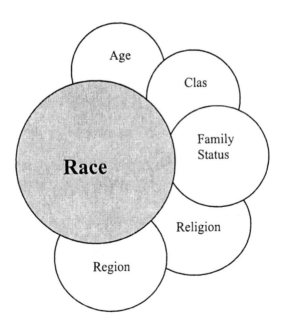

The ethnic identities of Greek and Turkish Cypriots seem to have become stronger through the last thirty years of conflict. Earlier in this century, while the ethnic identities were important sources of identity, a variety of other identities were also important and allowed Greek and Turkish Cypriots to live side by side and even intermarry in Cypriot communities. Today, along the Green Line that divides the island, billboards on both sides recount the horrible atrocities of the other ethnic group, portraying the other as monsters capable of gruesome murder. The similarity between the two billboards is striking. Before leaving each side of the island, billboards warn tourists and visitors of the evils of the other side.

In nonconflict environments, humans seem to perceive themselves and others as having different sources of identity based on their membership in crosscutting cultural groups. In societies without violent identity conflicts, people of different economic classes, ethnicities, religions, and so on, seem to have established relationships that cut across these divisions. In peaceful societies, identities are not dependent on a definition of an evil "other."

Issues of identity seem to become so central to conflict that it is hard to imagine the success of a conflict intervention that does not address them. If this is so, then the transformation of identity is necessary to reconciliation. Those people who have expanded their understanding of their own and their adversaries' identities and are able to find some shared identities seem to become the peacemakers. In the Middle East, Bosnia, Burundi, and Canada, people who have found shared identities with people across the conflict lines are doing the most to bring about reconciliation and peaceful coexistence in their regions.

Palestinian and Israeli women who have met each other and discussed the many shared aspects of their lives as mothers, widows, sisters, wives, and victims of a painful conflict have gone through a process of rehumanizing their sense of self and other. Together, they are in a stronger position to build peace in the region. People who share identities are able to form crosscutting groups to break down the psychological walls that perpetuate conflict.

Rehumanizing by Transforming Identities: A Matter of Context

People who have dehumanized each other through a protracted violent conflict will need to "rehumanize" their visions of each other in any reconciliation process that aims for sustainable coexistence. Rehumanizing includes increasing the flexibility of their understanding of identity.

An article in the *Washington Post* several years ago reported that women in some parts of India usually identify themselves as part of a certain caste or as members of a religious community before they identify themselves as women, because of the ongoing religious and caste conflicts. However, a group of Indian women crossed these identity boundaries, as they realized that they shared a common enemy: alcoholic men. This article gives a clear example of how identities may change depending on the context where the individual or identity group is located and as the definition of an enemy or an "other" changes.

> United by a common cause, high caste and lower caste village
> women who previously never would have shared a meal overcame
> traditional prejudice to work side by side . . . In many areas, Hindus
> and Muslims jointly shut down liquor shops (Moore 1993, A33).

These new coalitions of women seem to have revolutionized households in the region. "Women are not only stopping the hands of their own husbands [from drinking]. . . . If they hear any unpleasant shouting or beatings, neighborhood women come together to stop it" (Moore 1993, A38). Worldviews used to interpret the context shifted. Through the new conflict over alcohol, the women came to see their common identity as women, overshadowing other identities such as caste or religion, if only temporarily.

Perceptions of identity change according to both physical and relational contexts. When a person is at his workplace, he relates to others through his professional identity. When a person is in her own home, she interacts with others according to her family role as father, mother, daughter, son, and so on. Symbols in the physical environment help people know how to relate to each other and how to think and act in any particular context.

The typical negotiation room is often sterile. Tables and chairs are usually the central focus of the room. The lack of other symbols often creates a formal atmosphere. The formality can encourage people to identify each other as "negotiators" or members of only one identity group related to the conflict. Peacebuilders can intentionally create contexts where adversaries are encouraged to see themselves through a different lens that allows a fuller definition of both self and "other."

Constructing Contexts Conducive to Transformation

It appears as if perceptions of what constitutes an "enemy" are based on context. If this is so, it would seem that constructing contexts conducive to transforming perceptions of identity would be important to reconciliation processes. As noted above, the more crosscutting or "flexible" one's identity is, the less one will tend to cling to one identity factor and react violently when it is threatened. Individuals engaged in conflict patterns could be encouraged to strengthen other sources of identity by bringing them into contexts where they can more clearly see what they have in common. Processes aimed at dealing with identity perceptions in conflict could include placing antagonistic groups in a new situation where their old assumptions and perceptions about the identity of "the enemy" are challenged and transformed.

The study of ritual is the study of how to create transformative contexts. As noted earlier, *rituals are special contexts conducive to the symbolic transformation of identity and the reframing of conflict toward sustainable, coexisting relationships.*

The functions of ritual are included in this definition. Ritual shapes and gives meaning to a context, defines and shapes identity, and facilitates communication through physical actions and symbols that create changes in the ways ritual participants perceive the world.

Creating a World

Ritual environments are constructed with purpose and care. Symbols, objects, and people are placed carefully in ritual to give meaning and order to a setting. In ritual, humans create an idealized world.

Anthropologist Victor Turner speaks of ritual contexts as "liminal spaces," or as a "place in limbo." Ritual spaces are in-between, set-aside contexts where the rules for acting and interpreting meaning are different from the rest of life. These liminal spaces are thresholds between one social field and another (Turner 1988, 34). Often what happens in ritual is only allowed to happen because the space has been separated from the everyday, regular spaces where people interact.

Constructing transformational spaces for reconciliation processes is not a new idea. Many intervenors are already skilled in making sure that chairs are arranged in a circle or that round tables are used, as these both indicate and create equality and cooperation. Many successful international efforts at mediation have had major breakthroughs when the people in conflict were eating dinner, smoking a cigarette, dancing to music, or were in some location other than a negotiating room.

In the Cypriot workshops mentioned earlier, ritual spaces were separated from the daily workshop atmosphere. During the evening, the Cypriot participants spent time at a variety of different Mediterranean restaurants with white tablecloths, candles and soft lighting, and an array of aromatic food in front of them.

As the field of conflict studies progresses, we need to articulate and document the kinds of contexts we use to bring parties together. Rituals do not need to be formal or traditional. A ritual context can be improvised and constructed by conflict intervenors and/or the people involved in a conflict. Sensitivity and awareness of cultural norms are very important to the success of a ritual. When possible, reconciliation rituals should be constructed by participants and use symbols that are meaningful to all involved in the reconciliation process.

The first lesson in creating rituals is to pay attention to context. What does the room or location of a workshop, training, or negotiation communicate? Peacebuilders can create a "safe space" or an atmosphere conducive to transformation by finding an environment that holds warm, comfortable, and even sentimental feelings for all the people involved.

Transforming, Creating, and Healing Identity through Ritual

Ritual functions relating to identity seem to be important to the process of reconciliation in three ways. Rituals can transform people's identities, create new, shared identities for people in conflict, and heal identity wounds that may result from conflict.

From weddings to inaugurations, rituals are often used to mark and invoke changes in identities. Rituals may assist parties in conflict in the process of changing from being enemies to fellow problem solvers and/or victims to survivors. In other words, rituals can transform people's perception of identity from an exclusive focus on ethnicity to a full range of identity sources held by each participant. Peacebuilders can add rituals to reconciliation processes as a way to create a setting that serves as a passageway from dehumanizing and adversarial views of the other toward a rehumanization of the identity of the adversarial "other."

I observed a number of identity transformations during the Greek and Turkish Cypriot trainings. During daytime trainings, it appeared as if the workshop participants viewed each other by their ethnic identity as "Turkish Cypriots" or "Greek Cypriots." At night during the social rituals of eating and dancing together, the participants seemed to view each other by other identities: mothers, fathers, fellow victims of the war, teachers, musicians, dancers, and so on. One trainer noticed that

> they'd sing the same songs and dance the same way. Several of them
> said it brought them back to old times when they lived in the same
> village. And they knew they did the same things and were the same
> way. There's nothing on the island to reinforce that idea. I mean I
> can't think of any influence that would in any way suggest that the
> two sides are the same in any way. There's no contact, so there's no
> way of knowing. (Interview with James Notter 1995)

Engaging in rituals that reflected common identities seems to have emphasized their similarities rather than their differences. It may have strengthened their identity as Mediterranean islanders who had lived side by side for centuries. Dancing required individuals to play male and female roles, thus gender identities may have been more salient in this atmosphere as well. In addition, the interactions both in and out of the workshop setting helped create a group identity of Greek and Turkish Cypriots working together bicommunally.

Rituals can also be used to encourage and mark the creation of shared identities for people in conflict. Formal ceremonies can mark new identities that groups develop through reconciliation processes. In Cyprus peacebuilding processes, for example, "graduates" of bicommunal workshops were formally presented certificates and were dubbed bicommunal peacebuilders by the U.S. ambassador to Cyprus.

Ritual also acts as a way of promoting self-esteem and feeling good about one's identity, which may in turn fulfill the basic human need for identity and prevent destructive conflict from occurring. Driver describes the civil rights movement, for example, as a series of mass rituals where "African Americans demonstrated their equal and full humanity through demonstrations, lunch counter sit-ins and other nonviolent actions" (1991, 184).

Rituals that reaffirm or create identities may actually assist the healing process necessary for reconciliation and peacebuilding. Many women's groups in North America, for example, are creating new rituals to help their members claim the identity of being "survivors" rather than "victims" of domestic violence. Rituals such as holding a symbolic funeral and burying a childhood dress, for example, can help women move beyond their sense of victimhood into a more powerful identity of being a survivor.

In the United States, African Americans struggle to define themselves in a society that often imposes an identity upon them. While they share the same skin color as newer immigrants of Africa and many of the same economic and social concerns as other minority groups in the United States, the historical experience and the collective trauma of slavery created a unique identity for many Black Americans. Kwanza and other rituals that celebrate African American identity may increase the self-esteem and self-respect of African Americans without denigrating the identity of an "other."

Peacebuilders could help groups develop rituals such as these that help to heal "identity wounds" that may have resulted from conflict or violence. If there are no existing or traditional rituals that can provide a healing force to affirm identities threatened by conflict, peacebuilders can improvise new rituals that fulfill these functions.

Rituals create opportunities for people to see both their own and an other's full humanity. Peacebuilders can plan activities specifically geared toward transforming, creating, and healing identity. Activities such as sharing family pictures or childhood stories and visiting each other's homes might heighten awareness of interdependence to others and emphasize common identities that people share, whereas more formal rituals or ceremonies could be created to assist and mark changes in identity.

Rehumanizing Rituals: Other Ways of Learning and Knowing

Western theorists often dismiss ritual as being anti-intellectual. In the stark formality of many negotiating rooms, talking heads favor controlled rationality, emotions are banished, and only the most basic senses are employed. Assisting people in conflict to learn new ways of seeing themselves and their adversaries and invent new ways of coexisting should include pedagogies that engage people through multiple ways of learning and knowing. The use of rituals for reconciliation allows people to eat, drink, smell, dance, laugh, cry, and express the full range of human activity as they rehumanize both themselves and their adversaries.

Ritual communicates messages that sometimes have dramatic, transforming effects on the intellect. In the last two decades, cognitive theorists have concluded that the process of learning involves the whole body, not just the brain (Maturana and Varela 1980). Humans learn through action. What we learn through rituals, called "ritual knowledge" by theologian Theodore Jennings, often comes through the bodily expression of emotions, such as crying, anger, and joy, and senses, such as seeing, hearing, smelling, and tasting (Jennings 1996). Ritual makes use of the full range of ways people know and understand the world. It involves people's minds, bodies, all or many of their senses, and their emotions.

If individuals learn by doing, reconciliation could begin by enacting the desired transformed state of coexistence. It may be helpful for individuals in conflict to enact physically what they cannot verbally acknowledge at first. Shaking hands, sitting down to a meal together, or sharing a cigarette outside the formal negotiating room might physically symbolize a transformation of a conflict that may not be able to occur yet on a purely intellectual level.

A ritual environment created for people in conflict also helps them learn to empathize with the worldview of the other through the involvement of their entire bodies and all their senses and emotions, as opposed to Western notions of learning that involve solely rational, verbal modes. Activities that encourage people to interact physically and emotionally with each other and to act out new ways of being with each other can facilitate a shift in perception. This could include such varied activities as problem-solving games, informal sports, singing, watching movies, dancing, smoking, eating, going fishing, or cooking with each other.

Bicommunal groups of Greek and Turkish Cypriots created a sense of hope that the future could be different by planning joint music concerts, art shows, children's programs, and other cooperative ventures along the United Nations monitored Green Line (until they were stopped by the Turkish Cypriot authorities). These symbolic actions involved people's emotions, senses, and bodies while they set an example for coexistence and began to bring it into being.

Reframing Conflict

Conflicts are always complex and usually involve ambiguous definitions of right and wrong, enemy and ally, forgiveness and hatred, and so on. Rituals may be able to transform worldviews by holding together ambiguities, complexities, and paradoxes in a way rational, logical thought cannot. In conflicts, ritual appears to reframe our understanding of what is at stake, giving humans new lenses to examine competing interests, values, and perceptions.

Liminal space is by definition a place where transformation occurs, for it is "in between" one state and another. Ritual's "liminal" frame allows us to perceive the world differently (Turner 1969). Smith purports that each human "establishes and discovers," "invents and participates in," and "discovers or creates" his world through ritual (Smith 1973, 140). In ritual, humans are intentional about creating a context where transformation may occur. Ritual contexts allow and even bring about changes in how people perceive the world and, in particular, conflict.

Ritual has been used by both animals and humans to create ways of inter- acting when conflicting individuals or groups have competing interests (Lorenz 1966). Hunt claims that ritual tends to appear in situations where there is opposition, structured social antagonism, or potential conflict between structur- ally defined segments of society (1977, 144). Likewise, Moore and Myerhoff assert that ritual appears precisely when there appears to be the most conflict. "[Ritual] action itself may be soothing. . . . Ceremony can make it appear that there is no conflict, only harmony, no disorder, only order, that if danger threatens, safe solutions are at hand" (1977, 24). Ritual communicates a message that reframes conflict or danger.

Symbols are by nature ambiguous and allow for multiple interpretations. While individuals make unique connections with symbols such as drinking wine and listening to music in social rituals according to their worldviews, the experience can be equally significant. The symbolic nature of ritual allows individuals to come together and delicately dance around their differences while participating in a ritual that is meaningful to all, because it leaves room for multiple and even contradictory interpretations. While perceptions of peace and justice may be contradictory when expressed verbally, ritual communication may allow for new ways of thinking about conflict and may assist in finding joint symbols for peaceful coexistence.

Ritual is not a simplistic answer to life's most difficult conflicts, however. Obeyesekere sees ritual solutions "not [as] a cause before which the problem retreats as a consequence, but a message which declares *that in some contexts at least, the problem is not a problem at all*" (emphasis added) (Obeyesekere 1993, 124). Likewise, Bell claims that people "do not take a social problem to ritual for a solution." Rather, they create a "ritualized environment" that *transforms*, rather than resolves, the problem into some new social scheme (Bell 1992, 106).

Ritual does not solve problems by negotiating the best solution. It creates new symbols for interpreting or "framing" the problem.

The cultural interactions between the Greek and Turkish Cypriots described earlier seem to hold together a paradox. Both peoples have experienced great trauma, and since they were children both have feared and hated those from the other side of the island. How is it that in the ritual of eating and dancing together, there can appear to be such peace? Engaging in workshops complemented with evenings of social rituals seems to have brought about a transformation in the participants, holding the complexity and ambiguity of years of conflict and strife within a cultural setting that these two groups have shared for centuries. Greek and Turkish Cypriots have been neighbors, sharing culture for much longer than the political winds have divided them. Perhaps the ritual setting provided a way of seeing and creating a ritual "peace."

By creating new symbolic frames for thinking and holding together complex, dissonant, and conflicting perceptions of the world, rituals may allow for flexibility in thought and worldview changes to more comfortably allow dissonant or new information. Seeing a problem through a ritual prism may enable humans to address or even transform difficult conflicts. While the negotiation room may still be an important component of reconciliation efforts, peacebuilders also need to create a "ritual prism" to allow people in conflict to look at each other and their conflict through a different lens.

The Future of Ritual Reconciliation

The Western-based field of conflict studies has sought to bring some order to a world filled with chaotic violence. In seeking order and rationality, the field has neglected to see and use the oldest form of handling conflict: ritual. Rational and relational approaches to conflict are contributing to humanity's capacity for living a just peace. Yet if we are to create societies where coexistence is possible, we must find ways of working with people's emotions, perceptions, and worldviews, for they often appear as central to the cycles of violence and conflict. Humans need to find more ways of trusting and relating to each other that will move and align perceptions of justice and peace, allowing reconciliation to occur.

Ritual reconciliation holds promise for the growing number of peacebuilders around the world. But first, peacebuilders themselves, particularly Western peacebuilders who may have a bias against symbolic approaches to conflict such as ritual, need to undergo a transformation in their perception of conflict. What would happen if Western peacebuilders began to conceive the process of reconciliation as a process of changing worldviews, transforming perceptions of identity, and reframing conflict? What would happen if peacebuilders grew more intentional about the functions of ritual in their work and started to plan their reconciliation efforts to include more ritual? Can we imagine a group of peacebuilders from around the world gathering to share their experiences of using ritual in their communities? Can we imagine university courses on ritual reconciliation including when to use it, how to balance it with more traditional conflict resolution and reconciliation activities, and how to make sure it is used for positive rather than destructive purposes? The future of ritual as a vehicle for transforming identity, reframing conflict, and enhancing reconciliation processes involves reclaiming this discarded method from humanity's collective past. Humanity needs every tool for reconciliation available, including ritual.

References

Bell, C. M. 1992. *Ritual Theory, Ritual Practice*. New York: Oxford University Press.

Burton, J. W. 1990. *Conflict: Human Needs Theory*. New York: St. Martin's Press.

Campbell, J. 1988. *The Power of Myth with Bill Moyers*. B. S Flowers, ed. New York: Doubleday.

Cheal, D. 1992. Ritual: Communication in Action. *Sociological Analysis*, 53(4):363-74.

Coser, L. A. 1956. *The Functions of Social Conflict*. Glencoe, Ill.: Free Press.

Cragan, J. F., and Shields, D. C. 1995. *Symbolic Theories in Applied Communication Research: Borman, Burke, and Fisher*. Cresskill, N.J.: Hampton Press.

Diamond, L., and McDonald, J. W. 1996. *Multi-Track Diplomacy: A Systems Approach to Peace*. West Hartford, Conn.: Kumarian Press.

Docherty, J. 1998. When the Parties Bring Their Gods to the Table: Learning Lessons from Waco. Ph.D. dissertation, Fairfax, Virginia. George Mason University.

Driver, T. 1991. *The Magic of Ritual: Our Need for Liberating Rites that Transform Our Lives and Our Communities*. San Francisco: Harper.

Fisher, R. J. 1990. Needs Theory, Social Identity and an Eclectic Model of Conflict. In *Conflict: Human Needs Theory*. J. Burton, ed. New York: St. Martin's Press.

Fitzgerald, T. K. 1993. *Metaphors of Identity: A Culture-Communication Dialogue*. Albany: State University of New York Press.

Geertz, C. 1973. *The Interpretation of Cultures: Selected Essays*. New York: Basic Books.

Grimes, R. L. 1995. *Beginnings in Ritual Studies*. Columbia, S.C.: University of South Carolina Press.

———. 1996. Ritual Criticism and Infelicitous Performances. In *Readings in Ritual Studies*. R. L. Grimes, ed. (279-292). Upper Saddle River, N.J.: Prentice Hall.

Gurr, T. 1993. *Minorities at Risk*. Washington, D.C.: United States Institute of Peace Press.

Hunt, E. 1977. Ceremonies of Confrontation and Submission: The Symbolic Dimension of Indian-Mexican Political Interaction. In *Secular Ritual* (124-150). S. F. Moore and B. G. Myerhoff, eds. Amsterdam, Netherlands: Van Gorcum.

Jennings, T. W., Jr. 1996. On Ritual Knowledge. In *Readings in Ritual Studies*. R. L. Grimes, ed. (324-334). Upper Saddle River, N.J: Prentice Hall.

Laughlin, C. D., McManus, J., and D'Aquili, E. G. 1979. *The Spectrum of Ritual: A Biogenetic Structural Analysis*. New York: Columbia University Press.

Lederach, J. P. 1997. *Building Peace: Sustainable Reconciliation in Divided Societies*. Washington, D.C.: United States Institute of Peace Press.

Lorenz, K. 1966. *On Aggression*. New York: Harcourt, Brace, and World.

Maturana, H. R., and Varela, F. J. 1987. *The Tree of Knowledge: The Biological Roots of Human Understanding*. Boston: Shambhala.

———. 1980. *Autopoiesis and Cognition: The Realization of the Living*. Dordrecht, Holland: D. Reidel Publishers.

McManus, J., Laughlin, C. D., and d'Aquili, E. G. 1979. Concepts, Methods and Conclusions. In *The Spectrum of Ritual: A Biogenetic Structural Analysis* (342-62). E. G. d'Aquili, C. D. Laughlin, and J. McManus, eds. New York: Columbia University Press.

Montville, J. 1991. *Conflict and Peacemaking in Multiethnic Societies*. Lexington, Mass.: Lexington Books.

Moore, M. 1993. Indian Village Women Fight State, Husbands to Ban Liquor. *Washington Post*, December 19, A33, 38.

Moore, S. F., and Myerhoff, B. 1977. Introduction: Secular Ritual: Forms and Meanings. In *Secular Ritual* (3-24). S. F. Moore and B. Myerhoff, eds. Amsterdam, Netherlands: Van Gorcum.

Northrup, T. A. 1989. The Dynamic of Identity in Personal and Social Conflict. In *Intractable Conflicts and Their Transformation*. L. Kriesberg, T. A. Northrup, and S. J. Thorson, eds. Syracuse, N.Y.: Syracuse University Press.

Nudler, O. 1990. On Conflicts and Metaphors: Toward an Extended Rationality. In *Conflict: Human Needs Theory* (177-204). J. Burton, ed. New York: St. Martin's Press.

Obeyesekere, R. 1993. The Significance of Performance for Its Audience: An Analysis of Three Sri Lankan Rituals. In *By Means of Performance* (118-30). R. Schechner and W. Appel, eds. New York: Cambridge University Press.

Schirch, Lisa. 1998. Ritual: The New (Old) Tool in the Conflict Transformer's Toolbox. *Conciliation Quarterly*, vol. 17, no. 3 (summer 1998), 2-4.

Smith, J. Z. 1973. The Influence of Symbols Upon Social Change: A Place on Which to Stand. In *The Roots of Ritual*. J. D. Shaughnessy, ed. Grand Rapids, Mich.: Eerdmans.

Turner, V. W. 1969. *The Ritual Process: Structure and Anti-Structure*. Chicago: Aldine Publishers.

Turner, V. 1988. *The Anthropology of Performance*. New York: PAJ Publications.

Volkan, V. D. 1988. *The Need to Have Enemies and Allies: From Clinical Practice to International Relationships*. Northvale, N.J.: J. Aronson.

———. 1990. Psychoanalytic Aspects of Ethnic Conflicts. In *Conflict and Peacemaking in Multi-Ethnic Societies* (81-92). J. V. Montville, ed. Toronto: Lexington Books.

Part II

Practice in Reconciliation, Justice, and Coexistence: Selective Case Studies

9

Coexistence and Reconciliation in the Northern Region of Ghana

Hizkias Assefa

This chapter is a case study of a region in Northern Ghana torn apart by ethnic conflict and the efforts to restore and rebuild a peaceful coexistence. It illustrates a peacebuilding methodology that this author has developed over the past decade from experiences in a number of countries engulfed in civil war and has come to call "Process of Expanding and Deepening Engagement." The methodology offers insights into the interrelationship between the concepts of justice and reconciliation and provides an approach for attaining both objectives in large-scale conflict.[1]

Background to the Conflict—The Guinea Fowl War

The Northern Region, one of the six administrative regions of Ghana, covers almost a third of the country's land area and is inhabited by eighteen ethnic groups. In February 1994 a quarrel erupted in a small town between a man from the Konkomba ethnic group and another from the Nanumba group over the purchase of a guinea fowl, which eventually led to the killing of the Nanumba man. Almost immediately rumors began to fly that Konkombas had attacked Nanumbas. What had begun as a fight between two persons quickly engulfed two ethnic groups in armed conflict. Soon whole villages were aflame. Armed conflict had erupted in Northern Ghana four times since 1980, but this was to become the most devastating.

The conflict rapidly drew in other ethnic communities. The Dagombas and Gonjas, traditional allies of the Nanumbas, sided with them while the Basare,

Nawuri, and Nchumuru joined in on the side of the Konkombas. By the time the war was over, according to some estimates close to ten thousand people were dead.[2] Schools, clinics, and development projects estimated to be worth millions of dollars were destroyed. At least 423 villages were burnt or destroyed.[3] Some towns were "ethnically cleansed." The conflict left over 135,000 internally displaced people, out of an estimated population of close to 700,000 for the entire region. [4]

Issues of the Conflict

Traditionally, the social structure in the Northern Region has been divided into chiefly and acephalous societies. The former have organized themselves around hereditary chieftaincy structures that have a hierarchy from lower level chiefs to divisional chiefs, paramount chiefs, and even some that are superior to paramount chiefs who act like kings. Four ethnic groups, Dagombas, Nanumbas, Gonjas, and Mamprusis, organize themselves this way. The acephalous groups, such as the Konkombas, Nawuris, Basares, and Nchumurus, are segmentary societies that have not had hierarchical structures such as chiefs and chieftaincies.[5] To a very large extent they are migratory yam farmers who settle on a land and till it until it becomes less fertile, at which time they move on to other areas where the land has lain fallow for some time.

In most of the Northern Region, the traditional land tenure practice has not recognized individual ownership of land. Land ownership, to a very large extent, has been vested in paramount chiefs and is held in trust or on behalf of the ethnic groups to which the chief belongs. This, therefore, has restricted land ownership to the chiefly groups. These groups argue that they were the original settlers who allowed the acephalous groups migrating from other areas to settle on their land and farm there by permission. For this permission, the settlers pay tribute to the chiefs, although in many instances the tribute has become more and more symbolic.

The acephalous groups have resented the monopoly of land ownership in the hands of the chiefly peoples as well as the tribute that they are required to pay. Some of the acephalous people refer back to the sixteenth century to justify their claim that *they* were actually the indigenous people in the area and were invaded by the chiefly groups, who then took over the land and imposed their rule on them. The acephalous people insist on the creation of their own paramount chieftaincy that can hold land in trust for them.

Hidden under the issues of chieftaincy and title for land are deep resentments based on perceptions of economic and political inequalities, social and cultural prejudices, and competition for limited resources. Moreover, the era of multiparty politics in Ghana has made population a sensitive issue. The population of some of the acephalous people has been increasing rapidly, and this has meant more demand for representation in national and regional politics. This was threatening traditional authority in the area, which was based on ethnicity and control of land. To complicate issues further, religion also played a role in reinforcing the fault lines in the conflict. The leadership of the acephalous groups is predominantly Christian, having close connections with Western churches and missionaries, while the chiefly groups are primarily Muslim. Therefore, development or humanitarian assistance from Muslim countries to the Muslim population in Northern Ghana, or Bible translations in the local languages and vigorous distributions of these Bibles, fed into the fear of expansion of one religion at the expense of the other.

Government Response

Soon after the outbreak of the war in February 1994, the central government sent in the military to quell the conflict. Although the intervention was effective in stopping the fighting, in some instances the soldiers were drawn into the conflict and created more disaffection in certain areas. In April 1994 a high-level government commission, called the Permanent Peace Negotiation Team (PPNT), was appointed to mediate peace in the conflict area. The mediation effort did not make much progress, because the chiefly groups insisted on an acknowledgment of responsibility and apology from the acephalous groups before negotiations could begin, which the latter were unwilling to do. Although a cease-fire agreement was signed under the auspices of the PPNT in June 1994, unfortunately another armed confrontation was in the making.

Following the 1994 war, Konkombas who had to pass through Nanumba towns to go to hospitals, government offices, and other such public places were harassed, and a few were ambushed and killed by Nanumbas. This unleashed festering hostility and anger caused by the last war, and the Konkombas attacked, killing eighteen Nanumbas. The Nanumbas retaliated by attacking a Konkomba town, destroying it and killing its chief along with a number of Konkombas. The war immediately spread to a number of surrounding towns and villages. By the time the government military forces intervened and stopped it, about 150 people were killed, 14 villages were burnt, over 18,000 heads of cattle were looted, and about 21,000 people became displaced. Victims of the 1994 war who were just starting to rehabilitate themselves became victims again. Many say that they could have predicted that the March 1995 war would break out, since the skirmishes between the Konkombas and Nanumbas had been increasing and tension was mounting. But the agencies responsible for looking into these matters allegedly did not heed the warnings of the impending crisis.

Beginning of the NGO Peacebuilding Process

Several development nongovernmental (NGOs) operating in the conflict areas were concerned that not only much of the infrastructure they had built was destroyed but that the continuation of their work was rendered impossible due to the perpetuation of the conflict. So they formed a consortium[6] to develop collaborative responses to the problems they were facing. One of the consortium members approached this author requesting assistance in the reestablishment of peace in the Northern Region of Ghana. At that time, the author was Director of a Kenyan organization called Nairobi Peace Initiative (NPI). Based on that request, the author and a colleague, Emmanuel Bombande, a program officier at NPI and a Ghanian himself, left for Ghana in November 1994 to work with the consortium in order to develop a response to the conflict situation as well as to facilitate the peacebuilding work that might be necessary. Our first task was to assess, firsthand, the situation in the conflict-torn region.

Preliminary Explorations

During the first visit, we had extensive consultation with NGO representatives working in the conflict areas, church leaders, national level leaders of the youth associations of the conflicting ethnic groups,[7] government officials and ministers, and UN and other international agencies that were operating in the area or were engaged in providing humanitarian assistance. We visited the PPNT to learn what the team was doing and how NGOs might contribute to strengthen its initiative. It seemed that the PPNT was not eager to be associated with the exploration we were undertaking, but they cautioned us indirectly that we should move very carefully since the situation was very delicate.

We toured the conflict areas and held public and private discussions with, opinion leaders, paramount chiefs, district government officials, and various other people in the ethnic communities. It seemed that many of the actors were touched by the fact that Africans from another part of the continent had come to assist in resolving problems in Northern Ghana, and they received us with warmth and openness. Some of the discussions resembled town meetings. Not only the opinion leaders but also the general public came to tell us, sometimes in very moving ways, their stories about the conflict, the causes for it, the extent of their losses, and the sense of betrayal they felt from the other ethnic group with whom they had intermarried and shared their lives. The public meetings enabled us to hear directly from the people, allowing us to gather the various groups' prevailing perceptions about the conflict and of each other. The trust level we enjoyed among the people we visited allowed us to use these meetings not only to learn about the different views, but also to share with our audiences what we learned from the other ethnic groups about *their* perceptions of the causes and dynamics of the conflict. When circumstances allowed, we also used the meetings to challenge each group's perceptions of its adversaries' intentions and behavior as well as inject some conflict resolution concepts and approaches that we thought might be useful in laying down some ideas for future work.

We also visited divisional and paramount chiefs in their respective palaces, where they held court to gather the chiefs, subchiefs, elders, youth association leaders, and ordinary people from the communities to give us an opportunity to hear their stories. Most of the youth associations (which are organized along ethnic lines) had been active in the mobilization of people for the war effort by raising money (some called it war tax), recruiting fighters, and leading attacks and counterattacks.

The overriding message from many of our interactions during the visit was that the Konkombas and their allies had always been the aggressors, that they could no longer be trusted, and hence reconciliation with them was not possible. The youth associations from the chiefly groups demanded that the Konkombas and their allies acknowledge their faults, ask pardon from their former landlords, and pay compensation to the victims of their atrocities. They insisted that the Konkombas must acknowledge that they were settlers and abandon their demand for paramount chieftaincy. Some of the leaders brought in the religious dimension by indicating that meaningful agreement with those who did not share faiths was not possible.

These series of meetings and interactions were valuable opportunities for us to identify people who would be helpful in beginning to build bridges between these communities. Although most of the stories we heard were one-sided, usually presenting one side's grievances and hurt, portraying the other side as evil, and holding the other side responsible for the atrocities, there were a few people in every community who would acknowledge that there were some neighbors from the enemy group who offered them some protection or came to their aid when they needed assistance. We felt that some of those people would be the bridge-builders, and we talked with them in detail after the public meetings were over in order to discuss the conflict in more depth and obtain their commitment for the continuation of the discussion that had started.

We identified four people, elders and other influential people, from each of the four communities (sixteen in all) and invited them to attend a low-key consultation meeting under the pretext of "providing advice to development NGOs operating in the war-ravaged areas on how they could continue with their development work." The meeting was held in Kumasi, the capital of Ghana's Central Region, in May 1995. Kumasi was chosen because it was perceived to be a neutral site for all the conflict parties.

The Kumasi Meeting

Although the meeting was billed as a consultation between the invited participants and the NGOs, the real intention of the gathering was to give the participants a platform to talk about an issue (development) that seriously concerned all of them, and thereby use the opportunity to develop a common understanding of the conflict and the problems underlying it. The atmosphere upon arrival was very tense. There was no mingling among the participants across conflict lines, even at the meal tables. The Konkombas apparently felt outnumbered by the twelve people from the coalition of their adversary groups and were fearful. Later we were told that the four Konkombas slept in one room to protect each other.

Although we had called our meeting a consultation on development, it seemed that the parties came to do battle. The Konkombas were blamed for aggression and held responsible for the damages by the other groups. We organized the meetings in such a way that each group had an opportunity to tell the others how it perceived the conflict and how it suffered from it. The aim was to have the others hear the perspectives of their adversaries and eventually come up with some common definitions and understandings of the conflict and its dynamics. As outsiders to the conflict, we as facilitators also shared our observations about what we had heard and gathered from our tours of the conflict areas. Together, we analyzed the consequences of the conflict in great depth and what it had done to them as individuals and to their communities. There was a deep sense of loss and mourning about what happened.

A discussion then followed about the role that elders had played in conflict resolution in other parts of Africa where we have worked and observed. As a way of deepening the discussion, a reflection on reconciliation based on a monograph that this author had written, called "Peace and Reconciliation as a Paradigm," followed, which led to an exploration of the spiritual and secular understandings of reconciliation, the implications of these understandings, and what reconciliation might look like in the conflict situations in Northern Ghana. Both the Muslim and Christian participants began to share their respective understandings of the concept of reconciliation and discovered many commonalities about how it should be approached. Some of the challenges of reconciliation discussed in our formal sessions were apparently brought up repeatedly and discussed informally following the daily prayer sessions among the Muslim participants.

The Konkomba representatives, by and large, were younger than the other participants were, and since none of them was a chief, they enjoyed less prestige. This worked against them at the beginning. The chiefs talked down to the Konkombas, and the conversation was one-sided. But as the meeting progressed, particularly after our discussion of reconciliation, there was a change in the style of interaction. One prominent divisional chief apologized for the way he had been addressing the Konkomba representatives, pleaded with them to talk openly about their grievances against the three other groups, and requested that the others listen with sincerity. This changed the environment and gave the Konkombas time to detail their perceptions and complaints. The others listened with patience. In fact, whenever anyone from the chiefly groups would intervene to respond to the Konkomba allegations, the chiefs would censure the individual so that the Konkombas were not interrupted. Before this encounter, there had not been an opportunity for the chiefly groups to hear directly from the Konkombas about why the war erupted and how the Konkombas had suffered from it; nor was there opportunity for the Konkombas to hear directly from the chiefly groups about the material devastation and psychological damage that they had caused. One respected elder from the chiefly groups pointed out that there was enough fault on the side of everybody involved, and he suggested that all of them confess their disastrous roles and seek pardon from each other. He began indicating some things that other ethnic groups had done to the Konkombas that might have contributed to the conflict.

The hostile environment that existed at the beginning of the meeting was changing. The participants began to mingle and eat together. Both Muslim and Christian prayers were being offered at the beginning and end of our daily meetings. The adversaries began to sit with each other instead of in their separate corners. There seemed to be a great sense of relief among participants that it was not only possible to be in the same room with the enemy, but to talk in a candid and constructive way with each other. At the end of the meeting, the adversary groups affirmed that dialogue was possible, that the process begun here in Kumasi must continue and include more people. The participants committed themselves to working together to become bridge builders among the four ethnic communities.

The most important accomplishments of the Kumasi meeting were the changes in the protagonists' perception that there were some trustworthy people in the enemy camps; that the resolution of the problem must come by acknowledging each group's responsibility in the conflict, including one's own; that the adversaries would work together to avoid the repeat of the damages of the past; and that such collaboration was possible. A Peace and Reconciliation Follow-up Committee was created to continue the peace efforts begun in the Kumasi meeting, which came to be called Kumasi I.

The committee was made up of two participants from each of the four groups. It was agreed that the committee would work as follows:

a. Every committee member would go back to his or her respective ethnic community and find ways of sharing the insights gained from the Kumasi experience.

b. Where possible, public meetings would be organized to discuss the need for and possibility of peace with the opposing ethnic groups (which later on came to be called Peace Awareness-Raising meetings).

c. To the extent that it was safe, committee members from the adversary ethnic groups would be invited to the Peace Awareness meetings, so that people could see that there were elders even from the enemy group who were prepared to work for peace.

d. Committee members would identify people from the conflict region who should be invited to a follow-up meeting would be identified in order to advance the dialogue process that had just begun.

As a way of advancing the conclusions of Kumasi further, it was decided that a second meeting should be organized for district youth association leaders, chiefs, some influential opinion leaders, and district administrators from all the ethnic groups. The intention was to begin working at the local level and slowly move step by step to the district, regional, and then the national levels.

Unfortunately, just near the end of the meeting, there were rumors that a new outbreak of hostilities was brewing between the Konkombas and Dagombas because of a letter apparently written by the Dagomba Traditional Council calling the Konkombas aliens with no land rights in the area and, therefore, no right for paramount chieftaincy. Stopping this possible outbreak of violence became the first challenge for the peace and reconciliation follow-up committee. The fear was that if violence broke out this time, it might be even more destructive. People had vowed not to be victims again and had armed themselves. The senior Dagomba chief in the meeting took the matter up with the Traditional Council members and persuaded them to retract the letter, if indeed the letter was official. In the meantime, the Konkomba committee members, who also were leaders in the Konkomba Youth Association, quickly returned to their communities and began talking with different influential members of their communities. They urged people to remain calm, as a new outbreak would only make the situation worse. They also indicated that a new dialogue process had started with the chiefly people that might find ways for addressing grievances. Fortunately, as a result of these measures, the feared violence was averted.

The facilitating team revisited the conflict areas and shared the outcomes of the Kumasi meetings with people who were thought to be able to help move the process forward.

Kumasi II

Upon their return, the Kumasi participants began sharing their experience with other members of their respective communities. In the meantime, the follow-up committee had identified people to be invited to the next meeting. Those identified were individually approached and given a long and thorough explanation about the forthcoming meeting and the reason why they were chosen. Some of the youth association leaders said that they did not have a mandate from the national-level office to participate, but we insisted that they were invited because of their personal capacities and were not expected to make commitments on behalf of their organizations.

The Kumasi II meeting took place in September 1995 with about forty participants, including chiefs, district administrators, parliamentarians from the conflict areas, district-level youth association leaders, and opinion leaders. Here again, people who viewed each other with great hostility were brought face-to-face in a nonviolent atmosphere for the first time since the war. For the Nanumba participants the anger was still fresh, as it had only been a few months since the last outbreak of war with the Konkombas. The successive outbreak of war in the area in such short intervals had made the normal governmental administrative functions in the area very difficult, if not impossible. Thus the invited district administrators, by virtue of their position, were very much interested in the quick resolution of the problems and took an active and constructive role throughout the meeting. The parliamentarians and youth association leaders seemed the most bitter and uncompromising.

The Kumasi II meeting used basically the same process as Kumasi I. Although this group was more difficult to handle, slowly the accusations and counteraccusations began to give way to allowing space for each other to talk and listen. There was an exploration of the spiritual dimension, especially after the presentation of "Peace and Reconciliation as a Paradigm," and both Muslims and Christians were acknowledging that in their respective faiths "reconciliation with God" implied reconciliation with other human beings. This kind of reconciliation required protagonists to go beyond pointing out the damage that their adversaries had done to them, to also recognizing and admitting the damage that they themselves had inflicted on their adversaries.

One Muslim youth association leader captured the spirit of these reflections when he narrated a personal story. He had been actively involved in the war by raising money and mobilizing people. He was very bitter about the betrayal and cruelty he had experienced from Konkomba neighbors with whom he had grown up. He said his bitterness had made it impossible for him to even go through his daily prayer rituals since the eruption of the 1994 war. Anger, hate, and revenge dominated his thoughts, making prayers difficult for him. He said he was able to pray for the first time since the war after participating in Kumasi II. We heard reports that after Kumasi II he created a group that assisted the follow-up committee's peace awareness-raising work in the conflict areas.

At the end of Kumasi II, many participants expressed astonishment that they found themselves in the same room with their adversaries talking about the possibilities of peace and what needed to be done to bring it about. Some participants expressed their feelings in the following ways:

"In these meetings, many of us saw our mistakes. Some of us would not even greet each other. We learned the need for self-criticism in conflict situations."

"From their statements at the beginning, there were people from all ethnic groups who were hardliners when they first arrived. They now seem to feel and think differently. This means that this meeting has touched base with most people."

"I learned to tolerate and accommodate the views of other people other than my ethnic affiliation. . . . If the approach of these meetings continues, we can see peace in sight."

"I got to understand the viewpoints and demands of my contenders. . . . Having understood the root causes and the demands of the other ethnic group, I can explain to my people how to begin to make compromises."

"I leaned that I have to live a life that in itself will portray me as a peacemaker. We the people who participated in these meetings will leave here and go back home as peacemakers. Our examples will help others understand the need for them to also come together to talk about their differences without using arms. Thank you facilitators. . . . Allah bless you all."

"I appreciated most a meeting which created very healthy grounds for Africans to respect their true image as created by God."

Like Kumasi I, this meeting's participants resolved that they would talk to their chiefs, youth leaders and followers, opinion leaders, and respective ethnic communities about their experiences in Kumasi and mobilize people for reconciliation. The next step in the process was to expand the reach of the discussion. We felt that a good foundation was being laid, so we could risk reaching out to more powerful elements to bring them into the process. The facilitators also decided to include members of some other ethnic groups who had been implicated in the conflict, such as the Nawuris, Nchumurus, and Basares.

As a result of Kumasi II, a number of things began to happen. The follow-up committee decided to intensify its peace awareness meetings and campaigns. It prepared posters and T-shirts with peace messages, to be distributed during its campaigns. Some of them read: "Human beings cause wars and human beings can end them. Let us end our wars now." "All of us are created in the image of God, let us honor one another." Peace workshops were organized in the district capitals of Bimbilla, Salaga, Yendi, Saboba, Tamale, and Gushegu, where the different ethnic representatives of the follow-up committee gathered to talk to people about the need for tolerance and peaceful coexistence, free movement of people, and the opening up of markets. They were able to reach a large number of people (chiefs, elders, and different population groups) and challenge people's perceptions by the mere fact that the committee was composed of members of ethnic groups that were supposed to be enemies but were now working together for peace. The district administrators and the youth association leaders who had been at Kumasi I and II also began talking to their superiors, chiefs, and paramount chiefs and organizing their own peace awareness meetings in a number of towns. Slowly these meetings began to change the attitudes of the adversaries and helped them reach out to each other.

As an outgrowth of the Kumasi meetings, two former enemies, the Konkomba and Dagomba youth associations, were able to come together to undertake some joint tasks, such as helping to identify cattle looted during the war and return them to their legal owners. Some tractors, bicycles, and other personal belongings confiscated during the war were also returned. In some towns Dagombas and Konkomba villagers were coming together to rebuild schools destroyed during the war. Some Konkomba traders were beginning to come to Dagomba markets in Yendi and return without being attacked. Similar movements were observed regarding some Dagomba traders going to Konkomba markets in Saboba. In the Nanumba areas, the local youth associations organized meetings in four major towns, where they spoke with people about peaceful coexistence and encouraged the free movement of Konkombas as well as the resumption of trade between the two communities. The youth associations also began settling compensation claims between Konkombas and Nanumbas over looted cattle during the war. An agreement was reached between the Nanumba and Konkomba Youth Associations whereby Konkombas who had taken Nanumba land and houses while the Nanumbas were "in exile" were to return them to their previous owners immediately after harvesting the crops they had planted while the Nanumbas were away. Although on some fronts there were signs that the Kumasi process was beginning to have positive effects, progress on the Gonja-Konkomba front was facing difficulties.

From Kumasi III to Kumasi VI

Subsequent meetings began to focus on different strata and sectors of the society.[8] Kumasi III focused on national-level youth association leaders, divisional chiefs (the chiefs immediately below the paramount chiefs), and delegates from ethnic groups that had so far not participated, such as the Basare, Nchumuru, and Nawuri ethnic groups. We also began targeting the more extreme elements of the conflict parties and began to work with them. Some of these people were prominent lawyers and civil servants who had been identified with strongly held positions against the adversary ethnic groups; others were people who were identified as having led attacks against the other ethnic communities.

At the time of invitation, some of these participants said that they would not attend such a meeting; others said they would come for a day or two to present their cases and leave. Those who came appeared with all sorts of documents and maps, government commission of inquiry reports, investigations and findings of British and German colonial authorities, legal briefs submitted to the PPNT, and so on, in support of their peoples' grievances and positions. However, the process caught the interest of these participants, and they stayed, and at the end of the meeting many commented that the scheduled four and a half days for the meeting was not enough. During the meeting, there was much self-criticism, even among the most entrenched national youth association leaders. They acknowledged that they were to blame for the havoc and disaster that ensued and that they could play important roles in healing the societies in Northern Ghana.

In Kumasi III, the Nawuri and Nchumuru representatives did a splendid job in presenting their cases. In the past, their grievances had not usually been well understood. Their presentations in Kumasi III, however, were enlightening and even moved some of the participants to tears. Some people from the chiefly groups began stating publicly that they knew about the Nchumuru and Nawuri grievances but did not understand the gravity of the hurt or the depth of the concern. A sense began to develop that some of the grievances could not be ignored or avoided by legalistic sophistry and that everyone must collaborate to find solutions to these problems. People made repeated references to "conscience" as the guide to evaluating the claims, rather than the sophistication of the arguments. There were shared regrets about the damages the parties had inflicted on each other, and a realization that everyone ended up losing because of it. They detailed the damages suffered: the loss of close friendships, the breakup of ethnically mixed marriages, the horrors of the massacres, and destruction of the economic infrastructure, which had set development in the region back many years.

In the meantime, some specific NGO spin-offs from the Kumasi processes were beginning to take place. Catholic Relief Services (CRS) introduced peace education programs into the various Catholic Church dioceses in nine districts. Action Aid supported a joint Konkomba and Dagomba initiative to rebuild a school at a border area between the two communities, which required a great deal of communication and collaboration between them. The Ghana Council of Churches organized a number of reconciliation seminars, dialogue between Muslim and Christian youth organizations, interfaith prayer meetings, interethnic worship gatherings, and prayers at various locations in the conflict region.

Up to this time the peace process focused on laying the ground for peace in Northern Ghana. There was evidence that momentum toward consensus on the need for peace in the region was building. Increasingly, more and more people, even the extremist elements, were persuaded that dialogue and reconciliation were possible. It was felt that the time had come to go beyond this recognition and give a concrete definition to the kind of peace that the warring communities wanted in their region. So for Kumasi IV, we invited the delegates deputized by the conflicting parties to the PPNT mediation process (which had been attempted soon after the breakout of the war in 1994) to come together in order to arrive at a consensus definition of the issues of contention (building on the discussions, exchanges, and insights gained from the previous Kumasi meetings) and enter into a bilateral and multilateral negotiation process to seek solutions to the issues that underlay the war. In order to enhance the representativity and the mandate of each delegation, we asked that the original number of delegates to the PPNT be augmented by additional people who were respected, influential, and seen as good negotiators for the interests of their respective communities. Therefore, a number of outstanding women and lawyers were included in the teams.

In this meeting, we facilitated very intensive bilateral and multilateral negotiations among the delegates on the issues of the conflict. Each negotiation interaction came up with a set of agreements on identified issues of contention, except for the Gonjas and the Nawuris. The stipulations were then compiled in one common document, called the "Kumasi Draft Agreement on Peace and Reconciliation in the Northern Region of Ghana."

So that the agreement would not freeze on paper, it was deemed important to keep it alive by giving it some institutional embodiment. An organization was created that could capture the spirit of unity that was emerging and that could transcend the ethnocentric attitudes of the parties (identified by many participants as a major factor that had fueled the wars). The new organization was to be a multiethnic youth association composed of all the ethnic groups in the Northern Region, and it would focus on the common, overarching, and region-wide goals, concerns, and areas for cooperation. Among other things, it was decided that the new association would be charged with the following functions:

- Form peace committees to educate people in the region about tolerance and coexistence.
- Encourage free movement of people and commerce in the region.
- Create mechanisms for controlling rumors and misinformation that tend to create uncontrollable conflict situations.
- Develop ways for controlling the inflow of weapons into the region.[9]
- Be involved in the resettlement and reconstruction of the war-ravaged areas by mobilizing resources from NGOs as well as the government.
- Be a catalyst for the overall economic development of the Northern Region by galvanizing interest and assistance from inside and outside the country.

In order to ensure that the peace and reconciliation agreement that was just reached was something the overall society would identify with—rather than only those who participated in the Kumasi meetings—it was agreed that the document would be presented to the delegates' respective communities for extensive consultation and ratification. The delegates pledged to hold a series of meetings with chiefs, opinion leaders, youth associations, administrators, and the general public to invite discussion and comment on the draft agreement. The delegates also agreed to give each other one month for the consultation and then to come back with their feedback on the communities' reactions. In one instance the delegates reported that about five thousand people gathered at one place to discuss and comment on the draft agreements.

When the delegates returned for Kumasi V, they brought very strong support for the agreement from many sectors of their respective communities. However, they also came with amendments that required renegotiation of some of the stipulations in the draft agreement. Although the massive consultation process strengthened the legitimacy of the agreement by involving all the warring communities from the grassroots to the leadership levels, it also had the disadvantage of reducing the delegates' flexibility in the renegotiation process. Once the consulted constituencies demanded certain changes, the hands of the delegates were tied. It became difficult for the delegates to make any concessions. Thus, the negotiation of the amendments became even more difficult than the negotiation of the draft agreement. We began confronting deadlocks on a number of counts. After an excruciating process, the renegotiations were completed, and all the parties came up with the final agreement, which was called the Kumasi Accord on Peace and Reconciliation Between the Ethnic Groups in the Northern Region of Ghana. On March 30, 1996, all the parties signed the accord, and it became the official peace agreement, ending the hostilities between the warring ethnic groups and proposing new ways of governing their relationships with one another.

It was felt that the Kumasi Accord should be presented to the Northern Regional Administration as the government agency responsible for the peace and security of the region, and from whom we had received a great deal of assistance in terms of security and logistics during the peacebuilding process. We felt that through the regional minister, the accord could also be presented to top-level government officials, including the president of the Republic, for their official blessing as well as commitment for the great rehabilitation effort needed in the area to reinforce the peace accord.

Kumasi VI followed in October 1996. Here, all of the youth association leaders of the Northern Region debated and approved the draft constitution for the new organization, which was called Northern Ghana Youth and Development Association (NORYDA). Some referred to NORYDA as a "new structuring of political life in the Northern Region." In this meeting, we tried to identify the training needs for the NORYDA members so that they would be in a position to sustain the peacebuilding process. In the meantime, the NGO consortium undertook an assessment trip on how to rehabilitate the Northern Region now that a peace accord was signed and the participants were showing their resolve to stick to it. In December 1996, Ghana's second national elections took place. It is interesting to note that some of the people who were active in the Kumasi peace processes made "peace and development in Northern Ghana" their campaign platform, and some of them were elected into office. One even became cabinet minister.

Insights, Lessons, and Implications

After a long and protracted process, a significant milestone has been reached with the signature of the accord and the creation of NORYDA. But, by no means, is this the end of the journey. There is no end to this journey. One can only talk about opening a new chapter. The peace process leading to the accord has given the protagonists hope that what they thought was impossible in terms of positive relationships with their adversaries is indeed possible. It has given them a taste of what that new relationship could look like and to expose them to a methodology that could generate mutually satisfying results if they worked on their differences in a certain way. Once they caught that glimpse, even if they have setbacks in their relationships, and there will definitely be setbacks, the expectation is that the protagonists themselves will build on these new insights and conduct their future interrelationships in a different way. However, as we know from interpersonal relationships, nurturing these new insights once the major obstacles and hostilities are removed is very hard work. Social attitudes, perceptions, and behaviors acquired over generations do not change overnight.

They require constant work, vigilance, and support. Once the major hostilities are removed, inertia begins to set in. After the flurry of activities leading to the peace accord, the sacrifices people make in terms of time, resources, donor interest, and support tend to subside. There is therefore a great concern about how to keep the commitment going. Given that NORYDA would have less attention and support from the facilitators and the NGO consortium, how much commitment and sacrifice will it continue to manifest? What is the best way to support and encourage over the long term such social change processes as the Kumasi Accord was able to usher in? How do societies internalize new values and attitudes and begin to live them? These are still unanswered questions that the peace process in Northern Ghana has to wrestle with.

Notwithstanding, these questions, what are some of the insights that can be drawn from the Ghana experience?

Methodology of Reconciliation in Large-Scale Social Conflicts

The first lesson that comes out of the Northern Ghana case is methodology for working on reconciliation in large-scale social conflicts. Reconciliation is difficult enough in interpersonal conflict situations where there is more experience and precedence in terms of approaches and models. The problems multiply exponentially when working on reconciliation in large-scale conflicts where there are very few guides. This case illustrates a methodology that might be helpful in such cases. It demonstrates how it might be possible to start with a manageable number of actors and issues and then gradually expand outward to reach the whole community in order to address the multiplicity of issues in the conflict in a multidimensional and holistic manner. It provides some pointers on how to guide people through deep analysis of the problems underlying their common predicament and search for mutually satisfactory solutions in a spirit of self-criticism and mutual acceptance of responsibility. It gives some indications on how to facilitate a peace process which is owned by the community rather than by just the leaders and elites, as is usually the case in most peacemaking processes.

Protracted Civil Wars and the Grassroots Approach

An interesting feature of the Northern Ghana peace process is that it was a bottom-up approach. This type of approach could have the potential of mitigating the havoc many protracted civil wars cause in Africa and a number of other places. Many of these wars, which presumably begin with claims for liberation, autonomy, freedom, or unity of one people or another, seem to have lost their original purpose and taken on a life of their own. Although it is mostly ordinary people who are paying for these wars with displacement or even their lives, the very people in whose name these wars are being waged do not seem to be able to influence the duration of these conflicts, the manner in which they are fought, or the sacrifice the conflicts entail. The driving force behind the perpetuation of these wars seems to be the political ambition or economic gain of the leaders rather than popular commitment or support. Unfortunately, the culture of fear inculcated by the leaders in the population in the name of "security," "unity," "effective mobilization against the enemy," and so on, makes it difficult for the civilian population to challenge the wishes of the top leaders or to voice their preference for peaceful resolution. The Northern Ghana peacebuilding process suggests that one way of dealing with these kinds of conflicts might be to work at grassroots empowerment. By creating a forum for the grassroots where they are able to understand the conflicts, visualize alternatives, and articulate preferences, leadership can begin to emerge from below, which can influence top leaders' views and behavior. An active civil society begins to take shape that restrains the official leadership's commitment to perpetuating the conflict.

In Northern Ghana many top-level leaders were skeptical and even resistant to the peacebuilding process, while the people at the grassroots level were generally supportive of it. Eventually, the momentum created at the grassroots level began to gather force, pressuring the leaders to follow suit. Even the intransigent leaders came around and joined the process when they observed the enthusiasm and desire of their followers for it. They began to take cues from the people they were claiming to lead. Of course, these processes would have to be handled carefully, especially at the beginning, so that they are not seen as threats and are squelched by the top leaders. In the Northern Ghana situation, the process began in a very low-key, nonthreatening manner. The context for starting the work was "rehabilitation" and "development," to which most of the leadership could not object. By the time the impact began to be felt by the more intransigent leadership, the followers were already persuaded that the process must continue. Moreover, even the more intransigent leaders began to realize that the process had space for them. They were made to feel that even their adversaries could give a hearing to their extremist views as long as they were willing to be engaged and continue the dialogue. What proved fascinating later on was the "conversion" of the top-level leaders and their public confession of their responsibility for the role they played in the war and the destruction inflicted on each other's peoples.

The Coordination Dilemma

In many peacebuilding initiatives, especially those undertaken by NGOs, it is very difficult to get the breathing room needed to work systematically at a process over a long duration. As soon as the process begins to show signs of progress, it attracts a lot of competition from other peacebuilders, mediators, politicans, funders, and so on, each trying to influence it with an approach that may not be sympathetic with the one already under way. Alternatively, a parallel process might be started by other actors that begins to create confusion and at times even cynicism among the conflict parties and outside observers. There are many cases where signs of progress in the peacebuilding process trigger government intervention, which then prematurely takes over the process and risks losing the original vision or having it become politicized to the detriment of the process. This lack of incremental progress where new steps do not build on old is a cause of major frustration among practitioners in the field. In Northern Ghana, we were lucky to have the space to work at the peace process fairly intensively over a two-year period with little disruption and with the benefit of building on the momentum gained from previous steps. Part of the reason for this might have been because we enjoyed the respect of the parties and our partners, both of whom trusted us to lead the process as we deemed appropriate. Second, there was clarity of vision, concepts, and approach that struck a chord among participants. The "Peace and Reconciliation as a Paradigm" monograph that was widely shared helped participants to know where the facilitators were coming from and where they were headed. Third, the conflict was not a subject of much international media attention; therefore, it did not attract the interest of many project-hungry conflict resolution outfits. Although some tried to come in and start parallel processes, there was not much funding for their initiatives, and they didn't last long. Even the government's PPNT unintentionally gave us space, but for different reasons. It did not think that something useful would come out of what we were doing and left us alone until it saw the accord. We benefited from that space. One way of dealing with this problem of "space" and unhealthy competition could be creating mechanisms for coordination where different actors could work together or at least in a complementary fashion. However, the kind of coordination that seems to work best in peacebuilding and reconciliation initiatives is one that emerges organically out of a shared philosophy and methodology. Unfortunately, that does not come easily. When coordination is a result of a "marriage of convenience" or is overtly or covertly compelled by outsiders (like governments or donors), it becomes a difficult process, rife with conflict among the people expected to coordinate their efforts. It tends to take as much energy to manage the coordination (trying to make peace among peacemakers) as to do the work for which the collaboration is needed. It is a major challenge to encourage coordination that emerges organically.

Relationship between Justice and Reconciliation

In most deep-rooted social conflicts, issues of perceived or real injustice are invoked by one party against the other, if not reciprocally against each other. The approach to reconciliation used in Northern Ghana saw justice and reconciliation as inextricably intertwined. Any reconciliation that disregards issues of injustice underlying the conflict is not true reconciliation and will not be durable. It becomes appeasement by those who are benefiting from the injustice to calm down the "righteous indignation" of those who are suffering from the injustice. Reconciliation necessitates the transformation of unjust relationships to more just ones. That is why it is not easy. However, reconciliation and the pursuit of justice are not the same thing. Although justice is a necessary condition for reconciliation, it is not a sufficient condition. The aim of justice is equity, to address perceived imbalances in the relationship and grant the aggrieved their due. However, even if people might have equitable relationships or their rights are respected, their relationship may still be adversarial; full of fear, suspicion, anger, and hostility. Reconciliation goes beyond equity and tries to transform these negative relationships into more trusting, positive, and cooperative relationships. There lies the painful dilemma of reconciliation work—how to work at justice while maintaining or building positive relationships, how to look at the past and correct grievances while creating an amicable and livable present and future for all the protagonists. Therefore, reconciliation calls for a different methodology for working at justice than the typical adversarial approach that ordinary judicial process implies.[10] In the Northern Ghana situation, the underlying cause of the conflict was the injustice perceived by the acephalous peoples regarding land ownership and inequitable social status at the hands of the chiefly peoples. On the other hand, the chiefly peoples thought it was unjust for the acephalous peoples to claim land ownership when it had been the chiefly peoples' generosity that allowed them to settle on the land in the first place, and since their right to use the land has been guaranteed. The aim of the reconciliation exercise was to come up with creative frameworks where justice is done to the claims of the parties against each other while at the same time enhancing harmonious coexistence between them. Some of the outcomes of the Kumasi Accord were able to meet these two objectives. For example, among the Dagomba on one hand and the Konkomba and Basare on the other, the Dagombas conceded to create paramount chiefs for the latter two groups and to recognize their right to own land through these chiefs. Such recognition of land ownership also enhanced the political and economic status of the Konkombas and Basares. Lest the Dogambas who conceded to this right feel threatened by the creation of autonomous paramount chieftaincies in their region, the Konkombas and create a commonwealth by being part of the Dagomba Traditional Council, which is the traditional administrative organ for the region. This reaffirmed the traditional linkages that existed between the three groups and encouraged them to work together for the welfare of the region, which will benefit all three. What was particularly interesting about the Kumasi processes was how the issues of injustice were presented in such a manner that even those who were accused of being unjust publicly admitted it and took an active role in addressing it.

Reconciliation as Mediation between Tradition and Modernity

One interesting facet of the Northern Ghana experience was the significant role traditional institutions played in the peacebuilding and reconciliation process. Compared to many African societies, the traditional systems of social organization in Ghana are still intact and powerful. The institutions of chiefs and elders are still rich in culture, and they command great authority and influence in their communities. They were not only useful entry points for the peacebuilding and reconciliation process but also were critical in sustaining and reinforcing whatever peace resulted from the processes. We, as facilitators faced the dilemma of how to work with and through these institutions that appeared to have many autocratic features, which stratify people as rulers and subjects on undemocratic principles. In the last three decades of political and economic modernization processes in Africa, the prevailing view had been to present these traditional institutions as having nothing to offer and to reject them wholesale as backward and undemocratic. At first, we were similarly tempted to bypass these structures in this peacebuilding process, on the assumption that working with them was somehow accepting and reinforcing these negative characteristics. However, one of the lessons that has emerged from the failure of many modernization and development efforts of the recent past in Africa has been that ignoring or dismantling these traditional institutions has had serious detrimental consequences. Grafted systems from other cultures imposed on African realities have not only failed to take root and produce durable and positive impact, but have brought about alienation and confusion. We also realized that as peacebuilders and change agents in our own right, our strategy should be to identify the positive dimensions of these traditional institutions and strengthen them while mitigating some of their arbitrary, undemocratic, and unjust characteristics rather than undermine or bypass them entirely. In effect, then, in addition to mediating between adversaries, the peacebuilding processes in Northern Ghana became a mediating ground between modernity and tradition. The aim became how to reinforce positive traditional values of belongingness, meaning, stability, and cohesion by slowly infusing them with modern values of citizenship, participation, and equity. Some of the statements made by the chiefs during the Kumasi processes were illustrative of the kind of change that was beginning to take place. "As a chief, what I experienced in Kumasi will help me administer with justice all the ethnic groups I rule." "As a chief I have to meet my subjects on my return and brief them all on what have I experienced here, and teach them that there is need for reconciliation and peace in order to enhance development. . . . I shall organize the youth and educate them against misinformation, tribalism, and injustice." One celebrated chief suggested, "Let us get women to take part since women can talk to us to understand peace better." It was felt that as long as "justice," "participation," and "respect for people's rights" become major guiding principles, there would be major benefits in working within and strengthening the traditional institutions. Under these circumstances, something genuinely indigenous could develop that could continue to provide meaning and significance to the people but at the same time respond to their evolving needs. This approach has important implications for the development of African governance systems where the great preoccupation of the past decade had been the imposition of multiparty political institutions and processes with the total disregard for indigenous institutions that might be useful. In many instances, the new institutions have not produced the expected result but have also generated their own confusion and conflicts. There seems to be a need to build upon mechanisms that have been tested by time and to reform them with the desired values rather than destroy them with the hope that the new ones will work. The experience of how this was done in the peacebuilding process in Northern Ghana might be instructional in this regard.

Role of Religion in the Reconciliation Process

The conflict in Northern Ghana had a religious dimension. The two major protagonists were divided along religious lines. Although most of them shared various forms of African traditional religions, most of the chiefly groups such as the Dagomba, Gonja, and Nanumba are Muslims, while the acephalous groups are predominantly Christian, at least on the leadership level. Although the conflict was not about religion per se (where one side is trying to convert or impose its religious value on the other), religious differences served to reinforce the existing divisions between the groups. Both groups had fears about the expansion of the other religion, and some more fundamentalist preachers had sparked Muslim-Christian riots in the region. The methodology for the reconciliation process in Northern Ghana, which was inspired by the "Peace and Reconciliation as a Paradigm" philosophy, had a spiritual dimension. One of the strategies used in the process was to help the participants walk through various steps in the reconciliation process, such as honest self-examination, acknowledgment of responsibility, public admission, seeking apology, providing restitution, and so on. Both religions had well-adapted concepts and frameworks to do this. The concepts of confession, repentance, seeking forgiveness, mercy, and atonement are recognized in both religions. Also, both faiths acknowledge that people have accountability for their behavior to an entity greater than themselves, and that even if they managed to deceive each other, there was an all-knowing and all-perceiving being who challenges them to be honest. The reconciliation process fostered those common beliefs and helped generate an environment for very sincere self-examination and self-criticism. Both Christian and Muslim participants were able to go beyond their religious identities and meet at a spiritual meeting point where they could look critically at their behavior with, as the participants put it, "God as a witness." Exploring the religious and spiritual dimension allowed the process to move beyond the competitive and legalistic discussion and get to the bottom of problems. However, it is important to distinguish between religion and spirituality. Religion has been used as an instrument of division, and if the focus is on religion itself, it might be difficult to bring together adversaries who do not share the same faith. But focus on spirituality can enable people to transcend their differences in dogma or rituals and focus on the essence of all religions. If the process manages to get the parties to that point, there is a powerful meeting place there, which can unleash tremendous possibilities for honesty and reconciliation. Although this author was raised a Christian and practices that faith, in one of these workshops a Muslim Sheik commented to me: "You may not know it, but you are deeply Muslim." That was an indication that we were drinking from the same spiritual fountain, although we came at it from different religious entry points. That was the spirit of Kumasi. In a way, the Kumasi process was challenging people not only to come to resolve the specific problems of the conflict in Northern Ghana, but to also reflect on themselves and become better Christians, Muslims, or even human beings since the self-reflection, honesty, humility, and understanding of others are also signs of mature human relationships and healthy societies.

Notes

1. The peacebuilding process that this case describes took place between November 1994 and December 1996. I would like to thank Isaac Osei of Action Aid, Chris Bonuedie from World Vision, Jack Bochwe from Assemblies of God, Jessewuni Issahaku from BADECC, and Ben Pugansoa from Oxfam, who were not only great partners and team members on the ground, but also whose tireless follow-up and sense of humor made the process bearable and rewarding. Thanks also to George Wachira and Florence Mpaye, who gave a backing from the Nairobi office to the work that Emmanuel Bombande and I were doing in the field. I would like to express my deep gratitude to Ineke Van Winden of the Dutch Interchurch Aid, who provided encouragement for the initiative and was instrumental in providing financial backing for the work, as well as to my wife, Gretchen Van Evera, for her patient and helpful support during the peacebuilding work and for her editorial assistance.

2. Ada van der Linde and Rachel Naylor, *The Peace Process in Northern Ghana*, an unpublished report, p. 46. The authors report that the figures come from a National Mobilization Program developed in May 1994 to deal with the aftermath of the conflict.

3. Linde and Naylor, p. 47.

4. Linde and Naylor, p. 47.

5. However, this is slowly changing. In some areas which are densely populated by Konkombas, the paramount chiefs of the chiefly groups have appointed lower level Konkomba chiefs who pledge allegiance to them.

6. The members of the consortium were Action Aid, Action on Disability and Development, Amaschina, Assemblies of God, BADECC, Catholic Relief Services, Catholic Secretariat, Council of Churches, Gupgatemale, Lifeline Danemark, Pernoridas, Oxfam, Red Cross, TIDA, and World Vision.

7. Youth associations have very strong influence in their respective ethnic communities, especially on issues of the conflict. They were responsible for mobilizing people and resources for the war effort. Although called *youth associations*, most of the leaders are in their forties and fifties.

8. Due to shortage of space, the details of what transpired in the processes of Kumasi III up to Kumasi IV have been drastically summarized. More detailed discussion is provided in a publication by the author, called *Process of Expanding and Deepening Engagement: Methodology of Reconciliation Work in Large-Scale Social Conflicts* (forthcoming).

9. "There are more arms around in markets and they were being actively sold in Tamale, Accra, and other markets. The presence of arms seems to have been a cause or at least a heavily provocative factor in the conflict and in the spread of violence." A quote from an interview in van der Linde and Naylor, *The Peace Process in Northern Ghana*, p. 44.

10. See Hizkias Assefa, "The Meaning of Reconciliation," in *People Building Peace* (Utrecht, Netherlands: European Center for Conflict Prevention, 1999).

10

Reconciliation and Justice in South Africa

Lessons from the TRC's Community Interventions

Hugo van der Merwe

This chapter examines the impact of the TRC's (Truth and Reconciliation Commission's) work on reconciliation in two communities that were wracked by violence during apartheid, and it evaluates how the TRC's intervention contributed to resolving the problem of past injustices. The case studies raise fundamental questions about the meaning of reconciliation and conceptions of appropriate forms of justice, highlighting the top-down nature of the TRC process and illuminating what bottom-up reconciliation would involve. The chapter is based on interviews conducted with TRC staff, nongovernmental organizations (NGOs) involved in the TRC process, and members of the two communities (victims, ex-combatants, and community leaders).[1]

Background to the TRC's Community Intervention

The Truth and Reconciliation Commission was established by the South African government to deal with issues related to past human rights abuses during the apartheid era. It was tasked with uncovering the truth about past abuses, granting amnesty to individual perpetrators, and providing victims with a forum to recount their experiences.

The legislation that established the TRC was the outcome of a confluence of different political and social developments during South Africa's transition to democracy. The key political tension was between the demand of the outgoing government to protect their members from criminal and civil prosecution, and that of the liberation movements to hold the previous government accountable for past abuses. As part of the constitutional negotiations, both sides wanted the question of a truth commission to be addressed.[2] The exact balance between punishment and indemnity, accountability and impunity, had to be negotiated. The final product of constitutional negotiations presented a compromise that established an obligation to provide amnesty to human rights abusers by the new government, but left the details of the process to the new government. The granting of amnesty was thus an obligation of the new government in respect to both the criminal and civil liability of the perpetrators.[3]

Civil society structures (particularly nongovernmental organizations and churches) campaigned for the exposure of past abuses on all sides of the conflict, while also strongly urging the protection of the rights of victims. A compromise agreement that satisfied these competing demands was reached through a long process of debating, lobbying, and legislative negotiating. The resulting TRC legislation was shaped, however, more by national political agendas than the needs of victims and local communities.

The TRC was given the task of both granting amnesties and dealing with the legacy of these abuses. In an attempt to address the moral dilemma of impunity and to address victims' rights to compensation and dignity, the TRC legislation (the Promotion of National Unity and Reconciliation Act No. 34 of 1995) was formulated to provide a process of investigating past abuses and engaging communities in a process of public storytelling alongside the granting of individual amnesties.[4]

The initiative and momentum to establish a TRC in South Africa did not arise as a result of a grassroots and collective civil society groundswell. While there was significant civil society input into the process, the incentive for such a commission was rather the product of party-political concerns and negotiations. The TRC legislation was debated and passed by parliament during the period of consensus politics, when the African National Congress (ANC) and the National Party (NP) were partners in the Government of National Unity and pursued cooperative legislative development. The legislative process was thus one that attempted to encompass the needs of a range of political groups.[5]

While the TRC's mandate covered a range of responsibilities, section 3(1) of the act spells out its specific objectives:

> The objectives of the Commission shall be to promote national unity and reconciliation in a spirit of understanding which transcends the conflicts and divisions of the past by:
>
> (a) Establishing as complete a picture as possible of the causes, nature, and extent of the gross violations of human rights which

were committed by conducting investigations and holding hearings;

(b) Facilitating the granting of amnesty to persons who make full disclosure of all the relevant facts relating to acts associated with a political objective and comply with the requirements of this Act;

(c) Establishing and making known the fate or whereabouts of victims and by restoring the human and civil dignity of such victims by granting them an opportunity to relate their own accounts of the violations of which they are the victims, and by recommending reparation measures in respect of them;

(d) Compiling a report providing as comprehensive an account as possible of the activities and findings of the Commission . . . and which contains recommendations of measures to prevent the future violations of human rights.

The act is not clear on how these objectives could be achieved in a way that would "promote national unity and reconciliation in a spirit of understanding which transcends the conflicts and divisions of the past." Details regarding the kind of investigative and storytelling process that could establish a picture of violations and restore the dignity of victims were left open to the TRC commission to formulate.

The TRC operationalized the goals of uncovering the truth and restoring the dignity of victims largely in terms of engaging communities in a process of collecting statements from local victims and then holding a community (gross human rights violation) hearing. These community hearings became the dominant focus of the first fourteen months of the TRC's operation (April 1996 to May 1997). Altogether, eighty such community hearings were held in this period. These hearings were public meetings lasting between one and three days, during which ten to twelve victims told their stories to a panel of commissioners and a hall full of community members, local leaders, and local and international leaders.

These hearings served a number of functions for the TRC. First, the hearings focused on victims—giving them an opportunity to tell their stories. Second, they provided a space for open discussion in order to promote understanding among different groupings in local communities, between political parties or different races. Third, the community hearings provided a powerful media image that could be conveyed to the country as a whole—allowing the nation to confront its past, making it impossible for people to deny the suffering that had been caused by the conflict.

How these community hearings were used to promote justice and reconciliation was never clearly explained. They remained contentious concerns that were interpreted differently by various political parties and stakeholders throughout the life of the TRC. Fundamentally, the TRC was the embodiment of a denial of justice, because the amnesty provision in the constitution had robbed victims of their right to criminal and civil recourse. On the one hand, justice was presented as the price that had to be paid for reconciliation. Reconciliation was to be achieved through truth (particularly the public truth telling that occurred at the hearings) rather than through a retributive justice process. On the other hand, the TRC presented its work as an alternative form of justice, namely restorative justice. Rather than achieving justice through punishment, the TRC argued that restorative justice would be achieved through truth, dialogue, and reparations to victims from the state. This chapter examines how various stakeholders in two South African communities assessed this reconciliation and justice program, particularly in the light of the hearings that were held in two communities: Duduza and Katorus.

The East Rand: Duduza and Katorus

Background to the Conflict

Duduza and Katorus are two communities in what is called the East Rand of Johannesburg, an area that experienced extensive political violence between 1960 and 1994 (the time period covered by the TRC). Their political history is in many ways typical of numerous other South African townships. Their experience, however, is probably more intense—political mobilization was more extensive, and more lives were lost than in most other townships.

Both communities experienced some violence during the 1976 Soweto Uprising, in which a number of youths were shot and killed by the police. After a period of relative political calm, the community mobilized again in the early 1980s under the leadership of Civic Associations, locally based ANC-aligned political structures. In the mid-1980s violence erupted after police attempted to crack down on demonstrations that targeted local political structures and focused on demands for better services.

Police (many of whom were Black) and councillors living in the township were chased out of the area, and the townships were made "ungovernable"—state structures were effectively shut out of the townships. Police responses to protest action also became more drastic and ruthless. The experience of Duduza was particularly brutal. In one incident the police attacked the house of one of the Duduza Civic Association leaders; during the attack his two daughters were killed. In a revenge attack by Duduza youth, a white woman from a nearby farm was killed when her car was ambushed.[6] Police used detention and torture extensively and, in some cases, assassination in order to suppress political protests in the area. Police also infiltrated local political structures and orchestrated the "zero hand grenade" incident,[7] in which a number of Duduza activists were killed. Linked to these deaths was the murder in 1985 of an alleged police informant, Maki Skhosana. Rumors that she had had a relationship with one of the police operatives and had informed on the victims spread through the community. She was beaten and stoned to death by members of the community, and her body was set alight and mutilated. Several people were subsequently prosecuted and sent to jail for the murder.

Though Katorus experienced similar ANC-state conflicts, they were eclipsed in the 1990s by very intense fighting between supporters of the ANC and the Inkatha Freedom Party (IFP). While many observers point to the role of the security forces in fueling tensions and supporting one side (and some claim both sides) in numerous ways, including the supply of weapons, the community experienced a very clear internal division along political and (as the conflict progressed) ethnic lines.[8]

The ANC-IFP conflict in Gauteng erupted in 1990 when various violent incidents between residents of a hostel and a squatter settlement in Thokoza occurred. (These were replicated in other Gauteng townships such as Soweto, Sebokeng, and Kagiso.) After increasingly violent battles, the hostel residents were chased out, and the hostel was destroyed. The conflict continued to spread throughout the Katorus area as political parties fought for control of the area. The violence again reached a peak between July 1993 and April 1994, when close to 1,200 people died in the conflict (*The Star* 1995). In the four years of conflict, more than 2,000 people died in Katorus (*Simunye News* 1997).

The conflict led to the community being divided into clearly delineated IFP and ANC sections. IFP supporters within the community were chased out (and some killed), and hostels became virtual forts that were under direct political control of IFP *indunas* (traditional leaders). Residents in the houses around the hostels were evicted and replaced with hostel residents (or other IFP supporters). Dividing lines between IFP and ANC areas were no-go zones, often identifiable because the houses had been completely destroyed. A major effect of the conflict was that hundreds of houses were looted and destroyed, and many hostels sustained extensive damage. Whereas before the conflict residents of the community and the hostel mixed freely (socially and economically), the conflict made it impossible for any interaction (other than violence) to occur. Residents were sometimes killed simply for going into the wrong part of the township.

The conflict took on increasingly ethnic proportions as it intensified. Whereas Zulus were accepted in the community along with any other ethnic (or language) groups before the violence, Zulu speakers were increasingly treated with suspicion as the violence got worse. People were sometimes killed either because they spoke Zulu in the wrong area, or because they could not speak Zulu (fluently or with the right accent) in another area.

The continued violence led to the establishment of military-style units being formed in the respective areas. In 1993 Self-Defense Units (SDUs) were established in the ANC areas. These SDUs consisted of local youth (mainly teenagers) who received minimal military training but were expected to patrol the townships at night. The structures of control that regulated their actions were generally quite loose and ineffective. Shortly after the formation of the SDUs, the IFP also formed similar structures, called Self-Protection Units (SPUs), that performed a similar function for the hostels and the sections of the townships controlled by the IFP.

The role of the police and army in the conflict was a very controversial one. The ANC-aligned organizations had long been in a conflict with these structures. The IFP was known to have received assistance from the state, and in many instances it was reported that the police or army directly assisted the IFP in attacks on ANC areas. There have, however, also been many occasions during the conflict when hostel dwellers were killed or injured by security forces. The local police force was generally seen as completely ineffective in controlling the situation, and was often too scared to go into certain areas of the township. The Internal Stability Unit of the police, which had a reputation for extreme brutality and torture, played a more forceful role.

There have also been numerous reports of third force activities in fanning this conflict. While on the one hand providing assistance to the IFP in its fight with the ANC, the state—through its various clandestine security apparatus— was also instigating conflict through targeted assassinations and incitement to both sides to step up the violence.

The underlying causes of the conflict increasingly became obscured by the dynamics of violence and revenge. An SDU and an SPU commander give their respective reasons for involvement:

> After my brother was shot (dead), and his girlfriend was raped and the friend of his girlfriend was also raped and shot, I decided that there was no reason for me to sit down and relax while people were dying.

> If you're a Zulu, especially from Natal, even if you are a member of the ANC, its always suspected that you're an IFP, so I decided to stay with the Zulus. Most people who were dying here were Zulus from Natal—some were even my relatives. So I decided to stand and fight against the ANC. (*Simunye News* 1997)

Internal tensions within the broader camps, such as between the SDUs and sections of the ANC, between SDUs and the communities, and between the civics and the ANC, also sometimes spilled over into violence.

Similar ANC-IFP tension also arose around the presence of IFP supporters in Duduza hostels. In 1991 violence erupted in the hostels as IFP hostel residents from a neighboring township (where ANC supporters had chased them out) fled to the Duduza hostels. The conflict that emerged in Duduza hostels was both among hostel dwellers and between the hostel and community residents. During this conflict, members of the community burned down and demolished the hostels. The community absorbed some of the hostel residents, while others fled to other townships.

The picture painted here is of the broader visible dynamics of the conflicts. A direct result of the conflicts was that the internal cohesion among community members was also destroyed, as suspicions, allegations of complicity, retribution, and competition for leadership led to violent internal struggles and suppression of internal dissent. Both communities thus experienced various dimensions of conflict: conflict between the community and the state, conflict between political parties within the community, conflict within political parties, and conflict among community members who no longer trusted each other because of rumors, suspicions, and generalized fear.

The violence in Duduza subsided after the destruction of the hostels. In Katorus, the violence decreased significantly around the time of the first democratic elections of 1994. Political violence, however, flared up at various points over the next few years, but not to the same level as pre-1994. These communities now have democratic local government structures, and Katorus in particular has been targeted for development through central and local government housing and infrastructure projects. The legacy of the past, however, was still very strongly felt by respondents who participated in this study in 1997. Some saw the work of the TRC as opening old wounds, but for many community members it was only the first step in the process of making peace with the past.

TRC Involvement in Duduza

The TRC held a one-day human rights violation hearing in Duduza on February 4, 1997. The hearing combined cases from Duduza and the neighboring communities of Ratanda, KwaThema, and Tsakane. In preparation for the hearing the TRC met with various parties and individuals in the community. These included the local town council, the Civic Association, trade unions, and churches.

TRC statement takers came to the area and collected statements from the public on a specified day. Additional statements were collected by the Khulumani Victim Support Group, an independent victim support network that was not included in the TRC's consultative workshops with the community. The hearing was very well attended—the hall was filled to capacity, and speakers had to be set up outside the hall. The hearing was mainly attended by local Duduza residents, with a few people coming from Ratanda, KwaThema, and Tsakane. It appears that only one White person from the local historically White town of Nigel, a National Party councillor, attended. Of the ten cases heard on the day of the hearing, only three were from residents of Duduza. The witnesses from Duduza who told their stories were

1. victims of the zero hand grenade incident,
2. the sister of Maki Skhosana, and
3. a person who was tortured by police and accused by others in the community of being a police spy.

The other six cases were from the neighboring communities and represented a range of victim experiences spanning the last thirty years and representing various different political organizations.

TRC Involvement in Katorus

The hearing in Katorus was scheduled for the same week as that of Duduza. (The whole of the East Rand was covered in one week.) In preparation for the hearing, the TRC met with the leadership structures of the ANC and IFP in each of the townships individually. They also held a few meetings with churches and NGOs that were active in the area.

The TRC chose Vosloorus as the venue for the Katorus hearings, apparently for security reasons. The hearings were held over two days. Given the small number of IFP-aligned victims, who had made statements to them, the TRC had clearly made an effort to provide a balance in terms of the stories presented at the hearings. The hearings were not very well attended. The hall where the hearing was held was only about half full.

The following list of cases heard on February 7, 1997, demonstrates the range of experiences of victims who testified:

1. An IFP man whose brother was killed by ANC supporters (Vosloorus)
2. An IFP man who was shot by ANC supporters and whose brother was killed by soldiers (Thokoza)
3. An ANC supporter who was shot and blinded by police
4. A woman who told of her two brothers who were shot and killed by IFP supporters (Thokoza)
5. An IFP member who told of her brother and brother-in-law (both hostel dwellers) being shot by the police, and of a second brother-in-law being shot by township youth (Thokoza)
6. A woman who told of her husband disappearing after being abducted by hostel dwellers (Thokoza)
7. A man who told of being attacked by a group of Zulu-speaking people on a train on his way home to Thokoza (some fellow passengers were killed)
8. An SDU commander who was assaulted and tortured by police (Katlehong)
9. A woman who was assaulted by police and whose brother (an SDU member) was shot and killed by police (Thokoza)
10. An ANC member who was assaulted and whose friends were killed by an IFP member/gang leader (Thokoza)
11. A woman whose Zulu-speaking husband was shot by unidentified people (Thokoza)

The Amnesty Committee of the TRC also significantly engaged with the events in Katorus. Ten members of the SDU applied for amnesty for their role in killing ANC Youth League members. This was apparently in a conflict arising from allegations of SDU involvement in criminal activities. Over 150 residents also appeared in amnesty applications regarding their involvement in SDU activities. Applicants included the most senior SDU leaders, active members, and those who provided assistance to SDU members. While a significant proportion, these 150 applicants are nonetheless a minority of the total number of SDU members in the township. No SPU members appear to have submitted applications for amnesty.

Achievements and Shortfalls of the TRC Intervention

People had quite contrasting views about the appropriateness and effectiveness of the TRC's intervention in these communities. While some community members, particularly IFP leaders, opposed the TRC in principle, most community members had mixed feelings about the process. Almost every aspect of the TRC's engagement with the community caused some level of controversy.[9] The main areas of contention were as follows:

- *Public participation* in planning the hearings was limited mainly to political parties. Some victims felt that this was a deliberate attempt to suppress certain stories that might implicate present political leaders.
- *Public storytelling* was an important experience for those who got the opportunity to testify at the hearing. For many it was the first opportunity they had to convey their side of the story or talk publicly about their suffering. Less than 10 percent of victims, however, got this opportunity. (This is true for the East Rand as well as the country as a whole.)
- *Uncovering the truth*: The hearings were not an effective way of uncovering new information. Some new perspectives on past events did emerge, but in the eyes of the community, the complexity of each story was not sufficiently explored, and many other (maybe more significant) events were left untouched by the hearing.
- *Investigations*: The investigation capacity of the TRC was ultimately very limited. Most of the TRC's investigations were aimed at exposing broad patterns of abuse, corroborating whether the victims were in fact telling the truth, and checking the stories of perpetrators who had applied for amnesty. The victims who wanted the TRC to find out more information about their individual case (find a missing person, find out who was responsible for their victimization, or collect evidence to convict the perpetrator) were thus disappointed with the results.
- *Choice of cases*: Community members were disappointed by the limited number of cases that were heard. Many demanded that the TRC return to hear additional stories. They felt that the TRC or the community had not properly heard these stories, and that the TRC would not do sufficient follow-up work if things had not been properly aired.

- *Catharsis*: Victims often spoke of a sense of relief after talking to the TRC.[10] This should, however, only be seen as the beginning of a process that needs to be further facilitated. Victims spoke of the hearing as the *beginning* of a healing process rather than the end.

- *Victim Mobilization*: There had been several meetings of victims facilitated mainly by Khulumani (sometimes crossing previous divisions of the past) before and after the TRC hearing in both communities. Victims were able to submit their stories to the TRC statement takers in relatively large numbers. Victims felt that this was an opportunity to be heard and have their needs addressed. Khulumani was able to utilize the interest in the TRC to bring victims together and initiate an informal support network to address the various needs of victims. However, most victims felt that once the hearing was over, there was no longer space for them to influence the course of the TRC or to make an input regarding the handling of their own case.

Justice and Reconciliation

Engaging with the Ideas of Reconciliation, Justice, and Forgiveness

The publicity around the establishment and functioning of the TRC, as well as its operation within the two communities concerned, has, at the very least, forced people to examine their own understanding of what reconciliation, justice, and forgiveness means to them and their communities. For some it was mainly a mental exercise of looking at existing divisions and formulating some ideas about what should be changed—what a reconciled community would look like. For others it was a much more personal reflection regarding their feelings of hatred, guilt, and fear. Thinking about reconciliation meant thinking about a process of overcoming these psychological barriers that they had been living with, often for many years.

The messages projected by the TRC and the support given to the TRC by religious leaders and local politicians brought about some change in the way people view the idea of reconciliation. Many stated a clear commitment to a process of reconciliation, and contrasted this to feelings of hatred and a desire for vengeance that was previously their dominant attitude in response to their victimization. For some, the main factor in this change was the election of a new government, while for others, it was simply the passage of time. Some victims, however, attribute their change of heart to the work of the TRC.

While some victims still found the suggestion and insinuations that they should reconcile, and more particularly forgive the perpetrators, insulting, it appears that the TRC had built greater commitment to the process of reconciliation. It also created some space to pursue reconciliation. It was seen as a forum that provided a platform for storytelling, revealing of the truth, holding the perpetrator accountable, as well as for giving reparations, airing remorse, and potentially allowing forgiveness. These are steps in a multifaceted process that people now understand in much greater depth, and that they accept as legitimate. They are steps that involve a negotiated exchange between victim and perpetrator and between individual and state. Victims have developed a fairly clear idea of what would constitute a fair exchange for them as individuals, one that would involve both give and take.

The issue of justice was a key area of contention in the process of reconciliation. The TRC admitted that its existence was based on a compromise of justice. Nevertheless, the TRC attempted to promote an alternative model of restorative justice as a basis for reconciliation. The differing meanings of justice to the various stakeholders were, however, something that caused confusion and dissatisfaction with the TRC's delivery on its promises.

Broad Acceptance of a Restorative Justice Approach

While there were strong voices in the two communities that opposed the TRC as fundamentally unjust in its handling of past gross human rights violations, most victims and community leaders initially accepted the establishment of the TRC as a positive contribution. Whereas most people felt unhappy about the amnesty provision of the TRC, only a minority of victims completely rejected the TRC as unjust. For these victims, there was no way in which the injustice of amnesty could be circumvented or replaced by other forms of restorative justice. The lack of prosecutions was, to them, an indication of a lack of respect for their rights and their dignity. For them, retributive justice was a key demand, and they saw amnesty as a denial of this right.

> I want justice. The perpetrators should go to jail. I want the TRC to investigate my case. . . . I don't like the TRC, mainly because of amnesty. Police who killed children are now getting off.[11]

> If they are arrested they must be severely punished. If the person gets amnesty and I see them walking freely it will cause me a lot of pain. . . . I am willing to reconcile but first need reparations. I am constantly facing difficulties while the perpetrators are enjoying privileges. I am not able to reconcile while being deprived of my rights.[12]

While many victims did not have a strong opinion (especially those who did not know what had happened to their missing relatives), quite a few supported the concept of amnesty because of its potential benefits:

> If X applies for amnesty it would be good. We may then find out the truth (about what happened to my brother).[13]

Many victims, in fact, were hoping that their perpetrator would apply for amnesty so that the facts of their case would come to light and there would be some prospect for dialogue, apology, or greater public recognition. Most victims and community leaders accepted restorative justice as an appropriate or even preferable approach in addressing human rights violations. The question of what they understood by the concept of restorative justice requires some examination. Assessing whether the TRC had contributed to delivering restorative justice depends on whether one views restorative justice from a top-down or a bottom-up perspective. Victims' sense that the TRC failed to deliver on its promises is largely due to the differences between their understanding of restorative justice and that of the TRC.

Many victims, however, appeared to withdraw their support for restorative justice processes when the TRC did not provide significant truth or reparations. One study by Hamber, Nageng, and O'Malley (2000), for example, found much stronger resistance to the amnesty process. This appears to be directly linked to the victims' frustration at the TRC's lack of delivery.

Top-Down Conceptions of Restorative Justice

The TRC's (and the national government's) understanding of restorative justice is presented as both a necessary compromise—a way to make up for the lack of retributive justice—and as an ideal form of justice for a transitional political context. It is thus a combination (or confusion) of pragmatic and idealized notions of justice.[14] The extent of support within the TRC for restorative justice as the most suitable route to deal with past abuses is thus difficult to gauge.

The way that the TRC understood restorative justice was in terms of a national framework of repairing the damage of the past. The essential justice goal of the TRC was one of social rather than individual justice. Wilhelm Verwoerd (1997), a prominent TRC researcher, argues, for example, that "the TRC is also (primarily) making a contribution to 'justice' in the classical sense, namely at the level of the social order." He explains this contrast in terms of

> the fact that "justice" does not only operate at the more individual
> level, but also at the level of the social order. (This would mean that
> even if individual justice is limited, or even completely lacking in an
> institution dispensing amnesty, it doesn't follow that the TRC is
> "only a truth commission" or that reconciliation amounts to
> "no/cheap justice.")

The minister of justice also used this line of argument in relation to victims' compensation:

> We have a nation of victims, and if we are unable to provide
> complete justice on an individual basis—and we need to try and
> achieve maximum justice within the framework of reconciliation—it

is possible for us to ensure that there is historical and collective justice, for the people of our country. If we achieve that, if we achieve social justice and move in that direction, then those who today feel aggrieved that individual justice has not been done will at least be able to say that our society has achieved what the victims fought for during their lifetimes. And that therefore at that level, one will be able to say that justice has been done. (Omar 1996, xii)

TRC staff and commissioners also argued that justice could not realistically be delivered to each individual victim and that the focus should be on the broader picture:

> The TRC is not able to go into every single case and every community. It simply does not have the time and resources. We can only highlight key issues and thus throw some light on other more minor cases. Addressing these key issues will signal the way forward.[15]

Similarly, interpersonal reconciliation was seen as extending beyond the scope of the TRC:

> The TRC cannot be expected to achieve much in terms of reconciliation at the interpersonal level. Attempts have been made to bring victims and perpetrators together. These are mainly just symbolic processes. Extensive efforts go into it with very little results. It is not natural—only through great effort, and only with TRC prodding does it happen. . . . This symbolism of reconciliation means little. It appears forced.[16]

The TRC also presented itself as holding out the prospect of greater satisfaction for victims who turn to restorative options for addressing justice. The TRC approach was presented as of greater benefit to victims when compared to the "normal" prosecutorial route that would alternatively have been followed. The prospect for prosecutions was held out to be very limited (especially given the fact that many records had been destroyed, many offenses occurred years or decades ago, and the judiciary that has been inherited from the apartheid government has traditionally been conservative). Victims were thus faced with very limited prospects for retribution or truth through the formal legal system. Civil claims would also be similarly constrained. While admittedly reparations under the TRC would be very small compared to what a court of law would provide, it was argued that many more victims are likely to benefit from the TRC reparations than would have been the case had they all gone to court. The total probable benefits to victims are thus presented as having been increased by the introduction of the TRC.[17] The actual amount that victims will be paid is still undecided, however. The psychological benefits for victims to go through the TRC process rather than a court of law (where they would be subjected to hostile cross-examination) are also presented as a preferable route.

Through the introduction of the TRC, the state, in effect, attempted to engage victims, perpetrators, and society in a new justice contract. The TRC presented certain benefits to perpetrators, victims, and whole communities, and in return required them to provide cooperation in fulfilling its functions.

The underlying social contract between the TRC and victims is one of providing information (by the victim and communities to the TRC) and community engagement (by community leaders to the TRC), in exchange for recognition, truth, reparations, and the possibility of reconciliation. The victims and leaders of the two communities examined, while having bought into the contract, did not feel that the TRC came through regarding its end of the bargain.

Restorative justice, in terms of the TRC discourse, was thus an arrangement whereby the state took over the moral responsibility for reparations to victims from the perpetrators of these abuses and took on the task of rebuilding the moral order through symbolic actions (building monuments, renaming public buildings, and so on) which recognized undeserved suffering and victimization, and condemned actions which would be guarded against in the new social order.

What emerged as the final legislation and intervention policies of the TRC was clearly a mix of different interests that was ultimately shaped by political pressures, with only a secondary consideration given to victims' and local communities' retributive or restorative needs and demands. The main function of the justice model presented by the TRC appears to be one that was negotiated to minimize the likelihood of escalation of disputes involving criminal and human rights abuse allegations.

Bottom-Up Conceptions of Restorative Justice

The compromise of retributive justice brought about by amnesty was not the only (or necessarily the central) grievance of the respondents interviewed. Most victims interviewed had bought into the restorative justice deal held out to them by the TRC. Victims made their statements with the expectations of receiving some compensation and some recognition for their suffering, or with the idealistic goal of contributing to a new social order that would see their community coming to terms with the injustices of the past.

Victims' grievances regarding the unjustness of the TRC was mainly regarding its failure to deliver on its promise of restorative justice. On the one hand, the TRC was unable to get enough from perpetrators (information about who was responsible, admissions of guilt, commitment to a new social order, and so on) to deliver on its promise. On the other, the TRC's interpretation of its restorative justice mandate was one that was embedded in its own conceptual frames of reconciliation. This conceptualization, essentially built around a top-down approach to reconciliation, sets out different goals for proving its success as a form of restorative justice. The areas in which it does feel that it has delivered are thus not always recognized by the supposed beneficiaries. The provision and acquisition of acknowledgment, truth, restitution, and confessions were done within the ambit of its own top-down conceptualization rather than that of the consumers and beneficiaries at the community level.

Community members were also not always clear about the possibilities and limitations of the TRC. The TRC's model of restorative justice (its legal framework) confused some people, who did not accept it as a legitimate model of restorative justice. The issue that reparation would come from the state rather than the perpetrator was, for example, commonly raised by victims.

> With the TRC, the government compensates victims on behalf of the offenders. In our culture, however, the perpetrator must apologize to the victim and pay compensation. It is important for the victim that the perpetrator directly acknowledges their wrongdoing. Instead we now have the government taking the place of the offender. It would, for example, be more acceptable if the profits of the book that de Kock [a high profile security force hit squad commander] is writing were used to compensate his victims.[18]

Rather than accepting it as an ideal form in terms of their values regarding justice, restorative justice was thus accepted at a more utilitarian level: a contract from which they could gain some benefit. Restorative justice is not a self-evident or uniformly understood concept. It is given different substance within the specific local context and in relation to particular victimization experiences. For victims, restorative justice concerns are motivated by the following:

- The desire to confront the perpetrator with the consequences of their actions:

  > He (the perpetrator) must be informed of how he made me handicapped. He doesn't have problems; it is only I who suffer. If he doesn't have the money, his leaders who instructed him must bear the responsibility.[19]

- The desire to have the direct perpetrator confess (face-to-face):

  > I want them to apologize. I cannot forgive them until they come and apologize to me; both those who gave order and those who killed her.[20]

- The desire to make peace with those from the other side (or even with the perpetrator):

  > I want to confront them and ask them why they did this. . . . I want the TRC to look for the perpetrators. TRC must bring us together. . . . I want the truth. I want an apology. I just want peace to the people who shot my son because other people sent them.[21]

- The goal of establishing a unified, stable political community:

  > We have to find each other, to construct a commonly accepted value
  > system, to develop a system in which we can listen to each other and
  > meet each other halfway.[22]

- The desire to gain the respect of their neighbors and other community
  members:

  > After I had told my story, the commissioners asked the hall to stand
  > and observe a minute's silence. I was surprised that nobody hesitated.
  > It was very meaningful. Some people called me after the hearing to
  > ask that I forgive the community for what they had done to the victim
  > (my sister) and the family. People in the community had treated the
  > family with suspicion for a long time.[23]

- The desire to rebuild an environment of trust and interdependence among
  community members:

  > Reconciliation is about reconnecting relationships and rebuilding
  > trust. I cannot stay in a community where there is no trust. Talking to
  > others makes one feel less alone—regain the sense of community.[24]

  > The hostel dwellers are afraid of being in the location after dark. I
  > used to work with them and be friends. We have not renewed the
  > friendships. When we see each other in the street, we greet and pass
  > on. This is not as it should be.[25]

- The desire to see a new social morality for the community affirmed:

  > Reconciliation means recognizing our common humanity. It is the
  > same as "ubuntu."[26] Faith engages people in terms of these deeper
  > commonalties that are linked to one's heart and conscience. The
  > spiritual aspect of reconciliation is central. The government cannot do
  > this. They can recognize our role and support our work.[27]

From the TRC's perspective, the goals of restorative justice are defined more in
terms of national processes. Rather than have all the individual perpetrators at
the lower end of the command chain come clean about their past actions, the
priority is placed on the top end of the command chain. The politicians and
generals are the ones targeted as appropriate conveyors of information and of
statements of contrition and remorse. The search is for those who are willing to
take responsibility for perpetrating the policies of apartheid (generally regarded
as a crime against humanity by commissioners interviewed in this study) and for
giving the security forces the scope to commit gross human rights abuses.

The act of confession is also seen as a public impersonal message to the
country as a whole. The bond between perpetrator and victim is thus deperson-

alized, and the capacity for abuse is located within the political context of the past conflict. The perpetrator and victim are framed as actors playing a role scripted by the political struggle, rather than individual human beings.

Where the need for interpersonal reconciliation is recognized, it is seen as a symbolic interaction that is of significance more in terms of the way that it can be conveyed to the broader public. It is an image created for public educational purpose. Where the TRC did facilitate interpersonal exchanges, these were usually among people with a public profile, or done in the presence of the media. Community members, and particularly victims, saw reconciliation as something that had to be pursued at the national, community, and individual levels. While symbolic gestures and public images were seen as relevant, they did not replace the need for direct practical interventions.

The competing models of restorative justice are summarized in table 10.1:

Table 10.1: Top-Down versus Bottom-Up Models of Restorative Justice

	Top-Down	Bottom-Up
1. Understanding of Nature of Victim	category of people subjected to particular types of abuses	individuals who are experiencing certain forms of suffering
2. Understanding of Nature of Perpetrator	senior official—person with ultimate authority	person who was directly involved in abuse
3. Type of Relationship Targeted	structural relationship between institutions and sector of society	personal bonds between individual community members
4. Understanding of Moral Community	national society of citizens	local community of residents
5. Nature of Apology Sought	impersonal, public, and symbolic	personal, face-to-face
6. Narrative of the Past	key events or typical stories that mirror the country's story	particular, unique features that have meaning mainly to the particular victim
7. Audience	the public: particularly the groups to which the victim and the perpetrator belong	individual victim and the directly implicated perpetrator(s)—possibly the local community
8. Reparations	from the state (with voluntary, symbolic contribution by the perpetrator)	from the individual perpetrator
9. Process	done by predetermined formula, ritualized, formal	individualized, informal

Conclusion

The context of negotiations around the transition and the TRC legislation provided for a wide range of stakeholder inputs into the process. The outcome was a structure that attempted to satisfy a wide range of competing demands, but one that lacked a clearly articulated and coherent approach to the key questions of justice and reconciliation. The competing interpretations of these concepts created ongoing contentions around policy implementation within the TRC and between the TRC and local communities.[28]

A key dimension of the different approaches to reconciliation is the tension between top-down and bottom-up approaches. This tension also plays out in the way that the parties conceptualized justice. Even if parties can shift their goals toward more restorative conceptions of justice, scope for fundamental disagreements about the meaning and purpose of restorative justice remains. Local conceptions of restorative justice embody the need to deal with rebuilding the fabric that has been destroyed by the dynamics and culture of violence.

The TRC was an intervention that could only achieve a limited amount in its short life. Its national profile and extensive legal powers gave it clear authority unparalleled by the capacity of local reconciliation initiatives. This national legal authority and status, however, come with an agenda that was not always sensitive to local needs and priorities. This lack of local legitimacy was ultimately a serious obstacle in promoting community reconciliation. The task of taking reconciliation forward in these communities thus falls back on the processes developed by NGOs and churches operating in these communities. These processes, which are generally more sensitive to the complexity of local dynamics and local needs, operated alongside the intervention of the TRC.[29]

To understand the longer-term reconciliation process in local communities, both top-down and bottom-up processes must be more clearly evaluated. The way in which top-down and bottom-up processes of justice and reconciliation can complement each other in rebuilding communities destroyed by conflict particularly warrants further examination.

Notes

1. The data informing this study was the product of the author's doctoral research sponsored by the Randolph Jennings Program of the U.S. Institute of Peace. The sections of this paper dealing with the TRC's hearing in Duduza have been published in the TRC's final report (1998). More than one hundred community members and TRC staff were interviewed during 1997.

2. See Kollapen (1993) for more details about the background to these negotiations.

3. The relevant section of the interim constitution reads as follows:

> The adoption of this Constitution lays the secure foundation for the
> people of South Africa to transcend the divisions and strife of the

past, which generated gross violations of human rights, the transgression of humanitarian principles in violent conflicts and a legacy of hatred, fear and revenge. These can now be addressed on the basis that there is a need for understanding but not for vengeance, a need for reparation but not for retaliation, a need for Ubuntu but not for victimization. In order to advance such reconciliation and reconstruction, amnesty shall be granted in respect of acts, omissions and offenses associated with political objectives and committed in the course of the conflicts of the past. To this end, Parliament under this Constitution shall adopt a law determining a firm cut-off date, which shall be a date after 8 October 1990 and before 6 December 1993, and providing for the mechanisms, criteria and procedures, including tribunals, if any, through which such amnesty shall be dealt with at any time after the law has been passed. (Postscript, Constitution of the Republic of South Africa Act 200, of 1993, p. 180)

4. The TRC came into being at the end of 1995, and, while it released its final report in 1998, it continues to function in 2000 in order to hear all the amnesty applications that it received.

5. For more information about the legislative process of establishing the TRC, and the role of NGOs in this process, see van der Merwe, Dewhirst, and Hamber (1998).

6. This was the only report of a White civilian victim of political violence in the Greater Nigel Area.

7. In the zero hand grenade incident, two police operatives pretended to be Umkhonto we Sizwe (the ANC's military wing) members who had come to assist local activists with military training. They provided instructions to local youth on how to handle hand grenades and then helped them plan simultaneous attacks in three neighboring townships (Duduza, KwaThema, and Tsakane). When the attacks were launched, the hand grenades exploded prematurely in the hands of the youths. Some were killed and others severely maimed by the explosions.

8. See Taylor (1991) for a more detailed analysis of the underlying causes of the conflict and the way in which ethnic lines of divisions were manufactured by the state.

9. A fuller discussion of these achievements and shortfalls is provided in van der Merwe (1998).

10. Not all victims, however, shared this sense of relief. The frustration of not being given the space to tell his full story was, for example, a major frustration for at least one victim.

11. Interview with victim (Duduza, June 19, 1997).

12. Interview with victim (Katorus, September 18, 1997).

13. Interview with victim (Duduza, July 23, 1997).

14. On the one hand, the TRC described the amnesty as regrettable, but necessary to secure the transition to democracy. On the other hand, it presented the underlying ethic of confession and forgiveness, rather than retribution, as a healing process, and argued that the goal of uncovering the truth should be seen as a higher goal than justice. It demonstrated its support for amnesty most significantly by lobbying the government to extend the cut-off point for amnesty from December 1993 to May 1994.

15. Interview with TRC commissioner, June 1997.

16. Interview with TRC commissioner, June 1997.

17. Interview with Willie Hofmeyr, Parliamentary Portfolio Committee on Justice, March 3, 1998.

18. Interview with NGO staff member (October 2, 1997).
19. Interview with victim (Katorus, September 15, 1997).
20. Interview with victim (Duduza, May 21, 1997).
21. Interview with victim (Katorus, October 2, 1997).
22. Interview with town councillor (Duduza/Nigel, June 11, 1997).
23. Interview with victim (Duduza, May 21, 1997).
24. Interview with victim (Katorus, September 9, 1997).
25. Interview with victim (Katorus, September 16, 1997).
26. *Ubuntu*, a Zulu word describing the sense of connectedness among people where altruistic motives guide mutual interaction, was commonly inferred by respondents when describing the cultural basis for communal bonds. Ubuntu embodies the notion that human nature is fundamentally social—our humanity is expressed through our interdependence with others.
27. Interview with NGO staff member (September 9, 1997).
28. For a more comprehensive discussion of these different reconciliation perspectives, see Hamber and van der Merwe (1998).
29. Examples of such reconciliation initiatives dealing with conflicts of the past are the Wilderness Therapy Program (run by the National Peace Accord Trust), Simunye Media Project, the Video Dialogue Project (run by Wilgespruit Fellowship Centre), the Institute for Healing the Memories, the Ubuntu Project, and CSVR's community reconciliation workshops.

References

Hamber, B., and van der Merwe, H. 1998. What Is This Thing Called Reconciliation? In *Reconciliation in Review*, vol. 1, no. 1.

Hamber, B., Nageng, D., and O'Malley, G. 2000. 'Telling It Like It Is . . .': Understanding the TRC from the Perspective of Survivors. *Psychology in Society*, vol. 6.

Kollapen, N. 1993. Accountability: The Debate in South Africa. *Journal of African Law*, vol. 37, no. 1, 1-9.

Omar, D. 1996. Introduction. In *Confronting Past Injustices: Approaches to Amnesty, Punishment, Reparation and Restitution in South Africa and Germany*. M. R. Rwelamira and G. Werle, eds. Durban, South Africa: Butterworths.

Pigou, P. 1998. From Truth to Transformation. Paper presented at CSVR Conference, Johannesburg, South Africa. Unpublished.

Seiler, M. 1997. Building Community-Based Healing Efforts in Traumatized Communities. Paper presented to the South African Association for Conflict Intervention. Cape Town, South Africa.

Taylor, R. 1991. The Myth of Ethnic Division: Township Conflict on the Reef. *Race and Class*, vol. 33, no. 2.

van der Merwe, H. 1998. Some Insights from a Case Study of Duduza. Published as section of the *TRC Final Report*, vol. 5, chapter 9, pp. 423-429. Cape Town, South Africa: Junta.

van der Merwe, H., Dewhirst, P., and Hamber, B. 1998. Non-Governmental Organisations and the Truth and Reconciliation Commission: An Impact Assessment. *Politikon*, vol. 26, no. 1, pp. 55-79.

Verwoerd, W. 1997. Justice after Apartheid? Reflections on the South African Truth and Reconciliation Commission. Paper delivered at the Fifth International Conference on Ethics and Development, "Globalization, Self-Determination and Justice in Development," Madras, India.

Newspaper Articles

"Making Peace with Cameras," *Simunye News*, August 1997, Johannesburg, South Africa.
"SDUs Blamed for Killings," *The Star*, December 14 , 1995, Johannesburg, South Africa.

11

The Case of Land in Zimbabwe

Cause of Conflict, Foundation for Sustained Peace

Erin McCandless

I was born in Chiweshe, by the Mazowe River, in 1927. I am vana
vevhu, a child of the soil. I feel it in my body. It tells me I need to eat
fresh vegetables planted on my land. . . . Vana vevhu. . . . We fought
the Chimurenga wars for one thing: the land. All other reasons are
irrelevant. And we haven't got it yet. If no land is given this year, the
fighting and the crying will continue. Vana vevhu. If people think
with an open mind, they will understand why we Zimbabweans are
doing this. (Gertrude Gasa, PANA 1998)

Land has played a pivotal role throughout the history of Zimbabwe (formerly
Southern Rhodesia). Integral to imperialist and development policies of coloni-
alist rulers, the desire for land redistribution inspired and propelled the
revolution. Symbolically and practically, land issues drove postindependence
development policies and, twenty years later, continue to thrive as a primary
national development issue determining intergroup relations. That land needs to
be redistributed in Zimbabwe to ensure sustainable development and peace is
not, at least openly, in question. A small minority of White farmers
(approximately four thousand, or 2 percent of the population)[1] immeasurably
profited from the British colonial dispossession of majority Zimbabwean Blacks
from their homelands in 1980. Today, minority White farmers continue to reside
in Zimbabwe's most fertile farmland, while Blacks live in vastly overpopulated,
infertile communal areas.

The manner in which land reform is being undertaken, however, is highly contentious. After ten years of grudgingly pursuing a market-driven, peace agreement-mandated *willing-seller, willing-buyer* approach to land reform with little success, in 1990 President Mugabe adopted a *nonvoluntary land acquisition* approach. Unpopular with White large-scale commercial farmers as well as with the international diplomatic and economic community, Mugabe's approach has been further challenged by numerous economic and social problems. These include lack of funds to compensate for farms taken and a rising tide of unmet societal expectations from postwar promises. The current crisis characterized by war veterans moving onto thousands of White farms with Mugabe's consent illustrates the degree to which the issue has become politicized.

Zimbabwe's problems typify those experienced by many postcolonial and even postviolent conflict countries. Where primary resources are owned by a minority to the overt detriment of the majority, the potential for instability and violence is high. Often assuming an identity character, relationships between communities, rooted in colonialism, continue to be shaped and expressed around the availability and use of these resources. In such contexts, how can land or other resources be redistributed in a just manner and toward just ends? How can this be done in a way that fosters reconciliation and promotes sustainable human development?

Aiming to suggest new avenues for critical reflection and action,[2] these questions are explored through the case of land redistribution in Zimbabwe. A justice-reconciliation conceptual framework is proposed and considered alongside the reflections and analysis of different stakeholders in the conflict: White and Black farmers, NGOs and government officials. The hybrid justice-reconciliation approach proves useful in the case of Zimbabwe, where justice (both of means and ends) is necessary for reconciliation (conceptualized as the building and maintaining of constructive intercommunal relationships). Ascertaining the parameters and processes of justice and reconciliation, including their type and degree, are among the key challenges that will inform the usefulness of this hybrid model in different contexts.

Theorizing Justice and Reconciliation

While several bodies of literature are relevant to our problem, here we will discuss selected strands of reconciliation and justice theory that most effectively address the complexities of societies in transition from protracted social conflict (PSC). As defined by Edward Azar, PSCs are focused on religious, cultural, or ethnic communal identity, which in turn is dependent upon the satisfaction of basic [developmental] needs such as those for security, communal recognition, and distributive justice (1986). The proposed hybrid justice-reconciliation conceptual framework values both structures and relationships, while prioritizing material concerns: unequal and unjust structures must ultimately be identifiably under transformation before constructive intergroup relationships will develop.

Justice and Reconciliation: The Relationship

It has been frequently argued that significant tensions exist between a legalistic or rights-based approach to problem-solving and more reconciliation-based approaches.[3] Some argue that *how* one defines terms can generate this dichotomous view—for example, assuming a static or restrictive understanding of both reconciliation and justice.[4] The resulting perceived tension might account for the lack of quality research examining the relationship between the two.

A closely related discussion in the conflict resolution literature—relationships or structures as a source of conflict—provides insight. Proponents of the structure-as-primary-source identify social structures as the source of conflict, as it determines the distribution of valued resources and positions, denying particular groups access to power, resources, or other human needs (for example Mitchell 1981; Azar 1986; Galtung 1996). Relationships-as-source proponents alternatively focus on psycho-social explanations, in particular *perceptions* of difference as conflict-causing (for example Kraybill 1996; Laderach 1994). Many nationalism and identity theorists, as well as social psychologists, would agree.

This debate has implications for praxis. Structural injustices and economic inequalities that were primary causes for war take a priority for structuralists, whereas relationship theorists prefer relationship approaches. Van der Merwe notes that identity issues can be structural also, arguing for a complementary approach that steps beyond issues of causality (1999). Lederach and Galtung both illustrate this complementary approach in recognizing the importance of both relationships and structures in their transformation pursuits (1994; 1996).

In the reconciliation literature specifically, some discuss justice as a *component* of reconciliation (Lederach 1994), and others, as a precondition for reconciliation (Zehr 1990; van der Merwe 1999). Building on Zehr's argument that "a full sense of justice may, of course, be rare" and that "even 'approximate justice' can help" (1990), van der Merwe argues:

> For reconciliation to be promoted one must address the need for justice, i.e., overcome the injustices of the past. Disputants must, to some degree, be able to say that 'justice has been done.' For the creation of a unified moral order, this feeling of righting the wrongs has to be mutual. (1999)

In political conflict, he goes on, where both sides are likely to have suffered perceived injustices and both are, to some extent, responsible for excessive abuses, both then must to some degree "be satisfied with the mechanism(s) that are devised to address these injustices." A major challenge for peacemakers is designing justice processes capable of satisfying these needs, while not creating deep resentment by at least one group (1999).

Justice of Means and Ends

Justice is a complicated concept, holding a variety of meanings to all people. While it maintains great inspirational power for oppressed groups around the world, considerable doubt exists over whether a universal justice theory is useful, possible, or even desirable. Proponents point to the usefulness of an objective normative standard for creating and managing social institutions and practices. Opponents emphasize that for justice to be a meaningful measure for those it serves, it must contain presuppositions of social life derived from the social context (Young 1990). Both have implications for social life in the critical questions they beg. Who has the power, authority, and legitimacy to design and enforce an objective normative standard? How do we reconcile competing contextually or culturally defined models?

Transitional societies raise questions about the usefulness and viability of globally promoted models, to which domestic realities do not easily conform. *Transitional justice* has become a growing research interest among scholars and governments, as exemplified by a three-volume work published by the U.S. Institute of Peace (Kritz 1995). Aiming to illuminate practical questions and alternative solutions to justice-related issues, the three volumes examine "justice" vis-à-vis political issues and abuses, while economic considerations— often the cause of violent conflict—are conspicuously absent.

Assuming that transitional contexts demand creative thinking around justice issues, several categories of justice are proposed which encompass both the "ends" or outcomes of justice processes, and the "means"—the ways in which justice processes are undertaken.

Just Means—Social Justice of the Present and Future: Social justice usually refers to the structure and policies of a society, to its political economic, legal, and social institutions (Arthur and Shaw 1978). While many (often American) notions place emphasis on the *individual* and focus on the distribution of material goods, Iris Marion-Young (1990) follows the European leanings for the *collective*. She offers a vision of a heterogeneous public that acknowledges and affirms group differences and challenges institutionalized domination and oppression. Questions of need, poverty, and welfare are at the core of distribution concerns, as are issues such as decision making, division of labor, and culture. While this conception of social justice is arguably suitable for every multinational context, in postcolonial, unevenly developed Zimbabwe, it seems imperative.

Just Ends—Redistributive Justice: At the same time, a society's starting point must be recognized and addressed. *Redistributive justice*, particularly fol-lowing war or colonialism, should be considered material reparation, necessary for sustainable development (LTC 1994; Moyo 1995; World Bank 1999) and arguably for sustainable peace. Drawing on Rawls's popularized *distributive justice*—the distribution of economic goods in society—the hypothetical social contract becomes a useful tool for building consensus around fairness toward redistributive issues in society. Where the situation is one of vast inequality and disparity of material resources, for example, Zimbabwe, bringing the ahistorical *Rawlsian* approach into context spotlights material distributive justice concerns. Given that intercommunal identity is a factor in conflict and in marking disparity, a framework based on the social group rather than the individual, Young would propose, seems appropriate.

Relational Justice: Africa's rich array of justice approaches that prioritize the healing of relationships is an indigenous resource. Under the overarching concept of African Customary Law (ACL), these models focus on procedures that community members undertake to return harmony to the community, rather than "rules" or "laws" enforced by a judge. While some question the reliability and power imbalances maintained by these traditions,[5] their historical resonance with a broad cross section of people across Africa cannot be ignored. In South Africa, traditional approaches are taking on new life, combining with modern principles (e.g., women's equal rights), as communities recognize their utility and cultivate their peacebuilding potential. These hybrid models include *popular, community,* and *restorative* justice. They emphasize responsiveness to the needs of people in society, forgiveness, accessibility, participation in the administration of justice by those directly interested, and empowerment of citizens. They point to the need to address conflicts of interests rather than only those of rights, and the restoration of the relationship between the victim(s) and the offender(s) (see Twigg and van der Merwe 1996; Nina 1995). While in Zimbabwe such hybrid models are not flourishing, these examples illustrate the existence and practicality of people finding ways to balance and integrate reconciliation and justice. *Relational justice* also highlights an important facet of the African cultural context—that cooperative and forgiving justice models are valued. The challenge, of course, is ensuring that this is not abused.

Reconciliation: A Relationship-Building Process

At the national and intergroup levels of analyses, the idea that reconciliation is a *process* of building or changing relationships is growing. van der Merwe builds on Lederach (1997), pointing to the changing identity, values, attitudes, and patterns of interaction which contribute to a more cooperative relationship (1999). Others identify the process more with structures and procedures needed for establishing peace (Ackermann 1994; Feldman 1984).

What type of relationship are people desiring and capable of following violent conflict? Minimalists argue for "coexistence"—sharing space or tolerating each other in a way that appeals to self-interest while affirming the right of the other to life (Weiner 1998). While this rests on a pessimistic view of human nature, not aiming to address deep psychological or macrosocietal, political, economic, or structural injustice levels of the relationship, it is pragmatic and incremental, and an important stage in the humanization of a conflict (1998, 16). A slightly more optimistic approach comes from Montville, who emphasizes mutual respect and security (1996). Given the clearly stated bias here toward a "constructive intercommunal relationship" and the lack of theorizing in this area, Feldman's notion of political reconciliation provides a starting point for the Zimbabwe case. Political reconciliation, she argues, encompasses notions of *equality, trust, acceptance of cultural and political differences, partnership, active friendship,* and *mutual or joint interests* (1992). To note a few caveats: violent conflict situations are likely to offer less possibility for constructive engagement; relationships are conceived of quite differently in different cultures, and intercultural relationships are uniquely negotiated; and, while a type of desired relationship may be considered as the "ends" of a process, relationships are themselves dynamic and subject to change through time, changed circumstance, and overtures made and accepted.

Considering the question of praxis, many speak about *building* relationships alongside new peaceful structures and culture. For Lederach, mechanisms that engage conflict parties and activities are needed at three interdependent levels: top (or policy), middle-range (community), and grassroots. Encounters must address the past—creating opportunities for the expression of grief, trauma, and acknowledgment of past wrongs—as well as the future. Peoples' futures are intertwined and interdependent, bringing relationships and structures more fully together (Ackermann 1994; Feldman 1984; Galtung 1996). Feldman argues that a multileveled approach, whereby governmental and societal processes interact in political, moral, and psychological ways, eventually provides structures that contribute to sustainable peace. Ackermann's case of post-World War II French-German reconciliation highlights and elaborates on this theory (1994).

While some suggest steps or stages of a reconciliation process, involving areas such as truth telling, acknowledgment, forgiveness, mourning (Kraybill 1996, and see Montville in this volume and 1993)—a cultural critique could be made. Van der Merwe points to a nonlinear, interactive process that recognizes the role of religious, political, and cultural frameworks combining to construct a system of meaning that prioritizes various reconciliation needs (1999).

To summarize, our working justice-reconciliation conceptual framework is one that prioritizes justice concerns (of means, ends, and relational) in a process of constructive intergroup relationship building (reconciliation). It recognizes that the two share a dynamic interdependent relationship, mutually informing and benefiting each other. Let us now consider the case of Zimbabwe.

Zimbabwe's Land Reform

Zimbabwe has a long history of land-related injustice. Following the early seventeenth century Portuguese colonization and subsequent flight, the British South Africa Company (BSAC) followed in 1890. A treaty between British-backed missionaries and the allegedly misled (non-English-speaking) Ndembele leader Lobengula, gave missionary leader Cecil Rhodes rights to all metals and minerals situated within "his kingdom." The BSAC's Royal Charter granted the following year entitled Rhodes to oversee gold mining, make treaties, promulgate laws, maintain a police force, and undertake public works in what became Southern Rhodesia (Sylvester 1991, 17). Black families were forcibly moved without compensation from their ancestral lands to "native reserves," today's "communal areas." In 1898 order provisions from Britain, access to adequate land for cultivation, grazing, and watering was ensured to Blacks. As White, primarily Afrikaner, farmers became more influential in the BSAC, shifting the focus from mining to agriculture, these guarantees were eventually abandoned (LTC 1994, 9-10).

Postindependence 'Reconciliation' Policy

In 1980, when Zimbabwe gained independence following a decade-long struggle aimed at reclaiming the land for the "people of Zimbabwe," the new president, Robert Mugabe, and his Zimbabwe African National Union-Patriotic Front (ZANU-PF) overruled hardliners, creating a government of "national reconciliation." He brought in leaders of the liberation coalition force, Zimbabwe African People's Union (ZAPU), and Whites who had distanced themselves from Ian Smith's Conservative Alliance of Zimbabwe. Smith was permitted one of thirty seats reserved for Whites in parliament. A single national army was created with integrated forces. Ongoing problems, however, between the Shona-dominated Mugabe government and minority Ndembele-dominated ZAPU culminated in a violent, bloody search for Ndembele "dissidents" in January 1983. Politically, Mugabe secured his one-party rule through a constitutional amendment that replaced the role of prime minister with that of a strong executive president, banned ZAPU from organizing, and abolished the White seats of parliament.

While the policy of "Zimbabweanization" was managed quite successfully over time, effectively transforming the country's social and political structures, the establishment of new *economic* relationships and structures proved much more difficult. In addition to keeping their land, 100,000 Whites retained control over much of the country's industry, owning as much as 80 percent of the country's wealth (Cheney 1990, 126). Land specialist Moyo notes that a "generous reconciliation policy stance . . . demonstrated the Government's care for large White farmers . . . [but also] required the repression of Black demands for land and agrarian reform" (1995, 12). This approach, he argues, maintained a colonial legacy, one that assured large-scale White farmers preferential access to economic incentives.

Governmental Approaches toward Land Reform

Despite Mugabe's strong socialist ideals, with land reform and "justice for the people of Zimbabwe" at the top of his agenda, the terms of the British-negotiated Lancaster House Agreement at the time of independence prohibited the expropriation of private property and secured a *willing-seller, willing-buyer* approach to land reform. In the first decade, approximately 52,000 peasant families were resettled on 3.5 million hectares of land. This was far short of the 162,000 family target; approximately 4,300 Whites still owned about 40 percent of the land. About one million families remained in communal areas, with overpopulation increasing annually given a 3.5 percent communal population growth rate (Cheney 1990, 137; LTC 1994, 12). Displeased with the quality and quantity of land being offered, Mugabe took advantage of the expiration of the agreement to change direction.

The Land Acquisition Act (1992) (and the *nonvoluntary approach* generally) allows the government to acquire both underutilized and used lands for public good through a state-determined pricing mechanism. A "fair price" within a "reasonable period" is fixed through a committee of six persons through set (nonmarket-determined) valuation guidelines (Moyo 1995). The government has given compensation often above market value, and there has been little controversy over this aspect of the process.

In 1993, the government created the widely respected Land Tenure Commission (LTC) to examine the appropriateness of each of Zimbabwe's land tenure systems for its different farming sectors: communal, resettlement, and small- and large-scale commercial farming areas. Commissioners (including agricultural specialists, lawyers, academics, and traditional chiefs) undertook yearlong consultations with key government ministries and civic organizations (including human rights, development, and labor) and conducted public hearings at all levels. Comprehensive examinations of technical issues and implications, as well as land tenure systems abroad, were undertaken and a comprehensive Land Tenure Commission Report produced. In short, the LTC recognized the highly complex and contextual nature of land reform, deeming resettlement a necessary step toward relieving population pressures and promoting sustainable environmental management.[6]

Among commission recommendations were steps toward laying foundations for governmental follow-up actions, including the establishment of a Department of Lands and Technical Services, responsible for coordinating and implementing recommendations. A National Land Policy was aimed at widening benefits to the people, increasing consumers and producers, and generating overall economic growth. More technically, it introduced an agricultural land tax, streamlined land subdivision regulation, and introduced regulation on maximum farm sizes (World Bank May 19, 1999, 9). While a constructive approach was initiated and to some degree institutionalized, Mugabe's tumultuous relationship with the international community, combined with a widespread economic and political crisis, has placed great strains on his ability to manage the reform process.

The International Community's Role and the Present Context

On September 9-11, 1998, President Mugabe held a conference with international donors seeking support for his second phase of the Land Reform and Resettlement Program, a five-year program estimated at 1.5 billion Zimbabwean dollars for the resettling of 150,000 families on five million hectares of land (FES 1999). Without their assistance, he argued, the squatting phenomenon would turn into anarchy. Britain and the United States refused to fund the program, stating it failed to respect property rights and would not alleviate poverty (O'Loughlin 1998). The World Bank highlights consensus-oriented findings, notably an "inception phase" with a one million hectare target to resettle 34,000 farmers. The government would buy the 118 farms on the market for resettlement and make efforts toward market-based, beneficiary-initiated approaches, relaxing subdivision policies and imposing a land tax (World Bank May 19, 1999, 1).[7]

One month later Mugabe announced the government's intention to proceed with the second phase of its original plan—acquiring 1,471 farms (five million hectares)—vowing only to pay farmers for improvements made to the land and inviting the international community to assist with further finances. Various government explanations have been offered for the contradiction in word and deed.[8] Despite the competing agendas, the World Bank approved a $5 million credit to finance the inception phase in November 1999.

While the World Bank is keen to get started on a Third Structural Adjustment Credit for the country, since October 1999 the International Monetary Fund's (IMF,'s) stalled loans to Zimbabwe are impeding this. The IMF points to lack of transparency and accountability, particularly in terms of land reform, as well as cost overruns in Zimbabwe's military spending on the Democratic Republic of Congo war. At the same time, there is recognition that the IMF plan contained unrealistic assumptions, was based on flawed economics, and proposed unreachable targets (World Bank October 7, 1999; FG 2000).

These financial conflicts are exacerbating the worrisome economic situation. In August 2000 Zimbabwe is grappling with record-high inflation and interest rates of 60 percent, unemployment at 50 percent plus in the formal sector, mass poverty of 76 percent, and an unsteady local currency. Professor John Makumbe of the University of Zimbabwe's politics department notes:

> Mugabe has no logical answer to the land issue. On the one hand, he
> has no money to pay for the land. On the other hand, the ordinary

peasants are demanding land and moving onto commercial farms in
defiance of the Government. Things could easily get out of hand.
(O'Loughlin 1998).

And they have, as witnessed by the March-August 2000 war veteran takeover of
some 1,600 primarily White-owned farms. Moreover, it is widely believed that
the government was directing the farm invasions. While "designed to appear as
spontaneous demonstrations against the racial imbalance in land distribution,"
the government has arguably worked to create a political pretext for passing the
sixteenth amendment of the rejected Draft Constitution (Kahiya 2000). This
allows for the acquisition of lands without compensation—Mugabe's ticket to
winning votes and reelection, scheduled for late April 2000 (Kahiya 2000). At
the same time, the economy is severely affected, with invasions of farms
disrupting agricultural production, which accounts for 40 percent of Zimbabwe's
exports. White farmers claim that they have lost more than $75 million in
damaged crops and property, which will have a bearing on the stability of the
dollar (FG 2000).[9]

Challenges and Opportunities as Presented by Stakeholders

Aiming to elicit the views of people and representative organizations from
different stakeholder communities on the land redistribution process, intergroup
relations, and the prospects of a lasting peace, interviews were held with Black
and White farmers and NGO and governmental representatives.[10] Recorded here
are views of White and Black farmers, NGO representatives, and government
officials, organized thematically.

White Farmers

The White large-scale commercial farming community (LSCF) of about
4,500 farmers is represented by the Commercial Farmers Union (CFU). The
CFU is widely perceived to represent White interests, while maintaining a Black
membership of four hundred.

Among White farmers, strong and widespread critiques of the government's
unjust land distribution is reflected in two central concerns: illegitimacy of nonvoluntary acquisition process and lack of transparency and corruption of
process. CFU Deputy Director, Dr. Jerry Grant, explained: "The way [the land
reform process] is being handled by the government is causing conflict. . . . I
don't have a problem with the Land Acquisition Act. Every government has a
policy on this. I do have a problem with authority using the Act politically."
Specifically, farms are being designated on the basis of social and political

correctness—where White farmers had failed to act in accordance with social and political norms and interests of the government.

Others go further, challenging the constitutionality of the Land Acquisition Act as morally wrong, and even racially motivated. Unfulfillable postwar promises, one farmer noted, "tend to stir up a lot of racial hatred and confusion in the minds of the politically uneducated."

Lack of transparency and corruption in the acquisition process were also highlighted as problems. Dissatisfaction was expressed over the government's removal of White farmers from the Land Identification Committees. Not knowing their individual fate creates insecurity and makes it difficult to invest in their farms and harder to acquire investment capital necessary in planning for future production. Many farmers indicated that senior officials are being given vast tracts of land that are then left idle or underutilized, at best. Former Land Minister Kubirai Kangai was frequently noted for owning three farms, despite the "one man, one farm" policy.

In terms of sustainable development, White farmers consistently emphasized the very high rate of their productivity for national benefit, contrasted with the very low productivity of communal areas. They emphasized their ability to attract lucrative foreign exchange (47 percent of Zimbabwe's gross exports) needed for imports, while noting that they employ 200,000 to 300,000 people directly and that two million people's livelihoods are dependent upon them. They have built 5,700 dams and 8,000 schools. Mugabe's land redistribution proposals, they calculate, would cut commercial farm production by at least one-third (annual production worth 14 billion Zimbabwe dollars/US $100 million). By contrast, White farmers maintain, communal areas are totally unproductive and unsustainable.

A CFU former leader described communal farmers' attachment to land as a "mystical" one, rooted in another culture:

> To me, the real world is about business, if we want to survive into the millennium in a competitive world. . . . What country can afford to dismiss the skills of its farmers? What do you achieve by destroying a system that is, granted, a bit feudal and paternalistic, but that works economically? (PANA 1998)

In terms of relationship building, many White farmers described their relations with the Black farmers as good. Dr. Grant highlighted outreach and extension programs that commercial farmers are undertaking toward communal areas, including supplying bulls to facilitate breeding, offering low-price food supplies and fertilizers, assisting with transportation and financing. Still, one White farmer confided that the minority of White farmers who are still uncomfortable with these initiatives prevent their institutionalization as CFU policy. They are largely undertaken on a voluntary, individual basis.

Within the CFU, Black farmers keep a low profile, which one White farmer believed was due to conservative elements within the CFU. Dr. Grant, however, attributes this to pressure from Black farmers outside the CFU and political circles. CFU-Zimbabwe Farmers Union (ZFU) institutional relations were nonetheless described by Grant as very positive, with full communication between them from top to bottom.

Most farmers interviewed depicted problems between Black and White communities as occurring at the top, political level. Dr. Grant described the government reconciliation process as a political policy of "put up or shut up." The war was fought to "get back the land that was stolen." Some White farmers felt the situation had worsened, becoming more racially charged since Mugabe's recent election rallies where this theme had been so prominent. At the same time, Dr. Grant maintained that in recent years the CFU has worked toward building up relations with the government. He highlighted the CFU-arranged visit of forty-five members of parliament (MPs) to CFU projects, followed by a social event. White farmers do not seek to lobby against the government. They are "a community which is totally loyal to the country . . . I want to be considered a Zimbabwean. What is hurtful is when we are considered settlers and the problems of the past are laid at our doors." At the same time, Dr. Grant admitted, "we have been to blame in not coming forward earlier."

In a press interview, former leader of the CFU, James Sinclair, also expressed shock over the "nonindigenous" categorization, despite the White farmers' inability to hold other passports. However:

> I mean no criticism of the CFU leadership, but we have not maintained dialogue as we should. Some farmers have had a confrontational attitude toward the government. And Whites didn't do enough to mix. I guess it's the South African influence. Sure there is a gap between Blacks and Whites, economic, social, and cultural, and it is a shame. But we are citizens, entitled to a piece of land. There is a potential for working together on this issue. . . . There must be a meeting of minds—but it won't happen while the government is shouting at us. (PANA 1998)

Black Farmers

Black farmers comprise three land tenure communities: communal (formerly the Native Reserves), resettlement, and small-scale commercial farming areas. Zimbabwe Farmers Union (ZFU) most widely represents Black farmers with a union body of 200,000 members. Discussions were held with communal and resettlement farmers.

Perceptions of the justness of the land distribution process among Black farmers are best captured through the common sentiment articulated by Deputy director of the ZFU, Dr. E. N. Zhou, who explained that while compulsory acquisition has its problems, it came about because land was not forthcoming under the *willing-seller, willing-buyer* approach. "Some have an overabundance of land and will do anything to keep it. We do not expect for all of it to be redistributed, but if the government hits its target, this will be sufficient." Communal farmer Langton Musiwa emphasized, "White farmers who bought the land at market prices should be compensated, but not those who were given the land for free by the Rhodesian regime. I don't think Whites should leave Zimbabwe. But we must share the land. Some of the White people's dogs live better than Black Zimbabweans, and we are human beings" (PANA 1998).

Communal farmers also had concerns about the process by which farmers were chosen to move from communal to resettlement areas. Kadoma farmers felt that the process should be taken out of the hands of local counselors—"outsiders" with little knowledge of the land or other issues and an overriding interest in their own reelection. They proposed that a Resettlement Panel be created, comprised of union representatives, communal farmers, and agricultural experts.

For communal farmers the primary sustainable development concerns were related to the immense overcrowding of communal areas, problems stemming from the overgrazing of cattle, and the poor quality land. Resettled farmers emphasized a lack of developmental resources and the (still) poor quality of land. A fifty-five-year-old communal farmer with seven children spoke of never having had his own land in the communal area where he was born—an ever-worsening physical space problem compounded by children marrying and procreating. Squatters are an issue of tension, particularly in the grazing areas where allotted space is deemed extremely limited.

Resettled farmers, while more productive and in control of their resources, only have six hectares per resettled family[11]—insufficient, they felt, given the land's poor quality. One farmer spoke bitterly about how "they [the government] speak very nice in their offices, talking something very productive. But on the ground it is miserable." Insufficient and inadequate clinics and market places were highlighted by resettled farmers, as was the relatively new reality of expensive schooling. Several also expressed discomfort around the idea that while the "stand" they were given is theirs forever, they were not allowed to sell it.

On communal living, both groups expressed mixed feelings. One resettled Masvingo farmer described herself as happier, as the land and soil are more fertile, allowing for greater production. Describing the communal areas as crowded and scattered: "I miss the people of course, but if you are going to improve your life you go. Everybody wants development, something nice." Kadoma farmers expressed a desire to be resettled collectively, given the lack of cooperation when different cultures are resettled collectively.

Several of the Kadoma and Masvingo farmers expressed positive sentiments about the relations with White farmers. Some even claimed that there were no tensions between Blacks and Whites. Several expressed a desire for more help from Whites, in particular through investment. One Black farmer described his admiration for the efficiency of White farmers. "Our problem is that we are jealous amongst ourselves." At the same time a common frustration with White farmers was noted by Zhoe: "They could have sat down as a group and collectively offered and negotiated with us a long time ago."

NGOs

Concerns within the nongovernmental organization (NGO) community in Zimbabwe for the most part assume the goals of the redistribution process and focus on the process. Since the time of the 1997 interviews, NGO activity has flourished, while areas of advocacy and interest remain steadily on such critical issues as

- improvements in awareness-raising, education, and consultation with stakeholders;
- greater transparency and information-sharing;
- greater participation by women and addressing of women's lack of access and status, particularly with regard to inheritance rights in communal areas;
- addressing environmental and resource-management problems, such as overcrowding, overgrazing, rapid depletion of soils, environmental degradation, regular crop failure, and associated deepening poverty;
- overpopulation and lack of resources in the communal areas;
- exploration of alternative resource methods and sources.

Government

The government's attitudes to the justness of the land distribution process are reflected through all four government representatives who reiterated the failure of the *willing-seller, willing-buyer* approach and rejected the "political correctness" criteria accusation for land designation. Masvingo Rural State Land Officer Mr. Tendaupenyu pointed to their flexible approach—proven by the fact that 40 percent of designated farms have been "undesignated" following contestation since 1993. Dr. V. Hugwe, director of Land Management and Technical Services, spoke of difficulties in finding suitable resettlement areas which ensured people could remain in close proximity to buried ancestors— conflict prevention in the longer term.

Hungwe attributed the sluggishness of reform to the lack of institutional ca- pacity, compounded by a lack of resources. Recognition should be given, how- ever, to what has been accomplished, given the magnitude of problems with which they started. Senior Secretary of the Interior of the Ministry of Local Government, Rural and Urban Development, Mr. Chiwewe emphasized a bal- anced approach in choosing resettlement farmers, aimed at keeping some "good farmers" in the communal areas to maintain communal productivity. Both (the former) Land Minister Kubirai Kangai and Dr. Hungwe assured this author that government officials are not acquiring land through favoritism. Rather, they are competing fairly through the "indigenization program," which maintains a proc- ess of advertising, applications, interviews, selection, and lease through contract, and evaluation of performance after ten years before sale of title deed is considered. Hungwe expressed government intention for a highly participatory process where civil society stakeholders would have ample opportunity for intervention.

In terms of development, the government main policy is aiming to address land inequality while enhancing productivity, as Minister Kangai emphasized the importance of agriculture in the government's plans. In addition to investment into small-scale farming and resettlement, the government is developing rural "growth points" to discourage urban exodus.

Pointing to the U.K. Industrial Revolution, Chiwewe described the government's leaning toward village rather than individual title as one aiming to protecting the poor from having their land bought up by the affluent. While private enterprise makes sense economically, "where fortunes and misfortunes are so divided" it does not. Hungwe emphasized the long-term aim of increasing autonomy to the communal areas—this sense of ownership would create a more sustainable use of the resources. The land tenure system is not a static one, but responding with time to peoples' needs. Donor programs such as the Marshall Plan, Hungwe noted, are needed to assist in the development of these areas.

Speaking to government's attitudes on the issue of building relationships, Chiwewe noted,"Peace can only be sound if it addresses the day-to-day needs of local communities." Toward this end, strong local government is needed. The greatest threat to peace, he emphasized, is poverty, which the government is working to eliminate through education, health, and social welfare programs.

If White farmers had been more forthcoming in the past about offering up land, several interviewees noted, the government would have designed a more sensitive process toward White interests. A general feeling of optimism for the future was nevertheless expressed, as was an openness toward seeking creative alternatives with White farmers. Hungwe expressed hope and the need to map out areas of agreement between stakeholders.

Since the time of the above interviews, the local media expresses increasing mistrust of government motives and capabilities vis-à-vis the land project. Regarding its *ends*—that land should be redistributed—there still seems to be little disagreement. The *means* or processes of land redistribution remain controversial, particularly regarding a market-based-versus-nonvoluntary acquisition process. The issue of whom should be held responsible to pay for acquired land— the government, international actors, or some combination thereof—still appears to be divided along racial and colonial power lines. At the same time, there is a growing societal consensus on governmental mismanagement and corruption of the process. Simultaneously a rising political challenge is emerging through the Movement for Democratic Change (MDC), a coalition of civic forces whose leadership has come out of the Zimbabwe Congress of Trade Unions (ZCTU).

The government has made efforts to participate in "stakeholder" workshops and even to encourage dialogue through the creation of a National Economic Consultative Forum (NECF), which brings all major stakeholders together. Simultaneously, it states its position that "the land identification and acquisition process is the responsibility of the government" (Chairman of the National Land Acquisition Committee, Cde. J. W. Msika, FSE 1999).

Land Redistribution toward a Sustainable Just Peace

How one evaluates the success of reconciliation and justice approaches in Zimbabwe clearly depends upon one's experiences and conceptual framework. Discussions in theory and practice around whether and how to reconcile competing notions raise questions regarding process, capacity, and power. Who sacrifices, and how does power play into the adoption or promotion of particular approaches? The concluding analysis considers the above stakeholder views against the theoretical insights about reconciliation and justice toward offering practical recommendations for Zimbabwe's land redistribution challenges.

Building Constructive Intercommunal Relationships

At independence, reconciliation did not become a national project in the South African sense of public truth uncovering and apology, promoted by means of official policies and practices at all levels. Moreover, there has been little if any governmental effort to foster communication between the different communities. While the Lancaster House Agreement at independence assured that White interests would be protected, Mugabe's march toward one-party rule and intermittent inflammatory rhetoric over the years has arguably served to *create* tensions between Blacks and Whites. "Land is the main issue in which Mugabe has attempted to reduce a complex problem to Black against White," writes one journalist (Meldrum 1999).

Considering reconciliation theoretically as building constructive intergroup relationships, it seems clear that Black-White relationships go beyond mere coexistence, which is defined as sharing space and "tolerating" each other. From a (culturally biased and necessarily limited) outsider's perspective, there appears to be a good deal of acceptance of each other's right to exist in the geographical space of Zimbabwe. There also seems to be an acceptance of cultural and political differences, and even recognition that each needs the other. Given the colonial heritage and the still very stratified and separate existence of the communities, political reconciliation of the type Gardner Feldman describes clearly has not been achieved. The seeming lack of characteristics such as equality, partnership, active friendship, and trust, this author would argue, has to do with the fact that economic justice has in no way been achieved for the great majority of Zimbabweans.

Curiously, both Black (communal and resettlement) and White farmers tended to divert questions of relationships with the other group toward expressions of dissatisfaction with the government's process and the problems it created for their own community. Neither group targeted the other community's role in creating obstacles to a smooth process for the government. Rather, both Whites and Blacks spoke about their relationships with each other in friendly terms, expressing optimism for the ability for better relations and a willingness to do more toward this. In practice, however, political considerations come into play. White farmers have since offered an alternative land redistribution plan, which government officials resoundly rejected.

Although not raised by farmers, a common set of views emerging more recently in the press focuses our gaze toward class (PANA 1998). There is a new Black elite whose members intermingle relatively comfortably with Whites, and an increasing belief permeating society that Zimbabwe's poor masses have been left out of the transition. "Elsewhere, race relations are, on the surface, good. . . . But resentment breeds in the tremendous economic gap between the grinding poverty experienced by the average Black Zimbabwean and the comfort and luxury enjoyed by the majority of the White population" (Meldrum 1999). The class factor can be viewed as strengthening the argument that economic justice is a determinant in quality intergroup relations.

More promising phenomena for constructive intergroup relations are the coalitions of forces working for social and economic change. Growing dissatisfaction with Mugabe's rule is fostering cooperation among Blacks and Whites from various trade unions; churches; women's, gay, and human rights groups; as well as lawyers' associations. In addition to nonviolent antiwar demonstrations, people of all races have formed the National Constitutional Assembly, a group calling for a democratically drafted constitution, the Structural Adjustment Participatory Review Initiative, and the new political party, the Movement for Democratic Change. The strength here is that people from different communities are working together around various economic justice and good governance issues.

Justice and Redistributing Land

> Some donors and some governments keep telling us . . . to respect human rights and democratic values. But nothing is done to address the question of economic rights of the Black people. . . . It appears that in their eyes the rights of Black people to the resources of this country are not deemed to be human rights. . . . This is what the War of Liberation sought to redress and what we still seek to redress today. . . . The economic disparities that still exist seventeen years after independence are a tragedy. . . . How do we expect those who fought for land and do not have the land to respect the rule of law? The moment attempts are made to change the laws which preserve the economic supremacy [of Whites] a storm breaks out. . . . It is time we show the courage of our convictions and implement changes to give effect to the economic aspirations of our people. . . . The judiciary can still play an role in the process of change if it is a real peoples' judiciary. (Anonymous, *Herald* 1997)

Considering the three types of justice proposed at the beginning of this chapter, this profound plea touches upon each of them, expressing an increasingly vocal public sentiment. It emphasizes the need for *social* and *redistributive justice*, which addresses oppression and social inequality of the present, rooted in injustices of the past. It calls for recognition of economic disparity and inequality of particular groups, and of the ways in which the system preserves that inequity. It demands empowering solutions that engage institutions and people to create new opportunities for the reigniting of repressed aspirations. It gives voice to a justice of relationships founded on respect for human dignity.

As in South Africa, questions of economic justice are an increasing part of public discourse. Whether in the form of land redistribution, demand for jobs, housing, public services—the question of societal transformation toward a sustainable peace requires the meeting of peoples' economic needs and addressing the structural sources that prevent them from being met.

Lederach (1997) speaks about the need for spiritual and psychological dimensions of conflict resolution as moving beyond traditional statist diplomacy, providing seeds for sustainable peace. This author would add that a central reason for failed diplomatic efforts and agreements is that the justice needs of the oppressed or rebel groups are not fully taken into consideration. In theory and in practice, the focus is on the *process* of *conflict termination*, rather than the content of the peace agreement and the need to work toward a just outcome to sustain peace. In Zimbabwe, the Lancaster Agreement preserved White interests and economic power without providing adequate measures to address the cause of the war—the injustice of grossly unequal access to land.

At the same time, land must be redistributed via means that are perceived to be just by different stakeholders. This is by no means simple, given that different groups have different experiences, values, and perceptions of what is just and about the way things should be. The processes by which these different views are negotiated are central to the trust building needed for the development of a national identity that is inclusive of different communities. In Zimbabwe, the management of the land redistribution process has been deeply questioned by Whites and is increasingly being questioned by Blacks. This negatively affects people's perceptions about the ends of the process, as motives are increasingly questioned. In terms of relationship building, it could have both negative and positive implications; while relations between Whites and the government may suffer, coalitions of White farmers and sections of Black society are collectively forming to protest governmental corruption.

Sustainable Development

As several philosophers of peace tell us, we should not try to avoid paradoxes, but rather to seek the wisdom that lies in addressing them (Lederach 1997). In this spirit we might say that growth alone is no panacea to developmental problems; it must be balanced with equity concerns. The LTC's aim to "facilitate high and sustainable levels of production as well as enhanced social cohesion" (LTC 1) follows this thinking. Pursing these simultaneously, as with reconciliation and justice, is a task laden with challenges. Alternative development approaches will need to be actively pursued, and considered alongside dominant approaches, if a balance is to be struck in the name of sustainable peace. One critical area in need of thinking and action is communal and individual land title and rights—a wider question for all modernizing societies.

Other societal voices link development issues with reconciliation and peace. Sam Moyo, for example, writes that

> a reasonable climate for Black-White reconciliation can only be achieved through a more balanced redressing of the variety of land demands in Zimbabwe, in a manner which is transparent, equitable, and focuses on the productive use of land for agro-industrial and development purposes. (1995, 10)

The LTC emphasizes that redistribution and productive and sustainable use of the land are necessary for peace to be sustained in the country.

Justice and Reconciliation: Finding the Balance for Zimbabwe's Sustainable Just Peace

Following the logic of embracing both energies in a paradox, here it has been argued that a sustainable peace requires a balance of justice and reconciliation—they cannot be seen as mutually exclusive aims and processes. How does the case of Zimbabwe context help us to understand the paradox? Or: *How can reconciliation and justice be simultaneously pursued toward a sustainable peace?* First, two obstacles that have emerged throughout the analysis—one domestic and one international—need to be addressed.

Domestically, the primary obstacle is a lack of clear process. People from communal, resettlement, and White farming express confusion about the process and the reasoning behind different practices. While the LTC was a great step in the right direction, the lack of consistency in articulating and implementing follow-up has proved problematic, creating disempowerment and cynicism amongst stakeholders, and animosity toward the government. While the government has made steps toward consultation with stakeholders, the lack of consistency and clarity persists. At the extreme we have veterans squatting on farms, illustrative of the highly political nature of land reform—a pawn for Mugabe as he clings to power, yet a critical factor in maintaining societal order and peace.

External obstacles have manifested themselves in particular international community interests and institutions—that is, World Bank and IMF economic prescriptions which historically have failed to adequately consider the

Zimbabwean socioeconomic and political context, thereby exacerbating poverty, inequality, and social tensions. Critical awareness of the ways in which international political and economic norms, and the interests of particular actors, present challenges to the emergence and implementation of indigenous processes of reconciliation and justice is required. The international community is increasingly concerned about its rights and responsibilities with respect to interventions in conflict regions and related humanitarian and development assistance around the world. Why should it not practice prevention by simultaneously considering how its varied interests create and exacerbate conflicts and hinder the effectiveness of indigenous development and peacebuilding processes?

In a letter written to Zimbabwe's land and agriculture minister, Kumbirai Kangai, British International Development Minister Claire Short states, "I should make clear that we do not accept that Britain has a special responsibility to meet the costs of land purchase in Zimbabwe. We are a new Government from diverse backgrounds without links to former colonial interests. My own origins are Irish and as you know we were colonized not colonizers." Expecting a more sympathetic Labor government hearing, Kangai responded, "We are still paying for the debts incurred by Ian Smith. Some are ridiculous. Some were to borrow money to buy guns to kill us while we were fighting for liberation. If we recognize that we have an obligation under international law to pay the previous government's debts, the British government is obliged to meet obligations made by Mrs. Thatcher at Lancaster House. I don't see what that has to do with whether some British minister thinks she was colonized" (*Mail and Guardian*, 1997).

An alternative approach to the effects of colonialism worth considering is that of France in Cambodia. In the face of Cambodia's postwar economic crisis and debt burden, France paid off Cambodia's IMF debt, ensuring that Cambodia could borrow from international financial institutions, starting with a clean slate.

Both the domestic and international-level obstacles point toward the role of politics and power in any such peacebuilding process. Mugabe's unpredictable rule, accompanied by corruption and confusion in the land redistribution process, undeniably creates a climate of uncertainty for international or subnational actors. We must still ask, however: Would a national government be able to employ indigenous or unique notions of justice, even derived through democratic process, if the international donor community, for example, disapproved of the approach?

While obstacles and tensions clearly exist, it is worth reemphasizing the interactive nature of justice and reconciliation. If *just processes* are put into place, and people recognize a commitment to ensuring that processes that aim to rectify wrongs are maintained, their *sense of injustice* will begin to be placated, and trust will evolve within the system. This is turn should foster better cooperation and dialogue, contributing to the building of better relationships. Moreover, this should contribute to greater communication and understanding of different needs and interests, leading to an acceptance of less adversarial justice processes in a search for mutually satisfactory outcomes. Of course, the limits of this will be somewhat context-dependent, depending on a wide range of factors including the intensity of the conflict and how long ago it took place, the degree to which the system is trusted, the overtures that parties are making to each other, and the degree to which forgiveness is a cultural value.

At the same time, this case illustrates the need for both subjective (relational) and objective (structural) forms of justice to be addressed in some way; that is, even an *approximate justice*, before constructive communal relationships can substantially evolve.[12] If the structural violence that was an initial cause of violent conflict continues to exist in a postviolent conflict setting, it is unlikely that trust and cooperation and other foundational characteristics of constructive intercommunal relationships can be developed. This view ultimately questions the subjective/objective divide; people perceive inequalities and problems that are objective. However, one's standpoint—where one *stands* in the conflict—will affect how one perceives the justice or injustice of particular conditions.

Drawing from interviews, several themes evolve, around which concrete proposals can be made. Applying to the government in particular, and all groups generally, these are the need to:

- develop a shared understanding about the importance of land reform and a "just" way to move forward;
- ensure that different perceptions of justice, fairness, and reconciliation are recognized and included;
- increase awareness and different understanding of each community's relationship to and interest in the land (symbolically and practically) as well as development and productivity, and tradition and modernization;
- evolve an understanding about a shared history and national identity;
- ensure that ongoing perceptions of fair process are maintained, by ensuring transparency of the process, participatory process—design and implementation; and
- stop the production of enemy images.

Perhaps most important in our era of democratization is the need for all actors to take a proactive, mutually empowering role in the process. All communities interviewed seem to feel that there is more they could be doing to improve intergroup relations—an indicator of reconciliation being practical and possible. Better communication and more information sharing across these communities could provide opportunities for improved relations, and for shared land and development related projects. This would facilitate government efforts. NGOs can be involved to a greater extent, creating forums for this dialoguing and strategizing to take place. As people become more aware of the process, the challenges and complexities of carrying out such a monumental task will lessen. There will be less fodder for rumor and politicization of issues into competing camps, and more effective, cooperative implementation of policies. As people feel more ownership of the process, paradoxical tensions between reconciliation and justice will diffuse, strengthening foundations for building sustained peace.

The international community should take an active role in fulfilling moral and practical, historical and contemporary responsibilities. Pursing "national interests" is becoming less acceptable in an era where democracy demands fair process. If the international community seeks "peace" for countries facing numerous war and postwar challenges, then increasing and honest dialogue about the character of that peace, and means of achieving it, is central.

While drawing on theory to provide a loose conceptual framework, the subtleties of the Zimbabwe case reinforce the idea that a particular reconciliation/justice balance is ultimately situationally and indigenously defined. At the same time, conceptual insights from the literature usefully create an interactive normative and theoretical framework for analysis. Recommendations stemming from stakeholder analyses reflect many of the themes that particular reconciliation and justice theories grapple with. They offer transformative insights for Zimbabwe's situation, and food for thought for other cases facing similar paradoxes.

Notes

1. The White population was at its highest in the 1960s—about 275,000 people. Out of Zimbabwe's 11 million population, 9 million are Blacks, and approximately 100,000 are Whites (Cheney 1990; Meldrum 1999).

2. In the critical theory tradition, this research "seeks to elicit and promote normative ideals rooted in the experience of, and reflection about, the very society being considered" (Young 1990, 4).

3. Proponents include national leaders (e.g., Mandela and Tutu) as well as theorists (Lederach 1997; Nina 1995).

4. Sterba argues that relationship and justice are not always as distinct as Carol Gilligan (and others) argue. Rather, these theorists are working with a restrictive understanding of justice when they make comparisons (1998).

5. Anthropologist Nader has written extensively on justice norms in traditional cultural contexts, as well as impositional frameworks of justice and harmony ideology (Nader and Sursock 1986).

6. The LTC proposed a parallel path of growth and equity to "facilitate high and sustainable levels of production as well as enhanced social cohesion" (1994, 1). Proposals include: rural capital formation; greater rural employment; stimulation of public and private investment in land improvement; revitalization of agriculture; replacement of highly centralized and ineffective government structures with legal, administrative, and people-based institutional structures; and new capacity to implement and monitor land policies.

7. At the same time, the development of a UNDP coordinated Technical Support Unit, funded by Sweden and the United States, is under way to assist in preparing for the implementation of the land reform program.

8. These include "a legal requirement of the Land Acquisition Act (1992) which had to be completed by November 28, 1998" (Minister Kumbrai Kangai of Lands and

Agriculture, FES 1999); that these were not new farms, but the contested farms from last year's list (Minister Msika of the National Land Acquisition Committee ([FES 1999]). Both emphasized that this would be a fair process involving consultation with stakeholders.

9. As this goes to press, the situation has increasingly worsened. Mugabe has not moved to reverse the war veterans' action and is pursuing plans for an "accelerated land redistribution programme" which involves seizing 804 farms, followed by 3,000 more within months—without compensation. Moreover, he has drawn further criticism at home and abroad for election-related political violence. More than thirty Movement for Democratic Change (MDC) supporters were killed in the run-up to parliamentary elections, despite which the new MDC party won 57 of 120 seats—the first real challenge to Mugabe's rule. The fact that several of the victims of violence were White farmers has allowed Mugabe to claim the violence as land-related (McGreal 2000). While the current context demands new analysis that brings the war veteran element into greater focus, the reconciliation/justice analytical framework of this article remains critical in the search for a sustained peace in Zimbabwe.

10. Semistructured interviews were held May through June 1997 with the following: six White large-scale commercial farming community (LSCF) farmers in Masvingo Province and several high ranking Commercial Farming Union (CFU) representatives in Masvingo and Harare; twenty communal and resettlement farmers in Masvingo and Kadoma Provinces; five governmental representatives at regional and national levels in Masvingo and Harare; and twenty NGO representatives in Masvingo Province and Harare. Questions focused on the perceived justness (means and ends) of the land redistribution process; the importance of sustainable development and how to achieve it; and the state of intergroup relationships, the potential for peace, and how each community was actively pursuing peaceful relationships. Press quotes by government and farmers complement the interviews.

11. By contrast, LSWF are, on average, 2,550 hectares per farm, with many farmers owning several (LTC 1994, 13).

12. This is consistent with other postcolonial contexts, where indigenous peoples have resisted offers of reconciliation by their former oppressors—that is, in Canada and Australia. They want compensation for the lands and resources that were taken from them, and reimbursement for the exploitation of their labor over time.

References

Ackermann, A. 1994. Reconciliation as a Peace-Building Process in Postwar Europe, the Franco-German Case. In *Peace and Change*, vol. 19. no. 3, 229-250.

Azar, E. E. 1986. Management of Social Conflict in the Third World. Paper presented at the Fourth ICES Annual Lecture at Columbia University, New York.

Austin, W.G., and Tobiasen, J. M. 1984. Legal Justice and the Psychology of Conflict Resolution. In *The Sense of Injustice: Social Psychological Perspectives.* Robert Folger, ed. New York: Plenum Press.

Cheney, P. 1990. *The Land and People of Zimbabwe.* New York: J. B. Lippincott.

Feldman, L. G. 1984. *Special Relationship between W. Germany and Israel.* New York: Routledge.

Financial Gazette (FG) 2000. Staff writer. Bank Abandons Currency Controls. March 9.

Friedrich Ebert Siftung [FES]. 1999. Report on Land Consultation. Zimbabwe: FES.

Galtung, J. 1996. *Peace by Peaceful Means*. Oslo: Sage.

Gilligan, C. 1982. *In a Different Voice*. Cambridge, Mass.: Harvard University Press.

The Herald Newspaper Harare. 1997. Anonymous. "The Case for Redistributing Harare's Land." December 8.

Kahiya, Vincent. 2000. "Government Directs Farm Invasions," *Zimbabwe Independent.* March 3.

———. 1996. Ph.D. Dissertation, Eastern Mennonite University.

Kraybill, R. 1996. An Anabaptist Paradigm for Conflict Transformation: Critical Reflections on Peacemaking in Zimbabwe. Unpublished Ph.D. dissertation, Department of Religious Studies, University of Cape Town, South Africa.

Kritz, N. J., ed. 1995. *Transitional Justice: How Emerging Democracies Reckon with Former Regimes, Vol. 1*. Washington, D.C.: United States Institute of Peace.

Land Tenure Commission (LTC). 1994. Report of the Commission of Inquiry into Appropriate Agricultural Land Tenure Systems. Vol. 1, main report.

Lederach, J. P. 1997. *Building Peace: Sustainable Reconciliation in Divided Societies.* Washington, D.C.: United States Institute of Peace Press.

Lerner, M. J. 1980. *The Belief in a Just World.* New York: Plenum Press.

London Times. 1998. Staff writer. "IMF Tells Mugabe to Pay for Whites' Land." January 24.

Mail and Guardian. 1997. Staff writer. "Blair's Worse than the Tories, says Mugabe." December 22.

McGreal, C. 2000. "Regional Leaders Rally Behind Mugabe," *Guardian,* August 8.

Meldrum, A. 1999. "Zimbabwe Focus: Racism Lingers, but Class Divides," *Mail & Guardian,* March 30.

Mitchell, C. 1981. *The Structure of International Conflict.* New York: St. Martin's Press.

Montville, J. 1993. The Healing Functions in Political Conflict Resolution. In *Conflict Resolution, Theory and Practice: Integration and Application.* Ddennis Sandole and Hugo van der Merwe, eds. Manchester, U.K.: Manchester University Press.

Moyo, S. 1995. *The Land Question in Zimbabwe.* Harare, Zimbabwe: Sapes Books.

Nader, L., and Sursock, A. 1986. Anthropology and Justice. In *Justice: Views from the Social Sciences.* Ronald L. Cohen, ed. New York: Plenum Press.

Nina, D. 1995. Rights vs. Reconciliation. In *Alternative Law Journal,* vol. 20, no.12.

O'Loughlin, E. 1998. "Resettlement Plan Gets Short Shrift from West," *Herald Correspondent* September 14.

Panafrican News Agency (PANA). 1998. Staff writer. "This Land Is Your Land, This Land Is Our Land." May 18.

Sterba, J. P. 1998. *How to Make People Just: A Practical Reconciliation of Alternative Conceptions of Justice.* Lanham, Md.: Rowman & Littlefield.

Sylvester, C. 1991. *Zimbabwe: The Terrain of Contradictory Development.* London: Westview Press.

Twigg, A., and van der Merwe, H. 1996. Community Justice: A Restorative Vision and Policy Formulation Process. In *IMBIZO: Exploring Community Justice.* Community Peace Foundation.. January.

Van den Brink, R. 1999. Zimbabwe Land Acquisition Update. May 19. Washington, D.C.: World Bank.

van der Merwe, H. 1999. The Truth and Reconciliation Commission and Community Reconciliation: An Analysis of Competing Strategies and Conceptualizations. Fairfax, Va.: The Institute for Conflict Analysis and Resolution, George Mason University.

Weiner, E., ed. 1998. *The Handbook of Interethnic Coexistence.* New York: Continuum Publishing.

Williams, D. 1996. Popular Justice, Lateral Thinking and Believing the Impossible. In *IMBIZO: Exploring Community Justice.* Community Peace Foundation. January.

World Bank, InfoDEV. Zimbabwe's Reform Program Unwinds. <http://www.worldbank.org/develmentnews/index.html>

Young, I. M. 1990. *Justice and the Politics of Difference.* Princeton, N.J.: Princeton University Press.

Zehr, H. 1990. *Changing Lenses: A New Focus for Crime and Justice.* Scottsdale, Pa.: Herald Press.

12

Education for Coexistence in Israel

Potential and Challenges

Mohammed Abu-Nimer

A group of Arab ninth graders have just completed their first encounter with a Jewish group from a nearby town in the Galilee. The Arab children live two miles away from the newly built Jewish settlement. Fifteen years earlier, many parents of the Arab children were arrested because they protested the confiscation of their land by the Israeli authority to build this new town and settle the new Jewish immigrants or the parents of the Jewish children who participated in the encounter. The encounter lasted the entire day, and it focused on peace, culture, and coexistence. Throughout most of the day, the Arab children were in a well-maintained, state-of-the-art Jewish school. When they returned to their village, they complained about the lack of facilities and equipment in their school when compared to the Jewish school. One of the students even said, "They took our land, and they have better schools." The Arab teacher hushed him, declaring that "politics is not a part of this class or the Arab-Jewish encounter."

This event represents a certain type of encounter between minority and majority members organized around the world (e.g., in South Africa, Northern Ireland, Cyprus, Bosnia, or Washington, D.C.). The encounter's purpose is to educate the participants in order to achieve peaceful coexistence between the majority and minority groups. In itself, this purpose is a superior one, and it cannot be challenged by most people among the minority or the majority. However, there are many limitations and shortcomings that accompany such encounters. Such limitations are often related not only to the structure of the encounter or the nature of its participants, but extend to objectives, intended and unintended outcomes, process, content, role of the third party, and the encounter's consequences on the subordinate-subordinated power relations between the minority and the majority.

This chapter first discusses the nature of certain types of coexistence projects carried out in Israel by Arabs and Jews, who in most cases (if not all) face many challenges in their respective communities to even complete such projects. Second, it explores the encounter's limitations of such initiatives in terms of their goals, processes, structures, and content. Third, it focuses on the implications of such limitations on the concepts of peace, coexistence, justice, and reconciliation between Arabs and Jews in Israel. Finally, the chapter includes some suggestions for adapting such initiatives.

Arab-Jewish Coexistence Field in Israel

The Arab-Jewish field of coexistence is expanding, and its activities are tremendously diverse. Today, it includes joint projects of curriculum building, art and music, literature, computers and technology, career development, and so on. Nevertheless, the interethnic encounter is still considered a major tool for coexistence. An encounter is usually a project that brings Arab and Jewish participants together for a brief period of contact, which extends up to three days. Most of the encounters have been organized and conducted by nonprofit organizations in Israel. Since 1993, there are approximately forty-five organizations that have been active in this field (a few have been active since the early 1970s). These organizations are often led by an Israeli Jewish coordinator or director, who raises the funds from the United States (and, recently, European foundations) to support the Arab-Jewish encounter programs (Abu-Nimer 1999). Symbolically, those encounter programs are the most valuable and important aspects of the Arab-Jewish coexistence programs, if not all Arab-Jewish relations. They played a central role, for example, in fighting the racist movement of Rabbi Meir Kahana in Israel between 1982 and 1986 (Abu-Nimer 1999; Bar-On 1996; Hall-Cathala 1990).

Each encounter is often called by an Arab and a Jewish facilitator. The facilitators are trained and coached by the sponsoring organization in a specific model or approach. Most of the encounters' participants are students or teachers from Jewish and Arab schools. The organization's representative, who often meets with the school administration and secures their approval, recruits participants. The Ministry of Education or other government agencies usually encourages such encounters or projects.

In peace and conflict resolution theories and intervention models, there is no substitute for the work of coexistence and dialogue (Suanders 1999). Grassroots activities have to take place to promote tolerance of differences and respect for equal rights among Arabs and Jews in Israel. However, for Arab participants these programs have had another function; they provide Arabs with the only opportunity to interact with Israeli Jews without being accused, feared, or humiliated. The encounter is the only chance to present their ideas and perceptions of the conflict.[1] For the Jewish participants, the coexistence programs function as a safe window to look in depth at the culture and perceptions of Arabs.

The coexistence field can bring to Arab-Jewish relations in Israel great opportunities for reconciliation. Therefore, it is essential and necessary to continuously examine the work of these encounter programs by posing questions such as: What are the intervenors' goals when working in this field? Are such goals being achieved? What impact do these coexistence programs have on peaceful and equal relations between Arabs and Jews in Israel? How do coexistence programs relate to issues of justice among both Arabs and Jews in Israel?

Education for Coexistence:
The Encounter Programs

The field of coexistence in Israel can be captured through three phases: the first phase extends from the 1950s to the early 1970s, during which time organizations associated with the security forces (*Shein Biet*), "Histadrut" Israeli Labor unions, and Zionist political parties were created. Coexistence activities during this period were aimed at mobilizing Arab support and loyalty to the state. An example is the "society for friendship and understanding" (Abu-Nimer 1999). In this first phase, the aim was to preserve the status quo and to function as another arm of the security services—and thus as another tool for the political parties to mobilize Arab votes or supporters. Arabs in Israel understood that if someone supports coexistence, then he or she is loyal and not an Arab nationalist, Islamic fundamentalist, or communist.

The second phase took place between 1970 and the early 1980s, a period that characterized the discovery of the Arab minority by the Israeli government and public (after they were under military administration since 1948). Some minority leaders began expressing some interest in being integrated in the state. After the 1967 defeat of the Arab nations, many in this community realized that the "savior" would not arrive from the Arab countries (Lustick 1980). At the same time, the Israeli government increasingly began outlining the distinctions between Arabs in Israel and the Arabs outside of Israel (West Bank and Gaza). The new wave of organizations in this field, an extension of the Israeli Jewish public awareness, began exploring the other culture and working on cultural sensitivity issues. The Arab minority began functioning for the Israeli institutions as a window to understanding the Arab culture in general. These coexistence activities were the *Humus and Labni* meetings.[2] Jewish participants gained the chance to closely know the Arab culture through food, folklore dancing, and other practices. The primary activity of the coexistence field or the encounter during this period was twofold: (1) to help in drawing the green line between the territories and Israel, and (2) to reveal similarities between Arab and Jews in Israel by focusing on the interpersonal and cultural components.

The third phase of coexistence began in the early 1980s and extends to the 1990s. By the late 1970s and early 1980s, some organizations began using a prejudice reduction model that was imported from the United States (Sherif 1958; Amir 1969). Reducing stereotypes, and increasing cultural sensitivity and understanding, are the primary objectives of this model. This shift in coexistence approaches was due to the fact that the Israeli government partially institutionalized the field of coexistence. The Ministry of Education was motivated or threatened by the increasing support of Kahana's movement among Israeli Jewish youth.[3] In 1985 the government supported the notion that the destiny of both Arabs and Jews in Israel is linked and that the two groups will have to live together, formally declaring: "Arabs and Jews are destined to live together."

By the late 1980s few organizations began working on the analytical and conflict model of coexistence. Such organizations perceive the relations between Arabs and Jews as two ethnic groups who seek to live in an equal political system, rather than a Jewish majority-Arab minority relationship. This model aims to examine and confront conflictual issues, particularly political attitudes and ideologies. It requires Arabs and Jews to reexamine their ideological assumptions about the nature of the state. The main assumption of such a model is not cultural harmony, as in the second phase, but the existence of the conflict as an integral part of the Arab-Jewish relations. The model called for a "living with the conflict" approach (Bar and Bargal 1995). In 1997, only two programs were struggling with the attempt to incorporate conflict and difference into their work. These programs recognize the existence of the conflict, while other programs still adopt the notion of searching for similarities and avoiding conflictual issues.

Major Features of Arab-Jewish Encounters in Israel

The Arab-Jewish encounter starts with the *personal acquaintance stage*, in which participants are careful, hesitant, and show exaggerated politeness, reflecting the tension and difficulties of a direct encounter with the "other." Participants initially express the belief that they have no problem with the other side. A typical Jewish participant's statement at this stage is, "I have no problem with Arabs, in fact I have many Arab friends, and I visit in Arab villages," or, "I grew up with Arabs." Or an Arab participant would declare, "I have Jewish friends, and they have even visited my home." The participants show excitement at meeting the other and surprise from the kindness of others; they focus on exploring similarities.

The second stage of a direct encounter is cultural acquaintance, during which the tension continues, but participants begin learning and discovering the cultural differences and similarities, revealing stereotypes, and the setting becomes less threatening. In the cultural stage, participants get to know each other's cultural habits and values. The focus on similarities has characterized this stage of the encounter experience. Stereotypes and cultural prejudice can also be explored at this stage.

In the third stage, the focus is on political discussion. Participants explore political attitudes; as a result, their frustration and mistrust grow, and they exchange accusations and blame each other. Fearing the tense emotions and complexity attached to political issues, few programs move to the third stage of political discussion and exchanges of opinions. In addition, many encounter programs were presented as cultural rather than political. However, for those who discussed political aspects, during the 1980s, the Palestine Liberation Organization (PLO) and the Zionist nature of the state had been the main issues. In the 1990s, the questions of a Palestinian state and the national rights of Arabs in Israel are the main political issues. Identifying the different and similar political beliefs is the objective of this stage. At the end of this stage, participants, tired from arguing, discover and assure each other's differences. In the fourth stage, after being exhausted, the participants demonstrate less tension, more trust, and feel less threatened by the "others."

Participants search for agreement by focusing on separate or joint professional or instrumental tasks to accomplish (visits to villages or Jewish towns, education goals, or social or political actions). Usually, in this stage participants look for the similarities, common activities, and alternative resolutions to disputes.

Macrolimitations of the Arab-Jewish Coexistence Field

Scholars and practitioners have identified other shortcomings primarily based on large-scale evaluation of the Arab-Jewish programs. Some of these critiques and problems refer to the field of Arab-Jewish coexistence programs, and others refer to specific intervention models. Nevertheless, they all question the function of Arab-Jewish programs in the Israeli political context (Bar and Asaqla 1988a; Lemish, Mula, and Rubin 1989). Lemish and others (1991) argue that the "contact programs" (Arab-Jewish encounters) are another experience of asymmetry, because the primary reasons why Jewish participants take part in such activities are: (a) their need to present Israel as a liberal state and ease their consciences (e.g., Israel often used it as part of foreign ministry propaganda); (b) it is a test of their stereotypes (i.e., are they primitive or capable of rational reasoning?); (c) they must prove they are tolerant; and (d) they must test whether the Arabs are loyal to the Jewish state. In the encounter, the dominance of the Hebrew language causes Arabs to feel inferior, insecure, and alienated from the process, while Jews are very comfortable. Other research, however, concluded that the effects of the encounter programs contribute to the mutual acquaintance of both Arabs and Jews, increasing the knowledge and awareness of the actual relationship between the two groups and reducing estrangement and alienation feelings (Bar and Asaqla 1988b). Although these processes are also taking place among youth who did *not* take part in the encounter (the control group), the encounter group has a stronger effect on the feelings of participants' self awareness.

Kenneth Bandler (1991) describes the Arab-Jewish programs' function as a safety valve in that it provides the framework for dialogue rather than violence. Historically, in the 1950s and 1960s Arab-Jewish organizations were operated by government agencies as a part of the minority control system; today, another governmental policy adopted by these organizations is the division between Arabs, Druze, Christians, and Bedouins. Some organizations differentiate their programs according to these divisions; they do not question them. For instance, many programs and activities of these organizations are not directed or even marketed in the Druze schools.[4]

In terms of impact, Kuttab, who criticizes the dialogue and encounter groups of Arabs from the West Bank and Gaza Strip and Jews from Israel, provides a valid argument when applied to Arab-Jewish programs in Israel. He argues that

> when dialogue becomes a substitute for action, there are two results. First, it assuages the conscience of members of the oppressor group to the point where they feel they do not have to do anything else. The conscience is soothed and satisfied. On the other hand, for the members of the oppressed group it becomes a safety valve for venting frustrations. In both cases it becomes a means of reinforcing the existing oppression and therefore serves to perpetuate it. (1988, 89)

The prevailing assumptions of Arab-Jewish programs, which are accepted and not brought up during the discussion of Arab-Jewish relations in Israel, are (a) the legitimacy of the Jewish state as opposed to the state of its citizens, and (b) Arab-Jewish encounters are educational, and they should not have any political activity or consequences. This is based on the premise that education is a neutral act or process that should not take any political stand. In his critique of this field, in 1990 Hall-Cathala presented the following "radical" argument:[5]

> The coexistence programs that take place in the realm of Jewish state are simply an attempt to make Zionism more palatable for Palestinians by presenting the universal face of Israel. Instead, it is argued, they should be supporting the Palestinians' right for self-determination (in a state alongside Israel) or their right to live in a non-sectarian, secular Israel.

There are certain objective limitations to these encounters as identified by Hall-Cathala (1990, 135): (a) their development has been hampered by the lack of infrastructure and resources, and hence lack stability and professionalism in their operation; (b) they are extremely limited in reaching only a small part of the population; and (c) they lack institutional support and nationwide legitimization from the authorities and the public.

Finally, Bieran (1990), in her examination of the work of a newly emerging and promising Arab-Jewish project,[6] argues that for both sides there are components of *Hetnasaot*, or snobbish elitism. Arabs held Jewish views on female-male relations, issues of elder and children relations, and authoritarian figures in the child's life in contempt; the Jews looked down on Arabs in Israel because of the "power" image Jews developed after 1967. In addition, Jews are seen as trying to be affiliated with a Western mentality and lifestyle, due to the influence of Western Jews who control Israeli institutions and elite, and because of their Zionist movement ideology and history. Bieran (1990) argues that the encounter programs perpetuate the cultural dominance of the Jewish Western elite and place the Arab culture in an inferior status (by utilizing individualistic and rational rather than ritualistic and relationship models). In the workshops, participants and intervenors tried to reach understanding, empathy, and even "love." They spread flowers, but they ignored the difficult problems and the asymmetric power relationship. They did not talk about these issues until children exploded with hatred, violence, and rejection of each other.

The Arab-Jewish Encounter Model: Limitations

For the purpose of this chapter, the limitations of Arab-Jewish encounters or education for coexistence in Israel are classified into the following categories: design (assumptions, content, and process); organizational aspects (funding, administration, and so on); professional aspects (intervention and training models); and contextual aspects (political and social development).[7] The following limitations were identified in most of the examined encounter models.

Assumptions of Status Quo

The political and educational approaches that underlie the coexistence field were revealed through the participants', intervenors', and organization directors' answers to questions such as: What are the issues of the conflict between Arabs and Jews in Israel? Can Arabs and Jews become equal in the state of Israel? How does the organization perceive the Arab-Jewish relations? Is there a conflict? Are the issues cultural, religious, interpersonal, or political? Does the intervention program challenge or allow participants to question the assumption that Israel should be a Jewish state? Are the coexistence field and the specific project part of larger social movement in Israel, or is it a countersocial and political change movement? Are those who join the coexistence programs more or less likely to engage in political activity to change the status quo in Israel?

When responding to the above questions, it was clear that all the program's except Sekoi/Chance focus on the attitudinal changes.[8] They work on cultural sensitivity, prejudice reduction, and stereotypes. Organizations and projects have ignored the structural aspects of the Arab-Jewish conflict in Israel (institutes, ideology, and government policy). They have focused their work on the attitudinal level (stereotypes, prejudice, communication, misunderstanding, cultural sensitivity, and mistrust). The set of assumptions and principles underlying those encounter programs were asymmetric, corresponding more closely with the political consensus among the Jewish majority. For example, "Jewishness of the state" is an assumption that organizations or programs did not question, but rather accepted as a starting point for their operation. All organizations and their encounters adopt the notion that there should be a total separation between Arabs in Israel and Arabs in the West Bank and Gaza in terms of political and national aspirations. In addition, programs assumed that their intervention output and processes are apolitical. Most of the Jewish facilitators and the directors argued that the encounter should be based on an educational approach only.

Asymmetry in the Encounter Structure

There is a lack of preparation for such encounter programs. This is reflected in the lack of standardized frameworks. Neither Arab nor Jewish participants are required to meet separately prior to the encounter, for example. In the cases where they did meet, only a few hours were invested in such meetings. In addition, high and unrealistic expectations were expressed among intervenors as well as among the workshops' participants. Little care was given to the selection of participants. During the encounter, there was a clear imbalance of access to Arabic and Hebrew languages in the discussion: Arab students were not as comfortable as Jewish students in expressing their views due to the requirement or expectation to use the Hebrew as the encounter language. In all the examined programs, there were no follow-up activities for the one or two encounters conducted by the organization. Participants or schools were disconnected from the organization that conducted the encounter. This has been often an indicator of the lack of any continuing or comprehensive intervention plans by the hosting school or organization. Most of the organizations that conducted encounters had no research or any form of systematic evaluation of the postencounter experience. Some organizations even had no evaluation forms for the encounter itself.

Content and Process

Facilitators and directors often avoided political or conflict issues during the encounter. They focused on similarities between Arabs and Jews or interpersonal aspects. They avoided differences and overemphasized the cultural and professional similarities. Encounters ended with no common task to be accomplished or coordinated in the long- or short-term future. Thus most of the process focused on the experience of the encounter. The contact with the other was the main tool. Creating a positive environment on the interpersonal as well as professional levels was the primary focus of the facilitators in these encounters. There was also an imbalance in terms of content. Arab students knew more about the Jewish culture (at least in terms of information) than Jewish participants knew about the Arab culture. However, the assumption and programs' content were designed toward equal learning. Often there was no response to the differential needs of each group, particularly the Arab students, who as minority members had a natural disadvantage in such contact experience. Ongoing political events were neglected (even intentionally avoided) by intervenors as a result of the objective to keep the encounter positive, or due to the educational rationale of the sponsoring organization. For instance, discussions of the Gulf War and the Palestinian-Israeli peace process were ignored in such encounters.

Third-Party Role

There was an asymmetric role between Arab and Jewish facilitators. On many occasions, Arab facilitators found themselves acting as both translators and intervenors. The facilitators were less involved in the process and more focused on the content. They provided few reflections and little feedback on the process of interaction. When asked about their programs and rationale, facilitators and directors were unaware of the philosophical and theoretical details of the implemented models. Directors and facilitators of those programs held opposed and unclarified goals and assumptions due to the lack of interaction, training, and professional development in such organizations. Most facilitators complained about the lack of opportunities to discuss those issues with their program directors. This often resulted in the lack of common goals and interest among intervenors regarding their intervention. There was an unrealistic set of expectations for the workshop outcomes, particularly among Arab facilitators. In general, when asked about their perceptions of the Arab-Israeli conflict, intervenors were confused and had unclear perceptions of the conflict. For instance, the complexity of the conflict was not captured or presented by the intervenors in terms of issues, resolution, or the parties involved; instead, there was a consistent emphasis on the educational and stereotype reduction aspects of the programs.

Organizational Context

The contextual and interorganizational factors that influence and direct the programs' outcome were related to the following: (a) The need for all the organizations to obtain Ministry of Education's permission to enter the schools to recruit their beneficiaries, because these organizations and programs are mainly designed for the school system. Such conditions allow the Ministry of Education and other government agencies to oversee and monitor the work of those groups, limiting their scope and political orientation. (b) The fact that all the programs receive their funds from foreign sponsors (mostly Jewish), whose main interest and motivation is the promotion of a positive image of the state of Israel. In addition, they often encourage a harmony model rather than addressing conflictual issues. These funding organizations are usually in full agreement with the political and ideological principles of the mainstream Zionist values (e.g., most of those donors support the Jewishness of the state). (c) The lack of professional and academic experts involved in this subject. Such a lack of interest in these programs among the Israeli academic elite reduces their importance in the Israeli Jewish society. In addition, it reduces their credibility as an effective mechanism for improving Arab-Jewish relations. (d) The asymmetric division among Arab and Jewish intervenors who are active in the field of coexistence. Jewish intervenors in these programs are either directors, whose main job is to raise funds and administer the program, or university students, who consider their work in this program a short transitional period in their careers. On the other hand, Arab intervenors are in many cases educators who could not find a professional job or graduates whom the Ministry of Education did not accept as teachers or educators. Therefore, many intervenors lack the professional examination of their intervention models, and only a few are fully committed to the development of this field. Although the government, represented by the Ministry of Education, supports these encounters, there is a lack of continuous, serious, and deep commitment and support. For example, only a small percentage of the financial support for such encounter programs is given by the various governmental agencies. (f) The perception and understanding among Arabs that historically these organizations operated as a part of the ruling political party, which used these programs to mobilize political support in the Arab minority. Thus, certain political activists and parties avoid associating themselves with those organizations.

In summary, Arab-Jewish encounters produce a limited change on the interpersonal level, and a substantial part of these encounter programs are manipulated by Israeli control of the governmental system. Nevertheless, these programs are too valuable to be easily dismissed. They have a symbolic function and a role in the Arab-Jewish reconciliation process; they provide hope and the possibility for change. The following section discusses necessary changes and conditions to increase the impact and effectiveness of these programs in order to promote genuine justice, reconciliation, and coexistence between Arabs and Jews in Israel.

Coexistence, Reconciliation, and Justice: Basic Definitions

The dynamics of deep-rooted conflicts in divided societies underlie the need to clarify the relationship between reconciliation, justice, and coexistence. The fields of conflict resolution and peace studies attempt to provide tools and models to address such conflicts. The criteria and features of those concepts will be derived from the various theories and approaches in those fields. The following definitions are not based on a pragmatic, power paradigm or realpolitik approaches to conflicts. Instead, they are based on criteria of equality, structural change, and potential for transformation of the future relationship, rather than a temporary settlement of conflicts.

Based on the field of peacebuilding (includes peace studies and conflict resolution), for parties to reach a stage of reconciliation certain requirements and changes need to occur among them. Regardless, whether it is called conflict resolution or transformation, parties reach reconciliation when their basic needs are met (Burton and Dukes 1990). Structural changes are required outcomes for an intervention that promotes transformation or resolution. Reconciliation also includes the principle of establishing a conflict resolution mechanism or system that allows the parties to resolve and address their future conflicts in a manner different from confrontation, suspicion, and mistrust. Reconciliation is a place where parties of the conflict meet and are able to creatively examine their past, present, and future relationships through a cooperative and mutual recognition of their inevitable interdependency. Reconciliation is related to and dependent on the ability of the conflicted parties to redefine their contradictory sense of justice. For instance, the sense of justice which needs to be reframed by the parties is often reflected in their two options of either elimination of the other's existence or a full restoration of a reality that does not have any room for the current "other."

The state of reconciliation must also include elements of forgiveness. Parties to the conflict announce their ability to resume their collective life with a sense of contentment regarding what they have achieved through their reconciliation process. Forgiveness does not necessarily mean forgetting their past. On the contrary, for the parties to reach the stage of reconciliation, they should be able to walk together the path of the past and remember their historical injuries. The ability to remember the history and share it with the other, with its full intensity, is an element that relieves tension and anger in the conflict relationship. Thus, parties are not required to forget their victimhood, but to recognize it and be able to convey it to the other.

It is impossible to talk about reconciliation without addressing recognition as well. In most ethnic or deep-rooted conflicts, there is a need among parties for recognition of identity, victimhood, injustice, equality, and right for self-determination. Such recognition is essential for reaching the stage of reconciliation. The element of recognition demands confrontation of conflict issues and requires the parties to be able to address all the issues at hand. Those are often deep-rooted conflicts, and their causes and dynamics are not only related to misperception and miscommunication, or misinformation, but also to structural and institutional realities that impose their web of imbalances on the parties involved. Without addressing those structural issues, the conflict is left unaddressed. Under such circumstances, the minority, or the underdog party, will be disadvantaged.

Reconciliation is associated with the value of symmetry and equality. The outcome of a reconciling interaction ought to promote full and unconditional equality between the parties. One party of the conflict may not prevent the other from achieving its goals due to its inferiority, or special status or conditions. The reconciled relationship is based on full and equal national, economic, political, social, and cultural rights of the people involved. For instance, when a couple reconciles, the arrangement cannot be to continue a dominant-dominated relationship due to the superiority of one of the spouses. Parties reconcile because they believe in the equal rights of the other.

When reconciliation is achieved, the relationship between the parties is transformed or changed from its constant conflictual pattern into a new mode of interaction. Under the new conditions, the parties have developed a new sense of awareness for their dependent relationship. The norm is now to include rather than exclude the other. Under such conditions, the term *coexistence* means an arrangement between the conflicting parties that addresses their needs equally rather than providing a structural advantage for one or the other. The contract between the parties is now based on equal individual and collective rights. Coexistence means a full and possible inclusion of all parties in the political, social, and economic structures. Coexistence in this context also means the development of cooperative rather than destructive modes of interaction between the minority and the majority in order to realize the full potential of the two groups. Coexistence means recognition of the minority groups' rights for national and civic identity based on humanistic as well as pragmatic principles. Such arrangements would allow the minority members to determine their national, social, cultural, educational, economic, and all other aspects of their collective identities. In fact, the majority may function as a catalyst and supporter of such developments.

To reach such a place, the conflicting ethnic groups need to fully explore their conflict, confront it, and be able to realize their interdependency and humanness. Reconciliation becomes most crucial during a postsettlement phase when parties are engaged in processes of reconstruction and rehabilitation. Without a genuine process of reconciliation, postagreement efforts become additional methods for fortifying the ethnic divisions and walls that separate the conflicting communities (see Fitzduff in this volume). It is at this phase that the connection between reconciliation and justice is most crucial. By connecting the process of reconciliation with justice and focusing on the victimhood on all sides, parties and communities will be able to begin a process of genuine reconciliation for coexistence (see McCandless in this volume). In such a phase, Truth and Reconciliation Commissions (TRCs) are most needed and have been functional for the reconciliation process.[9] When reconciliation takes place, the sense of justice ceases to be associated with vengeful activities or desires. The other's existence, interests, and needs become an integral part of the new definition of justice.

Principles for Applying a Reconciliation Process

It is possible to identify eight principles to guide the design and implementation of the reconciliation process that may lead to a genuine and long-term coexistence between the conflicting parties or communities. It is the responsibility of the practitioners to ensure that such principles are integrated in their intervention or initiatives.

First, the purpose of any reconciliation process should be the realization that the nature of the relationship between the two conflicting communities has a complex and multidimensional set of causes, and therefore its resolution is complex and involves many forces, too. As a result, simple or unilateral solutions (such as territorial purification or deportation) are not the answer to a complex problem.

Second, any design or initiative to create long-term coexistence arrangements must be based on the principle of equality between the ethnic communities. Granting one community an advantage or superior position as a result of the coexistence arrangement does not contribute to a lasting coexistence.

Third, reconciliation is the appropriate channel to address different perceptions of justice. As painful as it will be, the two communities must redefine their sense of pure justice and make a place for the other in their sense of justice. Reconciliation and dialogue are the tools to begin such a process.

Fourth, the process of reconciliation only succeeds, develops, or gains momentum among the different communities if it is *not* divorced from structural arrangements. Reconciliation without addressing or beginning to address physical reconstruction of houses, returnees, infrastructural elements, redistribution of resources, and other economic needs will be resented if characterized as a sellout by a large number of the communities.

Fifth, understanding of the interdependency that ties the two communities together is crucial to the development of reconciliatory attitudes. The realization of such interdependency is a catalyst to seek alternative ways to coexist. Simple and unilateral solutions will not be applicable once a person has internalized the notion that his or her existence is dependable and interconnected with the other.

Sixth, the outcome of a reconciliation process should only empower; it should not bring helplessness and despair or a sense of betrayal to the communities. Empowerment is the feeling of strength and control over the process. Thus, material compensation or redistribution of resources should not be the only results of the reconciling process. Psychological security, recognition, and acknowledgment of separate identities should be included as well.

Seventh, reconciliation can only begin to take place if community members are willing to engage in a self-critique and recognition of their own deeds and responsibilities in the historical course of the conflict. Thus, reconciliation is not only the punishment of the other; it is not only intended to satisfy the need for revenge, restoration of old dreams, or any other expectations from the other (all of those are legitimate aspects of the reconciliation)—but it is equally important to confront the evil within. Every community has to look inside prior to their demands for outside restoration, redistribution, or punishment. Taking responsibility and acknowledging its role in the conflict dynamic is a major step in community self-awareness.

Eighth, coexistence, reconciliation, justice, and peace are all part of a framework or future vision. When reviewing all the above components of peacebuilding, the visions of pluralism emerge as the ultimate arrangement that divided communities seek. Unfortunately, today we do not have any ideal existing example in the world to point out as a perfect model to follow; however, there are many societies that have managed to apply pieces of this vision of pluralism. It is possible, too, that even if this is all that humans are capable of achieving at this period of history under our current economic, political, and social frameworks, it is still possible to hope for future integration of those principles of pluralism in our various communities. Identifying those abstract and ideal principles to guide the reconciliation process is not sufficient; it is necessary to move on to the practical applications of those principles in real-life situations or reconciliation initiatives. The following is an illustration of how such principles can be applied in the Arab-Jewish encounter program designs.

Principles and Guidelines for Designing Arab-Jewish Encounter Dialogue

Based on the above principles, for Arab-Jewish encounters to promote justice, reconciliation, and coexistence between Arabs and Jews in Israel, Arab-Jewish practitioners and organizations need to adopt some changes in their activities. The following is a partial list of recommended changes that can be viewed as guiding principles for interethnic dialogue encounters in other conflict areas as well.[10] Some of the suggestions and challenges are on the macrolevel of analysis; others are specific and aimed at improving the intervention program itself.

Education for coexistence and dialogue should not mean an indoctrination of the Arab and Jewish participants in certain political ideology. For instance, the Jewishness of the state is a guiding principle that restricts the membership of the Israeli Arabs in the state. This ideology contradicts the notion of democracy and equality; it is an assumption that assists in maintaining a level of suspicion and mistrust between members of the minority and the majority.

Arab-Jewish organizations have to reform their organizational arrangements to reflect their philosophy of equality and coexistence, even though the funds for the organizations are raised from Jewish communities outside of Israel and other foreign foundations. The directors and decision makers in these programs should not only be Jews. Arab trainers and activists must be partners, not just "tokens."

Funding and financial support for such initiatives ought to be the responsibility of both communities, even if the minority resources are often restricted or scarce. Nevertheless, symbolic contribution can be of major importance to the development of such projects or organizations. It will add to their credibility within both the minority and majority communities. For instance, lack of Arab financial support for such organizations contributed to the impression in the Arab community that these organizations are owned and run by and serve the Jewish community interests. Thus, funding for these programs should be expanded to donors from Arab countries. This would increase the support both financially and morally for the coexistence programs among Arab community leaders (politicians and municipal leadership).

Establishing the legitimacy and credibility of dialogue and coexistence programs is an important factor. Thus, organizations and donors should focus on such aspects in their activities. Increasing the academic legitimacy for the field of Arab-Jewish relations and coexistence has to be heightened. There are only a few studies on the encounter programs. In the universities and colleges, little is being done to promote this subject among either the faculty or the students.[11]

There should be a coordinating committee for Arab-Jewish organizations, which may contribute to their development and political influence. In addition, a coordinating committee may reduce the duplication of effort among the organizations. For instance, in one case three representatives of different organizations were sitting in a principal's office in hopes of working with this specific school that was receptive to the notion of coexistence. A coordination network is necessary to reach *different* communities of Arabs and Jews.[12]

Governmental support for such activities should be carefully viewed and weighed. Most of the governments in such a context are controlled and dominated by policymakers who continue the domination of the minority and are in charge of exclusion policies and ideologies. Thus, encounter and dialogue programs can be easily manipulated to meet the interest of such governmental policymakers. This does not mean to avoid receiving funds from the government or to boycott such resources. But the intention is to reject certain conditions that influence or limit the contribution of those programs to reconciliation and justice between the minority and majority as described above. For example, those who are supported by the government receive conditional support. They have to fulfill certain activities and comply with certain ideological assumptions (avoid politics; recognize and don't question the Jewishness of the state; establish mechanical separation between the Palestinians in West Bank, Gaza, and the Arab community in Israel).

The education for coexistence, if applied at school, should systematically target all grades. Thus, programs should be designed for kindergarten as well as university students. The goals of such education for coexistence should be equivalent in both communities, and such programs should not be used to facilitate the national agenda of one group or the other. For instance, the Arab students in Israel were educated for coexistence and democracy, while the Jewish students' education emphasized nationalism and Zionism.

At the same time, the long-term intervention focus can produce more impact than short-term activities. Instead of conducting twenty-five encounters each year (each one lasts two days) with twenty-five different groups, it is more effective to conduct four long-term encounters in which the organization concentrates on one region. Evaluation research has proven that the in-depth intervention produces more change in attitudes and higher commitment among the participants to take action or implement their ideas for change.

In terms of audience or target population for the coexistence program, the major challenge facing most of the programs is the element of "preaching to the choir." Arabs and Jews who oppose dialogue, coexistence, and reconciliation are out of reach for such programs. Thus, most of the intervention is often concentrated on those who are already favorable to the ideas. Very little attention has been paid to right-wing or even lower class communities. Most of the programs are focused on upper-middle-class communities, particularly within the Jewish majority.

Different programs should be developed for Arabs and Jews, or for minority and majority participants, due to the differences in their needs and priorities. For instance, Arab participants often might benefit from a separate program that will empower them *prior* to the encounter, due to the asymmetric starting points of the encounter. In such cases, strategies of uninational meetings prior and during the encounter period would increase commitment and effectiveness of the process among the participants. In short, the binational meeting should not be the ultimate means for the encounter or dialogue process.

Participants and intervenors in encounters and dialogue for coexistence programs often hold unrealistic and different expectations of the programs. For instance, Arab trainers and participants had unrealistic expectations, such as expecting immediate political change through coexistence activities. This misperception among participants, who regard the encounter as an opportunity to immediately and directly influence the status quo and bring equality or solve political problems that they face in their communities, can be addressed in uninational meetings and systematic preparation for those programs. Research indicates that encounters for coexistence carried out without such preparation may bring negative consequences in participants' attitudes. Facilitators, particularly from the minority, who presented social and political change as their primary goal of intervention, soon realized that their intervention can't provide an immediate, substantial, or direct contribution to the political change for which they strive. Many of them were frustrated and burned out. Such a mode of operation was obviously damaging their professional ability to intervene.

Staff and directors of these programs need to be trained professionally. In addition, cross-fertilization programs with other conflict areas are most enriching and encouraging for this type of intervention. Thus, practitioners of education for coexistence in Israel, Northern Ireland, South Africa, Cyprus, or even the United States can provide others with valuable resources by exchanging information and knowledge on intervention in divided societies. Unfortunately, most directors and trainers in these programs take trips only to raise funds to ensure their existence. Also, there is a pressing need to increase coordination and professional training for the facilitators, directors, and donors for such programs. Through professional training and development, programs might be able to cope with the high turnover and burnout among intervenors. In Israel, the coexistence workers are mainly Jewish students who consider the field a short stop in their professional careers. Most of the Arab facilitators are graduates who couldn't find work in their field and didn't want to be teachers.

Dealing with political reality and differences during the encounter is one of the most crucial elements of the process. Artificially detaching the participants from a conflict reality and placing them into a harmony model would only increase the possibility of backlash in negative attitudes toward the other community when participants return home. In addition, dealing with conflict reality and confronting it jointly with the other side is the most effective tool for promoting complex understanding of conflict, rather than the simplified and harmonious illusion. For instance, during the Gulf War, Intifada, and immigration of the Soviet Jews, many programs of coexistence in Israel detached themselves from the political context. The programs did not relate directly to the political environment, and thus some perceived the coexistence as an apolitical field, while others were afraid of funding problems. Nevertheless, such avoidance only adds to the mistrust and creates the illusion that there are no conflicting interests between the two communities.

Finally, structural conditions often constitute a major source of conflict between minority and majority groups. Power imbalances affect the perceptions of the conflict and its resolution, as well as expectations of the encounter; thus it follows that they should shape the expectations and outcomes of the encounter. An effective encounter program is one that is able to provide its participants with critical analytical skills to understand and systematically analyze the structural as well as the perceived causes of a conflict situation. To do so, the model of coexistence program should focus on power imbalance analysis, too.

The coexistence models of intervention in Israel were less analytical and didn't address the structural causes of the problem. Organizations fostered the perception that Arabs and Jews are two different cultures and that stereotypes, miscommunication, and interpersonal experiences are the sources of the conflict. In addition, in their approach to Arab and Jewish participants, the organizations equalized the minority's and the majority's responsibilities and the consequences of their actions. These assumptions ignored the structural responsibility of the dominant group for changing the current political, economic, and social arrangements.

The coexistence field can be used for a political manipulation function if designed according to the needs, desires, and values of one community only. On the other hand, if designed accordingly and, most important, jointly by the two communities, it can be a genuine tool to facilitate reconciliation. It is a powerful tool to educate for a different future, to bind the two fighting communities. However, to do so, the practitioners, as well as the theoreticians, must examine and integrate the concept of justice and values such as equality, empowerment, and democracy in their designs of coexistence programs and frameworks. In the case of Arabs and Jews in Israel, the coexistence field's primary task and function is to provide an opportunity for the two communities to examine, build, and create a shared future vision for their interdependent realities.

Finally, as in any other ethnic conflict, neither Arabs nor Jews can create that vision alone. The two groups need each other. Therefore, encounter programs, teacher training, curriculum development, and community meetings can all contribute to the creation of such shared future relations. This field can be a pioneer in generating new alternatives and options for Arabs and Jews in how to live together peacefully and equally. For example, a coexistence program can focus on the renegotiation of the existing Arab-Jewish contract of living together. The existing contract is dominated and determined by the mainstream and traditional Zionist Jewish majority. According to this contract, Arabs in Israel are under a continuous "citizenship loyalty" test. Arabs cannot be incorporated in the various departments of the state of Israel. Their non-Jewishness is an obstacle to full citizenship. The coexistence field can target such an unbalanced contract.

Notes

1. Arab teachers were prevented from political discussion or involvement until 1986, when the Ministry of Education issued a decree allowing the teachers to deal with current events. Teachers feared the Israeli security forces (*Shein Biet*).

2. Traditional Arab food served in many cultural encounters.

3. The Kahana movement was led by Rabbi Kahana, a religious right wing who called for the transfer of Arabs from Israel and called for a pure Jewish religious state rather than a democratic Jewish state. Some surveys in 1983 indicated that as many as 69 percent of Jewish high school students supported Kahana's ideas (Tzimah 1984 and Hareven 1984).

4. The Ministry of Education and other governmental offices established a separate school system and curriculum for the Druze community in an attempt to separate the Druze from the Arab community in Israel (Halabi 1989).

5. Political activists and intervenors who were interviewed for Hall-Cathala's book presented these arguments.

6. A clinical psychologist who criticizes one of the promising projects of Arab-Jewish relations, in which Arab students teach Jewish students and vice versa.

7. The research on this subject was conducted between 1991 and the end of 1997. Directors, trainers, and participants in 15 of these programs were interviewed, a total of 156 coexistence workers and participants. Those results are based on an in-depth research of seven Arab-Jewish encounter programs (interviews with directors, participants, and facilitators). In addition, there was a review of the activities of fifteen other Arab-Jewish organizations (a full list of those organizations is reported in Abu-Nimer 1999).

8. Sekoi/Chance is a nongovernmental organization that aims to promote the inclusion of Arabs in high-level governmental positions and seeks to highlight the lack of representation of Arabs in decision-making levels in all governmental institutions.

9. See more information on TRCs in South Africa, Guatemala, and Argentina. Also see current public debates of the need for TRCs in Northern Ireland and Bosnia.

10. It should be noted that some of the following challenges and suggestions have been implemented by some Arab-Jewish organizations since at least 1992; however, these organizations are the exceptions rather than the norm.

11. It should be acknowledged that in recent years there have been initiatives by the Wahat Al Salam/Neve Shalom team, who introduced the subject into Tel Aviv University and Ben Gurion University.

12. In mid-1987 there was an attempt to create *Reshet* (network), but it didn't achieve its objective of coordination because of internal organizational conflicts, and competition among organizations over resources and leadership.

References

Abu-Nimer, M. 1999. *Dialogue, Conflict Resolution, and Change: Arab-Jewish Encounters in Israel.* New York: State University of New York Press.

Amir, Y. 1969. Contact Hypothesis in Ethnic Relations. *Psychological Bulletin*, vol. 71, 319-342.

Bandler, K. 1991. *Jewish-Arab Relations in Israel.* New York: American Jewish Committee, International Perspective.

Bar, H., and Asaqla, G. 1988a. *Encounter Staff in Giva'at Haviva: Group Profile.* Jerusalem: Institute for Applied Social Research (Hebrew).

———. 1988b. *Arab-Jewish Youth Encounter in Giva'at Haviva: Evaluation of Attitudes Before and After.* Jerusalem: Institute for Applied Social Research (Hebrew).

Bar, H., and Bargal, D. 1995. *Living with the Conflict.* Jerusalem: Jerusalem Institute for Israeli Studies (Hebrew).

Bar-On, M. 1996. *In Pursuit of Peace: A History of the Israeli Peace Movement.* Washington D.C.: United States Institute of Peace Press.

Bieran, H. 1990. *Superiority and Inferiority Feelings: Obstacles to Dialogue between Arabs and Jews.* Unpublished paper.

Burton, J., and Dukes, F., eds. 1990. *Conflict: Readings in Management and Resolution.* New York: St. Martin's Press.

Halabi, O. 1989. *The Druze in Israel: From Religion to People!* Golan Heights: University Graduate Committee. (Arabic).

Hall-Cathala, D. 1990. *The Peace Movement in Israel: 1967-87.* New York: St Martin's Press.

Hareven, A. 1981. *One of Every Six Israelis: Mutual Relations between the Arab Minority and the Jewish Majority.* Jerusalem: Van Leer Institute.

Kuttab, J. 1988. An Exchange on Dialogue. *Journal of Palestine Studies,* vol. 17, no. 2, 84-108.

Lemish, P., Mula, W., and Rubin, A. 1989. *Cultural and Educational Struggle: A Model for Curriculum Development.* Paper presented at the Arab-Jewish Facilitator Conference, Nazareth.

Lemish, P., Mula, W., Sonnenschein, N., Gur-ziv, H., and Zaretsky, E. 1991. *Power Relationships in Divided Societies: The Case of Education for Coexistence in Israel.* Unpublished paper.

Lustick, I. 1980. *Arabs in the Jewish State: Israel Control of a National Minority.* Austin: University of Texas Press.

Saunders, H. 1999. *A Public Peace Process: Sustained Dialogue to Transform Racial and Ethnic Conflicts.* New York: St. Martin's Press.

Sherif, M. 1958. Superordinate Goals in the Reduction of Intergroup Conflict. *American Journal of Sociology,* vol. 43, 349-356.

Tzimah, M. 1984. *Attitudes of Youth in Israel toward Democratic Values.* Jerusalem: Van Leer Institute. (Hebrew).

13

The Challenge to History

Justice, Coexistence, and Reconciliation Work in Northern Ireland

Mari Fitzduff

From Violence to Politics

On Good Friday, April 10, 1998, after thirty years of a bloody civil war in which over 3,500 people had been killed, and after almost two long and weary years of political negotiation, the Belfast Agreement was finally signed by Northern Ireland's political parties.[1] In the agreement, the politicians appeared to have achieved consensus on the principles, and in some cases the practice, necessary to govern a society divided on constitutional, political, and cultural perspectives. Six weeks later, by a vote of over 71 percent, and despite the best efforts of fundamentalist nationalists and unionists to wreck the deal, the agreement was endorsed by the peoples of the island of Ireland, North and South. Northern Ireland appeared, at last, to be on the road from violence to politics. Undoubtedly, stormy years lie ahead. The bitter history of over eight hundred years of conflict has left a legacy of distrust that will take many decades to overcome. But the Belfast Agreement, with its combination of shared power arrangements, unique capacities for multilayered identity, and state loyalty possibilities, is likely to prove a turning point in the transformation of a bitterly divided state into one which has now, albeit hesitantly, started on the fresh and inclusively agreed task of a region that is beginning to be truly shared.

What had brought Northern Ireland to this particular turning point? What were the major developments in eventually securing such an agreement? And why had they taken so long? Such questions are the focus of this chapter, which addresses the extent and focus of the strategies of justice and equality work, of cultural coexistence initiatives, and of reconciliation approaches in Northern Ireland that have underpinned the developing political possibilities in the last decade of the conflict. This chapter argues that without such work, the political agreements would have been extremely difficult to achieve, as the historic contexts of inequality and cultural exclusion, and the lack of dialogue work, would have made the delivery of agreement by the politicians almost impossible.

A Divided Region

Since British plantation owners colonized the island of Ireland in the twelfth century, the struggle for political and cultural power on the island has remained continuous. Although these struggles eventually culminated in a regained independent status for most of the island in 1921, the agreement that led to such independence for twenty-six of the counties of the island excluded six northern counties, which remained British in nature. The reason for such a division was that the patterns of integration of the colonizers and the indigenous Irish developed differently in the northern part of the island. In the earlier plantations, on the rest of the island, colonizers were relatively quickly integrated into the life of the indigenous Irish. However, it had been a deliberate tactic of the seventeenth- and eighteenth-century plantation owners in the northern part of the island to ensure that communities developed in isolation from each other in order to maintain the dominance of the unionist planters over the indigenous Irish.

Hence, when the increasing independence of the island was agreed upon in 1921, it was resisted by Northern Protestants, who threatened violence if the northern counties were included in an independent Ireland. This threat resulted in the creation of the region of Northern Ireland, which retained its British status and established a relatively autonomous system of power in the region. Unfortunately, this new region of Ireland contained within its borders a substantial number of Catholics (32 percent) who were unhappy with the new order. Fearful of their own minority status on an island that was both Irish and (mainly) Catholic, the newly elected unionist government failed to sufficiently address the Catholics' concerns. The ensuing patterns of inequality; biased voting systems; unrepresentative policing; a maintenance of ghettoization in education, housing, and workplaces; and a significantly alienated minority created the context where such divisions successfully combined to create what LeVine and Campbell (1972) have termed a "Pyramid-segmentary" structure, that is, a structure in which different categories of a social, political, cultural, and theological nature rarely cut across one another. Discrimination and segregation in Northern Ireland became the norm. The civil rights movement in 1969, which happened in parallel to the international efforts of excluded groups elsewhere, such as women and ethnic minorities, set out to address this situation of inequality and exclusion. But the unionist government of the time was unable or unwilling to adequately address these demands, and republican/Catholic and loyalist/Protestant violence began to escalate. On the republican side, demands for civil rights escalated into demands for a united Ireland.

The inability of the unionist government to manage the divisions, as well as a disastrous security policy that showed the security forces to be unbalanced and biased toward the minority, meant that in 1972 security forces were dismissed by the British government. Direct political and security control of the region was then assumed from London. Republican and loyalist violence, however, rapidly escalated, reaching a height in the early 1970s, after which it abated somewhat. In the meantime there were several attempts at political agreements—mainly in 1974 and in 1982, both of which failed because of their exclusion of political groupings associated with the paramilitaries. A major turning point in the context for political development was reached in 1985, when the Anglo-Irish Agreement was signed, setting up a structure for security and political coopera-tion between the British and Irish governments. The agreement was applauded by the Social Democratic and Labour Party, a nationalist constitutional party whose goal was a united Ireland achieved through constitutional means and not through violence. It was rejected by Sinn Fein, the nationalist party associated with the Irish Republican Army, which also supported a united Ireland but was prepared to use physical force to achieve it. Both major unionist parties, the Ulster Unionist Party and the Democratic Unionist Party (led by Ian Paisley), rejected unequivocally the Anglo-Irish Agreement, which they saw as conceding sovereignty over Northern Ireland to the government of the Republic of Ireland.

Through the 1980s, it became obvious that neither the paramilitaries nor the security forces could achieve outright military victories, and in the 1990s, the initiatives were mainly of a political nature, against the background of continu-ing violence. The cease-fires of 1994, followed by the gradual involvement of those political parties associated with the paramilitaries, that is, Sinn Fein, the Progressive Unionist Parties, and the Ulster Democratic Party (both loyalist parties), led at last to the Belfast Agreement of 1998.[2]

Such an agreement was possible because of much of the contextual work, which had begun to significantly agree to address issues of justice and inequality and which had established the diversity of the region as a norm and a right and had also developed cross-community dialogue processes, which expanded and extended the range of political dialogue with communities and politicians alike.

Justice, Coexistence, and Reconciliation Work

Three approaches have significantly informed the work necessary to address the conflict in Northern Ireland. These are rights/equality work, which addresses issues of inequality and discrimination, coexistence/diversity work, which addresses issues of cultural and political inclusion, and reconciliation-interdependence work, which addresses issues of dialogue and reconciliation (Eybin 1997).[3] The emphasis given to each of these has varied over the decades. Reconciliation work, which focuses on issues of community relations and reconciliation, was the initial focus for public and community policy immediately following the civil rights campaigns, although in the subsequent decades it failed to achieve a sustained focus. Equality and rights work has dominated much of the 1970s and 1980s. In the 1990s there was a significantly increased interest in diversity/coexistence work, and once again in reconciliation work, which proliferated and developed many of the new dialogue processes among communities, paramilitaries, governments, and politicians, which were vital to securing an agreement.

Equality and Justice Work

Equality Legislation

In 1969, following the civil rights protests, the British government declared that every citizen of Northern Ireland was entitled to the same equality of treatment and freedom from discrimination as enjoyed in the rest of the United Kingdom, and a series of legislative reforms to address existing inequalities was introduced to investigate complaints of poor administration by government departments. In 1972 a commission was established to promote fairness in staff recruitment in the local councils, which had been so noted for their discriminatory nature, and to establish a working party to look at employment practices in the private sector. In 1973 the Northern Ireland Constitution Act provided for a legislative assembly to address discrimination on the grounds of religious or political belief; the act also established the Standing Advisory Commission on Human Rights to monitor the effectiveness of laws against discrimination. As discrimination in housing had been a major grievance, control of all public housing allocation was transferred from local council authorities to a regional authority. Voting reforms were introduced, that is, house ownership was no longer deemed a prerequisite for voting rights, and the multiple vote given to business owners was abolished, as both of these had effectively discriminated against Catholics. Local council boundaries were redrawn to more accurately represent the reality of citizen distribution, and a proportional representation system of voting was introduced that increased nationalist chances of gaining power where their numbers were substantial enough.

Employment Inequities

Major disparities in employment levels in Northern Ireland had been confirmed by the Cameron and other reports (Cameron 1969; Rose 1971). In 1971 it was estimated that 17.3 percent of Catholic males were unemployed, compared to 6.6 percent of Protestant males. In 1976 the Fair Employment Act was passed, making discrimination in employment on religious or political grounds unlawful, and a Fair Employment Agency (FEA) was established to investigate the extent to which there was inequality. This agency was eventually replaced in 1989 by the Fair Employment Commission (FEC), which was given extra resources and powers by the government to pursue its task of monitoring the religious composition of the workforce. Indirect discrimination was made illegal.

Targeting Social Need

However, by the early 1990s, after two decades of government attempts to address equity issues in Northern Ireland, the indicators still showed that the Catholic community in many areas remained seriously disadvantaged, for example, forty-five of the top fifty unemployment areas in Northern Ireland were almost exclusively Catholic. Faced with a major challenge of the continuance of marginalized ghetto areas (mainly Catholic, but also some Protestant areas) and the link between such areas and the use of paramilitary violence, the government decided that a major initiative was needed to address such alienation. The Targeting Social Need (TSN) program was set up to tackle areas of social and economic differences by targeting government policies and programs more directly to those areas or sections of the community suffering the highest levels of disadvantage and deprivation. Extra attention was also given under the TSN program to providing further opportunities for training, to increasing development work for indigenous industry creation, particularly in the most marginalized areas, and to ensuring that individual job creation agencies further biased their work toward those areas that were most seriously disadvantaged. In 1994 the government introduced a new initiative, called Policy Appraisal and Fair Treatment (PAFT), to ensure equality in policymaking and action in all spheres of government activity. These include legislation and strategic plans for the implementation of policy and the delivery of services, and they apply to all government departments and associated government bodies.

As part of the 1998 Belfast Agreement, it was agreed to set up a new Human Rights Commission for Northern Ireland to replace the Standing Advisory Commission on Human Rights. In addition, a new Equality Commission was established to replace the existing religious, gender, and race commissions, and to take responsibility for additional equality work in areas of disability, sexual orientation, marital, and parental status. The Equality Commission also had responsibility for ensuring that all public bodies implement an equality agenda.

Almost three decades later, under the jurisdiction of direct rule from London, many of the inequalities between the communities have been addressed. Complaints are no longer heard in Northern Ireland about rigged voting systems, unfair housing allocations, or unequal educational funding. Only primarily in unemployment—where levels of long-term unemployment among Catholic males is still twice as high as among Protestant males—does a significant problem remain, despite the various legal and social initiatives which have been undertaken to address the issue. Such advances mean that the anger and resentment many Catholics felt at being excluded under a unionist regime is no longer as potent a factor in continuing the support for violence. In addition, Catholics have increasingly assumed positions of responsibility in public, community, and business life, and an increasing number of institutions are beginning to assume a pluralist nature (O'Connor 1993). Such major developments have provided much of the fallow ground that has made the agreement possible.

Diversity/Coexistence Work

Cultural Diversity

For the entire period of the existence of the state, expressions of cultural and political identity have been contentious. Flag flying, the use of the Irish language, parading, and symbols have usually been seen as a threat to the political realities and aspirations of the other side. And in a contested territory, such expressions have a significant potential to accrue into civil disorder (McCartney 1994). Since 1921, many such expressions on the part of nationalists in Northern Ireland were deemed illegal. Several legislative acts (1951 and 1954) outlawed the flying of the Irish flag, and laws were also passed forbidding the use of Irish-language street signs (1949) or the use of any language other than English in court (1739). All transactions with the government had to be conducted in English. Such laws contributed to significant community tension and defiance—for example, by 1992 over 550 Irish-language street signs had been erected in nationalist areas in a clear challenge of the law. Many nationalists also began to use the Irish language and its lack of official support as a cultural weapon with which to challenge the authorities. Efforts were made, particularly by Sinn Fein, to encourage people to speak Irish as a political gesture.

Much of this context has now changed—mainly due to the work of the Cultural Traditions Group (CTG), a group of academics, practitioners, and policymakers, drawn from both the nationalist and unionist communities. Many within this group recognized that the negative government response to the issue of cultural diversity had been both shortsighted and unnecessary. They established and achieved government funding for the Ultacht Trust, a group set up on a nonsectarian basis to develop and fund the Irish language. The government was also persuaded to fund those schools that taught through the medium of Irish on the same basis as other schools, and to assist with the funding of a daily newspaper in Irish. In broadcasting, there were also many issues that were a source of considerable contention for the nationalist minority. There was an exclusion on the reporting of minority cultural issues, including sports, and the Irish language was banned from radio and television for almost the first fifty years of the Northern Ireland state. Following the civil rights campaign, the new-found culturally assertive capacities of the nationalist community began to achieve some successes in the early 1970s when the British Broadcasting Corporation (BBC) was persuaded to introduce occasional radio programs in the Irish language. Although there was considerable resistance from many unionists, the BBC persisted with the experiment and was eventually persuaded to introduce a regular Irish-language program in 1981, followed by some schools broadcasting in 1985. In 1991 the BBC broadcast its first television production in Irish. Eventually, in 1992, the secretary of state for Northern Ireland announced that where there was a local demand, street names in Irish could be erected alongside the English name. The government also now deals with correspondence in Irish, and official documents are published in Irish when requested, for example, the Belfast Agreement was published in Irish. The community is now used to hearing regular Irish-language programs on radio and television, the tricolor usually flies freely, without official interference, and street names in Irish are now accepted as delivery addresses by the postal services. The development of the above means that the use of the Irish language and expressions of nationalist/Irish identity have now receded as a significant source of political tension.

In addition to its work on the language, the CTG also helped to further develop the work of the broadcasting companies by encouraging, and in some cases funding, initiatives that exemplified cultural diversity programming and encouraged debate on political and cultural issues. Such work has assisted a context of diversity and challenge which has eventually led to a much healthier and open context for discussion on the many issues that were pertinent to the Belfast Agreement and the setting up of the subsequent assembly.

The CTG also significantly assisted the development of shared schools for children from different perspectives. In 1996, less than 4 percent of children attended shared, integrated schools.[4] The first such shared school was set up in 1982, and by the beginning of 2000 there were forty-two such schools. The CTG also helped to re-create a common history curriculum for schools, as well as programs for mutual understanding schemes, which are now obligatory for all children, in both segregated and shared schools.

Cultural Fairs and Exhibitions

In 1991 the CTG organized the first-ever Cultural Traditions Fair in Belfast. Through it they brought together about forty groups with very different cultural and historical perspectives for a few days to provide an open exhibition for each other and for the public. It was a unique undertaking, as it brought together groups that had been mainly suspicious and hostile to one another for most of the life of the state. The fair was subsequently repeated at many locations throughout Northern Ireland. The fairs provided not only an opportunity for each group to interact, however tentatively, but an opportunity for those interested in local studies to acquire information from a wide variety of sources for their burgeoning cultural traditions work. The fairs also provided visible evidence that differing traditions need not be perceived as necessarily hostile, but could together provide a richness that was greater than any single identity.

In addition to the cultural fairs, the CTG has organized a symbols exhibition, which has been displayed in most of the local district councils. This is a very colorful exhibition of the hundreds of artifacts from all traditions that are displayed in homes and halls and streets and on lapels in the island of Ireland, usually to proclaim a particular loyalty, and often relating to particular institutions. In most cases, such displays can cause offense or hostility (McCartney 1994). What the fairs and symbols achieved, as they moved through the towns and villages, was a safe opportunity for communities to understand each other's cultural and political differences, and to tentatively point to a richness of cultural and political diversity that is available to be creatively harnessed rather than used destructively.

Drama

Northern Ireland has always had a vibrant dramatic tradition—not just on the stages of its major city, Belfast, but also throughout its villages and towns, where local drama has had a significant place in the life of the community. Increasingly this tradition has proved to be of significance both in affirming a culture and in questioning its simplifications. A report released in 1994 (Grant 1994) showed how the work of local dramatists working in tandem with local dramatic groups can have a very significant effect on facilitating discussion about problematic issues both within and between communities. Such drama can help to pose fundamental questions about issues such as identity, social concern, and political possibilities that beset the conflict—in particular, when such drama picks up and deals with the very complex emotions surrounding local community dilemmas over, for example, paramilitary activity, dissatisfaction with policing, or social and cultural marginalization. It has an extremely engaging capacity that can be more powerful than many seminars and workshops. There are now many groups of drama facilitators who are working specifically with local groups to develop dramas that are particular to their needs and to their context in the conflict. When these groups work together on a cross-community basis and engage in performances with both communities, their capacity for dealing with complexity, and for emotionally mirroring for each other their communities' fears and hurts, is very powerful, indeed, and the groups are able to create significant degrees of empathy across the community divide.

Diverse Policing

A particular area where issues of diversity were exceptionally critical was that of policing. When civil unrest broke out in Northern Ireland in 1969, the fault lines within the police force were to render it in many cases counterproductive and inflammatory to the conflict. The force itself was largely Protestant, with a participation rate of only 10 percent Catholics in 1969, a rate which subsequently dropped to 6 percent by 1994 (Hamilton 1995). When the troubles broke out, it quickly became evident that the police were unable to react to the emerging law-and-order needs in a way that was professional and unbiased. The Cameron Commission, set up by the British government in 1969 to examine the causes of the troubles, implicated the police as a major problematic factor in the conflict; in particular, police acts of misconduct, assault and battery, and use of provocative sectarian and political slogans (Cameron 1969). Consequently, the reform of policing formed one of the main objectives of the British government. The police were to be disarmed, a police authority was to be set up to provide a buffer between the police and the unionist government, and a complaints system was to be developed. Although both a police authority and a complaints commission were eventually created, disarmament proved to be impossible to achieve in light of the continuing violence. Since the late 1970s, there has been a gradual professionalization of the police, which has helped to upgrade standards of impartiality in policing. Nevertheless, they are still viewed suspiciously by a sizable element within the Catholic community, partly because of historical attitudes, a perceived bias in their daily interactions with local communities, and their methods of interrogation, which many suspected went beyond the rule of law (CAJ 1992).

Since the early 1990s, under pressure from bodies such as the Community Relations Council (CRC) and nongovernmental organizations (NGOs) such as the Committee on the Administration of Justice (CAJ), the police themselves have begun to address more proactively the kind of training that could ensure that the interface between the security forces and Catholics (and, increasingly, working-class Protestants) did not continue to be a problem in fueling resentment and diminishing cooperation with the security forces. Both the Royal Ulster Constabulary (RUC) and the army have also taken steps to increase the quality of their recruits, and selection programs are now in place to try to identify bias on the part of would-be trainees. In 1993, the RUC, in cooperation with the CRC and NGOs such as the Mediation Network and other conflict resolution bodies, began to develop its own programs to deal with issues of sectarianism among the force, and to encourage a greater respect and understanding for the differing cultural and political traditions in Northern Ireland. Such programs are now an integral part of the initial training of all recruits entering the force, and the programs have also been introduced as part of the in-service training of established police personnel. In 1997 a fundamental review of policing was undertaken, conducted jointly by the Government, the

RUC, and the Police Authority, on the future policing needs of the community. And, as part of the Belfast Agreement, an Independent Commission on Policing for Northern Ireland was set up to inquire into policing in the region and to bring forward proposals for future policing structures and arrangements. This commission reported in 1999, with a wide range of suggestions about how to change and develop the RUC into a more modern, and more open and inclusive, force that could achieve the respect of all sections of the community. These reforms will gradually come into place in the coming years.

Interdependence/Reconciliation Work

Community Development/Community Relations Work

Following the reemergence of sectarian violence in 1969 in Northern Ireland, and particularly in the aftermath of the riots in Belfast and Derry/Londonderry in August 1969, the British Labour home secretary, James Callaghan, announced the establishment of a Ministry for Community Relations and a Community Relations Commission (Community Relations Act, 1969), which was charged with the promotion of policies that would improve community relations. The commission decided to adopt as its main strategy the initiation of local community development programs across Northern Ireland, based on the belief that communities that lacked self-confidence were more likely to relate aggressively to one another. Furthermore, it believed that the problem of relating to the structures of power, particularly for people in more socially marginalized communities, contributed to feelings of helplessness and resentment that in turn contributed to community tensions (Hayes 1972). The commission survived until the Sunningdale Agreement in April 1974, which resulted in a new power-sharing assembly for Northern Ireland. This assembly, in one of its first actions, abolished the Community Relations Commission. However, the process of community development remained an important method of facilitating communication within communities and between government and communities, and this process has continued to underpin many programs subsequently initiated and funded in the last two decades. Over a decade later, in 1985, the Standing Advisory Commission on Human Rights commissioned a report on the current state of community relations work and its potential for future development (Frazer and Fitzduff 1986). This reported on the underresourced, underdeveloped, and unstrategic nature of much of the work, suggested a theoretical framework for its development, and suggested some practical structures that should be considered if the government intended to take the work seriously. It suggested the creation of a specialist community relations unit within the government and the creation of an independent community relations body that would address issues of policy, training, and funding of community relations work. In 1987, the Central Community Relations Unit (CCRU) was set up, which was located at the heart of government, and in 1990 an independent body, the Community Relations Council (CRC), was established.

Community Relations, 1990-1998

In drawing up its initial strategic plan the CRC expanded its remit to include bodies that had not previously been working actively at peacebuilding, for example, business, church, and sports groups; health and education boards; and many groups from the voluntary and community sector. It also worked closely with the trade unions that had, since the late 1980s, been developing anti-intimidation and antisectarian programs for the workplace. Subsequently, there was a significant expansion of the number of groups working at peacebuilding, much of the growth of which was facilitated by a hugely increased financial investment in such work. By 1998 the number of civic groups engaging in contact work and developing programs and training to address issues of human rights, cultural diversity, cooperation on social and economic issues, single identity work, neutral venue work, and political dialogue had increased significantly—from 40 in 1986 to 150 in 1999. As the theoretical framework for such a focus expanded, the work also began to engage a much wider spectrum of people, including those who had previously been cynical of the "peace and doves" stereotype attached to the work (Fitzduff 1989a). It therefore became more possible to build a coalition of people and organizations addressing both the "softer" issues, such as understanding, dialogue, and cooperation, as well as the "harder" issues of inequality, rights, policing, and political and constitutional differences.

The development of such work was often extremely difficult—generally developed as it was amidst significant violence, where the workers involved in such dialogue work were often placed under threat by those who saw this work as threatening to their politics. The Peace and Reconciliation Group developed one such project in Derry/Londonderry.[5] Its work involved the verification of rumors emanating from either side of the divide, as such rumors often fueled street clashes, irrespective of their veracity. In addition, the PRG often provided "shuttle" mediators who could safely cross within and between communities to address impending tensions and difficulties that frequently occur in communities in a continual state of high alert. The group also worked with the police and army to ensure that their reactions to street tensions and violence were not counterproductive in terms of adding to street tensions.[6]

In many areas, women's groups were among the foremost to be involved in dialogue and cooperation work. Partly this was because they were seen as less threatening, and were less likely to be physically attacked if they crossed community divides. They were also the primary participants in the development of community work addressing social needs such as poverty, unemployment, and the welfare of children, and through such work they often formed connections that enabled them to address issues of differences between them in a way that was more difficult for men. Such connections were particularly useful in crisis work, for example, it was usually only the women, working in groups such as Women Together, who felt able to cross community lines to attend the funerals of the many victims of violence from all sides. Such developments among women were to significantly assist the development of the Northern Ireland Women's Coalition (NIWC), a cross-community political women's party founded in 1997.[7]

Another project with significant effect was the Interface project, which was set up in the mid-1990s to establish dialogue work along Belfast's so-called peacelines. These were very high walls, topped with barbed wire, dotted throughout the city to keep communities apart. These were erected by the government at the request of local communities, who felt they needed them to ensure their safety.[8] The Interface project built on the common social need of communities on each side of the peaceline walls. Separate consultations on such needs, which were followed by joint meetings between the communities as confidence was developed with civic leaders on both sides of the walls, gradually began to ensure that both sides began to understand and recognize each other's social, political, and security difficulties. Such work eventually led to a "mobile phone" project that ensured that as tensions arose, particularly over the summer months in the marching season, community workers from both sides were able to stay in contact with one another with the aim of reducing rising tensions and hostilities on the streets.[9]

The involvement of ex-paramilitaries who still identified strongly with their Republican or Loyalist communities, but who had abandoned violence as a tactic, was of particular assistance in developing many of the dialogue processes within and between local communities in the mid-1990s. On release from prison, many of these ex-paramilitaries involved themselves in the work of local community development programs, many of which had begun in the 1970s at the start of the conflict. Such work, in the absence of local democracy, had provided for community participation in governmental consultation processes about social, economic, and political issues. And in the mid-1990s, it helped to generate a new breed of "community" politicians who developed loyalist, republican, and feminist thinking in a way that significantly enriched the political mix of parties who were eventually able to sign the Belfast Agreement. Parties such as the PUP, the UDP, the NIWC, and Sinn Fein all have considerable experience at community and social politics.[10] Such experience has often provided them with fruitful contacts gained from their collective experience in addressing local social issues together, and should bode well for the social and economic tasks that face them as representatives in the new assembly.

Following the cease-fires of 1994, external assistance was also offered for peacebuilding by the European Union, which decided to help underpin the peace by allocating substantial funds to help build upon the economy and enshrine peace. Such funds have been useful, as their criteria for distribution included in many cases the development of local council partnerships that included business, political trade union, and community representatives, who were forced to work together on funding decisions. Such processes ensured that communities can no longer continue to be unaware of each other's social and economic needs, and have in many cases provided useful training for future collaborative government at both local and regional levels.

Lessons

As much of what has been achieved in Northern Ireland is as yet fragile, reflection upon experiences of conflict management and settlements achieved are still fraught with questions. Revisionism is ripe, and interpretations about causes and effects abound about how exactly the major violence, if not the conflict, has been brought to an end (e.g., Arthur 2000). And only time will test the validity and strength of many of the programs and processes outlined in this chapter. Nevertheless, despite such reservations, it may be useful to reflect upon some of the tentative lessons, gradually and often painfully learned, which have emerged from the experience of the conflict in Northern Ireland.

Peace by Piece

In many ways, developing peace at times resembles the task of assembling a massive jigsaw of needs, with the attendant frustration of attempting to decide, often in the midst of killing and bombings, what should be prioritized in order to achieve an end to violence. In dealing with intractable conflicts Kriesberg, Terrel, and Thorson (1989) have identified several strategies that may be usefully pursued in trying to free the gridlocks of a conflict. One approach is to try to find some areas of possible settlement, and work to attain them. Such has been a useful approach in Northern Ireland and has meant consistently identifying those areas where progress, with some energy and courage, appears to be possible to achieve. Such a multifaceted approach has also meant that at difficult times, when one area of work becomes too difficult or too dangerous to pursue, there are others where some success can be developed, and thus the momentum of progress can be retained. Also useful has been the recognition of the importance of the need to distinguish between the various phases of conflict, with each necessitating differing aspects of work. Thus, in Northern Ireland, the understanding of the need for preventative work in areas of high tension to prevent the escalation of violence after particularly difficult incidents of violence, or at volatile times of the year, has become extremely important. Similarly, anti-intimidation work within workplaces to prevent sectarian violence from occurring and possibly fueling community aggression has now been institutionalized. The management of ongoing conflict means that when hostilities are at their highest there is often a need for such things as rumor clarification and dialogue work by trusted mediators to bring about, for example, local cease-fires. Cross-community work that can mute revenge accruing from ongoing murders and maiming is also particularly important, and in Northern Ireland much of this work was carried out by women's groups who, as mentioned earlier, would travel on a cross-community basis to the funerals of all victims of violence. But also of significance is the medium-term work of training for facilitating difficult community and political dialogues. And without the development of the necessary longer term work, which can eventually help to transform the divided structures of society (for example, the development of integrated educational or housing facilities), a sustainable peace is less likely to be achieved. In Northern Ireland it has been found absolutely vital to work at all stages of a conflict in parallel.

Structural and/or Psychocultural Approaches

Unfortunately, fundamental disagreements between theorists and practitioners about priorities in the above aspects of conflict management and peacebuilding have often dominated the field, and in many cases have limited the development of the work. This was certainly the case in Northern Ireland, where throughout much of the 1970s and 1980s there was major dissension between those who see such work as primarily needing a structural approach to management and those who see the work as needing primarily a psychocultural approach. Those groups focusing on structural work—who saw the problem as one of incompatible interests that arise from the structure of a community—concentrated on issues of justice and rights, equity and political issues. Those approaching the work from a psychocultural perspective—which emphasizes the need to develop relationships between conflicting groups—concentrated in the first instance on eliminating the fears, ignorance, and hostility between communities through contact and cooperative possibilities, which provided groups with access to each other's histories, religions, cultures, and fears. Both approaches have their limitations, and tension between groups and institutions about prioritizing such approaches was both limiting and unnecessary (Fitzduff 1996). Eventually, groups focusing on relationship building began to energetically include dialogue on difficult issues of structural problems as part of relationship building, and those involved in such structural work began to avail themselves of the skills of those who could provide the productive context within which such dialogues could take place. The eventual recognition of such complementarity was vital to the recognition of the work.

A Multilevel Approach

The experience of Northern Ireland also suggests that it is usually vital to adopt what Lederach would call an organic approach to the management of diversity and division (Lederach 1998). Lederach suggests that there are three levels of diversity work that are necessary for a comprehensive approach to issues of difference and division, and he suggests that it is necessary, where possible, to tackle top, middle, and grassroots work simultaneously. Such was the case in Northern Ireland (Fitzduff 1996). It was necessary at the top level, for example, with the top power brokers, to work with governments, politicians, and, in some cases, paramilitaries in order to set the parameters for what was politically possible. At the middle level—for example, that of power holders—it was necessary to ensure the engagement of the major institutions involved in public life, in security work, education, the churches, businesses, and trade unions in order to deconstruct a societal and institutional life that was in many cases based on political and cultural inequality and exclusion. And at the local community level, where hostility was most often exemplified on the streets, it was extremely important to develop new paradigms of dialogue and coopera-tion, and to enable community leaders to transcend their particular community perspectives, in order to develop new possibilities of understanding between ghettoized communities. Without such an integrated approach, positive initia-tives on contentious issues such as equality, policing, and political options for Northern Ireland were much less likely to be effective and sustainable.

Reframe the Problem

A major factor in trying to end the obstacles to dialogue and agreement has been the attempts that have been made to circumscribe accustomed or declared stances on such issues as dialogue and constitutional possibilities. These have included, for example, the use of "unauthorized" and "deniable" contacts to facilitate dialogue where such was deemed either useless, obnoxious, or in some cases illegal; the presentation of a common social focus as an excuse for assisting talks between loyalist and republican community workers in Belfast; the use of win/win frameworks to issues of cultural diversity; the use of parallel or proximity talks as opposed to face-to-face talks, to ensure that all political parties could be included in discussions; and the frequent use of shuttle media-tion.

When very contentious issues arose in multiparty talks—such as decommis-sioning or policing—and began to slow down the talks processes, the use of independent commissions to deal with these issues was very helpful. Prime examples of these are the Independent Commission on Decommissioning and the Independent Commission on Policing, set up as part of the agreement. Such developments meant that these issues were not allowed to derail the various talks processes, or at least to make such derailment less possible. Perhaps the most major creative success is the Belfast Agreement itself, which has devel-oped a unique constitutional framework that secures a system of overlapping and interlocking national and cultural loyalties, and that has effectively brought an end to the idea of any possible identity or loyalty hegemony in Northern Ireland. All citizens can now legally hold British and/or Irish passports. People can choose to look to London or to Dublin—or to Northern Ireland—for their cultural identity and heritage. The agreement has broken the very much outdated notion—in this world of increasing ethnic mobility—that nationality, ethnicity, and territory are necessarily legally or constitutionally overlapping.

All Can Change

Inevitably, there are people for whom change is extremely difficult. Such resistance can be based upon a reluctance to lose power, while for many it is a fear of losing their identity. Some individuals and groups, whose core meaning has become bound up with their engagement in the conflict, may also resist its resolution, knowing (perhaps only at a subconscious level) that such resolution may leave them bereft in some way (Fitzduff 1989b). However, the experience of Northern Ireland would seem to suggest that there are few organizations or people that are not at some level capable of developing positive changes in their attitudes and behavior toward the outgroup, even when a conflict is in progress. The work also suggests that approaches for evoking such change must be flexible and sensitive to each group and situation. Even while such change is occurring, most individuals and groups can also act as positive change agents with others in facilitating further developments in attitudes and behavior that can gradually accrue and contribute to an overall shift in the conflict. While there have been valuable contributions to the facilitation of dialogue processes in Northern Ireland from externals, most facilitation of such work has come from those inside the conflict. Many indigenous models for dialogue have been developed, for example, the use of copartial facilitators, often ex-republican and loyalist prisoners, to facilitate discussions within local communities. Such copartials, many of whom have served prison sentences for political/sectarian murders, exemplify what have been significant change possibilities even in a society as conflicted as Northern Ireland.

The Future

It is a well-established fact to those of us working in conflict that in fact conflicts do not end—they just change. Undoubtedly, significant challenges remain to be addressed. These include the possible further development of some of the splinter groups that have split from the main paramilitary movements, and the need for the existing assembly parties to constructively and collectively deal with this challenge. There is the continuing difficulty of the possible destabilization of the assembly through the growth of more "antiagreement" representatives who could coalesce around such issues as dissatisfaction with the processes of decommissioning, prisoner release, and the difficulties in redeveloping a police service that is more acceptable to nationalists. On the positive side, however, much work has already been undertaken on the development of pluralist approaches to many of the contentious issues of equality and diversity, which have been so divisive in Northern Ireland. And in the Belfast Agreement, there is now in place a variety of mechanisms, such as weighted majorities for decision making, which have been designed to deal with the inevitable difficulties that will arise over the coming years.

The road to the agreement has been long, complex, and often bloody. Almost thirty years and 3,500 dead have been the result of the fear, discrimination, intransigence, anger, and violence with which politicians, government, and communities have limited their much surer and swifter progress toward peace. The peace has been long in coming, and hard in making. It does, however, at last appear that the hard work and courage of many creative approaches to justice, coexistence, and reconciliation work may have eventually yielded enough to take Northern Ireland to a future where politics, and not violence, will primarily prevail. If this happens, such will be truly a new beginning for Northern Ireland.

Notes

1. Also called the Good Friday Agreement, as it was signed on the Christian feast of Good Friday.

2. Loyalism is usually denotes a more fundamentalist form of Unionism, which is usually associated with violence. 'Loyal' usually means loyal to the Queen/King of Britain.

3. There is continual discussion in Northern Ireland (as elsewhere) about appropriate terms to use for such work. Over time, certain terms become more fashionable than others. By the late 1990s, the term *interdependence work* (to denote dialogue and cooperation) had become more common, and after the cease-fires of 1994 the term *reconciliation*, which previously had been used infrequently, had come to the fore. The term *diversity work* is now beginning to replace what was termed *cultural traditions work*, that is, work that focuses on validating differing cultural perspectives. More recently, the term *coexistence work* has been added to the vocabulary, but in Northern Ireland it is more usually associated with cultural validation work, and the implication of an acceptance of a toleration of a separate existence for communities, rather than a shared existence. In this context it is interesting to note that surveys consistently show that over 80 percent of people would like to live and work in shared communities, and approximately 70 percent would like to see shared educational systems, provided their personal security can be assured within such contexts. Such debates over terminology add significantly to the definition and redefinition about what is helpful in ensuring agreed goals, and effectiveness for such work.

4. These were mostly Catholics attending state schools, for reasons of convenience. Although state schools were nominally nondenominational, the fact that most Catholics felt obliged to attend Catholic schools meant that the state schools were essentially British and Protestant in nature.

5. The name of the city is contested—Catholics call it Derry, and Protestants usually prefer the term Londonderry.

6. Work with the police and army, even in trying to ensure the appropriateness and accountability of their actions, was particularly dangerous, as such was often viewed with

suspicion by Republicans, and frequently led to threats of violence, in many cases to expulsion from Northern Ireland, and in some cases to murder.

7. There are no women members of parliament representing Northern Ireland at Westminster, and only 10 percent of the local councillors are women. Angered by such statistics, and the refusal of existing parties to improve them, a group of women, who had mostly been involved in community work, formed the NIWC and subsequently secured two seats in the assembly which was set up after the Belfast Agreement.

8. Such fears are often justified; in one square mile of mixed Protestant/Catholic communities in North Belfast, there were six hundred murders during the course of the conflict. Most of these were believed to have been committed by neighbors from the diverse communities.

9. There are approximately three thousand marches every year in Northern Ireland. Most of these are by the Protestant Tradition. Some of these take place through what were previously Protestant areas, but have now become Catholic or mixed areas. While most of these are peaceful events, several dozen meet with hostile opposition from Catholic communities who often see such marches as continuing a pattern of dominance of their communities.

10. The PUP (Progressive Unionist Party) and the UDP (Ulster Democratic Party) were two small loyalist/unionist political parties with close connections to the loyalist paramilitaries. *Loyalist* is usually used to denote a more fundamentalist form of unionism, usually associated with violence. *Loyal* denotes loyalty to a British queen or king.

References

Arthur, P. 1999. Multiparty Mediation in Northern Ireland. In *Herding Cats: The Multiparty Mediation in a Complex World.* C. A. Crocker, F. O. Hampson, and P. Aail, eds. Washington, D.C.: United States Institute of Peace Press.

Cameron Report. 1969. Disturbances in Northern Ireland. Report of a commission appointed by the governor of Northern Ireland. Belfast: Her Majesty's Stationery Office.

Committee on the Administration of Justice (CAJ). 1992. Adding Insult to Injury, Belfast: CAJ.

Eybin, K. 1997. Training for Community Relations Work, Report to Central Community Relations Unit, Northern Ireland Office.

Fitzduff, M. 1989a. A Typology of Community Relations Work and Contextual Necessities. Belfast: Policy and Planning Unit, Northern Ireland Office.

———. 1989b. From Ritual to Consciousness: A Study in Change in Progress in Northern Ireland. Ph.D. Thesis, University of Ulster, Northern Ireland.

———. 1996. Beyond Violence: Conflict Resolution Processes in Northern Ireland. Series on Conflict and Governance. United Nations University Press.

Frazer, H., and Fitzduff, M. 1986. Improving Community Relations. Belfast: Standing Advisory Commission on Human Rights Report.

Grant, D. 1994. *Playing the Wild Card: Community Drama.* Belfast: Institute of Irish Studies.

Hamilton, A. 1995. Policing a Divided Society. Coleraine: Centre for the Study of Conflict, University of Ulster, Northern Ireland.

Hayes, M. 1972. *The Role of the Community Relations Commission in Northern Ireland.* (brochure). London: Runnymede Trust.

Knox, C., and Hughes, J. 1994. Community Relations and Local Government. Coleraine: Centre for the Study of Conflict, University of Ulster, Northern Ireland.

Kriesberg, L., Terrel, A. N., and Thorson, S., eds. 1989. *Intractable Conflicts and Their Transformation.* Syracuse, N.Y.: Studies on Peace and Conflict Resolution, Syracuse University.

Lederach, J. P. 1997. *Conflict Transformation.* Washington, D.C.: United States Instotute of Peace Press.

LeVine, R., and Campbell, D. 1972. *Ethnocentrism: Theories of Conflict, Ethnic Attitudes, and Group Behaviour.* New York: Wiley.

McCartney, C. 1994. *Clashing Symbols?* Belfast: Institute of Irish Studies, Queen's University, Belfast, Northern Ireland.

MacGinty, R. 1998. The Northern Ireland Agreement: Threats and Opportunities. Paper prepared for a seminar at the University of Kent at Canterbury, U.K.

O'Connor, F. 1993. *In Search of a State.* Belfast: Blackstaff Press.

Poole, M. 1990. The Geographical Location of Violence in Northern Ireland. In *Political Violence.* Belfast: Appletree Press.

Rose, R. 1971. *Governing without Consensus: An Irish Perspective.* London: Faber.

Ross, M. 1993. *The Management of Conflict.* New Haven, Conn.: Yale University Press.

———. 1998. Why Do They Do What They Do? Theories of Practice in Conflict Management. Paper presented to the European Conference on Peace and Conflict Resolution, Belfast.

14

Understanding Majority and Minority Participation in Interracial and Interethnic Dialogue

Amy S. Hubbard

Conflict resolution in general and grassroots intergroup dialogue in particular have a great deal to do with power—the attempt to prevent and stop the abuse of power, the use of effective techniques to wield power, and concerns about how the balance of power between the parties involved may affect their ability to reach a just, mutually agreed-upon solution to a serious long-term and painful conflict. This is particularly evident in grassroots interethnic and interracial dialogue. Many of us who come to work in this area are first genuinely moved to do so for social justice concerns. We seek ways of working out peaceful solutions between parties, communities, or nations in conflict because one or both parties to the conflict have been victimized by more powerful parties in the past or during the course of the present conflict. We seek ways to help the less powerful minority engage the more powerful majority in constructive ways to build a new, more peaceful, and more just future.[1]

We find dialogue groups particularly useful for this work, as they are a form of conflict resolution aimed at bringing ordinary people together at the grassroots level for discussion and possible reconciliation. The interaction is carefully structured through methods such as careful selection and balancing of participants or organizing discussion around a specific set of questions, which allow participants to discuss safer subjects like family background and ethnic foods first. The aim is to provide a safe space where participants can work through a carefully structured confrontation with each other. Dialogue group organizers hope that participants will come through the dialogue process (a) having become better advocates for harmonious relations between the parties and (b) having built bonds with one another that will help them work together to solve their problems jointly and to bring other members of their communities into the process.

But most of us would admit that there is an essential tension between working for peace and fighting for justice. Our views about the effectiveness of grassroots intergroup dialogue will be affected by the amount that we value one quality in relationship to the other. Will we contribute to harmony through conflict resolution but do so at the cost of accepting the continuation of some injustice? Or should we pursue justice for a particular group, knowing that this pursuit may increase conflict rather than resolve it?

Of course, some have argued, particularly with reference to the Israeli-Palestinian conflict, that peace and justice must be sought at the same time. Without one, the other can never be achieved. There is much that is attractive about this position. Nevertheless, we must acknowledge that the means to these two ends are often quite different. This is reflected, in part, in the different ways in which majority participants and minority participants view dialogue and use dialogue groups to pursue their goals.

This chapter presents a set of hypotheses about majority-minority relations in dialogue based on this author's previous research on long-term dialogue between Palestinians and Jews in the United States and current preliminary research on short-term Black-White dialogue in the United States. My observations suggest that majority participants and minority participants use dialogue differently from each other in part because their different levels of power lead to different levels of interest in peace and social justice. However, this is further complicated by the inherent tension between conflict resolution and social movement mobilization within grassroots conflict resolution exercises. Power imbalances between the parties do affect the dynamics of the process, but the dynamics of the process also have powerful effects on the power imbalance between the parties.

These observations were developed from 1984 through 1989, through participant observation in a long-term dialogue group of Palestinians, Jews, and other U.S. citizens living in a city in the eastern United States which has been given the pseudonym of Hartville (Hubbard 1997, 1999a, 1999b). The Hartville Middle East Reconciliation Committee (MERC) was formed in 1981 by Palestinians who were supporters of the Palestine Liberation Organization (PLO) and by Jews who supported the state of Israel. MERC also included a third group of non-Jewish, non-Arab participants such as this author, who for lack of a better term were called the "Others." In this post-Oslo Accord world, it is hard to conceive how difficult it must have been for MERC members to begin reaching out to one another across the lines of conflict—especially since not too long after MERC was formed, Israel invaded Lebanon, and, during the course of the conflict, the Israeli military allowed a Lebanese militia into Palestinian refugee camps, where the militia massacred the occupants. Nevertheless, MERC survived these difficult times and would survive other difficult times during the Palestinian uprising, or *intifada*, during the late 1980s and early 1990s.

Over the years, MERC developed a distinct pattern. In its early years, MERC members focused within the group in an attempt to resolve conflicts between Palestinian and Jewish members. After writing a consensus statement calling for mutual recognition and negotiations between Israel and the PLO, MERC members turned their attention to their home communities in an effort to build a peace movement that would pressure the U.S. government into playing a productive role in the peace process. But with the onset of the intifada in the late 1980s, MERC members found themselves once again pulled back into dialogue and conflict resolution as the conflict in the Middle East exacerbated conflicts within the group that had been left unaddressed during the social movement phase. MERC members were torn between the competing demands of addressing relations within the group and building a movement in the world outside of the group. It is this tension between conflict resolution and social movement mobilization in grassroots dialogue groups that must be addressed when discussing majority and minority participation in dialogue.[2]

This author's current research is in Black-White dialogue, working with an organization called Communities United (CU), which is based in a city in the southern United States with the pseudonym River City. In addition to the usual conflicts which complicate race relations in the United States, River City played a central role in the Confederacy, and conflicts over how the Confederacy is remembered are still being played out today. River City also has a central city with a large Black population, while its suburbs are largely White, and race relations are exacerbated by urban-suburban conflicts. CU staff members began working in race relations in the early 1990s when they decided that the city could not address its problems without addressing conflicts between Blacks and Whites.

CU staff members have developed a six-week dialogue program which has primarily focused on Black-White relations. The staff organized dialogue groups and provided trained facilitators and a manual to guide discussion. The manual begins with less confrontational questions such as where the participants' grandparents and parents grew up. The questions become more difficult later in the program when participants are asked whether they have ever suffered from discrimination or benefited from affirmative action. At the end of the program, participants are asked what kinds of changes are needed in their community in order to achieve genuine racial reconciliation.

The goal is to get participants to engage in "honest conversation" with one another about race, which requires that they address conflicts directly within the confines of the group. The CU staff members argue that everyone has been wounded by racism and that dialogue will help heal those wounds. Furthermore, participants can only build genuinely strong relationships if they work through this process. CU's long-term goal is to build interracial teams of people who can work together on community projects. However, they believe that those teams will flounder if they fail to do the difficult work necessary to create and maintain strong bonds with one another. Therefore, people must go beyond instrumentally oriented coalition building. They must have true, caring relationships.

CU's dialogue efforts have drawn heavily from the middle and upper-middle classes in River City. They have at various times brought corporate executives, local politicians, doctors, lawyers, local television newspeople, and social service agency officials into their dialogue efforts. CU has also had some success with local corporate support for various public events, such as a yearly breakfast meeting, which is attended by several hundred business and professional people. It sponsors other interracial events such as a walk around the city, which takes participants to infamous landmarks such as the docks where enslaved Africans were once brought to shore to be sold at market.

Unlike MERC, CU dialogue groups are meant to be short term, and the staff seeks to bring many people into dialogue for a short time rather than just a handful for a long time. But like MERC, CU dialogue participants face a similar challenge. What happens after the dialogue? Do people take the dialogue out into the community? Do they turn to political action? Are there differences in the way majority and minority participants use dialogue and what they expect to get out of it?

The term *majority* is used to describe those participants whose people or community or nation are in the relatively more powerful position and *minority* to describe those participants whose people or community or nation are in the less powerful position. Obviously these terms present some difficulty. In Black-White dialogue, it is easy to see that Whites are the majority party and Blacks are the minority party. However, with regard to Jewish-Palestinian dialogue, both Jews and Palestinians hold minority status in the United States. And while Israel is strategically, politically, and economically more powerful in the Middle East than the Palestinians, Israelis would argue that they are an embattled minority in the Middle East when compared to the Arab nations surrounding them. Nevertheless, few would argue that the U.S. Jewish community is not better organized and better established than the U.S. Palestinian community. As well, Palestinians as a group are in a less powerful position than the Israeli government.

But these terms could not easily be applied in other cases. For example, if Jews were to be in dialogue with Christians, Jews would be the minority rather than the majority. Or in cases of dialogue between Blacks and Latinos/as, for instance, it would be unclear who would be considered the minority and who the majority. Such a dialogue would no doubt reveal a different kind of dynamic from conventional majority-minority dialogue. These hypotheses may be most salient for dialogue between groups with clear power differences vis-à-vis one another. Therefore, for the purposes of discussing dialogue between groups with a clear power imbalance, the terms *majority* and *minority* are used in order to avoid the cumbersome phrases of "those from the more powerful community" and "those from the less powerful community."

Tension between Conflict Resolution and Conflict Waging

At the grassroots level, working for peace (or engaging in conflict resolution or dialogue) often means bringing people together to talk about the complexities of a situation in a quiet, safe place where they can confront each other successfully, work through that confrontation together, and then formulate a plan for peace. We bring the lines of conflict to the foreground, but only in order to reach across them and build a bond with someone who was once an enemy, so that the lines of conflict may fade. At the grassroots level, working for justice (or engaging in political action or social movement mobilization) often means finding effective ways to wage conflict and to bring allies into the struggle. We most often do that by simplifying issues to the level of the press release and the bumper sticker, and by exhorting our friends and comrades to be strong and prevail against the opposition in a very public manner. We bring the lines of conflict to the foreground in order to sharpen them, thereby building stronger bonds within our own circle.

Grassroots groups use both strategies in their efforts to expand their influence, starting with a *primary conflict strategy* and augmenting that with *alternative conflict strategies* when conditions change. Social movement organizations (SMOs), such as the National Association for the Advancement of Colored People (NAACP) local chapters, primarily use *conflict waging* strategies. Conflict resolution organizations (CROs), such as Communities United, primarily use *conflict resolution* strategies. However, both kinds of organizations at some point turn to alternative strategies when pursuing key goals. SMOs must use conflict resolution strategies in building coalitions with other SMOs or in negotiating with opponents. CROs must turn to conflict waging strategies when engaged in the reentry process, that is, when conflict resolution participants reenter their home communities. In the case of grassroots dialogue, this requires building a movement for change in the community at large.

Scholars and practitioners have been deterred from recognizing this by our tendency to separate these groups into different fields of inquiry. In the field of sociology, SMOs are well studied, but conflict resolution is rarely a concern. Some sociologists of social movements have addressed the challenges faced by social movement coalitions, but most have not addressed how the proactive use of conflict resolution strategies plays a key role in building coalitions (e.g., Benford 1993; Lichterman 1995; Staggenborg 1986; Hathaway and Meyer 1994).[3]

Fortunately, conflict resolution is flourishing both in practice and in theory as a field all its own. Scholars and practitioners have made tremendous strides in understanding how to resolve conflict at a variety of levels, from international negotiations over border disputes down to negotiations with your neighbor about who should repair a fence separating your yards. But what is missing is a systematic investigation of what happens next. What happens when participants in conflict resolution exercises reenter their home communities? Does success within the exercise translate to success in changing minds and behavior at homes?

Conflict resolution theorists and practitioners acknowledge this problem, especially with respect to problem-solving workshops—short-term meetings which bring together influential members of groups in conflict for the purposes of analyzing the conflict as a problem to which they can develop joint solutions (e.g., Azar 1990; Burton 1987; Doob and Foltz 1974). Some have considered it in structuring conflict resolution exercises. For instance, Kelman (1990) has emphasized that problem-solving workshops should be organized along group lines—so that participants are less likely to establish individual friendships which do not take group differences into regard. Participants cannot risk being viewed as people who became too friendly with people on the other side. Kelman has also discussed the importance of forming uneasy coalitions across lines of conflict (1992), since, once participants return to their home communities and address them, they must use words and symbols which will trouble their fellow participants in conflict resolution from the opposing side.

With regard to long-term grassroots dialogue groups, some scholars and practitioners have focused on the question of whether political action evolves from dialogue rather than on describing it as a reentry problem. Some have argued that it naturally follows as part of the dialogue group process (Breslow and Simon 1988). Others have argued that political action is problematic whether due to the personal flaws of the participants (Gordon and Demarest 1982) or the structural inequality between the participants (Abu-Nimer 1999; Kuttab 1988; Sharoni 1995).

But for the most part, reentry is a concern that is mentioned, yet rarely followed up on. This is not surprising because the process of getting people together and working out conflict successfully within the exercise itself is hard enough. Following them home, especially if they live in hostile territories, would be quite difficult.[4] Yet the reentry process is the central unsolved problem for grassroots dialogue. At the grassroots level, conflict resolution participants who wish to effect change in their home communities must necessarily switch from a *conflict resolution strategy* to a *conflict waging strategy*. Since they do not have the backing of powerful government officials in their negotiations, they must reach out to their home communities at the grassroots level. They must persuade the many rather than count on the clout of a few. This requires building a social movement for peace, which is an entirely different project from structuring a conflict resolution exercise. There are basic tensions between the two activities that are difficult to resolve. (For more on this, see Hubbard 1997, 1999b.)

Scholars must do more to investigate the reentry problem. We may be able to point to personal change among dialogue participants, and we can argue that

that in and of itself is a good thing. However, we would be fooling ourselves if we accepted that as sufficient, and, at any rate, we would then fail to answer the genuine criticisms leveled by the critics about the effectiveness of dialogue—that conflict resolution does more to co-opt the minority than to change the majority and that the price of building peace is the betrayal of justice.

Hypotheses about Dialogue

The following hypotheses fall into two areas: barriers to participation in dialogue by minorities and impacts of participation on minorities. The discussion of barriers draws primarily on the author's current research on Black-White dialogue. The discussion of impacts is based on this author's research on Palestinian-Jewish dialogue. This choice of data is related to the point at which this author entered these two research projects. Work was begun with CU during the first years of its dialogue group program, and research is still in the data-gathering stage. This preliminary work is best related to initial barriers to dialogue. Observations of MERC were initiated several years after it had formed, when it was entering its social movement mobilization phase. Therefore, most of the findings on MERC relate to the impact of involvement in long-term dialogue.

Barriers to Participation

Majority participants are more likely to approach dialogue with an interest in communicating with minority participants. Minority participants are more likely to expect political action to come out of their dialogue efforts.

Minority participants are more likely to know more about the majority participants' concerns and culture than vice versa. This is particularly true with Blacks and Whites in the United States. The fears and concerns of the White world are clearly reflected in the media and day-to-day life. Most Black Americans must contend with this every day of their lives, whereas Whites are considerably less knowledgeable about the challenges facing Black Americans. In a pilot survey of CU dialogue participants, Whites were more likely to say that they had learned something new about Black participants, such as, "I didn't know that some of the blacks continue to be hurt by the white majority."[5] Another said:

> I know I have not had the same experiences as minority members but
> I feel I'm more sensitized to issues.

Black participants did not report new learning about Whites but several did say they had become less judgmental:

> Although I am cognitively aware of the need not to judge others by
> their appearance, that was my greatest lesson in this experience.

Another said, "It made (helped) me really look at other people's perspective
without judging."

While some Black participants may find dialogue cathartic and healing,
others may tire of telling their stories over and over again to Whites who express
dismay and concern about the way the world operates but who take little
concrete action to change that world. For example, in the pilot study, some
Black participants were quite excited about their involvement in dialogue and
rated the success of their group quite high. Said one person who gave the group
a ten out of ten:

> I received positive reinforcement and support from members of my
> group and hopefully shared information that made the sessions mutu-
> ally beneficial.

However, other Black participants expressed caution. One person who rated the
group a five out of ten said:

> Nothing stated or heard was really new. The scale rating is modest
> because I can't really guess to what extent the majority participants
> were favorably affected or how.

Another, who rated the group a seven, said:

> While there were some learned insights which resulted from the dis-
> cussions, much of the discussion was extremely painful for the black
> male participants (all *three*). The white males' views basically re-
> mained the same as they saw the group males as exceptions to the
> "rule."

Such concerns reflect the approach that minority participants are more
likely to take toward dialogue. They are more likely to see it as useful if it leads
to concrete, genuine change, whereas majority participants are more likely to
see dialogue in and of itself as useful. In MERC, Palestinian participants were
more likely to express frustration over the lack of clear impact MERC had on
the Israeli-Palestinian conflict. Overall, one is more likely to encounter cynicism
in minority communities about the usefulness of dialogue. (See Abu-Nimer in
this volume.)

*Majorities are more likely use the conflict resolution frame when describing
race relations. Minorities are more likely to use the social justice frame.*

The different views about what the outcome of dialogue should be are also
reflected in the way people describe race relations within their community. The
conflict resolution frame suggests equality between the participants, in that
everyone must change in some way in order to bring about peaceful race

violations and state terrorism, Jewish members were careful about mentioning Palestinian terrorism. Nevertheless, while MERC members did not want to antagonize the local Arab community, the most care was taken to avoid alienating the local Jewish community. And in fact, the Jewish participants, while well-respected in Hartville, were not central figures in the Jewish community. In contrast, several Palestinian members were centrally connected to the local Arab community.

This can have the effect of muting minority participants who have strong social justice concerns. One Palestinian member had been quite vocal in the local community before joining MERC but reported that her involvement had caused her to "tone down" her statements:

> Going in and speaking with some control, a great deal of control,
> when in fact I want to scream and yell and vent against the injustices
> that I feel are being committed.

She was criticized by leading MERC members for a letter she wrote to the editor that was highly emotional and very critical of Israel. She left MERC some time after the incident, saying that she finally felt free to speak her mind again to call for justice for Palestinians.

On the other hand, another Palestinian member became adept at speaking to the Jewish community. He used the opportunity to learn how to speak to their hopes and fears, and he used the contacts he made through MERC to reach Jewish audiences that had been previously unavailable. Some Palestinians were critical of him, arguing that he had given up too much for the opportunity to form a dialogue. Whether this is true or not, for a Palestinian, he had a remarkable amount of access to the Jewish community.

Whether we join the critics or the supporters in our evaluation of this process, the fact is that behavior change does take place in long-term dialogue. The impact of this dynamic on CU's short-term dialogue remains to be seen and is a key concern in this author's current research. But whether this is a good thing or a bad thing, it does occur, and it occurs, in part, because of the dynamics of conflict waging and conflict resolution inherent in the dialogue process.

Majorities see the dialogue process as coming together to the bridge and returning home; minorities see the process as using the bridge to cross over and communicate with majority audiences.

However, while minority participants are more likely to be under pressure to change their behavior, this does not mean that they are the hapless victims of the majority. Minority participants use dialogue differently than majority participants (e.g., see Cohen 1994; Abu-Nimer 1999). The conventional image of dialogue is as a bridge where people arrive in order to negotiate or reconcile with each other. Then they go home and talk to their communities with the aim of bringing them to the bridge (e.g., Gordon 1991; Schwartz 1989). *Symmetrical constituent consultation and commitment* is the process most evident in formal negotiations between nations and bureaucratic institutions (e.g., Hopmann 1996; Moore 1996). However, at the grassroots level, conflict resolution participants are not official representatives of their constituencies. They cannot demand that their constituents commit themselves to the agreement. They can only persuade them to come along, and, as noted above, this is problematic (Hubbard 1999b).

This author's observations of MERC suggest that these dynamics led minority participants to concentrate on reaching out to the majority community more than reaching out to their own. Both Palestinian and Jewish members used MERC to reach out to the other side. A Palestinian member addressed a conservative Jewish congregation. A Jewish member spoke at a memorial service for an assassinated Palestinian-American. But Palestinian members saw their participation primarily as one way to reach the U.S. Jewish community, which they argued was a central pillar of support for Israel. They were less concerned with talking to Palestinians than they were with talking to Jews. As one Palestinian noted,

> The essence of dialogue, in my opinion, had been—if we expose the Jewish community in this country to what they haven't been exposed to, looking at the Jewish background and history, you find that the Jewish community in the United States is very liberal. And, therefore, it's very hard for me to believe that once you expose them to the truth, that they will keep on taking the positions that they're actually taking. . . . That has to change in order for the American administration and American policy in the Middle East to change.

Preliminary results in the CU research suggest that a similar pattern might hold true with Black and White facilitators. In an early survey, a handful of White facilitators either presented the conflict resolution frame or gave a combination of frames with the conflict resolution frame being predominant when describing race relations in River City. The handful of Black facilitators strongly held the social justice frame. We might expect that the Black facilitators would hold the conflict resolution frame. After all, they are committed to a strategy that is strongly based on that frame, but in fact they held the other frame. This would suggest that Black dialogue activists may enter into dialogue with an approach similar to some Palestinian activists—that of reaching the majority community rather than bringing the minority community closer to the bridge. However, this is still only speculation and requires further study.

Conclusion

If these hypotheses prove to be true, they raise serious questions about the reentry process. The assumption behind reentry as it is commonly discussed by scholars and practitioners is that the challenge facing participants is how to reenter and convince their own communities of the wisdom of working for peace. However, it's not clear that minority participants even focus on their own communities, choosing instead to reach out to the majority community. And if minority participants change their behavior in order to reach out to the majority community, they may lose important credibility within their home communities. Reentry, as it is commonly conceived, may be less than successful.

Furthermore, the dynamics of the reentry process for majority participants are less clear. Majority participants are more likely to focus on their own community than the minority community. It is less clear the extent to which they modify their behavior vis-à-vis either community. This is an area which needs further consideration.

It should be emphasized that these are only hypotheses—which will be further clarified at the end of a two-year research project for CU based on data from surveys, in-depth interviews, and participant observation. At this point, it is clear that power imbalances in dialogue can be problematic for some minority participants but also that minority participants can and have used dialogue to further their own ends in unexpected ways. Furthermore, we need to look at reentry as a central problem for dialogue, not a peripheral one—and look further to how grassroots groups use conflict proactively, not just to build harmonious relations between groups, but also to wage conflict against other groups.

Notes

1. The research in this chapter was supported by the American Sociological Association Spivak Program in Applied Research and Social Policy, the Walter Williams Craigie Teaching Endowment at Randolph-Macon College, and the Kellogg Foundation. The author also thanks the members of Community United for their help.

2. For other research on dialogue groups on the Israeli-Palestinian conflict, see Breslow and Simon 1988; Cohen 1994; Gordon 1986; and Schwartz 1989. For research on short-term encounter groups, see Abu-Nimer 1999 and Bargal and Bar 1992.

3. The exception to this is Hathaway and Meyer (1994), who described how SMO leaders structured their interaction so that they were successful at building and maintaining a coalition.

4. Also, how would we measure success? Doob and Foltz (1974) did follow-up interviews with participants in their Belfast workshop. They expressed the concern that some participants might have been telling them what they wanted to hear.

5. Spelling and grammatical errors have been corrected wherever they occurred in quotes.

6. In an analysis of seventy cases collected so far, Whites were statistically more likely than minority groups to say that being asked to join a dialogue group was less important in their decision to get involved. This confirms field observations that Black participants were more likely to say that they had been asked by someone connected with CU to participate.

References

Abu-Nimer, M. 1999. *Dialogue, Conflict Resolution, and Change*. Albany, N.Y.: SUNY Press.

Azar, E. E. 1990. *The Management of Protracted Social Conflict*. Dartmouth: Aldershot.

Bargal, D., and Bar, H. 1992. A Lewinian Approach to Intergroup Workshops for Arab-Palestinian and Jewish Youth. *Journal of Social Issues* 48:139-154.

Benford, R. D. 1993. Frame Disputes within the Nuclear Disarmament Movement. *Social Forces* 71:677-701.

Breslow, M., and Simon, L. 1988. *Dialogue Toward Israeli-Palestinian Peace*. Philadelphia: American Coalition for Middle East Dialogue.

Burton, J. W. 1987. *Resolving Deep-Rooted Conflict*. Lanham, Md.: University Press of America.

Cohen, C. E. 1994. Removing the Dust from Our Hearts: A Search for Reconciliation in the Narratives of Palestinian and Jewish Women. *NWSA Journal* 6:197-233.

Doob, L., and Foltz, W. J. 1974. The Impact of a Workshop on Grass-roots Leaders in Belfast. *Journal of Conflict Resolution* 18:237-256.

Gordon, H. 1991. Confronting Evil: A Prerequisite for Dialogue. In *Israel/Palestine: The Quest for Dialogue*, pp. 116-124. H. Gordon and R. Gordon, eds. Maryknoll, N.Y.: Orbis Books.

———. 1986. *Dance, Dialogue, and Despair: Existentialist Philosophy and Education for Peace in Israel*. Tuscaloosa: University of Alabama Press.

Gordon, H., and Demarest, J. 1982. Buberian Learning Groups: The Quest for Responsibility in Education for Peace. *Teachers College Record* 84:210-225.

Hathaway, W., and Meyer, D. S. 1994. Competition and Cooperation in Social Movement Coalitions: Lobbying for Peace in the 1980s. *Berkeley Journal of Sociology*, 38:157-183.

Hopmann, P. T. 1996. *The Negotiation Process and the Resolution of International Conflicts*. Columbia: University of South Carolina Press.

Hubbard, A. S. 1999a. Cultural and Status Differences in Intergroup Conflict Resolution: A Longitudinal Study of a Middle East Dialogue Group in the United States. *Human Relations* 52:303-325.

———. 1999b. Grassroots Conflict Resolution Exercises and Constituent Representation. *Peace & Change* 24:197-219.

———. 1997. Face-to-Face at Arm's Length: Conflict Norms and Extragroup Relations in Grassroots Dialogue Groups. *Human Organization* 56:265-274.

Kelman, H. 1992. Coalitions Across Conflict Lines: The Interplay of Conflicts Within and Between the Israeli and Palestinian Communities. In *Conflict Between People and Groups*, pp. 236-258. Stephen Worchel and Jeffrey A. Simpson, eds. New York: Nelson-Hall.

———. 1990. Interactive Problem-Solving: A Social-Psychological Approach to Conflict Resolution. In *Conflict: Readings in Management and Resolution*. John W. Burton and Frank Dukes, eds. New York: St. Martin's Press.

Kuttab, J. 1988. The Pitfalls of Dialogue. *Journal of Palestine Studies* 12(2):84-91.

Lichterman, P. 1995. Piecing Together Multicultural Community: Cultural Differences in Community Building Among Grassroots Environmentalists. *Social Problems*, 42:513-534.

Moore, C. 1996. *The Mediation Process: Practical Strategies for Resolving Conflict*. San Francisco: Jossey-Bass.

Schwartz, R. D. 1989. Arab-Jewish Dialogue in the United States: Toward Track II Tractability. In *Intractable Conflicts and Their Transformation,* pp. 180-209. L. Kriesberg, T. A. Northrup, and S. J. Thorson, eds. Syracuse, N.Y.: Syracuse University Press.

Sharoni, S. 1995. *Gender and the Israeli-Palestinian Conflict: The Politics of Women's Resistance.* Syracuse, N.Y.: Syracuse University Press.

Staggenborg, S. 1986. Coalition Work in the Pro-Choice Movement: Organizational and Environmental Opportunities and Obstacles. *Social Problems*: 33: 374-390.

15

Refugee Return in Bosnia and Herzegovina

Coexistence before Reconciliation

Barry Hart

Between 1991 and 1995 the various wars in ex-Yugoslavia killed approximately 250,000 people, wounded 200,000 people, and permanently disabled 13,000 people. Twenty to thirty thousand persons are still missing. The wars destroyed cities, towns, and villages and displaced millions of people, resulting in 1.3 million refugees in outside countries and one million internally displaced persons. Bosnia and Herzegovina (BiH) experienced the majority of this destruction and suffering, and three and a half years after the Dayton Agreement ended the war there, a plethora of structural problems and psychological issues continues to affect the region's Muslim, Serb, and Croat population.

Cooperative for Assistance and Relief Everywhere (CARE) International and other members of the international community, in partnership with national and local authorities and organizations, are attempting to address the postwar problems in BiH. Reconstruction and psychosocial projects, financial assistance to restart or rebuild local and national economies, and the creation of strong judicial and political systems are critical focus points.

For the past two years, there has also been a heightened effort by the United Nations High Commissioner for Refugees (UNHCR) and other international bodies to create avenues and means for return of refugees and internally displaced persons. (Return is seen as an integral part of the social, political, and economic rebuilding process.) In 1998, for example, 185,000 internally displaced persons returned home. Of this number, 35,000 were minority returnees, that is, persons who were either in the minority in their home communities prior to the war or are returning home to a community configuration changed by the war and therefore presently dominated by another ethnic group. In 1999 there was a goal of returning 120,000 internally displaced persons to their homes, 33,000 of which will be minority returnees (RRFT Report, November 13, 1998).[1]

Coexistence between the minority and majority members of the different ethnic communities is often highly problematic. The lack of political will and deep mistrust because of the events of war cause significant tension between them. Return has also been prevented for some of the same reasons. Prior to the war there was considerable tolerance and acceptance among members of the various ethnic groups in Bosnia and Herzegovina. Even today, one is regularly reminded of this by people from every side of the ethnic divide. It is also present in the fact that approximately 20 percent of the current population is from mixed marriages. Many people still say that they can live with others "if politicians and radical nationalists wouldn't interfere." But it can also be said that the war and the histories of distrust resurrected by it have done great damage to the relationship between Muslims, Serbs, and Croats—damage that will not easily be undone or reconciled.

A Short History

The relational history among Serbs, Croats, and Bosnian Muslims (also known as Bosniacs) has been mixed. It is not appropriate here to give a lengthy explanation of this history, with all of its social, cultural, and political variables, but an overview will provide a certain foundation for understanding coexistence issues and the CARE International Welcome and Information Center Project (WICP) involvement in the process of coexistence and reconciliation.

Serbs and Croats arrived in the Balkans in the early part of the seventh century. It is believed that they were two distinct but closely linked Slavic tribes with Iranian ruling castes, or that they were originally Iranian tribes which had acquired Slavic subjects (Malcolm 1996).[2] Their ethnic and linguistic impact on the Balkan region was significant. The pre-Slav groups, mostly of Illyrian, Celtic, and Roman heritage, were eventually absorbed by the new arrivals.

Serbs soon occupied and established kingdoms in what is now southwestern Serbia, Montenegro, and Herzegovina, while Croats settled the land of modern Croatia and most of Bosnia (Stovel 1998). Though they were pagan tribes when they entered the Balkans, both groups became Christians in the tenth century— the Serbs, Orthodox Christians; the Croats, Catholics. Islam came four centuries later with the invasions of the Ottoman Turks.

The independent state of Bosnia emerged in the 1180s and was "never a part of Serbia . . . since the Serb Kingdoms which included Bosnia at those times did not include most of what we now call Serbia" (Malcolm 1996, 11). This is an important element of the historical debate concerning Bosnia and to what ethnic groups the Slavs of the region truly belong. Although many Serbs and Croat historians (and politicians) argue that the Slavs of Bosnia "were really Serbs" or "really Croats," Malcolm replies that,

> As for the question of whether the inhabitants of Bosnia were really Croats or really Serbs in 1180, it cannot be answered, for two reasons: first, because we lack evidence, and secondly, because the question lacks meaning. We can say that the majority of the Bosnian territory was probably occupied by Croats—or at least under Croat rule—in the seventh century; but that is a tribal label which has little or no meaning five centuries later. (1996)

Malcolm (1996) and Judah (1997) reject modern revisionist history, which links ethnic identity of the Slavs of the region to present-day Croats and Serbs. Yet, the historical and cultural realities have been distorted in significant ways by all sides with myth and political interest constantly being injected into the debate. Therefore, the question of ethnic identity and related territorial claims remains an important one to analyze and address eight centuries later. For example, in the recent war in the region, Serbs and Croats fought for parts of Bosnia and Herzegovina to which they believed they had a historical and cultural claim. The fight was for the region (or a division of it between Serbs and Croats) that would marginalize Bosnian Muslims. In the postwar context the myths continue, and the fears, manipulations, and the demand for division remain.

Throughout the history of Bosnia and Herzegovina, Muslims, Serbs, and Croats have lived together and fought alongside each other. They have also fiercely battled one another—and at different times dominated one another. Outside forces have played a significant role in this political and relational history. In the twelfth century, for example, Hungary ruled Bosnia and from the fourteenth to nineteenth centuries, the Ottoman Empire dominated the region. In the early and mid-part of the twentieth century, the Austro-Hungarian Empire, Germany, and Italy exerted control over all or part of Bosnia and Herzegovina. Presently, the North Atlantic Treaty Organization (NATO) and organizations from other countries are involved in BiH in an attempt to help people in the region live together, while nearby Kosovo, Montenegro, and Serbia are caught up in ever-escalating conflict.

Yugoslavia was formed after World War I at the 1918 Paris Peace Conference. Originally it was called the Kingdom of Serbs, Croats, and Slovenes, but in 1929 it was renamed Yugoslavia, which means the "Land of the South Slavs." During World War II a Serbian monarch ruled over Yugoslavia, but in 1941 Nazi forces invaded the country, and many Yugoslavs, particularly Croats and Albanians, who resented Serb control, joined the fascist ranks. Hundreds of thousands of Serbs were killed. These acts of violence and those committed by Serb royalists against the Croats were never forgotten, acknowledged, or forgiven. Neither were the acts of the *Cetniks* (a Serb resistant force originally established to resist the Germans) who killed thousand of Muslims in southeast Bosnia in the early part of the war. Even with the victory of Tito's partisans and his call for "Brotherhood and Unity" during his rule from 1945 until his death in 1980, there were still issues of psychological pain, hatred, and desire for revenge that had been suppressed or not constructively dealt with. These issues were to emerge forcefully in the 1991 to 1995 wars in the region.

With Tito's death, the federation was severely weakened, and by the end of the decade the Soviet Union had collapsed and Eastern Europe was in turmoil or radically changing. These and internal political and economic factors helped weaken the Yugoslav Communist Party. Only the army remained strong, and the old communists were looking for new ways to control it and remain in power. Nationalism, which had been an issue since the founding of the state, became their new ideology—one that provided the leadership, especially in Croatia and Serbia, with a tool to revive past interests, wounds, and glories, but one that would eventually lead to war and the destruction of Yugoslavia.[3]

Two distinct nationalist policies have struggled for primacy since the founding of Yugoslavia. According to Pesic (1996), they consist of (1) Croatian separatism striving for an independent state, and (2) Serbian centralism striving to preserve the common Yugoslav state under its dominion.[4] In the later part of the 1980s, the new Yugoslav leader, Slobodan Milosevic (architect of the 1991 to 1995 wars and the crisis in Kosovo) wanted and sought the establishment of a greater Serbia. This was to include all Serbs in the Krajina, eastern and western Slavonia (regions within Croatia) and Serbs in and around Sarajevo in Bosnia.

Fighting began in Slovenia in 1991, soon escalating to a full-scale war with the Yugoslav Army siege on Vukovar in Croatia. Serbs made these first moves against the Slovenes and Croats and finally, as a mainly Bosnian Serb force backed by Belgrade, against the Muslims and Croats in Bosnia and Herzegovina. Croats and Muslims in BiH also went to war. In this case, Croatia didn't want to lose its Croat population there and so helped local Croats "protect" themselves from Bosnian Muslims. For some, this was seen as a fight initiated by Catholics to prevent Muslim expansionism in the region.[5] Serbs may have attacked Muslims (Bosniacs) for the same reason—remembering their loss at the Battle of Kosovo in 1389, a battle seen by them as a heroic attempt to stop Ottoman Muslims from entering Europe.

The Dayton Agreement and Annex 7

After forty-two months of war, the international community brokered a cease-fire that ended the conflict. In November 1995 the Dayton Agreement (named after the marathon negotiations that were held at Wright-Patterson Airforce Base in Dayton, Ohio) was signed. It included territorial and political decisions that divided Bosnia and Herzegovina into a federation of Muslims/Bosniacs and Croats and a republic with a mainly Serb population. The agreement also addressed police and military arrangements, economic and humanitarian concerns, and the declarations of the rights of refugees and displaced persons. The mandate of CARE's Welcome and Information Project in BiH is about these rights as well as the interests and needs of those people displaced and made refugees by the Balkan wars. Chapter 1, Article 1, No. 1 of Annex 7 states,

> All refugees and displaced persons have the right to return to their homes of origin. They shall have the right to have restored to them property of which they were deprived in the course of hostilities since 1991. The early return of refugees and displaced persons is an important objective of the settlement of the conflict in Bosnia and Herzegovina.

This article further says, "the Parties [signatories of the Dayton Agreement] shall ensure that refugees and displaced persons are permitted to return safely, without risk of harassment, intimidation, persecution or persecution on account of their ethnic origin, religious belief, or political opinion." The UN, the International Committee of the Red Cross (ICRC) and nongovernmental organization (NGO) bodies were given the mandate under Annex 7 to monitor human rights and help to provide or reestablish the basic human needs of the people of Bosnia and Herzegovina.

Annex 7 of the Dayton Agreement was the starting point for CARE's Welcome and Information Project. It provides both the basis for its development and structure as well as the framework for its mission, to help people return and aid them in reestablishing relationships with former neighbors. It should be noted here that many of the atrocities of the war were committed between neighbors because of ethnic/religious difference. It should also be said that a document such as Annex 7 is only a beginning in the long process of reestablishing these relationships destroyed by politically-motivated fear, hatred, and mistrust. These are some of the factors that helped create the wars in Yugoslavia and that traumatized its people, and in turn must be dealt with in the process of people's healing.

Since 1995 and Annex 7, other documents, such as the December 1998 Madrid Peace Implementation Council and the 1999 Reconstruction and Return Task Force (RRTF) Action Plan, set out intensive programs to address and strengthen the peace process and build democratic and market-oriented institutions in BiH.[6] The Madrid Declaration states that "in order to create a self-sustaining state of Bosnia and Herzegovina, action is needed in particular on: interethnic tolerance and reconciliation; the development of effective common institutions with powers clearly delineated from those of the Entities; and an open and pluralistic political life."

In order to build peace, the international community was being further encouraged through this declaration to join those people and institutions in BiH who desire to reconstruct relationships and rebuild the institutions and structures that will creatively support these relationships. In the end, it is humans-in-relationship that allows, and provides the energy for, the rebuilding of a society, leading to the "lasting peace" sought by the majority of the people in the region.

Obstacles to Reconciliation

Peace is not easy to accomplish, and a lasting peace is even more difficult to realize. Clearly, interethnic tolerance and reconciliation are a major challenge to peacebuilding and to the return process in Bosnian and Herzegovina. Capacity-building activities, says a 1998 UNHCR Regional Strategy Report, "particularly in the areas of rule of law, good governance, and community-based reconciliation" are essential to help meet this challenge. Postconflict reconstruction and sustainable peace in the region depends largely on what happens at the local level. In terms of reconciliation, the report insists that it is "community-based reconciliation activities, which foster openness, transparency, accountability, due process, impartiality and confidence," that will make a significant difference. It points to women's organizations and religious leaders as essential participants in this process.[7]

But all this takes time and major financial commitment, as well as a willingness on all sides to make things work. It also requires significant patience to work toward reconciliation through the multiple stages of tolerance building and coexistence. The international community realizes the long-term implications of reconstructing a postwar society—or it is learning this difficult lesson in new ways in Bosnia and Herzegovina. Yet, new crisis situations in other parts of the region (notably Kosovo) and/or the world, as well as "donor fatigue" and internal political blockages, may ultimately prevent capacity building and hinder the process of reconciliation. Without the financial and long-term commitment and local political will, reconstruction in BiH won't take place, return will be greatly hampered or stopped, and reconciliation goals will go unmet.[8]

There is another issue limiting coexistence and reconciliation attempts: minority groups often don't want to move back to unsafe physical and political conditions. An example of this is found in the January 17, 1999 ONASA News Report which says, "Ninety-eight percent of the 2,600 Croat refugees from the area of Banja Luka, who presently live in eighteen settlements in the Croatian Sunja municipality, said that they cannot or do not want to return to the Republika Srpska, 'under Serb power.'" And they fear for their future "in the case of a mass Serb return, [when they will be] forced to leave the Serb houses in which they are temporarily accommodated."[9]

Related problems may emerge as the NATO-led Stabilization Force (SFOR) takes a greater role in providing security for those wanting to return. For NATO, 1999 will be a "showdown year," where it is committed to "not . . . back off in the face of threats to public order from local radicals who will attempt to block minority returns" (ONASA, December 15, 1998). In 1998, for example, there were at least seventy incidents where Bosnian Muslims tried to return to mainly

Croat parts of southern Bosnia and were verbally and physically attacked. Moreover, many local police turn their backs when such incidents occur. It is not certain that this SFOR security involvement will aid the return process. Ethnic cleansing is not acceptable, but it is not clear that returning people under the protection of the gun will provide an environment for building tolerance between the majority and minority communities, let alone one that will nurture reconciliation.

NATO, the UN, and the majority of the international aid organizations on the ground are faced with the difficulty of establishing the conditions for tolerance and coexistence among a people divided by war. Their involvement is meant to help people feel safe and develop strong economic, political, and judicial structures. This is critical to the return process, as is their emphasis on aiding in the creation of multiethnic police forces and strengthening civil society. Also, action toward extending human and religious rights to all people is in process and is another critical factor in return.

Additionally, though, there should be a more systematic approach to addressing the psychosocial needs of returnees and those receiving them, one that more comprehensively factors in the trauma of war and its social development implications.[10] There also need to be new mechanisms built into the social framework for resolving or transforming conflict at all levels of society—particularly at the local level. Rule of law needs to be supplemented by analytical and practical tools to help restore not just formal judicial structures, but broken relationships.

CARE's Welcome and Information Center Project

CARE's Welcome and Information Center Project (WICP) attempts to address the obstacles and challenges to the long-term process of restoring people to their homes, helping heal broken relationships, and aiding social development. Established in mid-1997, the project has seven centers (soon to expand to nine) in Bosnia and Herzegovina. The focus of the centers' lawyers, communication officers, social workers, and trauma trainers "is to support return and community reconciliation by providing legal and social service information/liaison as well as trauma healing and problem solving counseling/training" (WICP Project Proposal, 1998).[11] This European Committee Humanitarian Office (ECHO)-funded project has recently added an additional component: training and support for basic financial capacity building—with small-income generation and small-business projects being the central focus.

WICP emphasizes the need for "timely and accurate legal and social and economic information/liaison support around return" (Welcome Project Proposal Paper, 1998). This legal aid and information related to the ownership and transfer of property, identity papers, and other legal concerns help people find their way through the web of political restraints and ongoing political turmoil. Access to this and other information related to social services and human rights issues helps returnees and displaced persons deal more effectively with the difficulties of return as well as the potentially hostile environment under control of the majority community. Financial assistance is seen to enhance the ability of returnees and their community to deal with the very practical and important psychological issue of income generation in a severely depressed economy.

The psychosocial component of the project was included due to the extensive postwar social and trauma needs. Social service and psychological help, though fairly well-developed in prewar Yugoslavia, did not exist, or couldn't meet the demand after the war. Moreover, it had an urban focus and the war affected an entire population, a large part of which is rural. International and local NGOs currently attempt to fill this gap. WICP's psychosocial services were created to ease the trauma and the stressors of war as well as tensions and problems in the community created through the return process. To do this it uses counseling or group therapy-oriented sessions, provides problem solving training for local authorities, such as municipal leaders and police, and helps local professionals develop a deeper understanding of the theory and practice of trauma healing and conflict transformation. There is also an emphasis on preparing people for return as well as those who would be receiving them, that is, members of the majority community. Practical as well as psychological preparation is the focus here.

Furthermore, the psychosocial component of WICP determined that work needed to be done with families of those individuals still missing due to the war. This effort is seen as essential to help break the tension between the various ethnic groups in the process of tolerance building and healing broken relationships.[12] Therefore, special counseling and problem-solving sessions are offered to these family members to help them speak about their grief and to more effectively express their anger and needs to local and international authorities working to locate missing people or their remains. And then there are the children and their trauma and needs. WICP also trains teachers and school pedagogues to deal more effectively with these needs, providing workshops on trauma healing, bias and prejudice reduction, self-esteem building, and communication and problem-solving skills.

Theory for Practice

What is painfully clear to any observer is the horrific suffering the war brought on the people of ex-Yugoslavia. As in every war, the suffering is physical, psychological, and spiritual. Everyone is a war's victim; its violence impacts everything and everyone. Gandhi once said, "I object to violence because when it appears to do good, the good is only temporary—the evil it does is permanent."[13] This author is aware of the arguments for stopping someone like Hitler and using force/violence to do so. But Gandhi's words are meant to take us to a deeper meaning, one of understanding ourselves/others and what we need to do, both individually and corporately, to seek and implement new value systems that prevent violent forms of conflict and stop our use of violence to deal with conflict. This is no easy task, but without a new set of values, insights, and theories, along with skills for implementation, the old and destructive ways will continue to define how we are treated and how we deal with our "enemy" (Volkan 1996).

For this author, the greatest crime of war's violence is the taking of life. Violence also destroys houses and villages, and in the process loved ones are separated and neighbors are alienated from each other. People are also robbed of years of their lives. In the case of ex-Yugoslavia, they lost four or five years—in other wars decades are lost. Safety and predictability are also victims of war, as is hope for the future in terms of friendships, jobs, and peace with justice. Furthermore, trust in others and possibly oneself is shattered.

Identity is also a victim of this violence, as it is threatened or stripped away by destructive words and actions. Northrup (1989) has defined identity as "a concept used to describe a person's sense of self and the relationship of the self to the world." Individuals as well as groups, such as families, and larger social constructs of people, such as ethnic and religious groups, need an identity, a sense of who they are in relation to their social, cultural, and political environment. Identity is a basic human need, and without it life is not safe or predictable in a social, psychological, and present historical sense. This can and often does lead to disorganization and results in death (Nudler in Fisher 1990).

Identity, specifically ethnic identity, in the crisis in ex-Yugoslavia is not the defining reason for the war there. We have already noted that the fall of communism, extreme nationalism, and related political power issues, as well as internal economic problems and external influences, helped create the conflict. But it should be clearly said that ethnic identity—with its religious and cultural components and its use within extreme nationalistic ideologies—played a significant role in the war (and continues to be a divisive factor in the postwar context). To understand this better, outlined below is a hypothesis in four parts which posits that the multiple set of identities people hold in peaceful times grow narrow and move to the level of an essential set of factors under the extreme conditions of conflict leading to and including war. This happens for the following reasons.

There is a sudden awakening in individuals and/or groups of a set of values or realities related to family/group connections, language, culture, and religion. The circumstances of escalating conflict and war bring these once unconscious factors of identity to consciousness. Political rhetoric and the use of music, poetry, religious symbols, and other cultural markers help create and heighten this awareness. Revision of myth and the creation of new ones add to this identity conscientization. The multiple identities, which individuals and groups have in times of peace, are therefore replaced in times of crisis by an essential identity that is tied to one's family, ethnic, religious, or national group.

Only with these people does life feel "safe" and predictable and can the needed sense of "belongingness" take place. Combined with survival identity—the need to stay alive during war, to be identified as an individual or group among the living—ethnic identity, with this essential set of factors, was a strong reason for the start, escalation, and continuation of the Yugoslav war. Without understanding this role of ethnic identity, we fail to grasp its power over the people in the region. We also fail to see how it becomes an important variable in the cause of trauma and in the process of trauma healing and conflict transformation and in the postwar return and reconstruction process.

The link between identity (ethnic and other identities) and the trauma caused by war and found in postwar contexts is complex. Experience tells us that war shatters hope and trust through the destruction of social relations, a primary value and source of identity. It also impacts the emotional state of many people caught in war's violence and postwar deprivation. This causes great stress and trauma, removing from people the sense of who they have been and presently are. Identity and other basic needs such as food, water, shelter, self- and group-esteem, recognition, and sense of purpose are often deeply threatened or taken away under these extreme conditions. When this happens, individuals—and possibly entire groups of people—enter a state of shock and bewilderment, leading to denial, anger, guilt, and a host of other psychological responses.

Of course, individuals or groups may also take on new and very strong identities in a war (or other extreme violent situations). They take on an increased sense of recognition and purpose as they defend themselves, their families, or homelands against enemy aggression or attempt to rebuild their lives after war. But many experience an unhealthy emotional and psychological reaction to the traumatizing factors of war and its aftermath. Furthermore, victims of violence are no longer who they were; their self-understanding and family and group dynamics have been greatly altered, and their future is uncertain.

Although not everyone is traumatized by war, or at least not right away due to circumstances such as distance from the fighting, personal characteristics and strengths, and so on, the trauma of war affects most people at some point during or after the conflict (or both). The intensity of their reactions to traumatic events depends on a number of factors, for example, how sudden or unexpected the death was of a loved one (if it was a death), the mode of death, the nature of the relationship, early childhood or social experiences, loss of social and economic support systems, and so forth. But when an individual, group, or an entire nation is "shocked" by physical and psychological abuse, when death hangs in the air and deep loss and grief are experienced, when hope is lost, there are clear physical and emotional reactions and consequences.

Being traumatized means loss, temporary or permanent, often leading to rage and a desire for revenge against those who caused this loss. One intense example of this is from another context: Liberia, West Africa. While working for a local NGO, this author and his colleagues did trauma healing and reconciliation workshops throughout Liberia. One was done for Christian leaders in the northeastern part of the country. One participant, the pastor of a local church, told how his parents had their throats slit in front of him by rebel soldiers and how this led to his hatred for the killers and the ethnic group they represented. All he could think about was avenging his parents' deaths. He could not shake this desire for revenge.

He was relieved to find out that this was one of the normal responses to an extreme and abnormal situation. Through participating in a listening process and being helped to name and express other responses to his loss and grief, he was able to see the possibility of movement out of his rage and away from the desire for revenge. He came to understand that it was also possible to eventually integrate his pain and move on with his life. He even spoke about the possibility of one day forgiving those who killed his parents. It was clear that he had taken the first and very difficult steps on the path toward healing.

Healing is not easy, but it is necessary, and if healing processes are done for large numbers of people in postconflict situations, they are potentially strengthened in ways that will allow them to rebuild their society politically and economically. Over the long term this healing may also prevent individuals and groups of people from seeking revenge, allowing them to risk the necessary emotional and practical steps to be taken to restore relationships.

An example that reflects the beginning of this process is given later in this chapter in the story of the women of Zepce. In the Balkans, this author has also witnessed midlevel leaders from different religious traditions meeting to restore relationships and determine their role in the rebuilding of their communities. In one context, a 1996 conflict resolution (and reconciliation) workshop held outside the region in Pec, Hungary, a Muslim and two Christians (one Catholic, the other Orthodox) pledged to work toward reconciliation in their region and be a united front in its rebuilding process. This was a bold step for these men from the former Yugoslavia, especially considering the timing of this pledge—so close to the end of the war—and the ethnic issues that underlie their religious affiliations.[14]

Practice from Theory

There is no simple panacea to healing trauma and reconciling people. For critical change to take place it is important for the people themselves to finally want it. Also, those of us attempting to help in this change process need to have the patience to be present with them over the long term. In Bosnia and Herzegovina, the WICP local staff members, often traumatized by the war and/or uncertain about their own futures, are asked daily to be deeply involved with displaced persons, returnees, and others under difficult postwar conditions. In this process they are also asked "to engender hopefulness and optimism rather than paralyzing apathy" (Clements 1997). The difficulties of this involvement and request are obvious. So from the outset, the WICP staff is the starting point in our goal to help others.

For those of us from other educational, cultural, and political realities, understanding local staff and issues is of critical concern. In some ways this author's four years in the region allows for a certain understanding of the context and in particular how local WICP staff members interpret their social and cultural environment. But no outsider will ever fully understand their history, pain, or worldview, and it is clear that outsider enthusiasm for peace and reconciliation in their country cannot be "transferred" to them.

To help bring new insights and change, there is the need for this author to constantly scrutinize his "psychological road maps." Moreover, listening, in both formal and informal ways, to staff concerns and needs helps strengthen relationships and leads to a certain amount of attitudinal change in us all. Trust, another essential element in our work together and with others, is also growing. It is an ongoing process, but one that makes the fieldwork possible and often creative.

Women of Zepce

Creative work of the WICP staff is reflected in Zepce, a small city in central Bosnia and Herzegovina. There, one of our mobile teams from Zeneca developed a training program on trauma healing and conflict transformation for two women's groups—one is a Bosnian Croat group, the other a Muslim/Bosniac group. Both ethnic groups have lived in or around Zepce for centuries, but the war deeply alienated them. And in the case of the Bosniacs, who mainly lived in Prijeko, just across the river Bosna from Zepce, many were killed, raped, and expelled from their homes by their Croat neighbors. Beginning in 1996, the Bosniacs began to return to their destroyed homes in Prijeko. They continued to distrust the Croats in Zepce and still hold a certain amount of fear of them due to what happened during the war.

This author gave a series of workshops to both groups of women, starting with the Bosnian Croats. Outsider involvement was important both practically and contextually, since an "expert" in the conflict transformation field was being called in to help these women and their families deal with their postwar problems. That this author was part of WICP, a program known in Zepce through our local staff, provided an element of respect and trust—although it was clear that international organizations and workers were often suspected of being uncaring or not very trustworthy. It was therefore a great help to have WICP team members, people who knew the author well, explain who he was, what he had to offer, and how long he had been in the region. This placed him solidly in context and gave him the base needed to provide the most constructive training and leadership in the situation.

The workshop topics included trauma awareness and healing, domestic violence, and problem solving related to these women's difficult postwar social and economic situations. With the Bosniac women, additional trauma issues were discussed concerning their being incarcerated, raped, and forced from their homes. During intervals between these workshops, our trauma trainer and social worker spent much time listening to the pain, fears, and needs of these women. Further trust was established over a three-month period through the workshops and visits, and it was suggested that the groups meet each other—ostensibly to discuss common interests and needs. There was also the hope that this meeting might be the first step in a reconciliation process.

The encounter took place on neutral ground in the city of Zenica. Several of the women had met before, but many were meeting for the first time since before the war. It was a surprisingly friendly and open meeting and one that produced an interesting and potentially significant outcome—they decided to form an official group, which they called "Women of Zepce." They agreed to work together to build relationships and a stronger economic base for themselves and their families. The WICP lawyer offered to research the legal implications of this union, and members asked WICP for information about starting a small business. The business was eventually established when an international organization gave the Women of Zepce several thousand chickens and help in setting up their business endeavor.

The bridge built across the river Bosna is still a foot bridge, but one that allows these women to reconnect in order to build more tolerance and trust and to acknowledge the reality of their coexistence. The physical, psychological, and spiritual aspects of this relationship will need ongoing work. They have been and will continue to be challenged by radicals and political forces that want the divisions between Croats and Muslims to remain. But an important step was taken in the healing process through this coming together, and these women will help in a small but significant way to transform the conflict in their region. It will no doubt be a long, even decade-long, process, but the values and attitudes are correct and may encourage others to risk creative coexistence and, over time, reconciliation.

Breaking the Cycle of Victimhood and Aggression

The Zepce women are an example of boldness of decision, of something far greater than the measured and destructive power decisions made by manipulative political entities. The WICP, albeit in a limited way compared to the regional need, encourages this boldness and provides some practical help in the decision and transformation processes. But to "push away the negative energy," as one of our staff said, there must be more acknowledgment of past wrongs and more relief of the trauma and other problems brought on by these wrongs.

One grandmother from Srebrenica, a mainly Muslim city destroyed by Serb forces in 1995, addressed these issues last year in a WICP workshop. She asked, "What should I tell my grandchildren about this war—who is going to tell what happened to their parents and why?" This Muslim woman, in her seventies, is raising two young grandchildren, because their father and mother were killed in Srebrenica. She is burdened with this reality and her grandchildren's practical and emotional futures.

There are no easy answers for her, and a response is made more difficult since she also is a victim of World War II—during which her father and brother were killed by a Serb military unit. After this tragedy, her mother told her she should "forgive the enemy." Although she now strongly believes that her mother was wrong, she is still struggling with what to say to her grandchildren. Her pain was evident as she asked for help.

The pain and questions of this woman typify the suffering and multiple questions concerning victimhood and aggression in the recent war in ex-Yugoslavia. What amount of healing is necessary, what sort of processes of acknowledgment, forgiveness, and justice are required in order to stop the victimization? What will break the cycle, which often causes victims of one conflict to be aggressors in the next? Moreover, how can the memory of war and its present historical distortions be challenged and prevented from emotionally crippling the region's ethnic groups well into the twenty-first century?

The WICP struggles to respond constructively to these questions. An important response by WICP and other international and local projects may be found in seeing social reconstruction as an equal partner, possibly even the cornerstone, to the important political, economic, judicial, and infrastructure reconstruction needs in Bosnia and Herzegovina. In this regard, civil society work is crucial and requires strengthening. This implies a need for people to be encouraged in social-psychological and spiritual ways that go beyond political and economic frameworks. Here, the people themselves define what they need, and are aided in attempting to meet these needs through the interventions of their peers and the constructive involvement of members of the international community.

The Zepce Women's group example above speaks to this social reconstruction, as do the WICP team members of Vogosca when they write the following:

> [The] Welcome program helps people in coexistence, building trust towards community, giving them the right information and psychosocial help and support, and very important moral support, showing them that they are not alone and forgotten—and in that way making their situation less difficult. We think the most important value of this project is that doors are open to everybody [regardless of] what religion or ethnic background they are from, or what political opinions they hold. (Hart 1998)

It is this kind of community-level work and attitude that requires further strengthening in the WICP and needs to be reflected on a greater scale in reconstruction efforts in the region. Refugee return clearly necessitates this manner of approach, as it attempts to enhance deeper group and cross-group understanding and healing.

Forgiveness and Justice

Cross-group understanding and healing can be furthered through forgiveness and creative justice processes. Forgiveness, as generally understood in a context reflecting Western values, means to effect change through a process of psychological and social healing and to restore broken relationships through just means. Forgiveness, from this perspective, necessitates that a wrong be acknowledged and that there be a willingness to right that wrong through confession and restitution. Therefore, the ultimate aim of forgiveness is to restore individual or group relationships. This is also the aim of justice. Justice, here, is understood as restorative justice, not just a punitive kind, or one that is solely focused on establishing blame and guilt. It is a justice that emphasizes the Golden Rule of "doing unto others as you would have them do unto you," not just the rule of law. Restorative justice, with its focus on listening, establishing facts, and acknowledging past wrongs, may be a strange concept when considered in the traditional or historical context of Bosnia and Herzegovina, but one recognized by many local people as needed to reconnect broken relationships and repair social injury.

An encouraging, but limited, move in the direction of a new kind of justice leading toward forgiveness and reconciliation is the effort being put into establishing a Bosniac-Croat-Serb Truth and Reconciliation Commission (TRC) for Bosnia and Herzegovina. Religious, civil, and political leaders met last year to discuss a TRC "to establish consensus on abuses suffered by victims from all ethnic groups in the recent war" (Peace Watch 1998). This commission would attempt to establish facts to aid in the understanding about victims on all sides and to help in the understanding that "individual by individual the victimization and suffering were exactly the same, while recognizing that more people in one ethnic group many have suffered than in another" (Peace Watch 1998). Furthermore, the TRC will document cases of heroism by ordinary citizens who risked their lives to save neighbors across ethnic divides. This will be done to recognize those who refused political, media, and other manipulation regarding ethnic cleansing and who "maintained their sense of humanity by demonstrating compassion for others" (Peace Watch 1998).[15]

The time may be ripe for this approach to healing and restoring relations, but will it actually happen, and is it enough? Will it and the punitive justice offered up by the local courts and International Criminal Tribunal for the former Yugoslavia at the Hague be enough to heal the wounds of a nation? Are these efforts, along with those of CARE and other international and local bodies, the necessary pieces to complete a complex peacebuilding puzzle in the Balkans?

We don't know, but we are certain that these and other efforts will require a long-term commitment to peace in the region. What took a relatively short time to destroy will certainly take several decades to rebuild.

Conclusion

To be a more effective part of this long-term peacebuilding and learning process, CARE's Welcome and Information Center Project will need to enhance its efforts. It can do this by

- further developing its theoretical insight regarding return, coexistence, and reconciliation, as well as the technical skills it uses for the practical work it does in these areas.
- developing ongoing evaluation processes that are for the people in the region. In this way the work of the Welcome and Information Centers will be scrutinized in the light of their needs and interests, not just organizational and funding ones.
- adding the evaluation information to the body of knowledge of organizations working on similar projects. In the case of the Welcome Project, its evaluation data on return and reconciliation should be shared with others in BiH working on similar issues. Moreover, this evaluation research can be tested in other contexts and eventually contribute to social science in general.
- building capacity for the future work of the Welcome Centers. CARE will leave Bosnia and Herzegovina one day, and it should therefore make every effort to help these centers exist beyond that point in time. The staff needs to be encouraged that it is both possible for the centers to continue and essential for them to do so—due to the long-term reality of the healing process.
- financial capacity training and scheduled workshops on proposal writing and management training at the centers. These are a beginning (if also applied to the staff and not just community groups). But they need to be coupled with other training approaches that emphasize creative and community-oriented capacity building. This training should also provide exercises and discussions on independence and possibility—often difficult subjects after historically strong socialist models and recent international organizational ones that have created a mentality of dependency.

Tolerance, coexistence, and reconciliation in Bosnia and Herzegovina depend on its people. Local WICP staff may prove to be part of the answer to these difficult problems. This necessitates capacity-building support for the future by CARE and other international organizations working with local partners. This is something that cannot be fully accomplished without a sense of history and a comprehensive approach to present and future realities. This author has argued that this approach should include

- giving full attention to ethnic identity and what threatens it.
- recognizing that ethnic identity and threat to it were factors leading to war and are part of the postwar reality in Bosnia and Herzegovina.
- linking identity threat and trauma to refugee return in order to address important historical and psychological aspects of the conflict.
- preparing for refugee return through psychosocial means—with both the returnees and those who receive them.
- understanding identity and nationalism, and power and nationalism, and where there is overlap and difference.
- recognizing the role of third-party "outsiders," and the difficulty of this role due to the lack of knowledge of the region, cultural issues, and the time needed to build trust.
- seeing the role of the outsider as a catalyst for change once trust is established.
- learning to listen and be present with people, and understanding that this is often related to the values brought to the context.
- understanding that reconciliation is a process that is often a complex mix of trauma healing, encouraging dialogue, and rebuilding relationships, as well as helping build civil society, supporting development work, and rebuilding political and economic structures.
- finding ways to support community-based cooperation when refugees return in order to develop tolerance and provide ways for coexistence to happen—remembering that reconciliation workshops may not be the first step.
- linking forgiveness to justice and reconciliation and being aware of how difficult and contextual this linkage and set of issues are.

In Bosnia and Herzegovina, refugee return work will not be as effective without this and other criteria actively addressing the postconflict issues. That there are political barriers to putting these understandings and suggestions to work is a reality. Long-term commitment is necessary, as is a related factor, patience, to do the work while at the same time not rushing it and putting returnees in harm's way. Political awareness is also essential, and building cross-border and ethnic relationships becomes a critical part of the humanization process needed to build peace in the region. If these forces can successfully be brought together over time, then reconciliation among the various factions may one day become a reality.

Notes

1. Under the regional authority of the United Nations High Commissioner for Refugees (UNHCR), the Reconstruction and Return Task Force (RRTF) operates across BiH and Croatia. It was created as a result of the December 1997 Social Policy Conference sponsored by the World Bank, the International Federation of the Red Cross (IFRC), the European Committee Humanitarian Office (ECHO), and CARE International. It developed a Provisional Action Plan for 1999 outlining an intensive program which emphasizes "space, security and sustainability" for returning populations.

2. Some historians believed that the Slavs came from the land between the Danube and the Carpathian Mountains, while the one late Renaissance historian, the Benedictine monk Mauro Orbini, believed that they were Goths frin Scandinavia. See Judah (1997, 7) and Malcolm (1996, 5).

3. Humanizing Nationalism is described by Wiehe (1996) as "a political expression of the desire among people who believe they have a common ancestry and common destiny to govern themselves in a place peculiarly identified with their history and it fulfillment." Nationalism, from a more radical Serb perspective, says this "place" can be anywhere that Serb blood has been spilt. This claim, along with the need to protect Serbs throughout Yugoslavia, became a justification for Serb expansionism leading to the 1991-1995 wars.

4. Although the first Yugoslav state (1918-1941) allowed the country's major ethnic groups to be constituted as nations within the new federation, Pesic (1996) believes that there were always "strident, ethnocentric [and] national ideologies . . . [which] preordained the failure of any attempt to constitute Yugoslavia as a modern unitary and liberal state."

5. In 1994, a coalition brokered by the United States was formed between Croatia and BiH to attempt to prevent further (Bosnian) Serb expansionism in the region. Militarily, this coalition helped equalize the balance of power in BiH and was a critical factor leading to the final cease-fire in October of 1995.

6. Section I, number 13 of the Annex to the Madrid Declaration on Peace Implementation states, "The Council is fully aware of the close link between progress in returns and progress in other crucial areas, such as the rule of law and economic reconstruction." It also acknowledges that returnees "need jobs, and a safe environment reliably policed."

7. The World Conference on Religion and Peace (WCRP), Moral Rearmament (MRA), the Center for Strategic and International Studies (CSIS), and other organizations have done significant work with religious practitioners and leaders. Long-term relationships have been formed and training for understanding and reconciliation offered in a multireligious effort at peacebuilding across BiH and the rest of ex-Yugoslavia.

8. The European Community has invested 700 million Euro ($750 million) in Bosnian reconstruction. Many hundreds of million dollars have been invested by other nations in BiH. Officials believe that the peace process is still struggling, and "the prospect for lasting success appear[s] shaky." See Barry James's article, "EU's Daunting Roadmap to Kosovo Peace: Bosnia," in the April 16, 1999. *International Herald Tribune*.

9. Two-way return is an essential factor for building tolerance, leading to coexistence and eventual reconciliation. The relatively quick development of property laws in the Federation part of BiH has been an important element in the return process. But instituting these laws has been long delayed in Republika Srpska (RS), the mainly Serb part of BiH, adding to the plethora of factors hindering minorities moving to and from the

RS. If these minorities cannot return to their homes in the RS or in significant numbers from there to the Federation, ethnic cleansing will have been successful.

10. There are different understandings of the extent of war trauma in ex-Yugoslavia as well as what the most appropriate methods are for working on this trauma where it does exists. Moreover, there may be little or no linkage of this work to social development in a postwar context. Stubbs (1997, 6) believes "psychosocial projects" are often formed by psychologists and NGOs who may have "crude psychologistic notions of 'war trauma' [which leads] to an inappropriate medicalization of the consequences of war." This in turn "distances NGO work from social development agendas."

11. WICP sites in Federation BiH include the centers in Mostar, Gorazde, Hadzici, Vogosca, Zavidovici (formerly located in Zenica), and two new centers soon to be established in Glamoc and Fojnica. In the Republika Srpska the centers are located in Doboj and Derventa. This proposal was written to the European Committee Humanitarian Office (ECHO) by CARE staff.

12. Amor Masovic (1998), director of the Bosnian government's exhumation program, believes that solving the missing persons problem will play the greatest role in peacebuilding in the region. With 20,000 officially missing persons (and 10,000 more believed to be missing), he points to all the persons affected by this painful reality and their need for closure on the subject. Until this happens, he believes, the wounds of war will remain open and the anger at the perpetrators never healed.

13. UNICEF Training Manual: Kukatonon: Training Manual of Conflict Resolution, Reconciliation, and Peace.

14. The Center for Strategic and International Studies does training in conflict resolution, trauma healing, and reconciliation with religious leaders in the former Yugoslavia. The strategy is to do city or regional seminars with mixed groups of Muslims, Catholic and Orthodox Christians, and Protestants. At the next level of the training representatives from the various places are brought together in a neutral venue. Pec, Hungary, was often used for these seminars.

15. Jezdimir Milosevic (1999), a Bosnian writer, recently published the book, *Svjetla u Tunelu* (*Lights in the Tunnel*), which tells the stories of those people who helped or protected members of other ethnic groups during the war in BiH.

References

Clements, K. 1997. Home Truths. New Routes (February). Peace Media Service.
Uppsala, Sweden: Life and Peace Institute.

Hart, B. 1998. Ethnicity, Politics and Fear: Conflict and Its Transformation in the Former Yugoslavia. Visiting scholar lecture. Harrisonburg, Va.: James Madison University.

———. 1998. Welcome and Information Center Project Staff Survey.

Holbrooke, R. 1998. *To End a War*. New York: Random House.

James, B. 1999. EU's Daunting Roadmap to Kosovo Peace: Bosnia. *International Harold Tribune. April 16.*

Judah, T. 1997. *The Serbs*. New Haven, Conn.: Yale University Press.

Malcolm, N. 1996. *Bosnia: A Short History*. New York: New York University Press.

Masovic, A. 1998. Interview with author, August.

Milosevic, J. 1999. *Svjetla u Tunelu*. Sarajevo, BiH: Protector.

Northrup, T. 1989. The Dynamic of Identity in Personal and Social Change. In *Intractable Conflicts and Their Transformation*. L. Kriesburg, T. Northrup and S. Thorson, eds. Syracuse, N.Y.: Syracuse University Press.

Nudler, O. 1990. Quoted in: Fisher, R. J. 1990. Needs Theory, Social Identity and an Eclectic Model of Conflict. In *Conflict: Human Needs Theory*. John Burton, ed. New York: St. Martin's Press.

ONASA News Agency Reports. December 1998 and January 1999. Sarajevo, Bosnia, and Herzegovina.

Peace Watch. 1998. Bosnia to Form a Single Truth Commission. Washington, D.C.: United States Institute of Peace Press, February.

Pesic, V. 1996. Serbian Nationalism. Peaceworks, no. 8. Washington, D.C.: United States Institute of Peace Press, April.

RRFT Report, 1998. United Nations High Commissioner for Refugees' Reconstruction and Return Taskforce. United Nations.

Stovel, L. 1998. Confronting Prejudice in a Post-Ethnic-War Environment: NGO Education for Peace in Bosnia. Master's thesis. Department of Educational Studies, University of British Columbia.

Stubbs, P. 1997. Forced Migration, Refuge and Repatriation in Croatia and Bosnia-Herzegovina: NGOs in the New Security and Development Paradigm. Article written for the project, "The Role of NGOs in the Repatriation of Refugees." Sited with permission from the author.

UNHCR Report. 1998. A Regional Strategy for Sustainable Return of Those Displaced by Conflict in the Former Yugoslavia. Developed for presentation to the Humanitarian Issues Working Group, June 26.

UNICEF Training Manual. 1993. Kukatonon: Training Manual of Conflict Resolution, Reconciliation, and peace. Monrovia, Liberia: UNICEF.

Volkan, V., and Harris, M. 1993. Shaking the Tent: The Psychodynamics of Ethnic Terrorism. Monograph No. 1. Center for the Study of Mind and Human Interaction, University of Virginia.

Volkan, V. 1996. *Mind and Human Interaction*. Vol. 7, no. 3. Center for the Study of Mind and Human Interaction, University of Virginia.

Wiehe, R. H. 1996. Humanizing Nationalism. *World Policy Journal*, winter 1996/1997. Vol 13, no. 4.

16

Justice and Reconciliation

Postconflict Peacebuilding in Cambodia and Rwanda

Wendy Lambourne

Since 1945, only one-third of the negotiated settlements of "identity civil wars" (or ethnic conflicts) have resulted in lasting peace (Crocker and Hampson 1996). Postconflict peacebuilding is evidently not a simple process. The efforts of the international community to promote peace in societies recovering from violent conflict are further complicated when there has not been a negotiated peace settlement, as in Rwanda after the genocide in 1994. In the aftermath of genocide, the peacebuilding process faces even greater challenges in dealing with the total devastation of societies and individuals physically, psychologically, structurally, politically, economically, socially, and spiritually. [1]

Postconflict peacebuilding may be defined as a set of strategies designed to promote a secure and stable lasting peace in which the basic human needs of the population are met and violent conflicts do not recur. This definition incorporates the goals of both negative peace (absence of physical violence) and positive peace (absence of structural violence). In order to be successful, postconflict peacebuilding must address the underlying causes of conflict in addition to the surface manifestations such as the military culture and proliferation of weapons. The peacebuilding process involves such activities as economic reconstruction and development assistance; refugee repatriation and reintegration; promotion of the rule of law and respect for human rights; development of police forces and judiciaries; strengthening of civil society; election monitoring; support for democratization; demining, disarmament, demobilization of militaries; prosecution of war criminals; and trauma healing and reconciliation workshops.

The international community (other than the nongovernment sector) has in the past primarily concentrated its energies and resources on other stages of the conflict cycle, including peacemaking, humanitarian intervention, and peacekeeping. Expanded peacekeeping missions such as that in Cambodia (1992-1993) have included many peacebuilding components, but mostly without the long-term commitment necessary to achieve lasting peace. The United Nations and international state actors have been reluctant to maintain support for postconflict reconstruction and development, and until recently there has been little emphasis on the need for justice and psychological reconciliation between peoples traumatized by ethnic or political violence.[2] These aspects have generally been left to the national government in question and nongovernment organizations (NGOs) to implement.[3] However, there are signs that the balance of focus is changing, as the international community becomes more involved in the implementation of accountability mechanisms in the pursuit of justice and reconciliation. For example, the extent of violence (and failure of the international community to prevent the escalation of that violence) in the former Yugoslavia and Rwanda triggered the establishment of the first ad hoc international war crimes tribunals since Nuremberg. An increasing number of international agencies are also promoting processes of reconciliation and healing in postconflict situations.[4]

There is, however, little clarity on definitions and insufficient analysis of the best means of achieving the goals of justice and reconciliation in different conflict circumstances and cultural contexts.[5] There has been a lack of discussion in policy circles about the relationship between mechanisms and desired outcomes in terms of justice and reconciliation. Assumptions are made about, for example, the impact of international criminal trials on national reconciliation. The question of "justice for whom?" and the role of indigenous concepts of law and justice are often not taken into account by international intervenors. This chapter explores the concepts of justice and reconciliation and their relevance to the international community's contributions to peacebuilding in two postgenocidal settings, Cambodia and Rwanda.

Justice

The need for justice is a strong motivating force in human life, whether it plays out in violent revenge or the application of legal principles in court. As a concept, it has been accepted as part of political discourse since the "golden age of Athens" (Shriver 1995) and is a central tenet of monotheistic religious doctrine. The definition of justice assumed in Western legal traditions is based on the ideas of retribution and restitution (or reparation). Retribution originally meant a settling of one's accounts, involving both the punishment of evil and rewarding of good deeds, but has become associated solely with punishment and revenge in common usage in the twentieth century (Borneman 1997). Restitution, meaning the recovery of losses or compensation to rectify harms, generally takes the form of a financial payment made to the victim either by the offender or by the state.

Some traditional justice systems (such as the *gacaca* system in Rwanda)[6] involve the concept of restorative justice where the emphasis is placed on restoring relationships between the parties in a conflict instead of inflicting punishment (Tutu 1999). Restorative justice is based on recognition of the humanity of both offender and victim, and the goal is to heal the wounds of every person affected by the conflict or offense (Consedine 1995). Options are explored that focus on repairing the damage, and thus the concept of restitution also plays a role in the implementation of restorative justice. Truth commissions can provide a form of restorative justice by allowing an opportunity for reconciliation between victims and perpetrators. Typically, victims are able to tell their stories and perpetrators acknowledge what they have done, often in return for amnesty.[7] Truth commissions can also contribute to achieving restitutive justice by providing compensation for victims. International tribunals, by contrast, are aimed primarily at achieving retributive justice and are limited in their ability to promote restorative justice because of their reliance on an adversarial approach to dispute settlement.

Another legal justice concept, procedural justice, is concerned with fair treatment in making and implementing decisions that determine the outcome of a court case. This type of justice is particularly hard to achieve in the aftermath of genocide or other mass violence when the police and judicial systems have been destroyed. This was true in both Cambodia and Rwanda, and thus, it can be expected that survivors will not be completely satisfied with the implementation of legal justice if it is perceived to be procedurally unfair or biased.

The other major category of substantive justice concepts relates to economic and social justice. Distributive or economic justice is concerned with giving each person his or her proper share and achieving a fair outcome, and is linked to both restitutive and restorative justice. In cases where one group has suffered economic discrimination over many years, economic justice may take the form of programs to lift the disadvantaged group out of poverty. There is clearly a link between people's desire for economic justice and the role of the international community in providing development assistance and the national government's promotion of socioeconomic reconstruction. Social justice is closely linked with economic justice and is achieved when socially disadvantaged groups are provided with some means (most commonly structural) of achieving social equality with the dominant group. For example, policies designed to ensure equal access for all to social services will foster a sense of social justice. Lack of socioeconomic justice is a major contributing factor in causing many violent conflicts and genocides, including those in Cambodia and Rwanda (Chandler 1996; Uvin 1998). Postconflict peacebuilding processes must therefore address the economic as well as legal justice needs of the population in order to promote the attainment of positive peace.

Finally, symbolic justice (as distinct from substantive legal or socioeconomic justice) also plays a role in promoting peace and reconciliation. Symbolic justice can be achieved when victims perceive that authorities or perpetrators acknowledge the injustice that they have experienced, even in the absence of substantive retributive or restitutive justice. This can be quite powerful, especially in cases where human rights abuses have been previously unacknowledged. Truth commissions that produce a public, official historical account of abuses and allow victims a chance to tell their stories can provide a sense of symbolic justice. Public apologies and commemorations are also aimed at achieving symbolic justice. If national or international trials of war criminals fail to deliver procedural or restitutive justice, or satisfactory retributive justice, at least they can contribute to achieving symbolic justice.

The various categories of justice identified above tend to overlap and interact, and any particular individual may value one type of justice over another at different times and in different circumstances. Added to this are the differing cultural interpretations of justice that need to be taken into account in designing postconflict peacebuilding programs to address the multiple justice needs of the population in question. Both Cambodia and Rwanda have traditional indigenous concepts of justice and legal mechanisms, but these have been overlaid with the European justice system brought by the French and Belgians, respectively, and, in the case of Cambodia, by the communist system introduced by the Vietnamese. This was reflected in the responses this author received when interviewing Cambodians and Rwandans about the meaning of justice.[8] For example, one Tutsi survivor defined justice, saying, "Somebody who is a victim of something gets compensation and the person responsible gets sentenced," clearly a combination of restitutive and retributive components, but not including the restorative component evident in the traditional gacaca system of justice. Similarly, one Cambodian described how the traditional justice system was restorative, while another defined justice in terms of retribution and restitution: "Truth first, then victims need to get redress and criminals need to be made to pay for their crimes." Many of the Cambodians interviewed mentioned socioeconomic justice as being important in addition to legal justice, while the Rwandans focused much more on the need for legal justice. It is therefore not a simple process to identify the most important justice needs in the aftermath of genocide.

Reconciliation

The concept of reconciliation had its origins in Christian theology, and only recently has the term found its way into political discourse (see, e.g., Frost 1991 and Shriver 1995). Reconciliation between individuals or groups requires the involvement of two or more parties in an interaction of apology and forgiveness and the willingness to embark on a new relationship based on acceptance and trust. The ability to forgive and reconcile with an enemy has been described as a profound process of psychological and spiritual healing and transformation (see, e.g., Borris 1997; Assefa 1993). The Rwandan definition of reconciliation, as expressed in the local language of Kinyarwanda, also implies a personal, two-way process. To quote from a Tutsi survivor: "Reconciliation should be between the victim and the person responsible—a new beginning because the relationship is broken and [one] should start anew and rebuild the relationship."[9]

The more secular definitions of reconciliation offered by authors such as Ackermann (1994) and Kriesberg (1998) seem to equate more with the idea of coexistence (as discussed later in this paper) than the type of spiritual transformation outlined above. For example, Kriesberg (1998, 1-2) defines reconciliation as "the process of developing a mutual conciliatory accommodation between antagonistic or formerly antagonistic persons or groups," while Ackermann (1994, 230) maintains that "reconciliation functions as a postwar reconstruction policy, designed to build peace among peoples with long-standing animosities by creating a political, economic, social and cultural relationship that is . . . ongoing and continuous." This approach seems to be more in line with the Cambodian use of the term *national reconciliation* which implies a more pragmatic, politically motivated group process of reconciliation. When Cambodians were asked about their definition of reconciliation they tended to equate the term *reconciliation* with *national reconciliation*, describing it as being "an act of compromise" to "avoid new war or new conflict" or "striking a balance of interest in pursuit of collective interest." One Cambodian interviewee explained how forgiveness and reconciliation are linked to Christian values and are not part of the Buddhist tradition.

It is understandably difficult for the survivors of genocide to contemplate the idea of forgiveness and reconciliation with the perpetrators. And yet, paradoxically, it is in this extreme case that forgiveness and reconciliation are most important. It is not easy, but it should be considered essential in the long term if the survivors and perpetrators are ever to come to terms with what they have suffered or committed. The individual who does not forgive and the group that does not forgive are likely to remain victims of their feelings of revenge or guilt. Not only will they not be at peace with the other, they will not be at peace with themselves. At a psychological level, they could be open to encouragement or manipulation by political or military leaders to wreak revenge on the other group. Cycles of violence can only be short-circuited if a process of reconciliation is entered into. Only by recognizing the sufferings and understanding the motives of the other group can a survivor of genocide ever live together in peace with members of the group that perpetrated the genocide. Similarly, only by acknowledging and expressing contrition for the crimes they have committed and the suffering they have caused can perpetrators ever hope to live together with members of the victim group.

All this does not mean that reconciliation should be equated with a culture of impunity or that perpetrators of genocide should not be punished under international law. Processes of legal justice and reconciliation need to go hand in hand and not be seen as alternatives. As described by Lederach (1995, 1997), reconciliation can be seen as the bringing together of justice and mercy in a process of understanding and forgiveness integrating both secular and spiritual aspects. Reconciliation implies the acknowledgment of wrongs committed, and compassion toward the perpetrator should not be equated with condoning the crimes committed. Without justice, forgiveness can perpetuate impunity. Individual perpetrators, and particularly the leaders and organizers, should be held accountable.

The complex interaction between the need for justice and the need for reconciliation is particularly difficult to manage in the aftermath of genocide. Because of the extremes of suffering and feelings of victimhood, and the legal obligation to punish the perpetrators, the pressure for criminal prosecutions is increased. Criminal trials for the key perpetrators provide a sense of retributive and symbolic justice that may be necessary before the survivors can contemplate reconciliation. However, this focus on retribution competes with the need for a public acknowledgment and reconciliation process that can heal the relationship between the victim and perpetrator individually or as a group. This tension can be seen in both Rwanda and Cambodia, where calls for legal justice have tended to overshadow the development of any mechanisms for dealing with the need for restorative justice. For example, both the international community and the Rwandan government had by mid-1996 established courts based on the Western legal system for dealing with the genocide perpetrators. However, it was not until early 2000 that, in the interests of promoting reconciliation, the Rwandan government reinstituted the gacaca system to deal with some of the backlog of genocide suspects being held in jails throughout the country.

Coexistence

Coexistence means "peoples of different political and social systems, living in mutual toleration" (*Concise Oxford Dictionary*). The use of the word *toleration* implies that people are willing to endure or permit others with different customs, beliefs, or values to exist without condemnation or persecution. As such, the goal of peaceful coexistence would be a minimum requirement of any multicultural society, where different ethnic groups are required to share the same geographical space, including in the aftermath of violent ethnic conflict or genocide.

However, peaceful coexistence, while necessary, is not sufficient for successful conflict resolution. In the terminology of John Burton, the goal of coexistence may be seen as equating with dispute management or settlement, but not resolution, as it does not deal with the underlying psychological causes of the conflict (Burton and Dukes 1990).[10] Achieving social and economic justice can promote peaceful coexistence, but the deeply held hatreds and view of the other as the enemy can only be changed with a complete psychological transformation that is part of the process of reconciliation. If the postconflict peacebuilding process stops at peaceful coexistence and fails to address the need for reconciliation, then the ethnic hatreds and desire for vengeance may simmer just below the surface, ready to reassert themselves in further violent conflict or even genocide some time in the future.

Reconciliation is thus a much more demanding and possibly unrealistic goal for postconflict peacebuilding, especially in the aftermath of genocide. The goal of peaceful coexistence may be seen as a necessary first step, but without some form of reconciliation this peaceful coexistence is unlikely to last (or even be achieved in the first place). Peaceful coexistence remains vulnerable to disruption and new outbreaks of conflict or violence if reconciliation is absent. Reconciliation, over and above peaceful coexistence, is necessary for people or societies who need to live or work together in the long term.

Cambodia

History of the Conflict and the Pol Pot Regime

Cambodia was once a great nation covering much of Southeast Asia, with its own distinct Khmer culture influenced by India's two great religions, Hinduism and Buddhism. Culminating in the Angkor dynasty, the glorious Khmer Empire lasted from the seventh to the thirteeenth century, after which it was progressively weakened by invasions from its neighbors Siam (now Thailand) and Vietnam. In 1863 Cambodia became a French protectorate and then colony until 1953, when King Norodom Sihanouk regained the country's independence.

After seventeen years of relative peace as an independent country, Cambodia became drawn into the Vietnam War. In 1969 the U.S. Air Force had begun secretly bombing Cambodia in an effort to eliminate the Vietnamese communist bases, and the anti-Vietnamese Lon Nol government took power in Cambodia (renamed the Khmer Republic). Sihanouk, now in self-imposed exile, forged a coalition with the communist-backed Khmer Rouge who fought a civil war with the U.S.-backed Lon Nol government. In 1975 the United States withdrew from Vietnam, Phnom Penh fell to the Khmer Rouge, and the Cambodian people were subjected to three years of the brutal Khmer Rouge regime led by Pol Pot.

The Pol Pot regime (Democratic Kampuchea) was reportedly responsible for the deaths of an estimated one to two million Cambodians (approximately 25 percent of the population), and the extent of human rights violations has been described as the worst to have occurred anywhere in the world since Nazism (Chanda 1986). As described by Kiernan (1997, 191),

> During the Pol Pot period, from April 1975 to January 1979, Cambodia was subjected to what was likely the world's most radical politi-

cal, social, and economic revolution. The country was cut off from the outside world; foreign and minority languages were banned; its cities were emptied; and all its neighboring countries were attacked militarily. Schools and hospitals were closed, and the labor force was conscripted. The economy was militarized, and the nation's currency, wages, and markets were abolished. Many of Cambodia's families were separated; its majority Buddhist religion, along with other religions and folk cultures, were destroyed; and 1.5 million of its nearly eight million people were starved to death or massacred.

In response to border incursions and military skirmishes, the Vietnamese mounted a full-scale invasion of Cambodia in December 1978. In January 1979 Phnom Penh fell to the Vietnamese, and the Khmer Rouge retreated to the Thai border. The Vietnamese-backed Heng Samrin government was installed in Phnom Penh, and the country's name was changed to the People's Republic of Kampuchea (PRK). The international community condemned the Vietnamese invasion, and the Pol Pot regime continued to be recognized as the official government of Cambodia by the UN. In 1989 the Phnom Penh government with Hun Sen as prime minister renounced communism and changed the country's name to the State of Cambodia, and the Vietnamese removed the last of their occupation troops. UN-sponsored peace negotiations finally led to the Paris Peace Agreement of October 1991 and elections in May 1993 under the supervision of the United Nations Transitional Authority in Cambodia (UNTAC). The election resulted in a coalition government with Prince Ranariddh (Sihanouk's son) and Hun Sen (leader of the pro-Vietnamese Cambodian People's Party) as co-prime ministers. However, following a coup against Ranariddh and his other opponents in July 1997, Hun Sen declared himself sole prime minister of Cambodia and remained so after the 1998 elections, despite allegations of electoral impropriety and failure to gain a clear majority of votes (Downie, 2000).

No Justice or Reconciliation

Following the genocidal Pol Pot regime, there were no significant or effective official public processes of acknowledgment, apology, or legal justice implemented in Cambodia, despite the numerous initiatives proposed by the international community and the Cambodian government. Nor were there any official international acts of condemnation or prosecution.[11] The PRK government did hold a trial of the Khmer Rouge leaders, Pol Pot and Ieng Sary, in Phnom Penh in August 1979, but the sentence (of death in absentia) was not recognized internationally because of due-process objections to the trial procedures and the diplomatic isolation of the PRK regime (Vickery and Roht-Arriaza 1995). The Khmer Rouge, meanwhile, was able to maintain its strongholds in towns such as Pailin near the Thai border, from which point it would continue its guerrilla activities with impunity for the next twenty years. The

Khmer Rouge remained a threat to the local populations as well as to foreign tourists and aid workers until the organization was formally disbanded in 1998 after the death of Pol Pot and the defections of two of the last of the former Khmer Rouge leaders, Khieu Samphan and Nuon Chea.[12]

Once the Cold War was over, the UN played a significant role in rebuilding peace in Cambodia, but the issues of justice and reconciliation were totally ignored in the final peace agreement. During peace negotiations, the Hun Sen government apparently stressed the issue of genocide and the need to bring the perpetrators to justice, but the United States and China supported the Khmer Rouge in blocking any moves in this direction. The final peace agreement did not preclude the Khmer Rouge from participating in the Cambodian elections, nor did it prevent former officials of the Khmer Rouge associated with the genocide from holding office in the future. Numerous Khmer Rouge leaders subsequently defected and joined the Cambodian government and military. In the interests of "national reconciliation," the Hun Sen government accepted the former Khmer Rouge and, in some cases, offered immunity from prosecution.

An International Tribunal for Cambodia?

Since early 1997, the UN has been trying to establish an international criminal tribunal for the Khmer Rouge, and in June 1997 the Cambodian government expressed its support for such a tribunal. U.S. officials continued to reiterate their commitment to bringing senior Khmer Rouge leaders to justice (despite the death of Pol Pot in April 1998), and in November 1998 a panel of UN experts visited Cambodia to assess the scope for an international genocide tribunal.[13] The Group of Experts' report recommended that the UN establish an ad hoc international tribunal covering the Pol Pot period from April 1975 to January 1979 that could charge the Khmer Rouge with offenses such as genocide, crimes against humanity, destruction of cultural property, forced labor, and torture.[14]

In March 1999, Kofi Annan submitted a proposal for an international tribunal to both the Security Council and the General Assembly, but the tribunal has not yet been established despite continuing negotiations between the UN and the Cambodian government.[15] Prime Minister Hun Sen formally rejected an international tribunal as being a threat to the country's fragile national reconciliation, and indicated his preference for national trials with foreign legal assistance.[16] The Hun Sen government is reluctant to cede control to the international community despite the commonly held belief that the Cambodian justice system could not deliver fair trials for the former Khmer Rouge. On January 6, 2000, almost twenty-one years after the end of the Khmer Rouge regime, the Cambodian government indicated it would approve a draft law setting up a tribunal to try the former Khmer Rouge leaders. The UN, because of legal flaws and procedural inadequacies, rejected this proposal, but the Cambodian government says it will go ahead with or without UN support.[17] A year later, the Cambodian government finally passed legislation allowing for the establishment of the tribunal. As of 13 January 2001, the U.S. government seemed confident that the outstanding issues would be resolved enabling a final agreement to be reached between Cambodia and the UN on the composition and functioning of the tribunal.[18]

Reconciliation Mechanisms

The UN Group of Experts recommended that Cambodia also set up a "process of reflection" and possibly a "truth-telling mechanism" dealing with the history of Khmer Rouge atrocities, but the United States rejected the truth commission approach as being an inadequate substitute for international accountability.[19] Following the UN Group of Experts' visit, Prime Minister Hun Sen spoke about the possibility of a Cambodian truth commission based on the South African model, but the proposal did not gain much support and was not acted upon.[20] The reaction of the Cambodians whom this author interviewed in October 1999 was mixed: some thought it was too late for a truth-telling mechanism ("we have been telling the truth all these years"), some thought it was too soon (a tribunal should come first), while others thought it would not work in a Buddhist country. Very few expressed any enthusiasm about the idea of a truth commission for Cambodia.

In the absence of such a formal reconciliation mechanism, nongovernment organizations (NGOs) such as the Center for Social Development have pursued other avenues to promote reconciliation. In early 2000, public forums on "National Reconciliation and the Khmer Rouge" were being organized. For the first time, the Cambodian people were given the opportunity to publicly debate the issues of justice and reconciliation. At the first meeting held in Battambang (near the former Khmer Rouge stronghold of Pailin), the majority of speeches were against a trial, but the 120 participants (including a large contingent of former Khmer Rouge cadre) voted in favor of a Khmer Rouge tribunal in a secret ballot at the end of the forum. Almost two-thirds believed a trial would be beneficial for national reconciliation.[21] This result is consistent with the comments made during this author's interviews in Phnom Penh: almost all said that the former Khmer Rouge leaders should be tried and punished for their crimes.[22]

One of the Khmer Rouge leaders who defected at the end of 1998, Khieu Samphan, apologized to the people of Cambodia, although it is not clear whether this was an authentic plea for forgiveness or a cynical ploy to encourage the Cambodian people to forget the past and any idea of trials.[23] Most of the Cambodians interviewed were skeptical about the authenticity of Khieu Samphan's apology ("saying sorry is simple," "it's just a word," "it doesn't mean anything"), and some suggested that he did it for the benefit of the international press in order to gain sympathy from the international community.

It seems that, even after twenty-one years, the Cambodian people are calling for justice before reconciliation can be contemplated.

There are, however, a number of foreign and local NGOs working to promote justice and reconciliation in Cambodia. Nonofficial investigations and documentation of the genocide have provided some form of acknowledgment of people's sufferings and hopefully a valuable healing opportunity. One of the most significant is the U.S.-funded Cambodian Genocide Program (CGP), which has been working since 1994 on producing a thorough documentation of the genocide, researching the conflict and undertaking training of Cambodian judges, lawyers, police, and human rights activists so they can participate effectively in achieving accountability of the Khmer Rouge (Etcheson 1997). However, the lack of public awareness of the Documentation Centre and its information resources is limiting its impact on the Cambodian people.[24] Other local projects have perhaps had more impact on the process of reconciliation, including Thai and Cambodian Buddhist monks organizing peace marches and assisting in revitalizing the Buddhist religion and temples (Colletta, Kostner, and Wiederhofer 1996).[25]

Culture of Impunity

The policy of impunity for perpetrators of genocide, and the inclusion of the Khmer Rouge in the political process, have arguably not aided the reconciliation process and have certainly not produced a lasting peace in Cambodia. The lack of firmness of UNTAC with the Khmer Rouge seemed to reduce the compliance of the new Cambodian government with the terms of the peace agreement, especially in relation to the implementation of human rights protection (Vickery and Roht-Arriaza 1995). There are continuing reports of government human rights abuses in Cambodia: prison conditions remain poor; arbitrary arrest is a problem; detainees have been tortured and killed; and the legal system is marred by inefficiency, lack of training and resources, and corruption (U.S. Department of State 2000). Government-sponsored violence continues, human rights protection mechanisms are ineffective, the government is unstable, no compensation has been provided for the victims of the Pol Pot era, and the Khmer Rouge leaders have not been held accountable. How can Cambodians be expected to respect the rule of law or be willing to embrace reconciliation if the perpetrators of such massive crimes against humanity are allowed to walk free, and in some cases are given "VIP treatment" (quote from a Cambodian interviewee)?[26]

In short, no sense of justice—retributive, restitutive or restorative, legal or symbolic—has been achieved for the Cambodian people. There has been little evidence of authentic atonement from the former Khmer Rouge.[27] The Cambodian people are aware of this, and the survivors still bear the scars. While some have expressed a spirit of forgiveness, there is a great deal of resistance to consider even a peaceful coexistence with the former Khmer Rouge ("They should be in jail"). The Cambodian people were not consulted during the peace negotiations. They were given a chance to vote for a government, but were not given a chance to express their needs and desires in relation to justice and reconciliation. The international community and the national government decided that a policy of impunity would best serve the interests of "national reconciliation." This definition of reconciliation ignores the needs of the people for psychological reconciliation—to heal the wounds of the past through a process of acknowledgment, apology, and forgiveness. The climate of impunity also denied the Cambodian people their right to justice—to see those who had harmed them held accountable and punished. There was a peace settlement and a peacekeeping mission, but no credible official justice or reconciliation process.

Rwanda

History of the Conflict and the 1994 Genocide

The precolonial history of Rwanda reveals a succession of interclan fighting and expansion of a dominant ruling class over a bonded labor class not unlike the British feudal system. Indistinguishable in terms of language and religion, but identifiable by their different physical appearance and occupational ties, the predominantly cattle-owning Tutsis achieved political domination over the majority Hutu agriculturalist population during the fifteenth to nineteenth centuries. However, this relationship was by all accounts more symbiotic than exploitative, and the categories of Tutsi and Hutu were treated as interchangeable according to a person's status rather than being seen as a fixed ethnic identity. Intermarriages were common. The interethnic hatred and cycles of violence and revenge between the two groups that we see today did not begin until the end of the colonial era.

Germany colonized Rwanda in 1885, but following World War I the colony became a trustee territory of Belgium. As in other parts of the world, these colonial powers followed the strategy of "divide and rule," reinforcing the division between Tutsi and Hutu. For the first time, identity cards were issued, so that the formerly fluid ethnic categories of Hutu and Tutsi became fixed. The Belgians used the Tutsi as the administrators of their harsh policies, and the Hutu became increasingly resentful—not of their colonial masters, but of the Tutsi monarchical system. The Hutus, encouraged by the Belgians in a policy turnaround, rebelled, and following a bloody civil war Rwanda achieved its independence and became a republic under Hutu leadership in 1962.

At the time of independence, an estimated 200,000 Tutsis fled the country and became refugees in neighboring Uganda, Zaire, Tanzania, and Burundi. The Hutu government maintained the ethnic identity system instituted by the Belgians and initiated a policy of discrimination against the minority Tutsi population in retaliation for the years of subjugation under Belgian/Tutsi rule.

The Tutsis of the diaspora tried on several occasions to return by force, but the Hutu government responded with periodic anti-Tutsi pogroms, a purge of Tutsis from universities, and a quota placed on Tutsis employed in civil service and teaching posts. In 1988 the Tutsi exiles and Hutu dissidents formed the Rwandan Patriotic Front (RPF), which launched several attacks on Rwanda between 1990 and 1993. The Hutu government conducted periodic massacres of Tutsis in Rwanda in retaliation for the RPF invasions. During this period of discrimination, violence, and exile, the ethnic identities of Hutu and Tutsi and cycles of revenge became entrenched.

A succession of cease-fire agreements and peace talks in July 1992 and March 1993 finally culminated in the Arusha Peace Agreement, signed in August 1993. But in April 1994 the presidents of Rwanda and Burundi were killed in a suspicious plane crash outside Kigali, triggering the onset of the mass killings by Hutu extremists of Tutsis and moderate Hutus perceived as their political enemies. The downing of the plane carrying Hutu President Habyarimana and the subsequent genocide appear to have been orchestrated by Hutu extremists determined to stop the power-sharing agreement about to be implemented by Habyarimana, as well as to eliminate the Tutsis from Rwanda once and for all.[28] The international community failed to intervene despite evidence of planned genocide, and the UN severely reduced its peacekeeping force after ten Belgian peacekeepers were killed (Feil 1998).

After three months of terror and violence in which thousands of Tutsi women were raped and between five hundred thousand and one million people were killed by the Hutu extremists and their followers, the RPF installed a new Tutsi-led government in July 1994.[29] As the RPF advanced into Rwanda, there were reports of revenge killings and human rights atrocities against the Hutu population. Thousands of Hutu refugees (including the genocide perpetrators) fled to neighboring Congo (former Zaire) and Tanzania, creating a massive humanitarian emergency that finally attracted some assistance from the international community. Most of these Hutu refugees have since been repatriated, although the extremists continue to be active in the border region. After thirty years of exile, many Tutsi refugees have also returned to their home country following the RPF victory, adding to the population pressures on this very small and very poor country.

The new Rwandan government comprises both Hutus and Tutsis, and its stated policy is one of inclusiveness, to the point where ethnic categories are no longer officially recognized. The stated aim of the government is to promote peaceful coexistence, but the fear of some is that denying ethnic differences may lead to greater violence in the future as a result of repressed ethnic tensions. Furthermore, the Tutsis retain effective control and occupy most of the key positions in the country, adding to the alienation and resentment felt by the Hutu population (Prunier 1997). The government's policy of achieving justice for the victims of the genocide is also seen as potentially divisive, as thousands of prisoners, mostly Hutus, are held in terrible jail conditions, facing unfair trials and possible execution.

Domestic Justice and Reconciliation

Legal justice is seen by both the international community and the national government as crucial to the peacebuilding process in Rwanda. A Rwandan law was passed in August 1996 authorizing prosecution of crimes committed during the genocide, but there are huge logistical problems in prosecuting all those accused. Rwanda's jails are overflowing with some 130,000 detainees, of whom about 2,000 have been designated as "Category One."[30] Some 95 percent of Rwanda's lawyers and judges were either killed or are in exile or in prison, making it very difficult for the criminal justice system to cope with the huge numbers of accused. As of December 1999, more than 1,500 of the accused had been tried and more than 300 sentenced to death, the first 22 of whom were executed in April 1998. In October 1998 the Rwandan government released 10,000 suspects, sparking fears of revenge killings, as reportedly occurred when some 1,500 detainees were released in 1997.

From the government's perspective, the detention and trial of perpetrators of the genocide are important steps toward ending the culture of impunity prevailing in Rwanda. The government sees legal accountability as an integral part of the reconciliation process.[31] This attitude was reflected by the Tutsi survivors and returnees interviewed by this author in Kigali in July 1998. While some did not agree with the Rwandan government's decision to hold the executions in public ("it is a continuation of the violence"), most of the Rwandans interviewed felt that justice demanded that the perpetrators of the genocide receive the death penalty ("I am against the death penalty in principle, but for the *genocidaires*, it is not enough"). The executions reportedly brought hope to some people in Rwanda, as they were able to see that the genocidaires would be punished. This contrasts with the official international response that such public killings could promote feelings of revenge rather than contribute to the process of national reconciliation.[32] In addition, the failure of the Rwandan government to prosecute RPF officers for massacres and other human rights abuses perpetrated during the invasion and subsequent years since the RPF has been in power, has led to the perception of "victor's justice" and criticism from both the Hutu population and the international community (Prunier 1997).

In an effort to deal with the overcrowded prisons and backlog of cases awaiting trial, the Rwandan government has taken steps to reintroduce the traditional gacaca system of justice. While the gacaca system will be community based, it will operate under a state law that was adopted by the Rwandan parliament in February 2000.[33] According to the vice-president of Rwanda's Supreme Court, Tharcisse Karugarama, "Rwanda is in desperate need of reconciliation . . . Going back to our traditional system—a system where both Tutsis and Hutus worked together—is one way of doing that."[34] It remains to be seen whether the gacaca courts as they are implemented will contribute to reconciliation, or become instruments of revenge and injustice as is feared by some commentators and Catholic bishops in Rwanda.[35]

The International Criminal Tribunal for Rwanda

Parallel international trials are under way in Arusha, Tanzania, under the auspices of the International Criminal Tribunal for Rwanda (ICTR). The ICTR was established by the UN in November 1994 to prosecute war crimes, crimes against humanity, and crimes of genocide committed in Rwanda during 1994. Its focus is on prosecuting the leaders and planners of the genocide, but, unlike the domestic judicial system, it does not have a mandate to impose the death penalty. After a slow start plagued with administrative difficulties and corruption, the ICTR has made significant progress and as of February 2000 had obtained custody of forty-five of the fifty-one suspects indicted, including the former prime minister, Jean Kambanda. The first two trials were completed and the judgements announced in September 1998. After pleading guilty to genocide, Kambanda was sentenced to life imprisonment, and Jean-Paul Akayesu, a former village mayor, begged for forgiveness and for a light sentence, but was ordered to serve three life sentences for genocide plus eighty years for other violations, including rape.[36] In February 1999, a former Rwandan militia leader, Omar Serushago, was sentenced to fifteen years in prison for crimes against humanity after pleading guilty and apologizing to the people of Rwanda for his role in the genocide. By January 2000, four more trials had been completed, resulting in three life sentences and one sentence of twenty-five years.

The establishment of the ICTR was specifically intended to help overcome the culture of impunity evident in Rwandan society and thereby to promote reconciliation and peacebuilding. The UN Security Council stated the aim of the ICTR as being, in part, "to contribute to the process of national reconciliation and to the restoration and maintenance of peace." One of the difficulties the ICTR faces in achieving this aim is the location of the ICTR in Arusha and the challenges inherent in communicating the proceedings of the tribunal to the Rwandan population. As a result, the proceedings of the ICTR have been seen as distant and irrelevant to most Rwandans.[37]

The lack of the death penalty and the slow pace of trials have also been a focus of Rwandan criticism of the ICTR and have significantly undermined the perception that justice is being done. On the other hand, the fact that many key perpetrators of the genocide have been arrested is a significant breakthrough in achieving accountability under international law and may in time contribute to peacebuilding and reconciliation in Rwanda. There is some recognition among Rwandans that only the ICTR could have arrested the so-called big fish who had fled the country, but there is also a perception that the accused are being held in comparative luxury. The penalty of life imprisonment in some comfortable Western jail is seen as insufficient and unlikely to satisfy the Rwandan people in their call for justice. The question of "justice for whom?" is relevant here. From an outsider's perspective, the ICTR has an important role to play in demonstrating equitable treatment of both sides in the conflict and hopefully providing some deterrence to future potential war criminals. In the short term, though, it does seem that the ICTR is doing more to assuage the guilt of the international community for not intervening earlier to stop the genocide than it is to promote a sense of justice for the Rwandan people.

Before the ICTR can contribute to the processes of justice and reconciliation in Rwanda, the public perception of the tribunal's deficiencies and the poor relationship between the Rwandan government and the ICTR observed during this author's visit need to be addressed. Significant steps in this direction have subsequently been taken, including the appointment of a Special Representative of the Government of Rwanda to the ICTR and the visit of a delegation of the Rwandan National Assembly to the ICTR in Arusha in October 1999. The delegation was reportedly impressed by the effectiveness and efficiency of the ICTR, and the Special Representative said that his government appreciated the "successes and improvements recorded by the ICTR in recent times."[38] It is hoped that these improvements in the functioning of the ICTR and the increased rate of prosecutions will have a positive impact on reconciliation in Rwanda.

One of the keys to reconciliation is the attitude and well-being of the survivors. And yet, the focus of the ICTR (like most Western courts of law) is on the perpetrator—proving his or her guilt or innocence—and on the upholding of the rule of law, rather than on the needs of the victims/survivors. Many of the survivors of genocide in Rwanda see the ICTR as a "waste of time and money." They are more interested in socioeconomic justice than criminal justice. Their needs are immediate and urgent—for health care and medicines, clothing, food for their children, housing, and for counseling to help them to deal with the trauma of being raped. Thus, in order to fulfill its mandate to contribute to reconciliation in Rwanda, the ICTR should provide its potential witnesses with physical and psychological support and some kind of reparations.[39] In this way, the survivors will have the opportunity to experience both retributive and restitutive justice, thus decreasing the likelihood that they will participate in retributive violence against the accused if they are released from the prisons in Rwanda. Only the survivors can forgive. Providing reparations and support mechanisms can be an entry point for the processes necessary for reconciliation.

A Truth Commission for Rwanda?

The process of reconciliation could be assisted by a truth commission modeled on the South African Truth and Reconciliation Commission (TRC), but with some important differences.[40] It would not be acceptable to the Rwandan people and the international community to allow amnesties in return for confessions due to the seriousness of the charges. Genocide, war crimes, and crimes against humanity are clearly breaches of international law and should not go unpunished. In both the local and international trials the focus is on the perpetrator. One advantage of a truth commission would be the emphasis on hearing and validating the stories of victims and survivors without needing to follow strict legal principles of admissibility of evidence. "A truth commission would be very important for Rwanda. Otherwise the people are closed up and could explode again in the future" (quote from a Tutsi returnee). The result could be a report that provides a unified account of the history of Rwanda and the injustices perpetrated against both Hutus and Tutsis. Such a truth commission could exist in parallel with the local and international trials, as was proposed in the former Yugoslavia.[41] However, attempts to establish a truth commission for Rwanda have not met with any success despite a visit by Rwandan officials to South Africa to examine the workings of the TRC, and a nongovernment project entitled "Conflict Prevention and Justice after Genocide" launched by a researcher in the Netherlands with the goal of establishing truth commissions and holding public hearings on the genocide in Rwanda.[42]

While the idea of creating a truth commission in Rwanda does not appear to have taken hold, the Rwandan government has encouraged prisoners to confess in return for reduced sentences. The assumption is that victims are more likely to accept lesser punishment if the perpetrators show remorse, thus facilitating the process of national reconciliation (Kritz 1997). At one of the first domestic trials, the defense lawyer said that the defendant should ask the people's forgiveness and be spared the death penalty, while the defendant himself told the court that "if his death would help bring about national reconciliation, then so be it" (UN DHA IRIN, March 7, 1997). To date, more than two thousand prisoners have reportedly confessed, but there are suspicions that their motives were to avoid punishment rather than to reflect true contrition for their crimes. Similarly, this author's interviews indicated that Rwandans regarded the confession of Kambanda during his trial at the ICTR as a cynical plea for mercy rather than an authentic expression of remorse: "Kambanda's confession didn't mean anything. He may be afraid of being killed. He deserves to be killed" (quote from a survivor). These confessions in the context of criminal prosecution are thus not expected to do much to further the cause of reconciliation in Rwanda: "Confessions made out of fear are not real and are therefore not useful for reconciliation" (quote from a Tutsi returnee).

> The thirst for vengeance in Rwanda is understandable. . . . The elimination of impunity is essential to ensure that the cycle of genocide is broken in Rwanda. National reconciliation will only be brought about when justice is seen to be done. . . . While doubting the main architects of the genocide feel any remorse for their actions, many Tutsis accept that they have to live side by side with their Hutu neighbours again, despite feelings of suspicion and mistrust. The tentative steps towards national reconciliation and rehabilitation must be respected and sensitively handled. (UN DHA IRIN, March 7, 1997)

Progress toward Justice and Reconciliation

It seems that the people of Rwanda are not yet ready or willing to embrace the concept of reconciliation on a large public scale. Allowing time for the healing or mourning process to reach a place of genuine forgiveness is critical (Montville 1993). Many survivors are not ready to forgive the perpetrators of the Rwandan genocide: "A Hutu asking for pardon should not be pardoned but should get justice" (quote from a Tutsi survivor). There are individual survivors who have forgiven the perpetrators and expressed their commitment to reconciliation, but they are in the minority.[43] Most of the survivors and returnees this author interviewed were not willing to reconcile; they were hurting and angry because of the betrayal by their friends and neighbors who killed, or they have not yet forgiven the Hutus for the years of discrimination and exile. The best hope for peace in Rwanda lies in time—to heal the wounds and to rebuild trust. The Tutsi survivors need to begin to trust their Hutu neighbors again, and the returnees need to overcome their fear of the return of majority Hutu rule, while the Hutus need to dissociate themselves from the guilt of being linked with genocide and to trust that the Tutsis will not take a bloody revenge. It was fear of the Tutsi invaders that enabled the Hutu extremist leaders to manipulate the masses into participating in their genocidal plans. Trust is therefore a key element in preventing a recurrence of such violence.[44]

A comprehensive sense of justice and reconciliation in Rwanda could be achieved by addressing the areas of legal justice, social and economic justice, and restorative justice. In other words, there is a need for the perpetrators of genocide to be punished in order to satisfy the retributive justice desires of the survivors; there is a need for social and economic programs to promote equality, nondiscrimination, and poverty reduction; and there is a need for relationship building, restorative justice programs which promote reconciliation between and within the two ethnic groups.[45] This author's observation was that such a comprehensive approach to peacebuilding is being implemented in Rwanda, albeit slowly and not without difficulty, and with insufficient attention to the restorative justice component. The government and international community are pursuing legal justice, and there are local and international NGOs involved in such projects as housing reconstruction, microcredit and economic empowerment, trauma healing, reconciliation workshops, joint Hutu/Tutsi activities, prisoner reintegration, health care, education, and youth programs. The Rwandan government has also recently created a National Unity and Reconciliation Commission with a mandate to encourage a culture of peace, unity, and reconciliation and to monitor government programs to ensure their observance of policies of national unity and reconciliation.[46] More resources are needed to support these programs, as well as greater trust and cooperation among the different sectors—government, NGOs, and the international community. My interviews suggested that this level of cooperation is improving, but there is still a long way to go, especially in terms of coordination and trust.

Conclusion

> With the aid of the international community, each society emerging from genocide, war crimes, or sustained mass repression will need to find the specific approach or combination of mechanisms which will help it achieve the optimal level of justice and reconciliation. (Kritz 1997, 23).

The approaches of the international community toward promoting justice and reconciliation as part of postconflict peacebuilding differed markedly in the two cases discussed. In Cambodia, the international community was at first deterred by Cold War constraints, political priorities, and respect for state sovereignty from condemning the atrocities of the Pol Pot regime. The 1991 peace agreement focused on economic reconstruction and the national unity and sovereignty of Cambodia, while the issue of legal justice was set aside because of perceived security dilemmas faced by the Cambodian people and the desire not to alienate the Khmer Rouge. The result was an expedient peace agreement that did not address the justice and reconciliation needs of the population and perpetuated a culture of impunity in Cambodia. Recent attempts by the international community to belatedly bring the former Khmer Rouge to justice have met with opposition from the Cambodian government, determined to protect its state sovereignty. By contrast, the international community's immediate response to the genocide in Rwanda was to establish an international tribunal aimed at achieving legal justice and contributing to reconciliation. However, the impact of the ICTR on promoting justice and reconciliation for the people of Rwanda has been undermined by the international community's inadequate understanding of these concepts, flawed implementation of the tribunal mechanism, and a lack of consideration for Rwandan approaches to justice and reconciliation (including the importance of reparations to promote socioeconomic justice).

There are also some similarities evident in the experiences of the international community in Cambodia and Rwanda that serve to identify further obstacles and challenges to the promotion of justice and reconciliation in the aftermath of genocide. In both cases, inadequate resources to ensure effective legal justice and a lack of coordination and cooperation between the national government and international community have compromised peacebuilding efforts. Also in both cases, attempts by the international community to promote the idea of a truth commission have been met with resistance because of the strong desire for retributive justice. Finally, and perhaps most significant, the promotion of reconciliation in both Cambodia and Rwanda has been slowed by the continuing violence, unwillingness of the survivors to forgive, and the perceived lack of authentic contrition on the part of the perpetrators.

It is clear from the experience in Rwanda that the holding of criminal trials is not in itself sufficient to produce a sense of justice and a process of reconciliation—other mechanisms are also necessary, as well as the conscious incorporation of the goals of achieving justice and reconciliation into the strategy of prosecution (Kritz 1997). As has been argued, there are a number of aspects of the domestic and international trials that may be seen as counterproductive in the quest for justice and reconciliation. On the other hand, more effective cooperation and communication between international and domestic accountability mechanisms could perhaps assist the ability of both to address the legal justice and reconciliation needs of the local population. Learning from these experiences in Rwanda could be critical for the effective implementation of international and/or domestic tribunals in Cambodia.

So, how can reconciliation best be achieved, especially in such cases as Rwanda and Cambodia, where the crimes have been so horrendous, and it is so difficult for the survivors to forgive, and the perpetrators have not sought forgiveness in a way that is perceived as being sincere? Some of the components of a successful reconciliation process that have been identified include time to heal, rebuilding trust, public acknowledgment, expressions of remorse, and justice in all its forms (legal, socioeconomic, and symbolic). As outlined above, some of the mechanisms that can promote reconciliation include truth commissions, reconciliation workshops, public apologies, equitable economic development assistance, and war crimes trials. It is important that the choice of mechanisms is based on the perceived needs of the affected population rather than expediency and political priorities (as in Cambodia) or simply applying formulae from outside (as in Rwanda). However, as indicated above, even if the needs of the community in question are taken into account, these needs are by no means clear or uniform. While some people may want economic justice, others may want a public or private process of apology and forgiveness, and others may not feel reconciled until the perpetrators are punished or even executed. A comprehensive reconciliation process therefore needs to take all of these needs into account.

Each conflict is unique and requires sensitivity to local and cultural factors in designing successful conflict resolution interventions. Despite this uniqueness, however, there are common experiences that people go through across different races and cultures if they have committed, suffered, and/or witnessed extreme violence in conflict situations. As suggested by Anderson (1996), "no matter what war, ethnic background or religion, in the struggle for justice, human rights and true peace and reconciliation there is much common ground." From the villages of Cambodia to the newly formed states of the former Yugoslavia to the hills of Rwanda, there are strong calls for justice emanating from the survivors and an obvious need for trauma healing and reconciliation among survivors, perpetrators, and bystanders in the conflict.

It has been argued in this chapter that reconciliation is a process necessary for psychological healing and the ending of cycles of violence based on ethnic hatreds, resentments, and revenge. However, there are also claims that the enmities and experiences of genocide make it unrealistic to expect the populations of these devastated states to aim for reconciliation; the best that can be expected, at least in the short term, is the achievement of peaceful coexistence. It seems that the focus on coexistence rather than reconciliation was not enough in

Cambodia to produce a peaceful society; the question remains whether ending the culture of impunity in that country may yet contribute to reconciliation. In Rwanda, on the other hand, attempts to end the culture of impunity are being undermined to some extent by the problems and challenges outlined above, and it is too early to assess the long-term impact of the ICTR and local trials on the process of reconciliation. However, it is hoped that the greater emphasis on justice and reconciliation in postgenocidal Rwanda will lead to a more stable and peaceful society than that which is evident in Cambodia today.

Notes

1. The research in this chapter has been funded by the University of Sydney and an Evans-Grawemeyer Scholarship made possible by the Honorable Gareth Evans, former Australian foreign minister, through an endowment from his 1995 University of Louisville Grawemeyer Award for Ideas Improving World Order. Much of the research was carried out while the author was a Visiting Scholar at the Institute for Conflict Analysis and Resolution, George Mason University, Fairfax, Virginia. The author would like to acknowledge Stuart Rees and Craig Etcheson for their valuable comments on earlier drafts of this chapter.

2. See, for example, Evans (1993) and Brown (1996). Evans (1993) includes two chapters on peacebuilding in which he identifies the many components of pre- and postconflict peacebuilding and indicates that they have not been clearly identified in the past and have therefore not received the attention they deserve (p. 40). Evans discusses the contribution of international legal regimes and justice including a reference to international war crimes tribunals (p. 43), but Brown mentions only economic justice (p. 610), and neither of them mentions the concept of reconciliation or the role of such mechanisms as truth commissions.

3. Various national transitional justice mechanisms (including criminal tribunals, truth commissions, administrative reforms, and reparations) have been implemented to deal with human rights abuses of former regimes in many countries (including those of the former Soviet bloc, Africa, and Central America) but generally with little or no involvement of the international community (Hayner 1994; Kritz 1995).

4. Fisher (1997) analyzes the various conflict resolution approaches that are being pursued by nongovernment or Track II intervenors as a contribution to peacebuilding in violent conflict situations, including problem-solving workshops and intercommunal dialogue.

5. Mani (1998) and Kritz (1995, 1997) are two researchers who are specifically studying the role of legal justice in postconflict peacebuilding. See also Pankhurst (1999) and Minow (1998), and the studies of particular postconflict transitions by Hayner (1999) on Latin American truth commissions and Frost (1998) on the South African Truth and Reconciliation Commission (TRC).

6. *Gacaca* is a participatory justice system that emphasizes reconciliation within the community along with punishment of perpetrators, thus incorporating restorative as well as retributive and restitutive justice components.

7. See Hayner (1994, 1996) for a comprehensive survey of truth commissions and how they function.

8. Unless otherwise indicated, this and other quotations from Rwandans in this paper are derived from interviews this author conducted in Kigali, Rwanda, and Arusha, Tanzania, in July 1998. The observations and quotations from Cambodians are based on interviews conducted in Phnom Penh in October 1999.

9. Not only is this impossible in the aftermath of genocide when the victim is dead, it is also highly offensive to suggest that the survivors should "shake hands" and become friends again with those who have murdered their family and friends (Drumtra 1998). For this reason, the use of the terms *peacebuilding* and *coexistenc*e have been substituted for reconciliation by many of those working in Rwanda.

10. It should be noted that not all theorists and practitioners agree with this definition of coexistence. For example, *The Handbook of Interethnic Coexistence*, edited by Eugene Weiner (1998), appears to assume a definition of coexistence that is more akin to the concept of reconciliation. It would be a pity if the two concepts of coexistence and reconciliation are used interchangeably, as this could lead to confusion and a watering down of the idea of reconciliation as a transformational process and promotion of the idea that coexistence (as this author has defined it) is necessary and sufficient for the attainment of lasting peace.

11. See Etcheson (1997) for a thorough analysis of the various attempts at redress or justice over the previous two decades and a comprehensive list of reasons for this failure to end Khmer Rouge impunity.

12. Ieng Sary had defected some years earlier, while two other former Khmer Rouge leaders, Ta Mok and Duch, were arrested by the Cambodian government in March and May 1999, respectively.

13. Craig Skehan, "Cambodia: The Long Road from Genocide to Justice," *Sydney Morning Herald*, August 29, 1998.

14. "Report of the Group of Experts for Cambodia Established Pursuant to General Assembly Resolution 52/135," A/53/850, United Nations, New York, March 16, 1999.

15. Any attempts to uncover and punish the crimes of the Khmer Rouge are complicated by the number of Khmer Rouge defectors who have joined the Cambodian security forces, some occupying senior positions, and Hun Sen's apparent reluctance to hold some of the former leaders accountable.

16. Associated Press, November 4, 1999.

17. *South China Morning Post*, January 7, 2000.

18. Agence France-Presse, January 13, 2001.

19. *Washington Post*, March 5, 1999; Reuters, March 17, 1999.

20. *Cambodia Daily*, January 21, 1999.

21. *Phnom Penh Post*, February 4-17, 2000.

22. Cambodians have previously expressed support for an international tribunal through a rally of five thousand people in August 1999 during the visit of a UN delegation to Phnom Penh (*The Australian*, August 27, 1999), and in a press release issued by the Cambodian Human Rights Committee, a coalition of seventeen Cambodian NGOs, in December 1998.

23. Associated Press, December 30, 1998.

24. The Documentation Centre was set up by CGP in 1995 but has operated as an autonomous Cambodian NGO since January 1, 1997. The author was surprised to find that only a small minority of the Cambodians interviewed in Phnom Penh had heard of CGP or the Documentation Centre despite the high level of media exposure in both Khmer and English.

25. See, for example, Yeshua Moser-Puangsuwan's account of the Dhammayietra movement, "One Million Kilometers for Peace: Five Years of Walking for Peace & Reconciliation in Cambodia," Nonviolence International Southeast Asia Office, Bangkok (1996).

26. See, for example, reactions to the welcome of former Khmer Rouge leaders by Hun Sen in December 1998 (*New York Times*, December 30, 1998).

27. See, for example, the comments made by Khieu Samphan and Nuon Chea indicating that they felt no guilt for their actions during the Pol Pot regime (*New York Times*, December 30, 1998).

28. More recent allegations have been made, however, putting the blame on the RPF for the killing of President Habyarimana. This issue has not been resolved (Sibomana 1999, 55).

29. See such books as Des Forges (1999), Gourevitch (1998), and Human Rights Watch (1996) for detailed accounts of the horrors of the Rwandan genocide.

30. The Rwandan legislation created four levels of culpability for the genocide: (1) the planners and leaders of the genocide; (2) others who killed; (3) those who committed other crimes against the person; and (4) those who committed offenses against property. Categories one through three are subject to full prosecution and punishment, although reduced penalty incentives for voluntary confession are available for categories two and three (Kritz 1997).

31. This is in stark contrast to the Cambodian government's approach to national reconciliation outlined earlier.

32. United Nations High Commissioner for Human Rights, Mary Robinson (United Nations Press Release HR/98/29, April 23, 1998).

33. The gacaca tribunals will try people accused under the second and third categories of Rwanda's genocide law. They will be held in Kinyarwanda, and families of victims will be allowed to speak. Punishment will be determined by a council of locally elected representatives, (IRIN-CEA Update 862 for the Great Lakes, February 16, 2000; Associated Press, October 8, 1999; IRIN Update No. 636 for Central and East Africa, March 24, 1999).

34. Associated Press, October 8, 1999.

35. IRIN Update No. 642 for Central and East Africa, April 1, 1999.

36. On May 1, 1998, Kambanda became the first person to accept culpability for genocide before an international court, and his conviction on September 2, 1998, was the first ever for genocide.

37. The ICTR is making some belated attempts to remedy this situation, including the transmission of judgments and other important judicial events to Rwanda in the local language, Kinyarwanda (ICTR Press Briefing, Arusha, February 17, 2000).

38. "Special Representative of Rwandan Government Visits Tribunal," Press Release ICTR/INFO-9-2-206.EN, Arusha, October 13, 1999.

39. The Security Council resolution establishing the ICTR did not specify reparations as a goal of its proceedings (Yacoubian 1998). However, the ICTR was planning to expand its functioning from "retributive justice targeted at the culprits" to include a "compassionate restitutive justice directed at the victims of genocide." To this end, a program of legal assistance, psychological counseling, and limited material assistance for the rehabilitation of victims was to be introduced (Kingsley Moghalu, "Justice Will Help Reconciliation in Rwanda," *Conflict Trends*, October 1998).

40. Sarkin (1999) presents a detailed case for a truth and reconciliation commission in Rwanda.

41. See report in United States Institute of Peace, *Peace Watch*, vol. 2, February 1998, pp. 1-2,7.

42. "Conflict Prevention and Justice after the Genocide in Rwanda," *AFB-INFO*, (Newsletter of the Information Unit Peace Research Bonn). February, 1995.

43. For example, one Tutsi survivor told this author how he had decided to devote his life to giving mercy rather than revenge.

44. The continuing extremist activity in the northwest of Rwanda and the reportedly violent response of the Rwandan government constitute perhaps the biggest threats to the rebuilding of trust and a climate of reconciliation (Prunier 1997).

45. Even the World Bank has acknowledged that its work on demobilization and reintegration needs to be accompanied by social reconstruction and reconciliation (Colletta, Kostner, and Wiederhofer 1996). Following the 1993 peace accord, the World Bank had planned a demobilization and reintegration program in Rwanda that was curtailed by the return to violence in 1994; it has been invited back, but this time social reconciliation will be part of the program.

46. *National Unity and Reconciliation Commission: Background, Functions, Structures & Responsibilities*, Government of Rwanda, Kigali (April 1999). See also Prendergast and Smock (1999).

References

Ackermann, A. 1994. Reconciliation as a Peace-Building Process in Postwar Europe: The Franco-German Case. *Peace & Change*, vol. 19, no. 3, July, pp. 229-250.

Anderson, M. B. 1996. *Do No Harm: Supporting Local Capacities for Peace through Aid*. Cambridge, Mass.: Local Capacities for Peace Project.

Assefa, H. 1993. *Peace and Reconciliation as a Paradigm*. Nairobi, Kenya: Nairobi Peace Initiative.

Borneman, J. 1997. *Settling Accounts: Violence, Justice, and Accountability in Postsocialist Europe*. Princeton, N.J.: Princeton University Press.

Borris, E. 1997. Forgiveness, Social Justice and Reconciliation. Paper presented at the Fifth International Symposium on the Contribution of Psychology to Peace, University of Melbourne, July.

Brown, M. E., ed. 1996. *The International Dimensions of Internal Conflict*, Cambridge, Mass.: MIT Press.

Burton, J., and Dukes, F. 1990. *Conflict: Practices in Management, Settlement and Resolution*. London: Macmillan.

Chanda, N. 1986. *Brother Enemy: The War After the War*. San Diego, Calif.: Harcourt Brace Jovanovich.

Chandler, D. 1996. *A History of Cambodia*. 2d ed. Boulder, Colo.: Westview Press.

Colletta, N. J., Kostner, M., and Wiederhofer, I. 1996. *The Transition from War to Peace in Sub-Saharan Africa*. Washington, D.C.: World Bank.

Consedine, J. 1995. *Restorative Justice: Healing the Effects of Crime*, Lyttelton, New Zealand: Ploughshares.

Cook, S. E. 1997. Documenting Genocide: Cambodia's Lessons for Rwanda. *Africa Today*, 44:2, 223-228.

Crocker, C. A., and Hampson, F. O. 1996. Making Peace Settlements Work. *Foreign Policy*, vol. 104, fall 1996, pp. 54-71.

Des Forges, A. 1999. *Leave None to Tell the Story: Genocide in Rwanda*. New York: Human Rights Watch.

Downie, S. 2000. Cambodia's 1998 Election: Understanding Why it Was Not a 'Miracle on the Mekong'. *Australian Journal of International Affairs*, vol. 54, no. 1, April. pp. 43-61.

Drumtra, J. 1998. *Life after Death: Suspicion and Reintegration in Post-Genocide Rwanda*. U.S. Committee for Refugees, Washington, D.C., February 1998.

Etcheson, C. 1997. Putting Pol Pot in Jail: Dilemmas of Accountability in Cambodia. Paper presented to the Annual Meeting of the American Anthropological Association, Washington, D.C., November 19-23.

Evans, G. 1993. *Cooperating for Peace: The Global Agenda for the 1990s and Beyond*. Sydney, Australia: Allen & Unwin.

Feil, S. R. 1998. *Preventing Genocide: How the Early Use of Force Might Have Succeeded in Rwanda*. A Report to the Carnegie Commission on Preventing Deadly Conflict, New York: Carnegie Corporation.

Fisher, R. J. 1997. *Interactive Conflict Resolution*. Syracuse, N.Y.: Syracuse University Press.

Frost, B. 1991. *The Politics of Peace*. London: Darton, Longman & Todd.

———. 1998. *Struggling to Forgive: Nelson Mandela and South Africa's Search for Reconciliation*. London: HarperCollins.

Gourevitch, P. 1998. *We Wish to Inform You That Tomorrow We Will Be Killed with Our Families: Stories from Rwanda*. New York: Farrar, Straus, and Giroux.

Hayner, P. B. 1994. Fifteen Truth Commissions—1974 to 1994: A Comparative Study. *Human Rights Quarterly*, vol. 16, pp. 597-655.

———. 1996. Commissioning the Truth: Further Research Questions. *Third World Quarterly*, 17:1, pp. 19-29.

———. 1999. In Pursuit of Justice and Reconciliation: Contributions of Truth Telling. In *Comparative Peace Processes in Latin America*, pp. 363-383. Cynthia J. Arnson, ed. Washington, D.C.: Woodrow Wilson Center Press..

Human Rights Watch. 1996. *Shattered Lives: Sexual Violence during the Rwandan Genocide and Its Aftermath*. New York: Human Rights Watch.

Kamm, H. 1998. *Cambodia: Report from a Stricken Land*. New York: Arcade.

Kiernan, B. 1997. The Cambodian Genocide. In *Genocide: Conceptual and Historical Dimensions*, pp. 191-228. George J. Andreopoulos, ed. Philadelphia: University of Pennsylvania Press.

———, ed. 1993. *Genocide and Democracy in Cambodia: The Khmer Rouge, the United Nations and the International Community*. New Haven, Conn.: Yale University Southeast Asian Studies.

Kriesberg, L. 1998. Paths to Varieties of Intercommunal Reconciliation. Paper presented to the Seventeenth General Conference, International Peace Research Association, Durban, South Africa, June 22-26.

Kritz, N., ed. 1995. *Transitional Justice: How Emerging Democracies Reckon with Former Regimes*. Vols. 1-3, Washington, D.C.: United States Institute of Peace Press.

———. 1997. War Crimes and Truth Commissions: Some Thoughts on Accountability Mechanisms for Mass Violations of Human Rights. USAID Conference, "Promoting Democracy, Human Rights, and Reintegration in Postconflict Societies," Washington, D.C., October 30-31.

Lederach, J. P. 1995. *Preparing for Peace: Conflict Transformation Across Cultures.* Syracuse, N.Y.: Syracuse University Press.

———. 1997. *Building Peace: Sustainable Reconciliation in Divided Societies,* Washington, D.C.: United States Institute of Peace Press.

Mani, R. 1998. Conflict Resolution, Justice and the Law: Rebuilding the Rule of Law in the Aftermath of Complex Political Emergencies. *International Peacekeeping,* 5:3, autumn 1998, 1-25.

Minow, M. 1998. *Between Vengeance and Forgiveness: Facing History after Genocide and Mass Violence.* Boston, Mass.: Beacon.

Montville, J.V. 1993. The Healing Function in Political Conflict Resolution. In *Conflict Resolution Theory and Practice: Integration and Application,* pp. 112-127. D. J. D. Sandole and H. van der Merwe, eds. Manchester, U.K.: Manchester University Press.

Pankhurst, D. 1999. Issues of Justice and Reconciliation in Complex Political Emergencies: Conceptualising Reconciliation, Justice and Peace. *Third World Quarterly,* 20:1, 239-256.

Prendergast, J., and Smock, D. 1999. Postgenocidal Reconciliation: Building Peace in Rwanda and Burundi. USIP Special Report, September, Washington, D.C.: United States Institute of Peace,.

Prunier, P. 1997. *The Rwanda Crisis, 1959-1994: History of a Genocide.* London: Hurst.

Ratner, S., and Abrams, J. S. 1997. *Accountability for Human Rights Atrocities in International Law: Beyond the Nuremberg Legacy.* Oxford, U.K.: Clarendon Press.

Sarkin, J. 1999. The Necessity and Challenges of Establishing a Truth and Reconciliation Commission in Rwanda. *Human Rights Quarterly,* 21:3, August 1999, pp. 767-823.

Shriver, D. W., Jr. 1995. *An Ethic for Enemies: Forgiveness in Politics.* New York: Oxford University Press.

Sibomana, A. 1999. *Hope for Rwanda: Conversations with Laure Guilbert and Harvé Deguine.* London: Pluto Press.

Tutu, D. 1999. *No Future without Forgiveness.* London: Rider.

United Nations, Department for Economic and Social Information and Policy Analysis. 1996. *An Inventory of Postconflict Peace-Building Activities.* New York: United Nations.

United Nations, Department of Humanitarian Affairs, Integrated Regional Information Network (UN DHA IRIN). 1997. The Rwandan Genocide Trials: Building Peace through Justice. IRIN Special Feature 1/97, February 19, 1997, reposted by Africa Policy Center, March 7.

United States Department of State. 2000. Cambodia, In *1999 Country Reports on Human Rights Practices,* Released by the Bureau of Democracy, Human Rights, and Labor, U.S. Department of State, February 25.

United States Institute of Peace. 1995. *Special Report: Rwanda: Accountability for War Crimes and Genocide,* Washington, D.C.: United States Institute of Peace, January.

Uvin, P. 1998. *Aiding Violence: The Development Enterprise in Rwanda,* West Hartford, Conn.: Kumarian Press.

Vickery, M., and Roht-Arriaza, N. 1995. Human Rights in Cambodia. In, *Impunity and Human Rights in International Law and Practice,* pp. 243-251. N. Roht-Arriaza, ed. New York: Oxford University Press.

Weiner, E., ed. 1998. *The Handbook of Interethnic Coexistence.* New York: Abraham Fund/Continuum Publishing.

Yacoubian, G. S., Jr. 1998. Sanctioning Alternatives in International Criminal Law: Recommendations for the International Criminal Tribunals for Rwanda and the Former Yugoslavia. *World Affairs*, summer 1998, pp. 48-54.

Conclusion: The Long Road to Reconciliation

Mohammed Abu-Nimer, Abdul Aziz Said, and Lakshitha S. Prelis

There are complex relationships among the four different but interrelated concepts of peace, justice, reconciliation, and coexistence. Therefore, through the collection of these chapters we attempt to shed some light on these relationships. In the field of peacebuilding (including conflict resolution and peace studies),[1] scholars and practitioners have used these terms interchangeably, without much attention to the different functions and relationships that exist among them.

The various contributors to this volume were asked to address these concepts on both the theoretical and practical levels. The cases that they analyzed, in this volume, were aimed to illustrate possible applications of these principles, and the obstacles facing practitioners when dealing with reconciliation, peace, or justice in inter- and intragroup or interethnic relations. However, there are many interpersonal and small-group examples in which reconciliation, justice, and peace have been the outcome after an ongoing conflict. The discussion shows that practitioners and scholars in peacebuilding are still at the beginning of the road in exploring the different and potential applications, as well as the conceptualizations of these four concepts.

Unfortunately, in the field of peacebuilding, practitioners as well as scholars have not yet mapped the various reconciliation methods that exist or have existed in human experience in resolving conflicts. As Galtung put it "Nobody really knows how to successfully achieve it." On the other hand, we have mapped and thoroughly studied war, conflict, and violence. Nevertheless, all the chapters stress the enormous potential for the transformation of interethnic relations when practitioners can manage to work out the relationship among reconciliation, justice, and peace. Thus, for a sustainable peaceful relationship to take place in an interethnic conflict, the parties must work out the relationship between reconciliation and justice.

Even the definition and the use of the terms can be confusing. For example, in this volume Galtung uses the term *reconciliation* as a generic term to represent all the twelve different strategies of peacebuilding that he is proposing; Estrada-Hollenbeck uses the term *conflict resolution* interchangeably with *reconciliation*; Kriesberg and Fisher assist in clarifying the different meanings of the terms *reconciliation* and *coexistence*; however, Kriesberg defines coexistence in various ways such that reconciliation can be one of the active coexistence relationships; Gopin presents reconciliation without much distinction from other cultural conflict resolution methods; Hubbard equates reconciliation with an outcome of the dialogue process; and Rasmussen addresses reconciliation as a continuation of the formal negotiation processes.

In general, there is an agreement among the contributors that *reconciliation*, as a process of peacebuilding, has more transformative connotations than the term *coexistence*. Reconciliation in its deeper sense, as described by Galtung, releases the parties from the trauma of violence. Schirch and others include transformation as a condition for genuine reconciliation. Rasmussen stresses, based on the Cambodian experience, that personal transformation of members of the political and military elites is an important factor in bringing reconciliation to the public level. While a coexistence relationship is a necessary condition for the conflicting groups to achieve on their way to reconciliation (termed as *passive coexistence* or *negative peace* by Galtung, Kriesberg, and van der Merwe), it does not necessarily allow for transformation of the relationship. Coexistence is not enough to ensure reconciliation. McCandless's discussion of the land issue in Zimbabwe illustrates how coexistence arrangements did not bring peace, justice, or reconciliation to White and Black farmers in the post-agreement phase.

Regardless of the different definitions of the term *reconciliation*, and based on the various lessons and conclusions presented by this volume's contributors, there are certain principles that come to the forefront which can guide peace-building scholars and practitioners alike. This concluding chapter focuses on some of those common lessons.

Common Lessons

Dialogue as a Necessary Condition for Reconciliation

Carrying out or engaging in a genuine dialogue is a necessary condition for parties to reconcile their relationships. Genuine dialogue occurs when parties of the conflict come together to engage in conversation with the intent of reaching agreement. Then, parties are capable of reaching reconciliation if they are assisted through dialogue. The sense of "togetherness" or the joint effort that characterizes the dialogue process is the core transforming force which changes the party's perceptions of each other. Fisher supports such a notion by suggesting that full reconciliation cannot be achieved without an adequate degree of genuine dialogue, which focuses on conflict analysis and mutual interactions. Hubbard and Abu-Nimer discuss three different case studies of dialogue between Blacks and Whites in Richmond, American Arabs and Jews, and Arabs and Jews in Israel. Although dialogue methods in these case studies were criticized, they were proposed as influential ways to reach reconciliation between the conflicting groups.

Addressing Emotions as a Necessary Condition for the Process of Reconciliation

To reach a new relationship between the disputing parties, feelings cannot and should not be ignored. Fisher, Montville, Abu-Nimer, and Hubbard provide good examples of how a lack of recognition of emotions can prevent reconciliation. In fact, Fisher suggests that the emotional and moral aspects of expression far outweigh that of rational calculation. In all the reconciliation and dialogue processes, self-disclosure and emotional expression are central to the healing of past and current injuries. In discussing the power of public acts of healing, Montville quotes Richard Goldstone, the head of the Hague tribunal for Bosnia and Rwanda: "The most important aspect of justice is healing wounded people. I make this point because justice is infrequently looked at as a form of healing—a form of therapy for victims who cannot begin their healing process until there is some public acknowledgment of what has befallen them." Thus, building trust in the relationship depends on a process of dealing with the parties' emotional expressions. Another example of addressing emotions and feelings in a public forum is the use of drama in the peacebuilding activities devised in Northern Ireland, as described by Fitzduff.

Reaching Reconciliation through Dialogue Requires Action

The perceptions of justice and reconciliation differ from one party of the conflict to another. Often those with less access and power expect structural changes, while those who have privileges of power tend to expect reconciliation to focus on attitudinal changes and harmony (see Abu-Nimer and Hubbard). In fact, Hubbard hypothesizes that minority members in a dialogue group tend to request social mobilization with an emphasis on justice, while the members of the majority perceive the dialogue as a way to bring communities together. Hubbard's hypotheses also raise the question of the reentry process and actions. One of the challenges facing many groups is how to best reenter their own communities and continue working for peace.

The peacebuilding practitioners in Northern Ireland, who combined structural with psychological approaches, also confronted such a dilemma. The Northern Ireland case (see Fitzduff) represents the possibility of integration of dialogue and activities to correct inequality (or the soft and hard approaches of peacebuilding). This combination is essential for addressing the different communities' needs. A good example of an action-oriented aspect of intercommunity dialogue is the mobile phone project in Belfast, which aimed to assist members from both communities in monitoring the events during a crisis or escalating tension. The Welcome Information Center Project in Bosnia, described by Hart, is another concrete illustration of dialogue and action. To be effective, reconciliation processes need to integrate changes in structure or other forms of action-oriented activities.

Contributions of Religious and Spiritual Aspects to the Process of Reconciliation

Religion is an underutilized and powerful tool to assist in resolving many of the intractable interethnic conflicts (see Gopin, Assefa, and Abu-Nimer). To rebuild injured relationships (healing and closure) and meet the needs of conflicting parties (in other words, to achieve reconciliation), disputing parties would need to have more than the typical and pragmatic approach of power negotiation or even interest-based negotiation. The use of symbols and rituals takes the interaction beyond words and tangible exchanges. Assefa's discussion of the peacebuilding process between the different Muslim and Christian tribes in Northern Ghana perfectly illustrates the potential constructive use of religious beliefs and rituals to enhance peace and reconciliation in identity-based conflicts (for example, the function of mutual prayers).

However, the application of such processes of public and collective rituals is complicated and raises serious questions. For example, Gopin challenges peaceworkers with a dilemma: How can we expect to transmit the apology of a few individuals to the group level, and at the same time challenge the expression of hatred carried out by a few people and transmitted to their collective groups?

A Single or Generic Method or Level of Intervention for Reconciliation

To create a reconciliatory relationship, practitioners and scholars need to consider multidimensional approaches. This means the need to combine spiritual, legal, economic, social, cultural, psychological, and political arrangements. The multidimensional approach of peacebuilding activities in Northern Ireland (see Fitzduff), including rights/equality work (employment and social needs), coexistence/diversity work (cultural diversity, rituals and symbols, drama, diverse policing, and language), and reconciliation/interdependence work (community development and relations), is an excellent example of the type of comprehensive, changing, and complementary ways of promoting peace in a divided society context.

A multilevel intervention (grassroots, middle range, and elite) approach is needed. Kriesberg suggests that when dealing with relations between large groups, a significant degree of reconciliation between the authorities on each side is crucial to public reconciliation. Others (Rasmussen, McCandless, Lambourne, Fitzduff, and Assefa) stress that intervention by the elite or official negotiations, alone, cannot bring peace, reconciliation, or justice. It has to be accompanied with intensive grassroots activities and the building of a strong foundation for civil society activities. Both Lambourne's and Rasmussen's case studies of Cambodia illustrate the danger of imposing a negotiated agreement without the involvement of the public in the implementation. Therefore, comprehensive types and parallel levels of activities in peacebuilding work are necessary to bring parties along the reconciliation path.

Local or Indigenous Cultures as Rich Sources of Reconciliation Processes

Utilizing indigenous methods, instead of relying on imported Western methods or on "modern" and pure legal practices of conflict resolution, can certainly be more effective, and oftentimes appropriate and necessary in reaching genuine and lasting agreements among the parties. The use of the Gacaca system in Rwanda (Lambourne), Sulh in Middle Eastern culture (Gopin), Ho`o ponopono in Hawaii (Galtung), and Chieftan system in Ghana (Assefa) provides excellent evidence on the power and potential impact of local cultural traditions in resolving conflicts.

Forgiveness is Only One Particular Component of Reconciliation

The discussions on forgiveness, in this volume, illustrate the principle that although there are certain stages or steps to reach reconciliation (acknowledgment, redress, forgiveness, assurance—see Fisher in this volume), or confession, repentance, and restitution (see Montville in this volume), practitioners should not rely on one model only. As proposed by Gopin, Lambourne, Galtung, and others, forgiveness and reconciliation may differ from one religion to the other (for instance, Buddhists do not make such a strong connection between forgiveness and reconciliation). In fact, different cultures have different expectations regarding the process of forgiveness and reconciliation. Thus, studying and mapping such processes in different social and cultural contexts would be more effective for peacebuilders than attempting to generate a standard process of forgiveness or reconciliation.

Rituals and Symbols as Tools and Concepts in the Field of Peacebuilding

Reconciliation and conflict resolution processes can be enriched and strengthened by integrating rituals as part of the resolution process. Schirch illustrates how, in interethnic identity conflicts, simple changes in the contextual arrangements can produce breakthroughs and change attitudes of participants.[2] Assefa's case study of the conflict resolution process in the Northern Region of Ghana illustrates the creative use and integration of rituals, both religious as well as cultural, in the process of reconciliation. Galtung recommends how a comprehensive method of reconciliation (Ho`o ponopono) is framed within a series of rituals carried out by traditional elders in Hawaii. Fitzduff describes the positive contribution of integrating national and cultural symbols in reconciliation work in Northern Ireland, in which Catholic and Protestant were asked to share their cultural and national symbols in joint meetings. Montville describes storytelling as a public form of ritual testimony that has healing powers.

Achieving Reconciliation, Justice, and Peace Is Connected with Meeting Basic Human Needs (Such as Security, Recognition, Equality, and Identity)

In all the case studies in this volume, contributors emphasize the notion that genuine reconciliation only takes place when the basic human needs of the parties are met. Understanding and further consideration of these needs in practice and theory will enhance the potential to resolve conflicts and transform relationships. Hart discusses the return of Bosnian refugees to their homes, and pointed out that without providing them with safe and secure homes there was no possibility for them to coexist or even consider living together with their enemies. Such principles have implications for the type of activities selected by the practitioners. For example, linking forgiveness to reconciliation is essential, but it cannot be addressed first or before the basic human needs are met, particularly in a development context. McCandless analyzes the impact of depriving Black farmers from their basic rights, and stated that without addressing these rights (through redestribution of lands) there would be no true reconciliation in Zimbabwe. And in the case of Palestinians and Jews in Israel, there would be no reconciliation without recognizing the national identity of the Arab minority in Israel (see Hubbard and Abu-Nimer in this volume).

The Sense of Justice Changes Over Time, and Such Change Is Necessary to Engage in the Reconciliation Process

In reaching reconciliation, parties redefine their sense of justice. Justice is never fully realized, as it has contradicting qualities and changing standards (see Kriesberg). Reconciliation processes seem to be more associated with restorative rather than punitive justice. Restorative justice (emphasis on building relationships) has been supported by scholars and practitioners as a more effective method to reconcile parties in a conflict (see Estrada-Hollenbeck, Montville, and Galtung in this volume). Others, on the other hand, argue that the punitive or restitutive approach can be necessary for parties to reach reconciliation (see van der Merwe in the case of South Africans opposing the Truth and Reconciliation Committee procedures; Lambourne's case of Rwandans and Cambodians opposing the reconciliation arrangements proposed by their governments). It is clear that, in many cases, reconstructing relationships is not enough, and the process has to include other aspects such as restitution or reconstruction of systems (see Schirch, Galtung, and Fisher in this volume).

However, one of the major dilemmas for practitioners and policymakers is to decide when and how to support which type of justice in a postconflict situation. For example, Lambourne suggests several forms of justice such as symbolic, restorative, retributive, social and economic, procedural, or legal justice as options to be considered in the process of reaching reconciliation. However, how we select the type of justice to focus on in our peacebuilding efforts is a question that has not yet been answered.

Truth and Reconciliation Commissions (TRCs) as a Healing or Political Manipulation Process

Like other forms of reconciliation, the complexity of the TRC needs to be further examined and addressed especially since practitioners and scholars are only now beginning to uncover and understand this complex process. The South African experience has provided us with solid examples of different reactions to the TRC process. On one hand, some victims perceived it as "the embodiment of a denial of justice . . . robbing victims of their right to criminal and civil recourse" (due to the amnesty provision—see van der Merwe in this volume). On the other hand, the TRC functioned as a process to uncover the truth, and an opportunity for public and individual catharsis, mobilization of victims, public storytelling, and participation.

In addition, a top-down approach in designing and implementing the TRC processes runs the risk of not being effective in bringing closure, healing the wounds of people, or achieving justice. It can easily become another form of dictating to the victims ways of dealing with their sense of injustice. van der Merwe points out that for some victims the lack of prosecution was seen as a lack of respect for their rights and dignity. He also argues that the "essential justice goal of the TRC was one of social rather than individual justice."

Lambourne provides examples from Cambodia and Rwanda to establish the notion that TRCs do not always work, particularly in a genocide context. Involving the public and adopting a bottom-up approach is a crucial step on the legitimacy and procedures of the TRC process. The cases of Cambodia, Rwanda, South Africa, and Zimbabwe, in this volume, support such principles.

Reconciliation as a Gradual, Slow, and Complex Process

There are no "easy shortcuts," as some politicians and practitioners might think. Thus, coordination and outside support (financial, as well as moral) are essential to the success of a reconciliation process. Lambourne's, Hart's, Rasmussen's, and van der Merwe's case studies clearly illustrate the complexity and negative impact that the lack of coordination can have on the process of reconciliation. However, the encouraging lesson from this volume is that regardless of the intensity, helplessness, suffering, and deadlocks that parties experience in a conflict, "all can change." This simple yet powerful principle is one of the primary qualities for scholars and practitioners to bear in mind, in order to be effective in assisting parties in their reconciliation processes.

What Lies Ahead

As noted in the introduction, the aim of this volume is to further clarify the connections between concepts of peace, justice, reconciliation, and coexistence; to generate potential and future research directions in the field of peacebuilding; and to strengthen the relations between practice, theory, and research in the field.

There are other future lessons and research questions that can be drawn from the case studies and examples presented in this volume by the various practitioners and scholars. For example, the role of the peaceworker in promoting reconciliation in intergroup conflict is complicated and challenging, but it is also crucial to the process. There are a tremendous number of factors and variables to be taken into consideration prior to and during the intervention. The outside intervention by a peaceworker can be central to the process of reconciliation, particularly if the peaceworker manages to take into consideration the previously mentioned conditions. However, like other aspects of this field, such principles need to be pursued further through research and practice.

Scholars and practitioners in peacebuilding just began to express interest and invest efforts in exploring the relationship between these concepts. Thus, further examination of the above principles and proposed hypotheses can advance the field and be more effective in responding to people's needs.

Finally, considering the theme of this volume and the nature of the conclusion proposed here, it is best to end this volume with the words of Abdul Aziz Said, who concluded the conference on Reconciliation, Justice, and Coexistence in February 1999.

> Peace is not a goal to be pursued. It is always in the making. It is a journey towards a place where there is trust, mercy, and justice. We may not get there, but the journey is important and is never ending. It is a process of being and doing. Peace is both task and experience. The task of peace is dealing with structural violence. The experience is self-knowledge. When we discover our authentic individuality we recognize the genuine uniqueness of others. We need to spiritualize our lives, in other words, we need to "sweat out" our spirituality, our personal experiences. With such experience, we can come to recognize that one's personal ideals cannot be another's ideal. Through forgiveness and coexistence we can create a new humanity. Everyone becomes a new person when new relationships are found. Through education we discover the sacred. We come to reinvest the sacred in our lives. The sacred is any process that links us to the greatest context to which we belong.

> Peace work literally means to get caught in a love triangle. At the outer top of the triangle there is "thought," on one outer base of the triangle there is "word" and on the other outer base of the triangle there is "deed." At the inner top of the triangle there is "love," on one inner base is "lover" and on the other inner base there is "beloved." The love triangle shows how our thoughts connect with our words and deeds: When our thoughts reflect love, our words are those of a lover and our deeds are directed toward the Beloved. We are peace. Love is a dynamic force, not a state we possess. It is a force passing through us. To receive it we have to give it to others. When peace emanates from us peace returns to us. It is well to think carefully about how we can build a world community—a just world order— one that is rooted in popular participation, that seeks to realize the dreams of the people of the world, and that creates mechanisms to regulate sustainable development. There are many roads to a just world order—and none of them easy nor amenable to quick resolutions. There is no one way, nor a magic formula.

Preparation for the journey toward a world community begins with irrelevant dreams. Dreams are imperfect and subject to contextual, cultural, and historical biases, yet they open the way for a future where we can shield ourselves from the disaster of chaos, take at least some small steps towards the alleviation of the massive misery, reduce the burden of the world arms race, and decrease the burden of repression on hundreds of millions of people. Utopias are useful tools to design intermediate steps, to know what is our hope, but utopias cannot be used to divert the energy of the world from the intermediate, small steps that are possible.

Notes

1. For further discussion of the nature of the relationship between those two areas of peacebuilding fields, see Hubbard in this volume, who emphasizes the common grounds shared by both peace studies and conflict resolution. In general, there is a set of perceived contradictions between peace studies (social mobilization and movements) and conflict resolution which often prevent cooperation among the various organizations or practitioners from these areas.

2. Schirch defines rituals as a "contextual frame which links people together in symbolic actions which communicate a transforming message" (in this volume).

Index

About the Contributors

Mohammed Abu-Nimer is an assistant professor in international peace and conflict resolution in the School of International Service at American University. His research interests include dialogue for peace among Palestinians and Jews in Israel, the application of conflict resolution models in nonwestern contexts, conflict resolution training models, and the evaluation of conflict resolution programs. Dr. Abu-Nimer has conducted conflict resolution training workshops in Israel, Palestine, Egypt, Turkey, Ireland, Switzerland, Sierra Leone, Sri Lanka, and the United States. He is the author of *Dialogue, Conflict Resolution, and Change: Arab-Jewish Encounters in Israel* (SUNY Press, 1999). He received his Ph.D. from George Mason University.

Hizkias Assefa is a scholar and an active international peacebuilding practitioner. He is a professor of conflict studies at Eastern Mennonite University and a Distinguished Fellow at the Institute of Conflict Analysis and Resolution at George Mason University. He works as a mediator and facilitator of reconciliation processes in many civil wars in Africa, and recently in Latin America and Asia from his base, the African Peacebuilding and Reconciliation Network located in Nairobi, Kenya. He is the author of several books, including *Mediation of Civil Wars, Approaches and Strategies: The Sudan Conflict* (Westview Press, 1987), *Peace and Reconciliation as a Paradigm: A Philosophy of Peace and Its Implications on Conflict, Governance, and Economic Growth in Africa* (Majestic Press, 1993), and *Process of Expanding and Deepening Engagement: Methodology for Reconciliation Work in Large-Scale Social Conflicts* (forthcoming).

Mica Estrada-Hollenbeck is a member of the Program on International Conflict Analysis and Resolution at Harvard University, where she received her Ph.D. in social psychology. She also teaches alternative dispute resolution at the California School of Professional Psychology in San Diego. Her research interests include the study of forgiveness, intergroup relations, and conflict resolution processes such as negotiations, mediation, and problem-solving workshops. She has helped conduct problem-solving workshops between Israelis and Palestinians under the auspices of Professor Herbert Kelman and has consulted on ethnic disputes in Cypress, Northern Ireland, the "former Yugoslavia," and Sri Lanka.

Ronald J. Fisher, currently a visiting professor in the Peace and Conflict Studies Division at Royal Roads University in Victoria, Canada, and the founding coordinator of the Applied Social Psychology graduate program at the University of Saskatchewan, is an expert on interactive conflict resolution and the social psychological dimensions of intergroup and international conflict. Dr. Fisher's most recent book is *Interactive Conflict Resolution* (Syracuse University Press, 1997). He received his Ph.D. in social psychology with a minor in international relations from the University of Michigan.

Mari Fitzduff is professor of conflict studies, and director of INCORE/UNU, an international United Nations Center for the study and resolution of conflict based in the University of Ulster in Northern Ireland. From 1990 to 1997 she was director of the Northern Ireland Community Relations Council, which developed and funded conflict resolution programs for Northern Ireland.

Johan Galtung is a professor of peace studies, offering instruction at various universities around the world, including Ritsumeikan and European Peace University, and is the director of Transcend: A Peace and Development Network. A native of Norway, he founded the International Peace Research Institute in Oslo and the *Journal of Peace Research*. He has been recognized countless times, including the Right Livelihood Award, the Norwegian Humanist Prize, and Bajaj International Award for Promoting Gandhian Values. His many writings include *The Way Is the Goal: Gandhi Today* (Ahmedabad, 1992), *Global Glasnost with Rick Vincent* (New Jersey, 1992), *Human Rights in Another Key* (Cambridge, 1994).

Marc Gopin teaches at the Fletcher School for Law and Diplomacy, is a senior associate in the Preventive Diplomacy Program at the Center for Strategic and International Studies, and a consultant and trainer in conflict resolution. As a rabbi in the Jewish community, he has applied Jewish values to peacemaking and war prevention, conflict resolution methodologies, and international development for the poor. He is the author of *Between Eden and Armageddon: The Future of Religion, Violence and Peacemaking* (Oxford University, forthcoming). He received his Ph.D. in ethics from Brandeis University.

Barry Hart is an associate at the Institute for Peacebuilding, Eastern Mennonite University, Harrisonburg, Virginia, and academic director of the Caux Scholars Program, Caux, Switzerland. He just completed four and a half years of work as a consultant and trainer for CARE International in the former Yugoslavia. In this context, he developed educational and psychosocial programs for children and adults. Through the auspices of the Center for Strategic and International Studies he also provided seminars on religious tolerance and conflict transformation for religious leaders of the region. Dr. Hart has done trauma awareness and conflict transformation work in Liberia during and after its civil crisis and recently led a workshop for Kenyan victims of the American Embassy bombing in Nairobi. He holds a master of divinity degree from Eastern Mennonite University and a Ph.D. in conflict analysis and resolution from George Mason University.

Amy S. Hubbard, an assistant professor of sociology at Randolph-Macon College in Ashland, Virginia, focuses on grassroots interracial and interethnic conflict resolution. She is particularly interested in the reentry process—what happens after dialogue participants reenter their home communities—and whether it leads to effective political action. She has studied long-term dialogue between Palestinians and Jews in the United States and is now working with Communities United on evaluating its dialogue program. She is studying the organization's short-term Black-White dialogue program in cities around the country.

Louis Kriesberg is professor emeritus of sociology, Maxwell professor emeritus of social conflict studies, and the founding director of the Program on the Analysis and Resolution of Social Conflicts (PARC) at Syracuse University. He continues as an associate of PARC and consults and lectures on peace studies and conflict resolution. He has written several books, including *Constructive Conflicts* (1998) and *International Conflict Resolution* (1992), and he has edited or coedited books such as *Intractable Conflicts and Their Transformation* (1989) and *Timing the De-escalation of International Conflicts* (1991). He received his Ph.D. in sociology at the University of Chicago.

Wendy Lambourne is completing her Ph.D. in the Department of Social Work, Social Policy and Sociology at the University of Sydney, Australia. She was a visiting scholar at the Institute for Conflict Analysis and Resolution at George Mason University from 1997 to 1998. She has degrees in psychology, international relations, and international law and has published articles on humanitarian intervention, United Nations reform, gender and conflict, Australian foreign policy, and East Timor. Her current research is focused on analyzing the concepts and processes of reconciliation and justice in different cultural contexts and conflict settings. Wendy also teaches in the postgraduate peace and conflict studies program at the University of Sydney.

Erin McCandless is conducting doctoral research at American University on civic challenges to economic reform in Zimbabwe. She is an executive editor of the *Journal of Peacebuilding and Development*. She also consults with the United Nations Conference on Trade and Development in its capacity-building mandate. In addition to leading students to Zimbabwe on an environment and development course, she has conducted research on reconciliation and justice and on broader development issues in the Southern African region on a number of occasions.

Joseph V. Montville, who defined the concept of Track II, nonofficial diplomacy, is director of the Preventive Diplomacy Program at the Center for Strategic and International Studies (CSIS) in Washington, D.C. Before joining CSIS in 1994, he served for twenty-three years as a diplomat with posts in the Middle East and North Africa, and worked in the State Department's Bureaus of Near Eastern and South Asian Affairs and Intelligence and Research. He is the editor of *Conflict and Peacemaking in Multiethnic Societies* (Lexington Books, 1990) and editor (with Vamik Volkan and Demetrios Julius) of *The Psychodynamics of International Relations* (Lexington Books, 1990, vol. 1; 1991, vol. 2).

Lakshitha S. Prelis is completing his master's degree in international peace and conflict resolution at American University. As an international student from Sri Lanka, in the United States, he has actively pursued and initiated coexistence initiatives in southern California and Oregon. His research interests are in conflict resolution and development efforts, genocide prevention efforts, and bridging public and private sectors in peacebuilding endeavors in divided societies. He is the cofounder of the International Peacebuilding Network (IPBN), an organization established in Ireland to bridge the private and public sectors in peacebuilding initiatives.

J. Lewis Rasmussen is a program officer at the United States Institute of Peace where he played a principal role in founding and developing the institute's international conflict management skills training program. The Institute's professional development seminars are offered to representatives of the U.S. government, foreign governments, regional organizations, and international governmental and nongovernmental organizations. His areas of responsibility include the interaction of political, military, and humanitarian actors in peaceoperations, cross-cultural negotiation styles, coexistence and community building, and public security in divided societies. Among his other publications is the award-winning book *Peacemaking in International Conflict: Methods and Techniques*, coedited with William Zartman. He is currently working on a book exploring the role of international civilian police in peacekeeping. He earned his Ph.D. in international relations at American University.

Abdul Aziz Said is the most senior ranking faculty member at American University, the first occupant of the Mohammed Said Farsi Chair of Islamic Peace at American University, the first chair endowed at any university in the United States devoted to the study of Islam and peace. Since 1987, he has been the founder and director of the International Peace and Conflict Resolution Program in the School of International Service at American University. Professor Said is a frequent lecturer and participant in national and international peace conferences and serves on the board of directors for various organizations including Search for Common Ground, Global Education Associates, and the National Peace Foundation. Author and editor of more than a dozen books, including *Concepts of International Politics in Global Perspectives*, 4th Edition (Prentice Hall, 1995), his forthcoming manuscript entitled *Minding the Heart,* and scores of articles on various aspects of world politics, Professor Said's deep commitment to human dignity, political coexistence, cultural diversity, and ecological balance has furthered the expansion of peace and conflict resolution as a field of study.

Lisa Schirch is assistant professor of conflict studies in the Masters in Conflict Transformation Program at Eastern Mennonite University. She has worked locally and internationally as a researcher, trainer, and facilitator on issues of civilian peacekeeping, nongovernmental organization security in conflict zones, environmental and economic growth, and indigenous rights. She received her Ph.D. in conflict analysis and resolution from George Mason University with a focus on identity, worldview conflicts, nonviolence, women in peacebuilding, elicitive cross-cultural training pedagogies, and the use of ritual in conflict transformation. She is currently working on a book that provides a framework for linking restorative justice, nonviolent activism, conflict transformation, development, and other social change activities.

Hugo van der Merwe is a project manager at the Centre for the Study of Violence and Reconciliation in South Africa. He has published numerous papers on the work of the Truth and Reconciliation Commission, covering issues such as community reconciliation, victim perspectives, restorative justice, institutional transformation, and the role of civil society. He received his doctorate in conflict analysis and resolution from George Mason University.